I0331807

Records, Recoveries, Remnants and Inter-Asian Interconnections

The **Nalanda-Sriwijaya Series**, established under the publishing programme of ISEAS – Yusof Ishak Institute, Singapore, has been created as a publications avenue for the Nalanda-Sriwijaya Centre. The Centre focuses on the ways in which Asian polities and societies have interacted over time. To this end, the series invites submissions which engage with Asian historical connectivities. Such works might examine political relations between states; the trading, financial and other networks which connected regions; cultural, linguistic and intellectual interactions between societies; or religious links across and between large parts of Asia.

The **ISEAS – Yusof Ishak Institute** (formerly Institute of Southeast Asian Studies) is an autonomous organization established in 1968. It is a regional centre dedicated to the study of socio-political, security, and economic trends and developments in Southeast Asia and its wider geostrategic and economic environment. The Institute's research programmes are grouped under Regional Economic Studies (RES), Regional Strategic and Political Studies (RSPS), and Regional Social and Cultural Studies (RSCS). The Institute is also home to the ASEAN Studies Centre (ASC), the Nalanda-Sriwijaya Centre (NSC) and the Singapore APEC Study Centre.

ISEAS Publishing, an established academic press, has issued more than 2,000 books and journals. It is the largest scholarly publisher of research about Southeast Asia from within the region. ISEAS Publishing works with many other academic and trade publishers and distributors to disseminate important research and analyses from and about Southeast Asia to the rest of the world.

Records, Recoveries, Remnants and Inter-Asian Interconnections

Decoding Cultural Heritage

EDITED BY

ANJANA SHARMA

ISEAS YUSOF ISHAK INSTITUTE

Published in Singapore in 2018 by
ISEAS Publishing
30 Heng Mui Keng Terrace
Singapore 119614
E-mail: publish@iseas.edu.sg
Website: <http://bookshop.iseas.edu.sg>

ISEAS Library Cataloguing-in-Publication Data

Records, Recoveries, Remnants and Inter-Asian Interconnections : Decoding Cultural Heritage / edited by Anjana Sharma.
1. Nālandā University.
2. Asia—Civilization.
3. Asia—Relations.
4. India—Civilization.
5. Nālandā Mahāvihāra Site (India)
6. Nālandā Site (India)—Antiquities.
I. Sharma, Anjana.
DS12 R29 2018

ISBN 978-981-4786-41-6 (soft cover)
ISBN 978-981-4786-42-3 (e-book PDF)

Cover images: *Top* – Student and faculty rooms at the Nalanda ruins.
Bottom – A Nalanda classroom.
Reproduced with kind permission of Gopa Sabharwal.

Typeset by Superskill Graphics Pte Ltd
Printed in Singapore by Markono Print Media Pte Ltd

To Sensei,
my eternal mentor,
with deep gratitude,
for teaching me the Buddha's way

CONTENTS

Contributors ix

Acknowledgements xv

1. Introduction: Records, Recoveries, Remnants and Inter-Asian Interconnections — Decoding Cultural Heritage 1
Anjana Sharma

2. Negotiating Place and Heritage: Creating Nalanda University 32
Gopa Sabharwal

3. India, Magadha, Nalanda: Ecology and a Premodern World System 51
Frederick Asher

4. Collecting the Region: Configuring Bihar in the Space of Museums 70
Sraman Mukherjee

5. Heritage Preservation in the Gaya Region 86
Abhishek S. Amar

6. Setting the "Records" Straight: Textual Sources on Nālandā and Their Historical Value 105
Max Deeg

7. "Central India Is What Is Called the Middle Kingdom" 141
Anne Cheng

8. The Object | The Tree: Emissaries of Buddhist Ground 160
Padma D. Maitland

9. Tracing Transregional Networks and Connections Across the Indic Manuscript Cultures of Nusantara (AD 1400–1600) 184
Andrea Acri

10. Seeking a Sufi Heritage in the Deccan 222
Kashshaf Ghani

11. Archaeological Remains at Nalanda: A Spatial Comparison of Nineteenth Century Observations and the Protected World Heritage Site 239
M.B. Rajani and Sonia Das

12. A Heritage Gem Sits in the Heart of a City, Unacknowledged, Incognito: The Case for Recognizing Kolkata Chinatown as a Historic Urban Landscape 257
Rinkoo Bhowmik

Index 271

CONTRIBUTORS

Abhishek S. Amar is currently working as an Assistant Professor in the department of Religious Studies at the Hamilton College, New York. After completing his PhD from SOAS in 2009, he was a research fellow at the Kate Hamburger project at the Ruhr University, Germany in 2009–10 and visiting Associate Professor at the Nalanda University, India in 2015–16. Amar has published a co-edited volume titled *Cross-Disciplinary Perspectives on a Contested Buddhist Site: Bodhgaya Jataka* (Routledge, 2012) and several peer-reviewed articles in journals and edited volumes. More recently, Amar has been directing a digital Humanities project titled "Sacred Centers in India", to create a database of temples, sculptures, and other remains of Gaya and Bodhgaya.

Andrea Acri was trained at Leiden University (PhD 2011, MA 2006) and at the University of Rome "La Sapienza" (Laurea degree, 2005). He is Maître de Conférences in Tantric Studies at the École pratique des hautes études in Paris since Fall 2016. Prior to joining EPHE he has been Visiting Assistant/Associate Professor at Nalanda University (India) and, since 2013, Visiting Fellow at the Nalanda-Sriwijaya Centre, ISEAS – Yusof Ishak Institute, Singapore. He has spent several years in Indonesia, and held postdoctoral research fellowships in the Netherlands, Australia, the United Kingdom, and Singapore. His main research and teaching interests are Śaiva and Buddhist Tantric traditions, Hinduism and Indian Philosophy, Yoga traditions, Sanskrit and Old Javanese philology, and the comparative religious and intellectual history of South and Southeast Asia from the premodern to the contemporary period. His publications include the monograph *Dharma Pātañjala* (2011) and the edited volumes *Esoteric Buddhism in Mediaeval Maritime Asia* (ISEAS – Yusof Ishak Institute, 2016) and *From Laṅkā Eastwards* (KITLV, 2011, with Helen Creese and Arlo Griffiths).

Frederick Asher is a specialist in South Asian art with special interests in India's visual culture in the larger context of the Indian Ocean. His most recent book, on the Buddhist monastery Nalanda (MARG) was published in 2016 year. He is now completing a book on Sarnath to be published by the Getty Research Institute. Asher has completed a term as Editor-in-Chief of *caa.reviews*, the electronic journal of the College Art Association, and a term as South Asia editor for *Archives of Asian Art*. He held various offices in the American Institute of Indian Studies, including Treasurer, President and Board Chair. He has also served as President of the National Committee for the History of Art and a member of the Bureau (Executive Committee) of the Comité International d'Histoire de l'Art (CIHA). He received the Morse Alumni Distinguished Teaching Award from the University of Minnesota and in 2015 was granted the Distinguished Contributions to Asian Studies Award from the Association for Asian Studies. His current research examines the visual culture of Indian Ocean trade, extending from the South China Sea to East Africa, a project to be supported with a Fulbright Fellowship in 2018.

Rinkoo Bhowmik, founder of The Cha Project (Cities • Heritage • Architecture), is a former print and television journalist and media entrepreneur. She first got interested in Chinatown during her stint at the Institute of Southeast Asian Studies (ISEAS), Singapore where she was involved in projects related to Kolkata. That research, initiated by the Nalanda-Sriwijaya Centre, grew into a passion for heritage conservation and urban planning, which she has now channelled into reviving neglected urban spaces.

Anne Cheng was trained in European and Chinese intellectual history at the École Normale Supérieure in Paris, at Oxford and Cambridge in Great Britain, and at Fudan University in Shanghai. After an academic career as a research fellow at CNRS (National Centre for Scientific Research), then as a Professor at INALCO (National Institute for Oriental languages and Civilizations), she currently holds the Chair of Chinese intellectual history at the Collège de France. Her main publications include a complete French translation of the Confucian *Analects*, a *Study of Han Confucianism* and a *History of Chinese thought*. She has also authored many articles and chief-edited several collective volumes on Chinese philosophy and Chinese thought, past and present, the most recent one being *Uses and Abuses of the Great Learning*. Since 2010, she has been directing a bilingual series of works written in classical Chinese and translated into French at *Belles Lettres*.

Sonia Das is currently working as Junior Research Fellow at the National Institute of Advanced Studies (NIAS), Bangalore, in a project titled "Advancing Landscape Archaeology Using High-resolution Digital Elevation Models" (funded by SERB-DST, Governemnt of India) studying topography of Bodhgaya, Vikramasila, Vaishali, Patna and their environs and pursuing a PhD in Trans-Disciplinary University. Her research interests are in the areas of geospatial and Non Destructive testing techniques for built cultural heritage. She has Bachelor's in Civil Engineering and M. Tech in Geo-informatics. She has co-authored research papers which include "Archaeological Exploration in Srirangapatna and its Environ through Remote Sensing Analysis" (2017) and "The need for a National Archaeological Database" (2017).

Max Deeg is Professor in Buddhist Studies at Cardiff University, U.K. He received his PhD in Classical Indology and his professorial degree (German Habilitation) in Religious Studies from the Julius-Maximilian-Universität, Würzburg, Germany, and has worked in different countries in the world. His main research interests are the history and spread of Buddhism from India to Central Asia and China. He has written numerous articles on Buddhist history in journals and edited volumes. Among his books are a German translation of the Lotus-Sutra (2007, 2nd ed., 2009), a (German) translation of the travelogue of the Chinese monk Faxian (2005), and *Miscellanae Nepalicae: Early Chinese Reports on Nepal — The Foundation Legend of Nepal in its Trans-Himalayan Context* (2016). At the moment he is working on a new English translation with an extensive commentary of Xuanzang's *Record of the Western Regions*.

Kashshaf Ghani is Assistant Professor at the School of Historical Studies, Nalanda University. His areas of interest include Sufism, Islam in South Asia, Indo-Persian Histories and Muslim societies with a focus on premodern India (1000–1800). As a fellow at the Maulana Abul Kalam Azad Institute for Asian Studies, his current project explores transcultural and transregional connections between Muslim societies in South and West Asia. His publications include *Exploring the Global South: Voices, Ideas, Histories* (2013).

Padma D. Maitland is a PhD candidate in the Departments of Architecture and South and Southeast Asian Studies at the University of California, Berkeley, and a Fulbright-Nehru Scholar. He is the co-editor of *Light of the Valley* (2012) and *The Object Emotions Dossier, symplokē* 24.1 (2016). Recent publications include: "Mandalas: Whole Symbols", in

Architecture of Life (2016) and "The Religious and Affective Actualities of the Yamuna: Conversations with Pandit Premchand Sharma, Nigambodh Ghat, Delhi", in *The Materiality of Liquescence: Water Histories of South Asia* (forthcoming 2018).

Sraman Mukherjee is Assistant Professor in the School of Historical Studies at Nalanda University (Rajgir, India). Graduating from the Centre for Studies in Social Sciences, and the University of Calcutta, he has held postdoctoral research positions at the International Institute of Asian Studies (Leiden), at the KITLV (the Royal Netherlands Institute of Southeast Asian and Caribbean Studies, Leiden), in the Department of Art History and the Institute for Advanced Study at the University of Minnesota (Minneapolis). He is trained as a historian of colonial and early post-colonial South Asia with research and teaching interests in disciplinary and institutional histories of archaeology and museums, modern biographies of sites and objects, the field of visual culture, and histories of Southern Asian Buddhism. He has published widely and is currently working on a monograph, *Inhabiting Ancient Pasts: Archaeology, Museums, and the Making of Bengal, Bihar, and Orissa.*

M.B. Rajani is working as Assistant Professor at the National Institute of Advanced Studies (NIAS), Bangalore, and was a Fellow at Nalanda University (2013–14). Her research interests are in Landscape Archaeology and geospatial analysis for cultural heritage. Her recent publications include *The expanse of archaeological remains at Nalanda: A study using remote sensing and GIS* (2016), *On the symmetry of the central dome of the Taj Mahal* (2016) and *Applications of geospatial technology in the management of cultural heritage sites: Potentials and challenges for the Indian region* (2017). Currently she is writing a manual on remote sensing and GIS applications to archaeology supported by Homi Bhabha Fellowship.

Gopa Sabharwal was the founding Vice-Chancellor, Nalanda University from 2010 to 2016. In this position, she was entrusted with the responsibility of giving shape to the vision of establishing a Nalanda for the twenty-first century — a task that resulted in the successful establishment of a unique international, research-focused postgraduate university with a focus on inter-Asian relations, an inter-disciplinary curriculum, and a unique pedagogy. Her research interests focus on ethnic groups in urban India, visual anthropology, and the history of society. Her books include *Ethnicity and Class: Social Divisions in an Indian City* (New Delhi: Oxford

University Press, 2006); *The Indian Millennium — A.D.1000 to A.D.2000* (2000) and *India Since 1947: The Independent Years* (2007). She was a Fulbright Scholar in residence in 2006, Chatham College, Pittsburgh.

Anjana Sharma is an Associate Professor in the Department of English and Founding Dean, Academic Planning Nalanda University (2011–15). Her research interests span the English Jacobin political and literary works in the 1790s, visual culture of late eighteenth century Britain and France, Indian Writing in English with a special focus on gender and culture. Another, more recent arc of her scholarship is related to examining the representation of the critical year in Indian history 1947, and the figure of MK Gandhi in the print media. Her experience at Nalanda awoke her to the rich seam of inter-Asian interactions and this shapes her current teaching and publishing. Some of her publications are co-editor, *Civilizational Dialogue: Asian Interconnections and Cross Cultural Exchanges* (2013), launched at the ASEAN Summit in New Delhi in 2012. Other significant works include the co-edited, *Agamemnon's Mask: Greek Tragedy and Beyond* (2007), the edited *Frankenstein: Gender, Culture, and Identity* (2004) and *The Autobiography of Desire: English Women Novelists of the 1790s* (2004). She was the recipient of the Fulbright Fellowship to Kenyon College, USA in 2001 and Senior Fellow, Nalanda-Sriwijiya Centre, ISEAS – Yusof Ishak Institute, Singapore, 15 June – 15 July 2016.

ACKNOWLEDGEMENTS

This collection of essays is a homage to the spirit of Nalanda which has brought into its embrace so many travellers over millennia; travellers drawn by its momentous vision and capacity to transform human life. I record my debt of gratitude to all who came as Seekers of the Great Law, Seekers tracing the pathways of humanity and peace, and Seekers whose minds were illumined by the transcendental vision of this ancient place of learning. This spirit of altruistic accommodation and shared struggle — that defines Nalanda — is best imaged through the iconic lines of the extraordinary world citizen, Rabindranath Tagore. His lines, written in the context of the Indian nationalist struggle, sit well with the Nalanda dream of being a university

> *Where knowledge is free;*
> *Where the world has not been broken up into fragments by narrow domestic walls;*
> *Where words come out from the depth of truth;*
> *Where tireless striving stretches its arms towards perfection;*
> *Where the clear stream of reason has not lost its way into the dreary Desert sand of dead habit...*

This volume is an attempt to retrieve the hope enshrined in these poetic numbers and a perfect way to retrieve the heart of Nalanda. It is also the time to thank some of those who have laboured hard to make the Nalanda vision one which will resonate globally. The first in this line of luminaries is the incomparable Amartya Sen, who never forgot the vision of a resurgent Nalanda he had as an eleven-year-old boy visiting the site of the ancient university with his redoubtable grandfather: a vision he silently nurtured through the busy decades of his distinguished transatlantic academic life. Gratitude also to the incredible George Yeo, who instinctively and absolutely understood the untapped potential of this icon of Asian renaissance, even though situated far away in his ministerial office in Singapore. Both have served as Chancellors of the revived Nalanda university: distinguished revolutionaries dedicated to establishing, and later, defending the core principles of knowledge based on dialogue, of respect for all, and of humanistic education as the fundamental legacy of the ancient *mahavihara.*

The first encouragement to put together this collection came from the memorable Wang Gungwu: a historian with a legendary body of work. I took his words to heart since, from my first meeting with him in a cool February in New Delhi in 2011, he was unfailing in his courteous kindness and intelligent advice. I thank him here for his words of wisdom and his affectionate care that went a long way to sustain the sometime flagging spirit of Vice-Chancellor Sabharwal and I. I would be remiss in my duties if I did not thank a Governing Board member who always rolled up his sleeves and toiled in the trenches with us with remarkable good humour — the irrepressible Meghnad Desai, whose fundamental egalitarianism quickly disproved his lordly title! He was the wall one could lean on when needed.

When I was an undergraduate student choosing which discipline I would graduate in with Honours it was a toss-up between my twin loves — literature and history — and I chose the former and throve. But, even in my own pursuit of higher education in English literature I found ways and means to keep my fascination for historicity and history alive and well. I owe a huge debt to my sojourn at Nalanda for giving me the opportunity to finally traverse — untrammelled — in the hills, plains, valleys and riverine basins of Historical Studies as Dean who was tasked to bring to life one of the first two Schools at Nalanda University — the School of Historical Studies. My new learning was in great part led by Sugato Bose (though he little knew it!), whose interdisciplinary readings of historical cycles and events spoke to me in manifold ways and shapes my own recent scholarship. So thank you Sugato for combining historical acuity with lambent prose! And Tansen Sen — a committed and thoughtful Sinologist — did much to sharpen my understanding through numerous exchanges via email and in person on inter-cultural Asian trails and their links with Buddhism. He was also generous in sharing ideas, networks and persons at all times to ensure that the Nalanda revival narrative reached far and wide.

There are many others who are part of the untold story of Nalanda and one of the foremost of these is Frederick Asher whose lifetime work as a distinguished art historian on the Nalanda ruins broadcast the greatness of this historic site long years before its actual reconstruction. I would not have had the good fortune of his loyal friendship and deep scholarship if it had not been for a late night conversation, in humid Kolkata, with Philippe Peycam, peripatetic Director, International Institute for Asian Studies, Leiden. So thank you Philippe for telling me that the *one* Nalanda scholar I could not do without was Rick. How right you were! I also thank him for ensuring that the first ever international conference in Rajgir got a head start because of the strong support of IIAS.

But all of these expressions of thankfulness would have been in vain without the timely offer of a most welcome Senior Visiting Fellowship by the Nalanda-Sriwijiya Centre at the ISEAS – Yusof Ishak Institute, Singapore in June–July 2016 which gave me the much-needed time and space to begin drafting this collection. My task was made easy by the timely help and support rendered by Ambassador Tan Chin Tiong, Director ISEAS – Yusof Ishak Institute with whom I had a wonderful conversation on Wordsworth in our very first interaction. This volume would not be in your hands today — literally — if it had not been for Terence Chong, Head of the Nalanda-Sriwijaya Centre, whose patience and support through the writing process has made it so much easier to soldier on. A special thank you, Terence!

Words of appreciation are due to all the contributors who worked with one mind to make sure that we have a first rate collection and who, moreover, put up with my queries, comments and editorial interventions! However, my final words of thankfulness are reserved for my friend, colleague, fellow traveller and foot soldier, Gopa Sabharwal, with whom I had the happiness and privilege of contributing — just a little — to the (re)founding of Nalanda.

1

INTRODUCTION
Records, Recoveries, Remnants and Inter-Asian Interconnections: Decoding Cultural Heritage

Anjana Sharma

I met a traveller from an antique land
Who said: Two vast and trunkless legs of stone
Stand in the desert. Near them on the sand,
Half sunk, a shatter'd visage lies, whose frown
And wrinkled lip and sneer of cold command
Tell that its sculptor well those passions read
Which yet survive, stamp'd on these lifeless things...

Percy Bysshe Shelley, *Ozymandias*,[1] 1818

So why begin an introduction on the contours, memories and cascading narratives of an inter Asian cultural history and heritage making with the sonorous words of the quintessential British Romantic poet, Percy Shelley, writing of a lost and unknown king, one who is possibly an Egyptian tyrant in an ancient time? A poem which takes at its point of entry the view of "a traveller from an antique land", one, it is clear, who has no direct links with this land but is encountering an unknown, unreadable culture and is seeking to decipher and decode the lost civilizational history from a Eurocentric, colonially shaped imaginary.

So is it a sense of historical myopia and twisted irony, to choose as an epigraph this iconic poem, one that is symbolic in literary history of the opaqueness of cultural encounters? More so given that many essays within the pages of this volume directly disagree and debate on how history is manifested, absorbed and then concretized into a narrative that feeds a culture's — any culture's — sense of hegemony: accounts that have the common seam of being dialogic and interrogative, and, fundamentally, anti-colonial.

However, the views that emerged in the works of a Shelley, or others I will cite/site later on in this introduction, sit well with the arc of the narrative that many of the cultural theorists, Sinologists, historians, art historians, interlocutors of heritage and culture, its practitioners, religious study experts and social anthropologist engage with in this collection. At the heart of these contestations lie the vexed questions of cultural heritage, its complex and multivalent legacies, its deep fissures, its ruptures indicative of ideological schismatics and political shifts, its historical reconfigurations and altered meanings and symbolic "value" across time. In fact, as we read through this collection, we find that the drum beat of a lost time echoes in different ideational registers till today. Echoes bringing with them responses that are still locked in an emotive — and sometime resistant — account of what it means to "own" a monument, a ruin, a tree, a bark, a brick, a leaf, a space, a temple, a temple that was a not a temple at one time, or a manuscript, that, for example Andrea Acri's unknown "cultural brokers" circulated and transmitted, and unwittingly, preserved.

Shelley, as we know through the long history of the nineteenth century British-led colonial charge in India, was only speaking of concerns that despite the gap in the spatial location(s) — Europe and Asia — shaped how culture and heritage were made and remade from the vantage point of the colonial master. Some of these colonial master narratives that Sraman Mukherjee and others refer to, namely, Francis Buchanan-Hamilton, Alexander Cunningham, and Alexander M. Broadley that becomes the common referent for many as they dismantle the colonial "heritage" narrative. Critical commentary on how they constructed (and thus deconstructed) a material and textual "history" of ancient India (that was in line with their own positioning as colonial administrators) is hence a consistent theme. Thus ancient India, of course, in the view of these three Victorian gentlemen archaeologists was none other than Bihar, or, more accurately ancient Magadh: a variegated space from where opium, indigo and the Buddha all travelled to both the Eastern and the Western edges of the Empire.

And it is Bihar and its centrality in a multi-religious cosmology that we explain, explore and elucidate in this volume in a small way. So what of this Magadh-Bihar typology that confronts us when we dwell on how the regional and the transregional, the ancient, the medieval and the modern, now work within a space which is constantly being mapped and defined depending on which "traveller" is the current resident of the space? As we time-travel we ask: what of the time of the Chinese monks, Xuanzang, Faxian and Yijing, that Max Deeg and Anne Cheng principally, and to a degree, Frederick Asher, concern themselves with? What of the impact today of the aforementioned Broadley, Cunningham and Buchanan, Victorian gents all? Additionally, what of the valuable counter culture narrative and politics of the Sri Lankan monk, Anagarika Dharmapala — who almost the same time as the British imperialists as Padma Maitland tells us — was doing his own revisionist history of the spiritual and cultural ecology of the Mahabodhi temple in Bodh Gaya? And what, specially, of the subaltern narrative of the unnamed villagers of the region, with their everyday interventions and assimilative practices that reshaped Buddhist iconography and history through the lens of their lived Hindu traditions in the words of Abhishek Amar?

Going beyond the sacred geography of the Magadh-Bihar matrix lies a connection across the seas — of Srivijaya, far away from the kingly Magadh where the Buddha walked and preached. Srivijaya, a space which nurtured and protected ideas of an Indic heritage even when it lost it's lustre in its own sub continental homeland. How does one find links between the Buddha world, and what Frederick Asher and Andrea Acri define as the Sanskrit Cosmopolis, worlds far distant but which, nevertheless, deftly wove the travelling accounts, for instance, of kingship derived from the epical Indic textual world to create their own transregional variants? And finally, what of the relationship of travel, time, traveller, memory, memorial, text, context, History and history, shared heritage and inter-Asian interactions, and most significantly, the evolving patterns of religious practice with the compelling memory of the ancient Nalanda *Mahavihara*?

All of this and more became the substratum for the humanist vision of a shared heritage that underpinned the revival of the new Nalanda university in Rajgir, Bihar in the twenty-first century. Nalanda university, as many know now, is a revival project that brings with it old time and new, and had its founding mentors from Europe, the United States, East Asia and Southeast Asia, and, of course, India. A university designed to encourage the study of new disciplines grafted onto the lineage of an ancient tradition of cutting-edge knowledge. It is a narration fittingly put together in this collection by Gopa Sabharwal, the Founding Vice Chancellor.

This collection of essays has its beginning in all of these questions; interrogations that became the intellectual space from where I organized my second international conference, while discharging the role of Dean, Academic Planning, at the fledgling Nalanda university. In 2014, eight months before the first set of students and faculty came to live and learn at Nalanda university — after a gap of eight hundred years — I, along with the Vice Chancellor Gopa Sabharwal and a few intrepid Nalanda Fellows — Michiel Baas, Eleonor Marcussen, Aviram Sharma, M.B. Rajani — and with the able support of Tansen Sen, Governing Board member, and Philippe Peycam, Director of the International Institute for Asian Studies (IIAS) Leiden, conceptualized a collaborative, truly international and interdisciplinary conference in Rajgir, Bihar. It was, on my part, a leap of faith, to bring to the as-yet-to-be inaugurated university a set of scholars from places near and far, many of whom, like Anne Cheng, came as pilgrims, some as curious travellers, as would-be-faculty as it turns out, to the conference on "Cultural Heritage: Environment, Ecology and Inter-Asian Interactions" in a briskly cold but salubrious January of the year 2014.

It was only natural that I chose a subject that lay at the intersection of all that Nalanda and its networks have resonated with: movements of people and hence movement of cultures; heritage anchorage in spaces that transcended the geographical borders of Nalanda. Additionally, it engaged with ecological concerns and political dynamics that changed not just Magadh-Bihar, Rajgir-Nalanda, Bodh-Gaya and its environs (a process trenchantly described by Frederick Asher in his essay), but also shaped the cultural economies of the medieval Deccan region in India (Kashshaf Ghani) and of medieval Nusantara (Andrea Acri). And at the heart lies Nalanda: a place that resonated with not just the message of the Buddha, but also the spirit of a monastery, or a university (there are many views on what exactly) still suffused with the memory of a time when, to quote Kakuzo Okakura (1904), when "Asia is [was] one" (ibid., p. 1).

It is this sense of Nalanda shared across Asian countries — before and after colonialism — that helped to create a unique initiative, spearheaded by Singapore's former Foreign Minister, George Yeo and Nobel Laureate, Amartya Sen, the Founding Chancellor to begin drawing on a *tabula rasa* the broad brush strokes of the new Nalanda university. And later — post the historic revival of the Nalanda university on ground — this partnership across countries, helped to draw fresh attention to the crying need to have the ancient ruins of Nalanda, only about 10 kilometres from the site of the new university, to be considered worthy of being listed as a UNESCO World Heritage site. It is important to point out that the debate on "why not Nalanda ruins too?" came at the same time as the founding of the university. Finally, in 2016, almost fifteen years after Bodh Gaya was listed as a UNESCO World Heritage site in 2001, and almost two years after the formal beginning of classes at Nalanda university in 2014, the excavated remains of ancient Nalanda were finally inscribed. A listing that brought with it a sense of well-being and achievement for Bihar and for Rajgir-Nalanda as evidenced from the many congratulatory messages we at the university received.

In this context, I share a snippet from the dossier which was submitted for evaluation and which — despite some reservations expressed by those who worked on this on behalf of the university — was eventually cleared for approval for listing. In the section entitled, in pared down bureaucratic terminology, as "Justification for inscription", the Nalanda dossier (2014) states:

> The textual evidence, including inscriptions, about Nalanda that appear in Tibetan, Chinese, and other East Asian records suggest that it was a leading site for intra-Asian interactions. No other place in Asia seems to have attracted such immense notice and imagination of people living in far-flung regions of the continent.
>
> The influence of the revival of Nalanda as a full-fledged modern university with a unique heritage is also evidenced by the following evaluative statement: "... Nalanda symbolized the multiplicity of knowledge production, the innovative processes of the organized transmission of ideas through education, and a shared heritage of people living in multiple regions of Asia (ibid., p. 105).

Additionally, and this is moot, under Criteria vi — *"to be directly or tangibly associated with events or living traditions, with ideas, or with beliefs, with artistic and literary works of outstanding universal significance*" (ibid., p. 109) the dossier states

> Moreover, the systems of education and administration apart from architecture and planning were the basis on which later Mahaviharas at Vikramashila and Odantapuri in India, Jagaddala and Paharpur in Bangladesh were established by the Pala dynasty between 9th–12th Centuries. Nalanda Geidge in Sri Lanka stands testimony to Nalanda Mahavihara's influence in higher education. The continuity of its systems is also evident in contemporary monasteries in Tibet and Nepal.

> In fact, the term Nalanda has become synonymous with aspired standard of education as evidenced in 21st century namesake institutions such as ... Nalanda University in India, the Nalanda Buddhist Society in Malaysia, the Nalanda Monastery near Toulouse in France, the Instituut Nalanda in Belgium, and the Nalanda cultural festival, organized annually by Dongguk University, Korea's largest and most prominent Buddhist University (ibid., p. 110).

Many commentators in this volume, and elsewhere, are deeply critical of the whole UNESCO driven socio-economic-historical-political-cultural intent behind heritage classifications as being reflective of a continuance of colonial hierarchies of power vis-à-vis culture and heritage. However, the experience of those who are close kin and neighbours to heritage sites can sometime belie this — a response briefly spelt out by Abhishek Amar. Thus, while I partly concur with Chiara Bortolotto's (2007, p. 22) observation that

> the UNESCO approach to cultural heritage, as fostered by the Convention Concerning the Protection of the Natural and Cultural Heritage (Paris, 17 October 1972), was limited to the traditional categories of "classical" art history and shaped by Western museological principles ...

the actual impact on those who have tended and honoured some of these "heritage" sites very often comes as a personal validation of long years of unmemorable foot soldiering.

Having said that, there is no way of eliding the colonial impulse that is the shaping influence behind the still largely Eurocentric view on *who* determines *what* constitutes heritage. This persists despite — as David Lowenthal (2015, p. 11) points out — the diminishing returns on heritage today

> Additionally, calendric happenstance imposes a *fin-de-siècle* sense of change – we are no longer twentieth- but twenty-first-century people, denizens even of a new millennium. Like post-French Revolutionaries of the early 1800s and *fin-de-siècle* survivors in the early 1900s, we feel marooned in fearsome novelty. The past is not simply foreign but utterly estranged, as if on some remote planet. Our exile from it seems total, lasting, irrevocable.... In the twenty-first century being nineteenth century seems appealing but impossible. Irrelevant and irretrievable as the past may seem, it is by no means simply sloughed off. To assuage the grief of loss, the pain of rupture, the distress of

> obsolescence, we cling avidly to all manner of pasts, however alien or fragmentary. We also add to them in ways evident and extraordinary. Newly augmented and embellished pasts cannot replace the traditional ... But they comprise a complex of histories and memories, relics and traces (ibid.).

But, for our purposes, and certainly large parts of the Asian world (Lowenthal is situating his remarks in the context of his American experience) the past is not a lost world. To elucidate this we loop back to the nineteenth century and its desire for collecting, displaying, labelling and classifying. It is this political drive, masked as a saving impulse of a fast-vanishing heritage, on the parts of the colonialists, that sits at the heart of Sraman Mukherjee's essay "Collecting the Region: Configuring Bihar in the Space of Museums". The account critiques the colonial "master" narrative of nineteenth century Bihar with a specific focus on Broadley and his privateer urges, urges that were a direct result of the unquestioned authority vested in him as representative of British imperial power

> Framing nineteenth century Bihar as a land of wilderness, a region wrecked by lawlessness, and inhabited by natives with a disregard for their own past, enabled the colonial narratives of discovery of Bihar's ancient history. It is against these narratives of loss that colonial officials, archaeologists, and antiquarians like Broadley would stage their labours of recovering ancient pasts.
>
> In his capacity as the Assistant Magistrate of Bihar, Broadley conducted surveys, excavations, and built up a substantial antiquarian collection which found their way into the Bihar Museum established in the town of Bihar Sharif. As the earliest museum collection of nineteenth century colonial Bihar, the Broadley Collection emerged during 1870s and 1880s as the site of rediscovered ancient Buddhist Bihar protected from the ravages of "nature" and "natives".

Mukherjee's reading is echoed by Amar, whose own surveys of the region of Rajgir-Nalanda-Gaya-Bodh Gaya are indicative of a counter culture "native" narrative that continues through the colonial era and after. What emerges in his essay, "Heritage Preservation in the Gaya Region" is the direct opposite of the colonial history of discovery of lost Indic heritage, particularly Buddhist. Instead, Amar explores the disjunct between lived heritage and textual heritage and comments on the layered contexts of the lived traditions in which this "heritage" lay, and sets it off against the ascription of "true" value by the enlightened, esoteric and culturally sophisticated imperialists.

It is small solace to know that this sense of cultural superiority was not something the British colonialists only felt in colonies they had founded, so to say. For the nineteenth century British of a certain class and education, much of the world they controlled — and did not — suffered from what David Lowenthal (1998, p. 243) evocatively names "heritage blindness"

> Heritage blindness was imputed not only to savages but to civilized Europe's archetypal heirs, the Greeks. Debased 18th-century Athenians strolling "with supine indifference among the glorious ruins of antiquity" struck Gibbon as "incapable of admiring the genius of their predecessors." As classicism gained devotees, more and more of them found modern Greeks unfit guardians. The "rightful inheritors" of Hellenic legacy, in Woolf's words, were in London, Paris, and Berlin. They were truer heirs not only because they cared and knew more about it, but because in their hands it became truly universal — a legacy inspiring philosophers and statesmen, poets and architects everywhere. "We are all Greeks," Shelley declared; "our laws, our religion, our arts have their root in Greece." (ibid.)

But, as we now well know, it was not just Greece that the English could truly value as vaunted roots of European classicism, but also others parts of the world, even the several worlds of India. It is India, more than any other part of the British Empire that witnesses the successful charge of the Light Brigade of administrators, amateur collectors, Indophiles, archaeologists, epigraphists, philologists, linguists, art historians, Sanskritists, breakers of the Brahmi code, and creators of the first museums, especially the redoubtable Calcutta Museum. And, unsurprisingly, as all of this army of colonials made camp in Indian terrains, in Indian texts, in Indian monuments, and in Indian mounds and ruins, they saw each and every one of them through the panoptic vision of an European imaginary.

Such a hegemonic and flattening perception would, naturally, make it possible for a Cunningham or a Buchanan (a quick shorthand for so many others like them) to decide, unilaterally, how precisely "heritage" was to be protected, preserved and memorialized. If you see the world, as these British did, as object and text, as something that needs to be codified, explained and *removed* beyond its contemporaneous value, then you would wrench, extract, remove all *object de arts* of an ancient time into the police version of a "safe house" — a museum, a library, a private collection. Or, as it did over and over again, ship them "back home" in the manner of the famous collection of Greek marbles brought back to London by the nineteenth century aesthete, the wealthy English aristocrat, Lord Elgin. Or, even better, house them in the greatest monument of England's imperial might: the British Museum with its Egyptian, its African and Asian rooms, among others.

What would such as world view know of matters of what Amar sees as a resituated and assimilative practice of those who live, literally cheek-to-jowl with hoary antiquity and lost religions? However, it is this lived tradition that has, as Amar reaffirms repeatedly, ensured the survival of shrines, temples, and sculptures by villagers, who, while they could not tell you about their "meaning" in historical or cultural terms, could certainly value them as symbolic of grace and beneficence that lived beyond its taxonomy in altered historical times

> These remains were either appropriated or resituated in new socio-religious contexts at their site of discovery or in proximate distance, which indicates an ongoing dialogue between the extant communities and the past.... It was this assimilative practice, as the paper argues — based on the interaction between extant communities, local knowledge, and material-remains (sculptures and temples/shrines) — that resulted in their reuse and their subsequent preservation. Hence, it also illustrates an awareness of the historic potential and heritage value of material remains amongst the local inhabitants.

Amar also comments on how history is differently apprehended and hence valued, by those who live in close proximity with it, and those others who are trained to "read" history; essentially, practitioners of lived history versus believers of documented History

> This also explains why the dialogue between the villagers and Buchanan emphasized the different understanding of history that they both had. For Buchanan, what mattered was the origin and primary identity of sculptures, whereas the local inhabitants were not interested in configuring these questions. For them, the temple constituted a part of their daily experience as well as a living reminder of their past.

Jacob N. Kinnard (1998), too, bears out this way of apprehending how we see lived traditions, peoples and their interactions with what to them is also heritage, but heritage in a deeply personalized yet, simultaneously, communitarian manner

> The whole question of the identity of any single image in India is, I think, in serious need of revision. There can be no question that Indian images, be they Buddhist or Hindu or Jain, have always been made for specific purposes, made by and for specific people, and made to function in specific contexts. But we would do well to heed Davis's words about obsessing about original intentions. For as he

> has demonstrated in his *Lives of Indian Images*: "Even as the images hang on to their distinctive insignia, they may find themselves carried off to new places, where they encounter new audiences, who may not know or appreciate their earlier significance. Or, even staying in their original locations, the images may take on new roles and new meanings in response to the changing world around them (Kinnard 1998, p. 822).

To extend this argument: this "new audience" could also be widely separated by age, by disposition, by race, by country of origin, by politics, and by religion. Hence, for example, for the nineteenth century antiquarian, the historical "archive" of ancient Magadha, specifically *Buddhist* Magadha, would be, to quote from Keats' *Ode to the Grecian Urn* (1820), possibly a thing of rare beauty indicative of a lost, desirable world. Or a place from which their minds could seek to decipher an ancient, impenetrable age. Certainly, worthy of preservation, but, at the same time removed from their European experience. Yet, as we witness again through poetry, through art, through architecture and archaeology, through historical writing and so much else that originates from the nineteenth century imperial space, it was this shock brought on by this intercivilizational and intercultural encounter that eventually became the intellectual bedrock of their newly globalized world view.

Nevertheless, in a curious twist, it is a few lines of this poem which I will just quote from, that make the views of the European colonizer and the colonized Indian villager come together in unexpectedly similar ways of seeing. It really — as I see it — does not matter that one had access to a treasure trove of material to "read" the sculpture of say a Buddhist deity, and the other had no knowledge that it was even a Buddhist sculpture! For, at the end both were as mystified as Keats when he first saw the famous Elgin Marbles in a private exhibition in London and sought to recreate a heritage and civilization that was far removed from his own one that was rooted in urban, industrial, nineteenth century London. Thus, in their own ways both the colonial master and the native subject confront the same conundrum when they encounter time past in its material reality, by, possibly thinking along such lines

> Who are these coming to the sacrifice?
> To what green altar, O mysterious priest,
> Lead'st thou that heifer lowing at the skies,
> And all her silken flanks with garlands drest?
> What little town by river or sea-shore,

Or mountain-built with peaceful citadel,
Is emptied of its folk, this pious morn?
And, little town, thy streets for evermore
Will silent be; and not a soul, to tell
Why thou art desolate, can e'er return

So how do we truly "know" a past from which no "can e'er return"? And, if this past has to be recovered and reinscribed, is the "native" understanding a better repository of cultural heritage than that of the "outsider"? Do changed times, changed contexts, changed cultural and political prisms only reflect an unending struggle between hegemonic and counter-hegemonic discourses? Or, can there be meeting grounds where the imperial agenda works to secure the ownership of the sacred heritage by some others, who are also colonised, as in the case of the historic and sacred Mahabodhi Temple at Bodh Gaya, Bihar?

Padma Maitland's account of the struggles of what precisely was the spiritual legacy of the Mahabodhi temple — Indian, Hindu, or, Sri Lankan, Buddhist — is a good example of the convoluted and contested history of spiritual legacy, religious practice and transregional bid for ownership of spaces that are seen as lying beyond the geographical boundaries of where they are actually spatially located. The essay details the highly successful manoeuvring of the Sri Lankan monk, Anagarika Dharmapala who fought for control of the Mahabodhi Temple, and successfully wrested it, for a time, from its Hindu trustees. What Maitland explores in his essay is the inheritance of an interregional Buddhist heritage and its linkage with Buddha, the sacred ground of his Enlightenment, and its roots (pun intended) in the Tree of Trees — the magical, mystical, ever living symbol of the presence of Buddha in a particular space: the much venerated Bodhi Tree at the Mahabodhi Temple in Bodh Gaya. This connection between the inner core of Bodh Gaya and its Buddhist edges is, in the words of Kinnard (1998, p. 819), reflective of "the multivalent complexity of Bodhgaya itself".

At the opening of the introduction I had spoken of how cultural heritage can be linked with the ecological space via a tree, a bark, a leaf. What I had not spoken of then was how critical origination narratives are to deciding who really owns what? Two essays in this collection — Maitland's "The Object | The Tree: Emissaries of Buddhist Ground", and Acri's "Tracing Trans-regional Networks and Connections Across the Indic Manuscript Cultures of Nusantara (AD 1400–1600)" — pay close attention to the ecological origins to weave a narrative of inheritance and legacy.

Maitland traces the struggles of ownership not only between the British and the Indian on heritage meaning and ownership, but between two sets of colonized peoples — the Hindu Indians in whose land the Mahabodhi Temple exists, and the Buddhist Sri Lankans whose Bodhi tree it apparently is. What Maitland's essay uncovers is how Buddhist networks can and are created not only through the materiality of shrines and temples, the corporeality of Buddhist relics, but also through the circulating ecology of the many Bodhi trees with multiple significations all of which create a Buddhist cosmology and "sacred ground" in disparate parts of Asia

> Despite the common use of the term, bodhi trees are not technically "bodhi trees". They are a variant of the fig tree known as the *ficus religiosa*, and sometimes known as a *pipal* tree, *bo* tree, or *ashtvatta*....
>
> While it is possible to talk of one Bodhi Tree, it is more correct to talk of many bodhi trees. While the bodhi tree that the Buddha Sakya Muni is said to have sat beneath died many years ago, saplings and cuttings of the original — or of its decedents — have been planted in Sri Lanka, Japan, India, Europe, and the United States.

The present tree at Bodh Gaya — the object of deep venerations for not just Buddhist of many hues, but also those who come to pay obeisance to the life of the Buddha from different faiths — is a cutting from one in Anuradhapura in Sri Lanka. A cutting that returned "home" after centuries to the parent, or originating space, from where it first went as a sign of the body of the Buddha and the sap filled living icon of Buddhist heritage.

It is this re-turn that also signals how the powerful Sri Lankan monk, Dharmapala, could make a highly successful bid for Sri Lanka to become the *authentic* inheritor of the Mahabodhi Temple, and not Hindus who worshipped the Buddha as an avatar of Vishnu, for instance. It was a historical reading that found favour with the Buddhist oriented Europeans who supported the claim. As a result, "by the nineteenth century", Maitland explicates, "the bodhi trees of Bodh Gaya had become important objects in debates over ritual, rights, and space. Legal battles over Bodh Gaya continued for years until finally the Mahabodhi Temple was entrusted to a committee of both Hindu and Buddhist representatives."

However, despite the legal tussles that Maitland shares what is beyond question is how the living, thriving presence of Bodhi trees — across countries — signalled towards the Buddhist orginary core in Magadh. It is the space from which Buddhist values spread in Asia from ancient times

> The conflation of the tree with multiple narratives — historical, botanical, religious — and with figure and ground, make it a prime object for considering the ways Buddhism spread around the world and its modern return to India. Just as Buddhism experienced periods of transformation at the hands of new ways of seeing and studying, bodhi trees have been caught up in multiple discourses and modes of figurations related to efforts to conceptualize India as a Buddhist territory. In particular, the continued presence of bodhi trees at Bodh Gaya has been vital to arguments about Buddhism's enduring connection to its original landscape.
>
> [For] when planted as part of the creation of new Buddhist landscapes, bodhi trees legitimize each new locality as sacred space, invoking the Buddha and fostering an equivalence between that spot and the ground where the Buddha achieved enlightenment. Through the planting of bodhi trees, sites become linked to much longer histories of Buddhism. They become part of a network of Buddhist sites and cultures, each unique, yet linked by a common invocation of the Buddha as a teacher and Bodh Gaya as his seat of liberation.

Moreover,

> The movement of bodhi trees has played a crucial role in the preservation of Bodh Gaya and in perpetuating conceptions of India as a Buddhist holy land. They have acted as ambassadors, helping to instill Buddhist ideals and a sense of community, *sangha*, abroad. More recently, bodhi trees have been used to revive notions of Buddhist ground and sangha in India, redefining cultural and ecological landscapes in South Asia.

These struggles to correctly reflect what is the spatial and spiritual topology of colonial India's greatest export — the Life of the Buddha — is best showcased by how British colonialists living in India sent back an "authentic" record to their British brothers living in Victorian England. An England plagued by the cankerous spread of doubt in the efficacy of religion post mid-1900s, thanks to the separate but combined assault of the naturalist Charles Darwin's *On the Origin of Species* (1859) and Karl Marx's three volume magnum opus *Das Kapital:* the first part of which was written in London and published in 1867.

Though the cultural and theological impact of Darwin's revolutionary text is well established, what is often not remembered is what led him to create his scientific document is none other than travel beyond the shores of Great Britain. Like many other British of a certain disposition in the nineteenth century, Darwin too was bitten by the voyaging bug and his scientific temper led him to embark on a five-year survey voyage around the world on the HMS *Beagle*. His studies of specimens around the globe led him to formulate his theory of evolution and his views on the process of natural selection.

What is readily accessible from the two quick examples of Darwin and Marx is that Victorian England was undergoing ideational tectonic shifts that would be soon characterized in literary parlance as the Age of Faith and Doubt. So Doubt we have in the interventions of the aforementioned duo, but what of the faith that was steadily ebbing with the advance of science and industry? It was a terrible time where God the Father seemed an image created by hapless Man to keep him warm in the cold winter of his harsh life on this earth. The answer to this, it seems, lay with the figure of a man with god-like attributes, one who was born in an ancient time, but whose life and words and examples could possibly inspire, for a while, the late Victorian public: Gautam Buddha.

Philip Almond's work — cited by Mukherjee in his essay — on *The British Discovery of Buddhism* (1988) works well to explain why all things associated with the Buddha and Buddhist lore — text and monument — captured the Victorian imagination. And, at the centre of this "discovery" was Bodh Gaya. How strong a pull this exerted in late Victorian England — and not only on those who found themselves now ruling in the veritable Land of the Buddha — but on the home-bound others is evidenced through the numerous literary accounts of the life of the Buddha that were in circulation in British print culture. The three best-known ones, which ran through several editions are still well known today: Richard Phillips' *The Story of Gautam Buddha and His Creed: An Epic* (1871), Sir Edwin Arnold's long poem, *The Light of Asia: Being the Life and Teachings of Gautama, Prince of India and Founder of Buddhism* (1879), and the winner of the Newdigate Prize in Oxford, Sidney Arthur Alexander's verse narrative, *Sakya-Muni: The Story of the Buddha* (1887). It is the last, written as the inner flycover tells us, by a "scholar of Trinity College" that provides a verse-drawing of the Buddha image enshrined in the inner sanctum of the Mahabodhi, thus placing the Buddha in a new "home" of the Victorian reading public. A short section of this long poem very effectively conveys how heritage is transposed, nay, transliterated from the space from where it materially exists to one where it is part of the heritage imaginary of those who can evoke its richness within the lines of their poetic renditions.

The Story of Buddha

And, passing inward, you will wonder there
At lofty pillars, carved and sculptured fair,
And fretted work of silver — shrine by shrine,
Reaching to where in majesty divine
Great Buddha, wrought of gold, looks down on all.
And there is silence, till the trumpet's call
Thrice rings out sharp on the untroubled day,
And thrice loud echo sells and dies away:
Then, wending voiceless down the long-drawn aisle,
The priests of Lhasa in slow-moving file
Part the translucent gloom, and darkly seem
To move like figures in a painter's dream,
Mystic and lovely, in that mystic place:
And then the hymn and prayer for Buddha's grace
Spring from a thousand voices, and the air
Grows heavy with faint clouds of incense rare,
While dim lamps, lifted high above the throng,
Shine through the dusk, and mingling with the song
Make strange sweet union of sound and sight. (Alexander, 1887)

However, long before the over-arching narrative of British colonialism and its connections with heritage, particularly Buddhist heritage, there were ancient, inter-Asian interconnections that took the story of the Buddha back to their own countries, lands contiguous to India, namely China. Two articles in this volume, Anne Cheng's and Max Deeg's, tell the story of the Buddha, of Buddhism, and most significantly of the Rajgir-Nalanda core in the spread of Buddhism to China and from there onto Korea and Japan. As inheritors of the twisted legacy of colonialism, we postcolonial millennials, know little of the deep historical and spiritual links between India and its Asian neighbours, connections forged not just by the circulation of Sanskrit texts, but the more enduring ones built on the transmission of Buddhist philosophy.

It was this cultural loss of memory that is a crucial part of the revival mission and vision of Nalanda university: to re-tell the story, for instance, of the ancient travels of the Chinese monks and seekers of the Law. This foundational narrative is explored in the aforementioned essays by Max Deeg and Anne Cheng. However, while both Cheng and Deeg provide a close examination of original textual Chinese sources to explicate how they view the relationship between the Chinese monk travellers accounts of their travels to India, they hold widely divergently views on how this heritage was received, interpreted, and codified, and then transmitted in future times.

Cheng's essay, "Central India is what is called the Middle Kingdom" provides a fresh take on how exactly we are to view the notion of an ageless Chinese cultural, political, social and spiritual heritage in contemporary geopolitics. Cheng takes as her point of departure, the contemporaneous Western capitalist inspired narrative — between the Chinese dragon and the Indian tiger — as a way of reading historical interactions from a non-Orientalized, pre-colonial perspective. In fact, Cheng makes her own location in the latter part of the essay eminently clear to show how she reads the India–China dualism by stating

> In 1882, Friedrich Maximilian Müller, the renowned Sanskritist of German origin, gave a famous series of lectures at the University of Cambridge entitled *What can India teach us?*, and proceeded to show in detail in what way India was at the source of numerous aspects of European languages, cultures, religious beliefs, etc. In that respect, Max Müller's question was raised from a European point of view. Being born and bred in France, but of Chinese ancestry, I would personally raise the question both from a European and a Chinese viewpoint.

Cheng's viewpoint, thus, sees the ancient Chinese world view of themselves in a way that runs counter to the normative contemporaneous Chinese narrative. By closely examining textual sources, Cheng affirms that ancient Nalanda, is a space

> redolent with the memory of the historic endeavour of members of the Chinese elites to leave behind their Chinese heritage in their quest for something other than what had so far constituted the Chinese civilizational centrality and self-proclaimed superiority.

Far from being just an emotive statement from one, who in 2014 came to Rajgir, to the Nalanda university conference with the heart of a "pilgrim", the careful analysis of textual sources related to the travels of Faxian and Xuanzang bears out her assertions on how India was, in a particular historical time, the Central kingdom to which Chinese came seeking spiritual knowledge and salvation. In Cheng's account India, particularly Central India is the heart of culture, of knowledge, of heritage, of spirituality and much more, and the Chinese travellers convey through their travelogues a sense of being from the margins of all of this.

> As was noted by Abel-Rémusat, Faxian seems to consider as a matter of fact that the Chinese designation *Zhongguo* can only refer to *Madhyadeśa,* which is confirmed by the fact that he and his fellow-monks consistently refer to themselves as coming from the "borderlands" (*biandi* 邊地, literally "lands on the margins")

Hence, according to Cheng, there can be only one possible way to read the centre-margin cultural discourse: the identity of "*Madhyadeśa"* as the only possible "Central country or kingdom" (*Zhongguo*) is a clear referent to *India's* centrality.

> And as Abel-Rémusat specified in his footnote, the Chinese monks never use *Zhongguo* to refer to their homeland, but persistently identify themselves as coming from the land of such and such a dynasty, e.g. "the land of Qin" (Qindi 秦地), "the land of Han" (Handi 漢地), or "the land of Jin" (Jindi 晋地, Jin being the Chinese reigning dynasty at the time of Faxian).

Indeed, as Cheng posits, many ancient Chinese travellers to India display an acute sense of cultural inferiority — "the borderland complex" — coming as they do from "the land of Han" (*Handi*), that wretched 'borderland' (*biandi*)". Why? Because they were not karmically lucky enough to be born in the land of the Buddha! The only way to fill this lack is to work towards learning all they can in India, take it back to China, and thus provide "enlightenment to the Chinese who were not lucky enough to be born in the right place."

Max Deeg's essay, on the other hand reads with scepticism another aspect of the China–India linkage, even as it employs the same methodology of reading textual sources as Cheng does. His, provocatively titled essay, "Setting the 'Records' Straight: Textual Sources on Nālandā and Their Historical Value" tilts at many windmills and questions accounts related to Nalanda. Referring to the UNESCO World Heritage inscription and the attention that it has garnered for the Nalanda ruins, Deeg critically examines the textual, "archaeological and art-historical evidence" — principally Frederick Asher and Mary Stewart's seminal work — and the uses of evidentiary material "made on the basis of the old nineteenth century translations of the most extensive texts on Nālandā, the Chinese records, and of the Middle-Indic (Pāli, Prākṛt) and Tibetan sources". His essay sets up a sort of fact-finding mission — to "set the record straight" — from a "textual-philological point of view" in order "to give contextually informed translations and discussions of the relevant textual sources".

His argument primarily focuses on the textual materials and their translation by those whom he — rightly — considers "the ones deemed to be most informative and reliable ... Chinese records of Xuanzang 玄奘 (600/602–664), of his biographer(s), and of Yijing 義淨 (635–713)." The choice is a natural one for Nalanda: "both monks resided and studied in Nālandā for several years." The problematic lies not with their originary texts, but, as Deeg painstaking unravels, because of the manner in which "the information extracted from these sources, digested mostly from the nineteenth century translations by Beal and others, [and thus] feed[s] rather uncritically into the major historical narrative of the monastery, pushing its existence even back to the time of the Buddha."

Deeg's essay deconstructs the hagiographic accounts around the highly privileged status of a very successful Nalanda *Mahavihara*, its immense success creating a back story that even has the Buddha himself imparting knowledge there! This telling amply proves that what the British did with the history of ancient Maghadh was something done centuries earlier by others by those who knew how to create legacies and interconnections across regions, spaces, times. In this context, he too strongly resists — as do Cheng and Asher — the "fact" of their being 10,000 students at Nalanda in its prime and links it to later histories, post the destruction of the monastery.

> The tendency to make the monastery bigger than it was ("ten thousand monks") is also found in Tārānātha's history when it states that at the time of Nāgārjuna a certain "Suviṣṇu, a *brāhmaṇa* of Magadha, built one hundred and eight temples at Śrī Nalendra."

Deeg's comments on the actual size of the monastery are borne out by the essay that moves to quite a distance from reliance on textual and philological sources to ones based on the most recent technological advancement and their indubitable service to imaging the very ground from where the heritage site is spatially located. M.B. Rajani and Sonia Das's essay, "Archaeological Remains at Nalanda: A Spatial Comparison of Nineteenth Century Observations and the Protected World Heritage Site" signals towards the new pathways that are now being taken by those who work with heritage, with ecology and environment and their hitherto concealed histories that are now, for the very first time in human history, revealed with a degree of fullness not before encountered either by those who work in the textual or the material archive.

The duo, trained in first-rate scientific institutions, reveal how the new depths (literally) that the use of LIDAR (Light Detection and Ranging) and other scientific tools gives to us new ways of seeing the old. Ways that are, moreover, seemingly not subject to the degree of individual and cultural biases that other disciplinary trainings seem to be often ransomed to. Indeed, through their highly specialized examination of the physical site of the Nalanda ruins — using geospatial imagery — the authors provide a picture, or pictures, that add a whole new dimension on how we "read" a historical, heritage site that is overlaid with centuries of textual interpretative narratives.

However, and this is moot, they too begin by looking at "the graphical and textual records of archaeological ruins in Nalanda's vicinity made in the nineteenth century". In addition, they use as their base data

> all features recorded therein, and precisely locate these archaeological remains in Nalanda's environs by correlating historical information with recognizable patterns in a variety of satellite images and report the current condition of every location through on-ground observations.

Furthermore, they place "this information in geospatial context with the core and buffer zones of the inscribed property as specified on the UNESCO website".

However, more than the questions of core and buffer — what technology does in the context of the Nalanda ruins — is to determine exactly how large was the expanse of the old Nalanda; though the initial ground for the aerial research, as suggested above, is squarely based on the study of the nineteenth century maps drawn by Buchanan and Broadley. As the authors state, this new technological arm of heritage preservation uses

> remote sensing images obtained from satellite/aerial platforms in this study (to) augment traditional techniques, especially when synoptic, multispectral views can discern tell-tale signs of archaeologically interesting features that are invisible to observers at ground level.

Also, this scientific way of seeing is done without the burden of history, or so it seems. Thus, they provide credence to Deeg's closing argument, that an authentic account of Nalanda must not only require the union of architectural and textual sources, but also the added frame of technological advances.

What emerges then if we put together the multiple approaches to heritage and culture making is that they are most likely to be "authentic" if we go beyond the disciplinary hermeticism and ideas that segue not just between defined disciplines — viz. history and art history and archaeology, epigraphy and philology, linguistics and literature — but also embrace the immense contribution of science and technology. It is possibly exactly this kind of unified vision, one that the pedagogical practice of new and old Nalanda seem to be aligned to that may allow us to get beyond Deeg's concerns when he has to reconstruct the history of the ancient Nalanda *mahavihara*. An account that can accommodate, for instance, this kind of anomaly:

> In contrast to Xuanzang's brief description, Huili's aggrandizing and Daoxuan's idealizing depictions of Nālandā, the other famous Chinese traveller Yijing gives a very elaborate, in fact the longest, description of the monastery, its monastic organization and its history in his "Biographies of Eminent Monks" where he indirectly compares the architectural structure and the organization of the Indian monastery with the different layout and monastic functions of Tang monasteries," or the Tibetan hagiographic accounts post the destruction of Nalanda where "Tārānātha states that Śāriputra was born and attained *parinirvāṇa* in Nālandā (Nālendra) and ascribes the foundation of the first monastery there to Aśoka."

With Deeg's mention of King Ashoka we come to another extremely significant aspect of heritage-making: the dynasts whose immortal deeds signified through their large territories leave a human trace that is soon transformed, through bards and their books, into a tangible cultural heritage that is then enshrined and unquestioned. It is this aspect that Deeg, Acri, Asher, and in altered context Kashshaf Ghani expiates upon. In the context of Nalanda, Deeg avers "Nālandā became prominent as a transregional centre of Buddhist monasticism and learning at a time when India was prospering under the rulership of a dynasty which presented itself officially as prominently non-Buddhist and dedicated to major Hindu deities: the imperial Guptas."

It is this trajectory of the imperial Guptas, and other empire builders such as them, which is the opening argument of distinguished art historian Frederick Asher's essay: "India, Magadha, Nalanda: Ecology and a Premodern World System". Asher argues that it is the sea routes that these empire builders had access to that were the crucial components in the transmission of ideas on kingship, on culture and even on the material reality of art and architecture in Southeast Asia (ideas shared by Andrea Acri).

Both Asher and Acri clearly establish how the circulating Sanskrit texts established the concepts of a venerable and divine idea of kingship in Southeast Asian culture, and thus ensured the continuing traditions —

albeit altered over a period of time — of Indic cultures. However, going beyond those tropes, Asher's reading of why Buddhism expanded at such an extraordinary speed at a particular moment in inter-Asian history touches on questions of real politics and building of structures of power and prestige. His comments lead to a very shrewd conclusion:

> But there were things a landlocked power such as the Guptas and their contemporaries, the Vakatakas, or somewhat later Harshavardhana, could do to foster an international profile, and high among those things was support for Buddhists and Buddhist institutions such as Nalanda or Ajanta, in the case of the Vakatakas. In other words, it was not just great benevolence that led these dynastic powers to promote places for Buddhist learning. It was, rather, considerable pragmatism. Buddhism had a pan-Indian footprint and regular traffic in both directions between India and East Asia.

This reading is, as mentioned above, is both espoused and developed in scholarly detail by Acri in "Tracing Transregional Networks and Connections Across the Indic Manuscript Cultures of Nusantara (AD 1400–1600)". The great attractions of the divine right of kingship as extolled in Sanskrit manuscripts is something that even endures in cultures that move — in this instance — beyond the Hindu textual and spiritual traditions of a Java and Bali in Indonesia and continue to live on in a newly emergent Islamic culture in the same space. Why? Because they endorse and protect the new Islamic sovereigns in the same way as they did their Hindu predecessors. While the paper focuses on the "manuscripts and textual practices in the Java, Bali and Sumatra in the period going from the fourteenth to the sixteenth century", it goes beyond them to highlight

> not only the shared, Indic-derived tradition of text building, but also the common religious imaginaries. My aim has been to reconnect what are often perceived as "local" and disconnected historical developments in the Javano-Balinese world and the Sumatran highlands on the one hand, and the cosmopolitan centres and the peripheries within those regions on the other. In doing so, I have stressed the continuities and changes between the Hindu-Buddhist and Islamic epistemes in the production and consumption of knowledge during the crucial centuries that led to a religious and socio-cultural paradigm shift in Nusantara.

What Acri and Asher also reflect upon (to different degrees in their essays) is how the inter related thematics of human power, of religious variants, of temples and monasteries, of scriptural and manuscript survival and circulation, of transregionalism and transnationalism are all subtly but critically linked with the questions of environmental, ecological and climatic factors. Hence, ideas cannot be located in some transcendent space but are literally rooted in specific locales which either can ensure their survival or literally cause them to decay and die away.

Take the case of another compelling Asian heritage site: Angkor Wat. Marika Vicziany (2013), in her seminal essay "'Indianization' and the Religious Sites of South East Asia", discusses the decline of the temple complex in terms of environmental changes; shifts that impacted the very survival of the site. Thus, going beyond the historical factors and depredations due to war which form the core account of the decline of Angkor, Vicziany, turns to the "environmental, spatial, palaeological and new archaeological data", that melds "multidisciplinary approaches and multiple technologies to generate a complete and holistic perspective on what Angkor Wat was and meant". Simply put, it became environmentally unsustainable for such a huge community to continue living in the environs of the sacred site.

This account of the reasons why Angkor Wat was first established in the place it was — well-irrigated agricultural lands — is apposite when we look at the story of the founding of Nalanda in ancient Magadha too. Asher — stepping away from the accounts of spirituality and kingship that characterize conversations around Nalanda — comments thus:

> Nalanda was established in Magadha, not only because Magadha was the homeland of Buddhism — after all, Nalanda was not a site associated with the life of the Buddha, although nearby Rajgir was. But there was also the economic infrastructure to support an enormous monastic establishment, and that required a sort of climatic benevolence, that is a climate that could support cultivation sufficiently well that there would always be an agricultural excess sufficient to generate profit and give to the maintenance of the monastery.
>
> What then about ancient Nalanda? The monastery must have had a dynamic relationship with the surrounding region, not just with towns such as Rajgir and Bihar Sharif but also with the agricultural lands outside of the towns. While the region may have prospered from the endowment wealth of Nalanda, the great monastery in turn was heavily dependent on goods and services from the region. Food alone would have been a major enterprise.
>
> In fact, one explanation for the concentration of Buddhist monasteries in Magadha might be the ability to supply food for large concentrated populations of monks who provided neither goods nor services to the community but rather were exclusively consumers.

This linkage between ecology and heritage and its survival is also dwelt upon by Acri in his account of how certain manuscripts survived the depredations of time and changing religious practices and others died away. Consequently, is its not only heritage that is built of materials such as brick and stone that is subject to environmental challenges, changes that are usually placed within the cyclical histories of dynasties and religions — as in the case of Nalanda — but also the more fragile history of a tree or a bark that is subjected to a historio-environmental processes that have not often been read in their completeness. Acri's examples work well here:

> The ecological considerations by van Lennep (1969, pp. 16–17) and van der Molen (1983, p. 88) contrasting the thatch-palm, generally growing only in a humid climate along muddy coasts, beaches and lagoons (West Java), to the *lontar* palm, thriving in drier climates (Central and East Java, Bali, Lombok), appears to be still valid with respect to the *talipot* and *lontar* palms. These ecological considerations may explain why the number of *gebang* or *śrītala* manuscripts that have survived until today is very small compared to the number of *lontar*s, and none of them has been recovered from East Javanese or Balinese collections. Similar considerations could be applied to Sumatra, where the *daluang* or tree-bark is the commonest writing material while the *lontar* palm is unknown except in the dry part of Aceh.

While the introduction has so far largely dealt with questions of the circulation and transmission of tangible heritage there is also the question of intangible heritage and its link with orality and performance traditions that are subject to individual whimsicality and the nebulousness of changing tastes. How does cultural interchange and transregional dynamics get reified in for instance, in verse, song, dance and spiritual ecstasy? Moreover, how does the dissemination of cultures attempting to occupy a new space — both literally and figuratively — in a socio-religious and politico-geographical context work out to temper and complicate our understanding of cultural heritage? These and other such concerns lie at the core of Kashshaf Ghani's "Seeking a Sufi Heritage in the Deccan".

Ghani's essay goes beyond both the British colonial rule and its interface with Indian art, architecture, its texts and the overarching rubric of Sankritized cultures and the spread of Buddhism, and engages with an intrinsic element of Asian culture — the syncretism that allowed for Hindu, Buddhist, Jain and Islamic cultures to co-exist in a simultaneity rarely found in other parts of the blue planet. Traversing the spatial geography of the Deccan area in Central India, Ghani deliberates on the steady growth and development of Islamic culture in what was hitherto a Sanskritized space. His essay looks

> into certain aspects connected to the rise of Sufi activities in the Deccan in the thirteenth and fourteenth centuries, at a time when Deccan's Sanskritized cultural world experienced the coming of a North Indian Persian tradition. In spite of some obvious similarities with the Iranian situation, the focus will be less on such sweeping categories as "renaissance" [but] will seek to engage with a different set of questions that have a more direct relevance to the creation of a Sufi heritage in the Deccan.

A heritage, most interestingly, that certainly has the material reality of a shrine but is more often to be found in the "intangible idea of mystical rituals and practices, like *sama*?" One that, additionally, reflects the trans regional dynamics of Persian culture and its assimilation in a Sanskritized culture. The carriers of this are Sufi saints, who go beyond the brief given them by their Sultans and chart a whole new path that assures that the Sufi tradition becomes secularized and indigenized, creating, what Homi Bhabha (1994, p. 55) denotes as the "Third Space", a space that is beyond regulation and control of those who first sanctioned it.

This narrative of heritage construction and cultural exegesis centres around the Sultans who became the newest arrivals in the Indian subcontinent, and like others before and after them, were first overwhelmed by the cultural richness of the lands they now controlled and then began to seek to overlay their own cultural signatures upon it. Thus, it comes about that in 1327

> after becoming the Sultan of Delhi, Muhammad bin Tughluq set up an administrative centre in the Deccan that would, in all senses, operate as the second capital ... renamed Daulatabad in 1328. A successful completion of this project was done through the physical transfer of the Muslim elite from Delhi to the Deccan. This involved the movement of intellectuals, scholars, clergy, administrators, warriors, revenue officers, poets and artisans to the Deccan capital, who, it was expected, would inaugurate a new era in the socio-cultural and political life of the region. Sufis formed a considerable section of this migrant population who were expected to spread the worldview of Islam in Daulatabad, and subsequently the larger Deccan region, thereby advancing the agenda of the Sultan to fuse "Islamic religious symbolism with the rhetoric of empire".

While successful in manifold ways, this enterprise to host "Persianized political culture" met the countervailing views and understanding of the very Sufi saints, the redoubtable Chistis who were only appointed to take forward the imperial agenda. Their contributions ensured that the enduring Sufi tradition seeped not only in the Deccan area but also beyond — travelling through the riverine network to coastal Malabar, the Konkan region and Bengal — and became part of the heritage of a whole intra-Asian region long after the demise of the Sultanate.

Discovery and demise, space and signification, textured heritage and civilizational interchanges that live on long after the fading away those who contributed to the physical, tactile reality of ordering the buildings of monuments — small and large — becomes even more evocative when we turn to the transregional imperatives that finally led to the revival of Nalanda university. In the light of the severe treatment meted out to British colonialists by many of us post colonials, it now behoves me to say in their defence that if it had not been for Alexander Cunnigham's ability to see mounds as not just earth hillocks but as more, we would never actually had a Nalanda *Mahavihara* model to emulate. It is his determined and dogged efforts that gave to us the excavated revelations of the Nalanda *Mahavihara* in all its red brick, geometric, stupa filled glory. An actuality that had, moreover, before him only lived in esoteric accounts of Chinese and Tibetan scholars. A tactile reality furthermore that had, stunningly, no presence in the lives of the many who lived, loved, married and died there for centuries with scant knowledge of the sacred ground beneath their feet and its immense, impeccable inter-Asian heritage.

And it is this place — Rajgir-Nalanda — that is examined in great detail through the lens of sociology, history, archaeological and textual accounts — by Gopa Sabharwal in her exhaustive commentary on the carefully thought out choice of reviving the new Nalanda in the aforementioned site only some ten kilometres or so from the majestic ruin of the ancient one. In "Negotiating Place and Heritage: Creating Nalanda University" she elaborates on her role as the Founding Vice Chancellor, Nalanda University. In essence, the role — as she brought it to life —ensured that the vision behind the reconstruction of Nalanda — as idea and practice — drew its *raison d'etre* from the very land in which it is founded anew, even as it sought to connect with networks — old and new — that are designated as "the Nalanda Trail".[2]

The essay begins with a set of questions: "Does place matter? Does it matter in all instances? When locating new institutions does place matter beyond conventional issues of logistics, or will institutions achieve the same outcome irrespective of locale?". It then goes on to state, with absolute certainty, that the close linkage between old and new Nalanda and the unique character of Rajgir as a multi religious site with a rich and varied history of cultural exchanges and ideational flows is the *only* space in which this university can be brought to life again.

This assertion is backed up by data that relies on multiple sources — material and textual — that state, that despite the visible drawbacks of being non-metropolitan and mofussil, Rajgir still has strengths that shore up its pan-Asian profile. Additionally, it also has the benefit of historical, ecological and environmental factors that shape the university curricula.

> By situating itself in a living historical and ecological laboratory, Nalanda university is uniquely placed to draw upon the richness of the locale and to bring to it scholarship and engagement which will further the research on the area and simultaneously expose students to the research process, encouraging them to move outside of the classroom. The Nalanda academic community is engaging with Rajgir and fulfilling its mission to link research to the community and its needs through a range of activities.

What is readily manifest is that this mode of direct intervention takes cultural heritage and situates it within the heart of a university, and in and through this process, travels beyond the existant paradigms of preservation and conservation, of display and ownership, and possibly, most critically, beyond the borders of governmental and State controls. Instead, by initiating a programme of learning — immersion — dissemination into the community and *for* the community, Nalanda's research ambit breaks new grounds. The university then becomes not an entity that is first built and then endorsed by the legacy of a sacred site and its historical tapestry, but a continuum that nurtures and fosters in ways that connects the community of scholars and students *and* the community of those who either reside in its environs or come as visitors to this place. It is this manner of integrative, holistic curricula development that is imaged in collaborations such as the ones mentioned here by Sabharwal

> At a more formal level, the university is taking its research objective further by launching the Rajgir Archaeological Survey Project (RASP) in collaboration with the Bihar Heritage Development Society, (an autonomous society under the Art, Culture & Youth Department, Government of Bihar)... RASP will examine the multi-phased and multi-layered development of Rajgir as an urban, political and religious centre.In addition, the university... conducts the Rajgir Heritage

> walks in association with the Bihar Heritage Development Society on separate routes namely, historical Rajgir, new Rajgir, Ecological Rajgir and multi-religious Rajgir. These have commentary in English and Hindi for both domestic and international visitors.

The inter-linkage between environs and university building is not confined to academic programming alone: the dossier for the master plan and design components of the university directly pay homage to the sense of place that the university is coming to life within. It's a rare case of synergy between history and legacy, between idea and practice, and most of all, between principles of sacred ground of a kind mentioned by Maitland that has anchored the care filled and exemplary values of the Nalanda Masterplan:

> The site of the university runs parallel to the Rajgir hills that stand as sentinels in the background. Given the immense historicity of those hills and the Buddhist Councils and other events there, the university took two decisions — one, that all vistas in the Campus will have a view of the hills or look towards the hills and second, that no structure on the land will attempt to dwarf the hills. Thus buildings are going to be generally a maximum of four storeys height. It has also been a stated philosophy from inception that even though 450 acres seems like a small township, the university intends to be outward looking in its lived philosophy. Walls if any will be porous: the university will not be an ivory tower looking out at the world but an institution that has a harmonious relationship between what has traditionally been called the "town and the gown".

In brief, it will endeavour to breathe the heart and soul of the ancient *Mahavihara* with its Buddhist belief in the sanctity of all life and the shared relationship between culture, heritage, ecology, environmental sustainability and human beings into one integrative and powerful whole. Truly build, in every way, a Nalanda for all times and for all peoples.

CODA

For the illustrious Irish poet, William Butler Yeats, writing during the interregnum of the two world wars, history was a nightmare where the cycles of destruction had unleashed a nightmare spectacle of senseless destruction. In this slaughterhouse, all that is of "value" in human society could — at least for Yeats — only be secured through the profundity of poetry that strives to conserve and preserve fast vanishing myth, history, folklore, heritage and culture. For Yeats, thus, the only way to preserve cultural heritage and contain the toxicity of political, sociological and environmental abuse was through writing illuminating verse. But, the Yeatsean project of revival, reconstruction and rescue, as we have seen in the body of many of the accounts shared by the scholars in this selection, can also be built *on the very ground in which it was first destroyed*: say, in the case of the preservation of the Mahabodhi Temple, or, in the conservation of the Nalanda site.

Rinkoo Bhowmik's crisp, anecdotal and passionate account of a few — too few — socially and culturally invested individuals with few monetary resources but huge emotive and intellectual ones, is a fitting Coda to this collection to my mind. The Singapore-based CHA (Cities, Heritage, Architecture) Project, which is led by a combine of heritage practitioners, university-bred academicians, and those who literally live within this heritage, provides a heartening account of how a small band of like-minded folks — from different parts of the globe — can soldier on to resurrect, for instance, what Bhowmik describes as "a heritage gem that sits in the heart of a city". It is none other than Kolkata's Chinatown, a Chinatown that Bhowmik swiftly but effectively shows us as very different from the image in the public consciousness of generic Chinatowns across the world, and is, furthermore, "one of the oldest and the only surviving one of its kind in South Asia".

A forgotten place, even if not buried under a mound, Kolkata's Chinatown is a lingering presence of a treacherous arc of Southeast Asian history, in particular the migrations that occurred in the wake of the decades of bloody struggles for power in Mainland China. Kolkata, or erstwhile Calcutta, a port city, functioned for these Chinese exactly as it had done for the British when they came into India first — a safe haven, a place that accommodated multiple ways of living, of eating, of building, of praying, and of performing. It is a city that encouraged the spirit of commerce and enterprise regardless of points of origin of its new denizens.

It is this new history of one of the most recent *émigrés* that the CHA Project is concerned with: to recover, preserve and conserve a relatively new but vital aspect of an inter-Asian connection. It occurs in the first half of the twentieth century when Chinese semicolonialists are provided refuge in an India that has not only won its freedom from colonialism, but is also now sees itself, under the broad and encompassing vision of a Nehruvian India, as a place from where the Asian recovery of old friendships, interrupted dialogues can be begun anew. And so, initially it welcomes the Chinese diaspora into its own national boundaries and gives them a home and an identity, but with the outbreak of the 1962 Indo-China war the same Indian State withdraws its patronage and rejects the values of Asian syncretic cultures and spirit of multi-ethnic and multi-religious accommodation and corrals and pens and up the self-same Chinese. The effect of this historical accident — as Bhowmik spells out — is then lived out in the slow but steady decline of the Chinese heritage in Kolkata. A Kolkata, which now retains only a wispy memory of the genial spirit of shared cultures and connected histories between India and China: the Middle Kingdoms twain of Cheng's account, but torn asunder.

Bhowmik's pithy account traces the history of this cultural encounter and unveils how the forces of geopolitics decide what heritage lives and what has to be erased. And it does by choosing as the nomenclature of its endeavour the acronym "CHA"

> Chiya.Chaha.Chaya.Theneer, Tī. Many different words for tea in different parts of India. Interestingly, in Bengali (spoken in Kolkata) it is Cha. As it is in Chinese. Although CHA primarily stands for Cities, Heritage and Architecture, it takes on an acronym that is really the essence of the project — a revival through teashops and cafes. Tea has had a rich legacy of being a catalyst for communication, culture, and creativity, bringing people, even nations, together, and it is through cafes and tea rooms that the project plans to revitalize the neighbourhood turning neglected by-lanes into vibrant food streets and night markets.

What even then, in conclusion, is the relationship between this spirited endeavor and the critical analysis of "Heritage" experts such as David Lowenthal? How do we reconcile the Lowenthal vision of the burdens of and indecipherable past with its sheer foreignness and the pointlessness of bodies such as the much-maligned UNESCO, a Moby Dick-like creature fated to die despite its size?

There are no easy answers here, but, given the myriad examples that the many essays place before us in this volume, it would not be over optimistic to state that the human race will not easily bury and forget much of its past (even as it chooses to do exactly that with some parts of it). To conclude then, the business of understanding our own selves must necessarily be done with the added and necessary recognition of where we come from, or where we were *told* we came from. To my mind, only in looking back can we move forward. For, in the words of T.S. Elliot (1943): "In the end is my beginning."

Notes

1. *Ozymandias* is one of Percy Bysshe Shelley's best-known poems. It was written sometime between December 1817 and January 1818, and was probably the result of a sonnet competition between Shelley and his friend Horace Smith, who stayed with the Shelleys at their home Marlow between 26 and 28 December. In such competitions two or more poets would each write a sonnet on an agreed subject against the clock. *Ozymandias* was first printed in *The Examiner* on 11 January 1818; Smith's sonnet, also entitled *Ozymandias* was published in the same newspaper on 1 February. Shelley's poem was the last of the "other poems" he included in *Rosalind and Helen*, published in 1819.

   In 1812 Shelley ordered a copy of Diodorus's forty-book *Bibliotheca historica* (*Historical Library*), and in 1814 an English translation, *The Historical Library of Diodorus the Sicilian*, by George Booth, was published in London. See more at <https://www.bl.uk/romantics-and-victorians/articles/an-introduction-to-ozymandias#sthash.VRtUIKKj.dpuf>.
2. "The Nalanda Trail" was a specially curated exhibition hosted at the Asian Civilizations Museum in Singapore that was inaugurated in late November 2007 to underscore the Government of Singapore's immense and early contribution to the revival of Nalanda university. It traced the Nalanda footprint across Southeast Asia, India and China and displayed the spread of Buddhism across these regions and their connection with ancient Nalanda through the travel accounts of Chinese travellers such as Faxian, XuanZang and Yijing. Artefacts from Indian museums — such as the Nalanda copperplate from the ninth century Pala times — were loaned for this exhibition.

Bibliography

Almond, Philip. *The British Discovery of Buddhism.* Cambridge: Cambridge University Press, 1988.

Arnold, Sir Edwin. *The Light of Asia: Being the Life and Teachings of Gautama, Prince of India and Founder of Buddhism.* Donohue Bros, 1879.

Bhabha, Homi K. *The Location of Culture.* Routledge: London and New York, 1994.

Bortolotto, Chiara. "From Objects to Processes: UNESCO's 'Intangible Cultural Heritage'". *Journal of Museum Ethnography*, no. 19 (March 2007): 21–33. Downloaded from 210.212.129.125 on 4 March 2017.

Davis, Richard. *Lives of Indian Images.* Princeton: Princeton University Press, 1997.

Elliot, T.S. *Four Quartets.* New York: Harcourt, Brace and Company, 1943.

John Keats. *Ode to A Grecian Urn.* 1820.

Kinnard, Jacob N. "When Is The Buddha Not the Buddha? The Hindu/Buddhist

Battle over Bodhgayā and Its Buddha Image". *Journal of the American Academy of Religion* 66, no. 4 (1998): 817–39 <http://www.jstor.org/stable/1466173> (accessed 4 March 2017).

———. "The Polyvalent Pādas of Viṣṇu and the Buddha". *History of Religions* 40, no. 1. Buddhist Art and Narrative (August 2000): 32–57 <http://www.jstor.org/stable/3176512> (accessed 4 March 2017).

———. *Places in Motion The Fluid Identities of Temples, Images, and Pilgrims.* New York : Oxford University Press, 2014.

Lowenthal, David. *The Heritage Crusades and the Spoils of History*. New York: Cambridge University Press and Free Press, 1998.

———. *The Past is a Foreign Country — Revisited.* New York: Cambridge University Press, 2015.

Okakura, Kakuzo. *The Ideals of the East: With Special Reference to the Art of Japan.* New York: E.P. Dutton & Co. 1904.

Phillips, Richard. *The Story of Gautam Buddha and His Creed: An Epic.* London: Longmans, Green & Co., 1871.

Sidney Arthur Alexander. *Sakya-Muni: The Story of the Buddha.* A. Thomas Shrimpton, 1887 <https://archive.org/search.php?query=publisher%3A%22A.+Thomas+Shrimpton%22>. Digitizing sponsor <https://archive.org/details/googlebooks>.

UNESCO Website for Dossier of World Heritage Nomination. "The Nomination Dossier: The Excavated Remains of Nalanda Mahavihara". Submitted to UNESCO by Archaeological Survey of India, Ministry of Culture, Government of India <http://whc.unesco.org/en/criteria/> (accessed 5 March 2017).

Vicziany, Marika "'Indianization' and the Religious Sites of South East Asia". *Civilizational Dialogue: Asian Inter-connections and Cross-cultural Exchanges*, edited by Anjana Sharma, pp. 212–13. New Delhi: Manohar, 2013.

2

NEGOTIATING PLACE AND HERITAGE
Creating Nalanda University

Gopa Sabharwal

Does place matter? Does it matter in all instances? When locating new institutions does place matter beyond conventional issues of logistics, or will institutions achieve the same outcome irrespective of locale? These are some of the questions that emerged when two places with seemingly long histories and identities seemed to come together in the (re)creation of a new Nalanda university for the twenty-first century. These two places were of course the original Nalanda university or *Mahavihara*, the archaeological remains of which still exist as testimony to the greatness of what it symbolized, and the settlement of Rajgir, inhabited since prehistory, where the new international Nalanda university was to be located.

The identification with and choice of Nalanda was of course deliberate: Old Nalanda was the inspiration for the establishment of the new university. Old Nalanda, as we well know was one of the flourishing citadels of intellectual pursuit in the world way before organized transmission of knowledge became codified in formal university structures, and it symbolized academic rigour of the highest distinction. Added to this was the evocative symbolism of an interconnected Asia and the journey to Nalanda undertaken by Asian scholars seeking knowledge and learning they could carry back to their regions. It was this voyage that inspired George Yeo, the then Foreign Minister of Singapore, to forward the Nalanda proposal to the Government of India sometime in early 2006. He envisaged a new Nalanda university could once again be

> an icon of the Asian renaissance in the 21st century and should draw students and scholars from everywhere, as it once did. It should be a centre of civilizational dialogue and inter-faith understanding, as it once was. It should again make available for the common betterment of all human beings knowledge already existing in the world (Yeo 2011).

Later that year, in March 2006, while visiting Bihar, the then President of India, Dr APJ Abdul Kalam said how impressed he was to learn during a state visit of Singapore's commitment to the project. And it was only because it involved re-establishing a Nalanda for our times, that Amartya Sen agreed to chair the Mentor Group that would guide the project. Enthused by the idea, the State Government of Bihar, decided proactively to explore the setting up of a new Nalanda university. The project finally came under Government of India as a centrally funded project realizing the idea of re-establishing a Nalanda for the twenty-first century. The fact that the Central Government and the State Government of Bihar — both of which belonged to different political parties — worked in tandem on this project is a testimony both to the power of the Nalanda idea and the leadership of then Prime Minister Dr Manmohan Singh and Chief Minister Nitish Kumar.

The crucial decision of where to locate new Nalanda was settled when the State Government of Bihar announced that it would acquire land for the new university in Rajgir. The land was duly acquired and 450 acres of land was handed over to the new university in February 2011, thus firmly rooting new Nalanda in Rajgir and bringing into the story the place where this dream would be realized. So what do these two places mean for the new Nalanda university and how has the university engaged with them? As a sociologist, focus on places has been just as important to my work as focusing on the people who inhabit these places (Sabharwal 2006, pp. 44–76). An understanding of social geography is crucial to making sense of how the past has impacted both the physical landscape and the social fabric of a locale. The present encounter with place, while focused as it was on locating an institution, nevertheless required an understanding of place as crucial to the outcome.

Rajgir, literally translated as the Abode of Kings, lies almost 110 kilometres south east of Patna, the capital of Bihar state in eastern India. It is a place that has a long and varied history and seems to have been inhabited since pre-historic times, as evinced from tools and other objects uncovered during excavations (Jha 2011, p. 5). The most significant mention of Rajgir in the historical period is in the sixth and fifth century BCE with the founding of the Magadh empire by Bimbisara, who is believed to have ruled his kingdom from this fortified city. He was followed by his son Ajatashatru in 491 BCE, who built the first fortification in Pataliputra (present-day Patna) where the capital of this empire was later shifted. Ancient Rājagṛha (Pali: Rājagaha) was not only the first capital of the Magadh empire, it is believed to represent an early example of Indian urbanization, finding mention in an early Pali text as one of six great cities.[1] It is considered to have been a flourishing city during the Buddha's time (ibid., p. 2).

The Magadhan capital was considered socially and ideologically very open and non-conventional and seemed to have encouraged and sustained a large population resulting from the presence of an organized production system and an agriculture that produced surplus (ibid., p. 3). Rajgir is also listed as one of the sixteen *Mahajanapadas* — or great cities — in Buddhist and Jain literature. Palaeobotanical studies in the Gangetic plain show the area sustaining large settlements backed by agricultural production which included double cropping and the cultivation of crops introduced from West Asia, South Europe and the Western Ghats and Southern India (ibid., p. 4). The presence of beads and semi precious stones also point to linkages with other areas and the presence of trade or other networks (ibid.). "Rajagrha, close to the southeastern corner of this (middle Gangetic) plain, could have hardly remained untouched with the contemporary current of changes" (ibid., p. 5). Pataliputra, the succeeding capital of the Magadh empire, became a major administrative and commercial centre. However, it is believed that Rajgir continued to be a "subsidiary administrative centre ... and a commercial transit point ... being relegated gradually to the centre of religious interest, shortly after the Maurya-Sunga phase was over" (ibid., p. 7).

In terms of places in the neighbourhood of Rajgir, the remains of old Nalanda university which existed from 499 CE to 1199 CE lie at a distance of 12 kilometres north. At a distance of a further 12 kilometres north from old Nalanda lies Pawapuri, the final resting place of Mahavira, the last of the Jain *Tirthankaras* (believed to have attained enlightenment in 527 BCE). Bodh Gaya, the site of the Buddha's enlightenment is 80 kilometres distant in the southwestern direction. Twelve kilometres before Bodh Gaya is Gaya on the banks of the river Falgu (known as Niranjana in Bodh Gaya), an important site for essential Hindu rituals pertaining to the salvation of the souls of the dead. The myth of this river links it to the epic *Ramayana* and one of its protagonists Sita. The district headquarter town Bihar Sharif, a distance of 30 kilometres northeast from Rajgir, is a medieval settlement with some important Islamic shrines.

Rajgir has historically been referred to by many different names — Girivraja (signifying it being nestled within the valley of five hills — Vaibhargiri, Vipulagiri, Ratnagiri, Sonagiri and Udayagiri), Kuśāgrapura (in Xuanzang's account signifying the presence of a particular grass), Barhadrathapura (in Mahabharata), Vasumati (in *Ramayana*) and of course, Rājagṛha (the abode of kings) (Amar 2016). Present-day Rajgir, constitutes a modern settlement, market and fortification ground and a concentration of historical and religious sites inside the valley. While a division may be made between the valley nested within the hills and the modern town which has evolved around the boundaries of the fortification wall on the eastern, northern and western sides, with the southern side leading to the valley and multiple religious sites surrounding the hot water springs on the Vaibhargiri and Vipulagiri hills, this divide is not considered historically valid and most scholars today consider the division artificial (ibid., p. 1).

Rajgir's presence in prehistory finds mention in the epic *Mahabharata* and Puranic literature, as the capital of the cruel king Jarasandha, believed to be the person responsible for Krishna fleeing Mathura to found a new city in Dwaraka on the Gujarat coast. It is believed that Krishna returned to Rajgir with the Pandavas, Arjun and Bhim where the latter slayed Jarasandha. Sites ascribed to Jarasandha are still believed to be present in Rajgir such as his wrestling ground (*akhara*) and the place where Bhima ripped his body into two parts at the end of fourteen days of battle, shedding so much blood that the land must forever remain red (*ranbhoomi*) (ibid., p. 53). The temple attributed to the female demon now regarded as a goddess — Jara who joined Jarasandha into one after he was born in two halves, thus giving him his name (literally one joined by Jara) — sits at the entrance of the old city, albeit in renovated form.

Following the shift of the capital to Pataliputra, Rajgir, witnessed a change in fortune, but, it resumed the status of capital once again, for a short while during the rule of Sisunaga (accession 411 BCE) who founded the new Magadhan dynasty (Jha 2011, p. 10). He too however later shifted his capital this time to Vaisali, a city from where his mother hailed. Rajgir did not totally lose out in importance thereafter and there remain records of activity in the area in subsequent years. Sometime in the third century BCE, Ashoka is believed to have constructed a *stupa* after taking out the Buddha's relics from the *stupa* originally built by Ajatsatru (ibid., p. 10). The city was regarded as a trading centre up to the Kushana period in the first and second century CE, and is apparently mentioned as a military garrison during the invasion of Magadha by Kharavela (ibid., p. 10). One of the Son Bhandar caves is believed to have been built during the early Gupta period (fourth century CE) and the Maniar Math, another unique structure, has a construction period that stretches from BCE to the post-Gupta period (ibid., p. 10). Rajgir is mentioned as a district (*vishaya*) in the Nalanda Copper Plate of Devapala suggesting that old Nalanda was under its jurisdiction (ibid., p. 10).

Rajgir seems to have always maintained its attraction to pilgrims and seekers, especially with regard to its five surrounding hills with their rich cultural ecology, and as a transit point in trade mainly due to its location. Buddhists, Jains and Hindus of various shades continued to frequent Rajgir. Rajgir also finds mention in both Buddhist and Jain historical texts under different names and there is mention of the Buddha having been here, both while searching for enlightenment and afterwards, especially during the rain retreat. Similarly, the twentieth Jain *Tirthankara* Suvrata was believed to be born here and the last Mahavira spent fourteen monsoons in Rajgir. For the followers of orthodox Brahmanism, Rajgir was a place of pilgrimage with centres emerging around the hot springs in the Vaibhara and Vipula hills. "All the religions in Rājagrha, especially the newly emerging heterodoxical ones, got generous moral and material support from both the ruling elites as well as the ever greater stronger trading community" (Jha 2011, p. 11). Jha postulates that this accommodating social ambience promoted upward social mobility of the trading community, which was an emergent community of the time" (ibid., p. 11). Despite these competing cults, local cults such as the snake-worshipping Naga cult as symbolized by the Maniar Math continued to flourish (ibid., p. 11). Much later in history, the founder of Sikhism — Guru Nanak — is also believed to have visited Rajgir in 1506 CE or thereabouts, en route to Gaya and to have blessed a cold water tank for people to get a cold water source amidst all the hot springs.

In medieval times, Islamic saints were attracted to Rajgir. Of them Makhdum Shah Sharf'Ud-din was the most prominent. The cave where he meditated is an important shrine and pilgrim centre. Jha sites Faxian as having noted in the fifth century CE that the inner city of Rajgir was desolate, a sign that Buddhist presence was on the decline. However, Xuanzang in the seventh century CE seems to list places of Buddhist importance some of which are not mentioned by Faxian when he visited in 415 CE. Xuanzang is believed to have noted that the inner city had been taken over by the Brahmanas whose importance seemed to have enlarged in medieval times (ibid., p. 12). The construction of the Maniar Math which is interpreted as a local ethnic cult transforming itself into a Shaivite shrine during the Gupta period (fourth and fifth century CE) is illustrative of this takeover. Jha summarizes this period thus

> The Jain and Brahmanical idols continued to be installed and shrines were built in stages from the Gupta period down to the late medieval and early modern periods. The adjacent cave of Son Bhandar, which initially was probably excavated for the Ajivakas, was taken over in turn first by the Jains and then by the Vaishnavas. But then the Jains seem to have reclaimed it once again during the Pala (800 to 1200 AD) period. (Jha 2011. p. 12)

The emergence of the original Nalanda university or *Mahavihara* in the fifth century CE, led once again to the revival of "Rajgir's importance owing to its Buddhist association. But the importance remained primarily religious and not scholastic" (ibid., p. 12). Rajgir once again became a pilgrim centre for Buddhists apart from Jains and Brahmins. There is evidence of the installation of many statues of Buddha particularly on Griddhakuta, the sixth hill considered sacred to the Buddhists. Similarly, there are many Jain religious structures belonging to the late medieval and modern periods, but because of the fact that much of the local building was done in mud and timber no buildings remain. As described above, some sites fell into neglect and were appropriated by others probably more than once, or have been overlaid by others and building materials of one have been utilized in another or used by locals in constructing homes in neighbouring settlements.

Given the size of Rajgir, even a brief listing of historical finds establishes the high density of sites and the richness of the landscape. To begin with there is the cyclopean wall, a massive fortification of crude stone masonry comprising single huge undressed stones, atop the hills — considered a unique architectural feat which stretches a length of 48 kilometres (ibid., p. 23). The stones seem to sit in a very neat and compact manner despite the fact that no mortar or cement has been used to bind these walls. The walls seem to be interspersed with bastions — some of which are clearly visible while others seem to have been appropriated for other uses. The same holds true for what are believed to be watch towers, two of which can be seen on Vaibhara hill and some others identified on other hills. On Vaibhara hill the watch tower is also referred to as *Jarasandha ki Baithak* or Jarasandha's seating area, otherwise referred to in Buddhist sources as Pippala Cave. While there are believed to be two ancient Jain and Shaiva temples close by on Vaibharagiri hill, the watch tower on Vipulagiri hill has been almost taken over by a newly constructed Jain temple on it (ibid., p. 27). Also identified is Bimbisara's jail of which no certainty can be established except that Griddhakuta can be sighted from there. It is believed that when Bimbisara imprisoned his father Ajatashatru, the only favour his father asked was to be able to see the abode of the Buddha at Griddhakuta.

In the area around Jethian valley, in Rajgir is Jarasandha's wrestling area or *akhara*, another stone masonry platform quite like the watch tower or the bastions, with the site of his death close by. Yashtivana or Latthivana in the Jethian valley is where the Buddha is believed to have been staying when Bimbisara invited him to come to Rajgir with great pomp and show. Moving on from Jethian one gets to the Banganga: a river that derives its name from the *Mahabharata* legend. It is said to have emerged when Bhima hit a rock with an arrow (*ban*). There are shell inscriptions on the rocky surface near Banganga, which are yet to be deciphered and the marks of what are considered chariots wheels from the time of the *Mahabharata* on another rocky surface. Nearby is another structure like a two storey stupa, excavated by the Archaeological Survey of India (ASI) as recently as 2001.

The most important Buddhist site in Rajgir, namely Griddhakuta, is on the sixth hill, attached to Sailagiri which houses the caves occupied by the Buddha and Ananda, and the place from where the Buddha is believed to have preached the Lotus Sutra (*Saddharma Pundarika Sutra*). The identification of the hill is reminiscent of Basso's *Wisdom Lies in Places* (Basso 1999), and the description of how places get their names. We have seen some examples of how places in Rajgir have got their names due to mythical occurrences, but here, it is the vertical, sharp edged, grey coloured rocks of Griddhakuta creating the "visual impression resembling ... perched vultures" (Jha 2011, p. 67) that alone would have given this hill its name vulture peak. The remains of some structures are believed to be scattered in and around these hills. The first structure that appears leading up to the hill has been identified as the monastery and the mango grove of Bimbisara's physician Jivaka. There are also the remains of where a deer park stood at the base of the hill near where an ancient path ascends the hill connecting "a host of Buddhist relics, scattered over slopes, terraces, flat tops, summits and in caves" (ibid., p. 65). Bimbisara is believed to have had the pathway up the hill constructed to make it easier to ascend the hill to hear the Buddha preach.

On another hill are on the Saptaparni caves where the first Buddhist Council was held around 486 or 483 BCE, shortly after the death of the Buddha (ibid., p. 92), with the aim of compiling the teachings of the Buddha into the *Pitakas.* It is believed to have been attended by 500 monks and presided over by Mahakasyapa, the foremost disciple of the Buddha. This space is believed to have been constructed by Ajatshatru. On Vaibhara hill the largest of the Rajgir hills, lies the Son Bhandar cave believed to be hiding treasure, and another adjacent cave. The two are different and appear to have been carved many centuries apart. There are clear Jain linkages with the caves (Jha 2011, p. 86). The Vaibhara hills also have two ancient Jain temples and an ancient Shiva temple close by. Vipulagiri is an important hill with Jain linkages and is dotted with late medieval and modern Jain temples and more seem to be being built even now.

The famed hot springs of Rajgir lie on the Vaibhara and Vipula hills, and draw large numbers of visitors mainly from Bihar. There are places of worship linked to these springs some of which still exist. The largest is Brahma *kund* into which seven springs drain, and on the opposite side the Surya *kund* has five springs clustered together (ibid., p. 99). Further away on the same hill is what now stands as Makhdum *Kund*, named after the Muslim saint Hazrat Makhdum-ul-Haq, believed to have been appropriated sometime in the Middle Ages. Near the Surya *kund* is believed to be the remains of the stone house of Devadutta — cousin and disciple of the Buddha, and the place he entered into *samadhi*.

Moving to the plains area, one encounters the famed bamboo grove known as Venuvana, gifted to the Buddha by Bimbisara. Its importance lies in the fact that this was the first fixed place for the Buddha and his disciples to live in Rajgir (ibid., p. 105). It is also believed that at its entrance a stupa was built over the remains of the Buddha's trusted disciple Mudgalayana, which now lies in ruins with the top now occupied by graves of Muslim saints. There are other monuments and remains including some rock paintings too on a hill further away.

This whistle-stop tour of Rajgir and environs amply illustrates the dense archaeological richness of the landscape of Rajgir and also reveals it as a site of multiple religions and sects. These multireligious sites bear witness to the words of Jacob N. Kinnard that

> although the western Orientalists who have studied space and place in India, in particular, have gone to great lengths to fix their identities, to demonstrate their origins, and thus to constitute them, discursively and physically, as singular and thus fundamentally monosemic, the

> spaces themselves, and very often the identities of the various people who lay claim to them, are inherently polysemic, dynamic, and ... fluid. These are places in motion (Kinnard 2014, p. 4).

Rajgir is a classic case of a place in motion. Its rich multilayered past and present make it an interesting space in which new structures are constantly being added and old ones are being reinvented or converted anew into something else. In the last century, following surveys many of which came to identify Rajgir as a predominantly Buddhist site, there has been construction of new international Buddhist temples and monasteries, each in their own distinctive architectural form adding diversity to the built form visible in Rajgir. These include sects from Japan, Myanmar, Thailand, Vietnam, among others and the construction of the heritage ropeway to the top of Ratnagiri hill where a Japanese built peace pagoda resides. A Jain monastery Veerayatan run by a venerable Jain priestess, established in 1973, is probably the largest single private enterprise in Rajgir at the moment, running not only a charitable eye clinic and a school and an education college and nursing college in Pawapuri, but also a museum on the life of Mahavir. Given this overwhelming identification of Rajgir with enterprises of peace, religion and philosophy it is somewhat ironical that the largest single entity in Rajgir, set up by the Ministry of Defence, Government of India in 1999 is an Ordnance Factory spread over 3,000 acres. While the factory is still to begin full production, an entire defence township has been laid out. There is also a central school on campus which serves children of government employees in the area. An international convention centre and a park named Pandu Pokhar at a spot where the Pandavas are believed to have bathed before challenging Jarasandha to battle (ibid., p. 114) have been built by the government.

Rajgir continues to attract large numbers of visitors many of them pilgrims but are also tourists who come to visit the sites — the bulk of domestic tourists are from within the state while international visitors belong largely to East Asia. Rajgir and Bodh Gaya —along with the heritage Nalanda ruins — are the leading Buddhist attractions in the state; most tourists on the Buddhist circuit visit all three places. These sites, old and new, and others in the vicinity are also of historical and academic interest to many people. It should come as no surprise that Rajgir has since the 1800s attracted historians, scholars of religion, art historians, archaeologists as also geographers and geologists due of its historical and physiographic richness and depth. Many of its sculptures and other antiquarian remains have been moved to museums and often put together in a pattern that defies any interpretation of the original space and its usage.

HISTORY, HERITAGE AND REVIVAL

Into this ever-changing and dynamic landscape of Rajgir, the new Nalanda university is now being born and carving out a presence and an identity for itself. How is the university positioning itself in this milieu and how is it engaging with the place dimension of its existence?

At 450 acres, on the Chabilapur State Highway leading from Rajgir to Jahanabad, the new Nalanda will be the second largest single entity both in spatial and human terms, second only, ironically, to the aforementioned Ordnance factory which is at the opposite end of Rajgir on the road leading to Bihar Sharif. New Nalanda's location is also going to mean that Rajgir will grow in another direction away from the city along the State Highway 71. To build the university in physical terms has meant that much thought be given to what already exists and how the physical structure wants to engage with the place in general and the site in particular. The site of the university runs parallel to the Rajgir hills that stand as sentinels in the background. Given the immense historicity of those hills which hosted the Buddhist Councils and other events, the university took two decisions — first, that all vistas in the campus will have a view of the hills or look towards the hills; and second, that no structure on the land will attempt to dwarf the hills. Thus buildings are going to be generally a maximum height of four storeys. It has also been a stated philosophy from inception that even though 450 acres seems like a small township, the university intends to be outward looking in its lived philosophy. Walls if any will be porous: the university will not be an ivory tower looking out at the world but an institution that has a harmonious relationship between what has traditionally been called the "town and the gown".

Determined to draw upon the learnings from the land and the ruins of old Nalanda the university embarked on a global design competition to select architects for its master plan and design after articulating the architectural vocabulary for the new campus. In a first, Nalanda University, with technical assistance from the USAID-led bilateral Partnership to Advance Clean Energy – Deployment (PACE-D) Program, is striving to be a *Net Zero Energy, Net Zero Emissions, Net Zero Water*, and *Net Zero Waste* campus, the first of its kind in India. By phrasing a net zero energy vision for the university, an attempt has been made to tie up the historical legacy inherited by Nalanda University with one of the most urgent contemporary issues that needs to be addressed, namely, environmental sustainability. The architectural design follows the logical sequence of achieving Net Zero Energy Building (NZEB) status — focusing on building form and orientation to reduce energy loads, resource efficiency, energy efficiency, and low-energy comfort systems and then strategizing to meet the residual load through renewable means, mainly solar energy.

The core philosophy of the design is water conservation, since Rajgir is entirely dependent on rainwater for all its water needs. The university will have a 13-hectare lake at its centre, with many holding ponds in the outlying areas which will hold excess water and also feed the lake when its level dips (see Figure 2.1). This central water body draws upon traditional Indian design, of the central water tank in many places of worship that sustain large populations. The earth excavated for the lake will be sufficient for raising the plinth level of all the roads and buildings on campus with enough soil left over for making bricks on site. Nalanda has chosen to move away from burnt brick for the cladding of the walls to using instead, Compressed Stabilized Earth Blocks (CSEB). This unique brick will be manufactured on site thus further reducing the carbon footprint of the construction process.

The endeavour is that through the use of responsible architectural philosophy, Nalanda University campus will demonstrate the feasibility of implementing and operating NZEBs in India and create awareness amongst the building industry and be as cutting edge in a new domain of sustainability, as ancient Nalanda was in other domains. Already, since the launch of the Nalanda design process, other institutions have not only asked for support to understand the whole process followed in running the competition for choosing the architects and masterplanners but have also been enthused to walk the path of Net Zero. With construction having begun on site, it is a matter of time that this unique campus will become a reality. Also on display after due testing will be the Dessicant Assisted Evaporative Cooling (DEVAP) Towers based on special external combustion engines.

Conceived as a research university in a very specific culture and environ, Nalanda recognizes that it has both academic and societal roles. Thus, apart from engaging in research and introducing students to the culture of research, is the commitment to the needs of society. These ideas have informed all development activities at Nalanda, be it the academic core, the governance structure, the faculty and student recruitment and of course the infrastructure. Given that it is virtually impossible for any university today to be truly universal and teach the full range of all academic disciplines

FIGURE 2.1
Master Plan of the Nalanda University

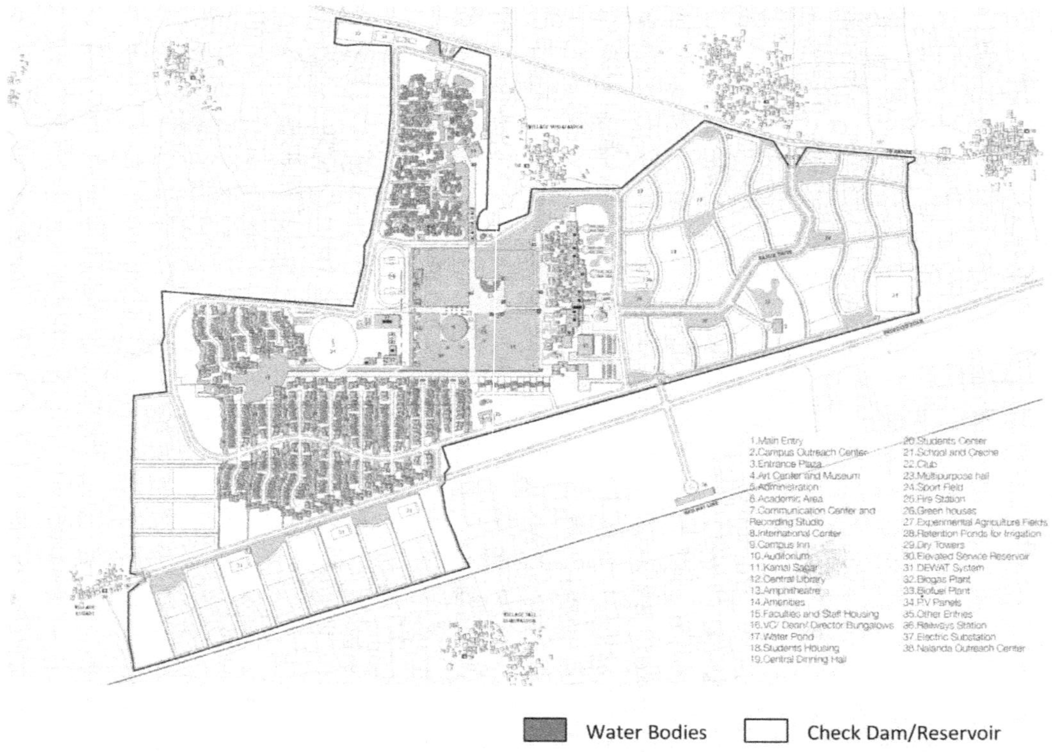

Source: Vastu Shilpa Consultants, Ahmedabad.

from A to Z, the university decided to focus at the core on disciplines that resonate with the idea of Nalanda and which will impact the setting of the university, i.e. the place. The list of schools decided upon include the Schools of Buddhist Studies, Philosophy and Comparative Religion, Historical Studies, Ecology and Environment, International Relations and Peace Studies, Languages and Literature, Information Technology and Economics to which the School of Public Health was later added.

It was decided that the university should begin with the Schools of Ecology and Environment Studies (SEES) and the School of Historical Studies (SHS), in the first instance, since each of these schools would immediately cover the continuum from the old Nalanda — archaeology and historical Asian interconnections — to the most pressing concern on the planet today, namely environment and ecology. The schools would also be ideal vehicles to make an impact on the actual locational space and would serve as examples of the kind of learning Nalanda is trying to impart. A third school titled Buddhist Studies, Philosophy and Comparative Religion (SBS) was launched in August 2016. It complements well the other two schools and already there are courses that are cross-listed across SHS and SBS with SEES hoping to join the mix.

Led by Dean Anjana Sharma, the academic programmes were planned around concept notes, formulated with inputs from experts in the field. These were discussed and approved at the Board level. Using these as base documents, the focus areas of each school was arrived at after further discussion with experts in the field and alongside were also developed some of the other givens of the academic curriculum. These included the idea of Asian interconnections and inter-disciplinarity. Viewing the university as a space that must engage with its surroundings and the context of its setting, it was also decided that an essential component of being a Nalanda scholar would be to move outside the confines of the classroom and to engage with the real world. To further that idea, the focus areas of the schools were defined in a concentric circle approach as moving from the immediate surroundings to regional, national and international perspectives on issues. SEES focuses on issues such as human ecology, hydrology, disaster management, agriculture, climate change and energy studies which are all areas of concern in the region. Similarly, SHS focuses upon Asian interconnections, archaeology, art history, global history and economic history. SBS focuses in Asian connections, the spread of Buddhism, Buddhist archaeology and art, South and East Asian religious traditions, interactions of religious traditions and theory and method of religious studies. For this academic vision to be realized, it needed to be communicated to the faculty to ensure that they would respect this philosophy and vision and give it life as would the students. This has been done consistently.

This said, it needs to be pointed out that new Nalanda university is unique in relation to other institutions of excellence in India, in that its geographical location is far removed from an urban centre, which has traditionally been the case with all such Central Government institutions. Almost all the Higher Education Institutions in India tend to be concentrated in urban centres and state capitals. Nalanda by virtue of its historical legacy and the desire to be located close to the remains of the original centre of learning, has been located in Rajgir, which is a small habitation with a population of 26,000 people, most of whom run small establishments or other business largely catering to the local tourists who throng to Rajgir to visit the local sites.

The location aspect of new Nalanda, did come in for some comments from those involved with higher education. There were some who while being supportive of the idea of the new Nalanda, were sceptic of the location of the new university in a remote area (Altbach 2012) and wondered whether the lack of amenities and distance from other academic networks, museums. etc., will be a hindrance in recruitment of faculty and students. However, while there is merit in this view in terms of general planning and these factors are relevant specially so for any green field university project but not quite so in the case of this historic revival project. Nalanda university is not just another new university — it is a heritage-inspired university where the location is of prime importance to achieving that outcome. Yes, the remote rural location of Rajgir poses problems with regard to urban amenities and givens like medical care, places of entertainment, good schooling and big stores; but these problems are not insurmountable and reason enough to relocate to the crowded capital of Patna!

By situating itself in a living historical and ecological laboratory, Nalanda university is uniquely placed to draw upon the richness of the locale and to bring to it scholarship and engagement which will further the research on the area and simultaneously expose students to the research process, encouraging them to move outside of the classroom. The Nalanda academic community has engaged with Rajgir in fulfilling its mission to link research to the community and its needs through a range of activities. These include ecological walks in the hills, listing of biodiversity projects studying water contamination, analysis of post-harvest loss, environmental effects of tourism, problems of garbage disposal, an analysis of historical sites, looking to train tourist guides at Nalanda, collecting biowaste to make electricity, pioneering a project that has mounted a small dynamo on the horse carriages to store electricity which the *tonga* owner can use later at home and having organized for the first time ever, in the fundamental spirit of Buddhist and Jain respect for all forms of life, a health check for horses that pull the *tongas* in Rajgir.

Simultaneously, the university is also becoming part of the cartography of Rajgir, and is being regarded as one of the local establishments albeit with an international focus. Until the buildings on the 450-acre campus come up and the university shifts to its permanent home, it is functioning from temporary premises spread all over Rajgir. This includes university offices, class rooms and residences in one campus and three student residence halls and another office complex. In criss-crossing Rajgir, frequenting the shops and eating places, seeking other services, etc., the university community is making itself accessible to the residents of Rajgir and demystifying the university as the community makes its home in Rajgir. The community has also built links with the craftspeople in neighbouring villages and not only procured much of their produce but also introduced design elements, allowing the weavers to weave certain material exclusively for the university. This initiative, wholly driven by some of us at the university, seeks to empower and protect fast-vanishing intangible forms of heritage.

At a more formal level, the university is taking its research objective further by launching the Rajgir Archaeological Survey Project (RASP)[2] in collaboration with the Bihar Heritage Development Society (an autonomous society under the Art, Culture & Youth Department, Government of Bihar). The partnership is part of the strategy of the university to involve certain established institutions in the region in research activities, so as to both gain from them and help them upgrade their research potential. This project will undertake an archaeological survey of Rajgir to better understand the archaeological landscape of this historical city through available antiquarian remains. RASP will examine the multiphased and multilayered development of Rajgir as an urban, political and religious centre. In this process, it will study the settlement history, its connection with hinterlands, and the nature of early state/capital city along with the religious histories.

The Project entails a micro survey of the archaeological site of Rajgir — the ancient capital of Magadha. The site though excavated in the early twentieth century, most identifications were based primarily on texts. The current project aims to move away from textual archaeology, to document every man-made feature on the ground through a careful survey of the valley and the fortified mound area. The list of features to be covered would include: regional context and relationship with hinterland; local setting; settlements, roads, temples/shrines, and fields in relation to the city and natural landscape; evidence for forms and scales of production (pottery, metal, trade, etc.); long-term political and religious history (specifically after the transfer of capital to Pataliputra) and evidence for later Buddhism (Amar 2016). The survey will draw upon the methodology adopted for the Vijaynagar metropolitan survey project conducted by Carla Sinopoli and Kathleen Morrison (2007) over a ten-year period.

In addition, the university conducts Rajgir Heritage walks in association with the Bihar Heritage Development Society on four separate routes namely, historical Rajgir, new Rajgir, Ecological Rajgir and multireligious Rajgir. These have commentary in English and Hindi for both domestic and international visitors. It is also trying to create a living archive of Rajgir in a multimedia project that has the potential of becoming over the years an important documentation of a living place and changes in it.

At an international level, the university has signed an agreement with Peking University, which among other things, will support the setting up of the Xuanzang Centre for Asian Studies on the Nalanda campus. This, in effect, will revive and build upon the old connections of the Chinese monk-scholar to the space from where he set forth on his return home with the *sutras* and the knowledge acquired at Nalanda university.

While the association with Rajgir has been that of locational place, that with old Nalanda has been about situating it in its heritage. Considering, the manner in which old Nalanda lives on in the shared memory of South and East Asia, if not beyond, this focus on Nalanda as common heritage (and the need for its conservation) is completely to be expected. Thus, the university's engagement with Nalanda has been at many levels. It has hosted scholars who are experts on Nalanda — Max Deeg, Rick Asher, Anne Cheng to name a few — supported and encouraged others to work on Nalanda (M.B. Rajani), engaged with the ASI and the tourist guides at the site in discussions about how the university may help specially with the cataloguing of material in the Nalanda museum, and of course hosted more than one seminar on heritage and one in particular with ASI on the heritage of old Nalanda.

In dealing with the heritage aspect of old Nalanda one needs to keep in mind that the heritage aspect of Nalanda plays out in various ways and at various levels. There is the telling of the tale of its greatness and size which is reverential at one end and on the other, based on a literal reading of the sources, estimates a size and numbers so large, that experts find hard to explain in terms of sheer sustaining power of the land and resources. There is also the story of its destruction which claims that the famed library being set on fire burnt for anything from three days to six weeks or more. There are those who insist that Nalanda did not come to an end in 1199 CE but continued as a centre of learning for many years after that. Then there are those who contrary to the Buddhist tradition of dialogue, regard themselves as the exclusive keepers of both Buddhism and the Nalanda tradition, and believe that their views — sound and unsound — on the heritage of old Nalanda should be taken on board. Emotional and biased though some of these views may be, yet they all reflect the fame and importance of Nalanda and the desire in people's minds to be connected with it or control it in some sense.

The new Nalanda university, as mandated, has encouraged scholarship to both consolidate and address new areas of research on the Nalanda tradition and on Xuanzang's record of the *Journey to the Western World.* At some point in the initial years of the university's revival, it was remarked, that while the fame and influence of Nalanda were unquestioned in the Asian world at the very least, Nalanda had not quite got its global due since it was not included in the UNESCO World Heritage list, regarded by many as the official global recognition of cultural greatness. In fact, Nalanda was not even on the proposed list of Government of India. The last could be explained by the fact that given the number of historical sites in India, there are regional pulls and tugs and the government has to pick and choose which nomination to send forth when.

Be that as it may, the new Nalanda University was requested to support the application by Government of India for the inscription of the *Excavated Remains of Nalanda Mahavihara,* in the UNESCO World Heritage List. The university put together scholars who could help with the dossier that needed to be submitted and also organized a workshop in Rajgir for all stakeholders on the Indian side to come together and deliberate upon the various dimensions of this application. What became clear very early on in the process was that the UNESCO Dossier is not an academic document — it is a bureaucratic document that needs to be filled as per pre-set guidelines. The application process seemed to rest most importantly on which category was chosen to make the application for inscription.

To those of us who were involved in such an enterprise at a close level for the first time, particularly for Dean Sharma and I, it opened up a whole new vocabulary and paradigm on how culture and its outgrowths may be categorized into a universal standard framework. The whole enterprise of inscription seemed to rest upon the description of the category "outstanding universal value". This meant setting out what was unique about the remains of old Nalanda that they be considered a part of world heritage. The statements of "Outstanding Universal Value" are made up of several elements: a brief synthesis of the property, justification of criteria, a statement of integrity, a statement of authenticity, requirements for protection and management. To be included on the World Heritage List, sites must be of outstanding universal value and meet at least one out of ten selection criteria.

> The nomination was finally made under two criteria (iv) and (vi) which read as follows:
> (iv) to be an outstanding example of a type of building, architectural or technological ensemble or landscape which illustrates (a) significant stage(s) in human history;
> (vi) to be directly or tangibly associated with events or living traditions, with ideas, or with beliefs, with artistic and literary works of outstanding universal significance. (The Committee considers that this criterion should preferably be used in conjunction with other criteria); (UNESCO Website).

It was an educative experience and while experts may have views on various statements both historical and otherwise, made in the dossier, the fact remains that if the UNESCO listing is the final stamp of global significance then, a site like Nalanda should be on it. The inscription is a matter of pride for those in Nalanda and in Bihar and will hopefully act as an impetus for further archaeological investigation around the site. For the new Nalanda university, the inscription process coming through in 2016 just as new Nalanda graduated its first batch of students, was a perfect coming together of history, heritage and place.

Notes

1. These six great cities are Rajagrha, Champa, Sravasti, Saketa, Kausambi and Kasi as listed in the Digha Nikaya, a part of the Pitaka literature.
2. This project was written up largely by Dr Abhishek Amar from Hamilton College, USA while he was Visiting Associate Professor at Nalanda University in 2016.

Bibliography

Altbach, Philip G. "Right Concept, Wrong Place". *The Hindu*, 2 July 2012.

Amar, Abhishek. “The RASP document”. Unpublished document for Nalanda University, 2016.

Basso, Keith H. *Wisdom Sits in Places: Landscape and Language among the Western Apache*. Albuquerque: University of New Mexico Press, 1999.

Jha, Satyendra Kumar. *Rajagrha The City of Eminence*, Patna: K.P. Jayaswal Research Institute, 2011.

Kinnard, Jacob, N. *Places in Motion The Fluid Identities of Temples, Images, and Pilgrims*. New York: Oxford University Press, 2014.

Sabharwal, Gopa. *Ethnicity and Class, Social Divisions in an Indian City*. New Delhi: Oxford University Press. 2006.

Sinopoli, Carla M. and Kathleen Morrison. *The Vijayanagara Metropolitan Survey*. Memoirs of the Museum of Anthropology. University of Michigan. Memoir 41. 2007.

UNESCO Website for criteria of World Heritage Nomination <http://whc.unesco.org/en/criteria/> (accessed 5 March 2017).

Yeo, George. “Nalanda and the Asian Renaissance”. *Straits Times* (Singapore), 14 April 2011.

3

INDIA, MAGADHA, NALANDA Ecology and a Premodern World System[1]

Frederick Asher

My recently retired colleagues at the University of Minnesota, Carla and Wim Phillips, have asserted, "By the late fifteenth century, the ocean had ceased to be a barrier and had instead become a highway or bridge to what lay beyond."[2] That may pertain to Europe and the voyage of Columbus, about whom they were writing, but in Asia, way before the late fifteenth century, water created a trading network — at the very least a proto-world system. In fact, as early as the third millennium BCE we have evidence for trade by sea, and a flourishing trade network is documented by the first century BCE.

Around 2500 BCE, when we first can document cross-cultural sea trade, civilizations with access to the ocean could enhance local economies through trade, providing not only a means of selling locally produced goods to a vastly expanded market, but also providing a means of importing luxury goods and expanding the repertoire of products locally available. Sea trade created a system linking a huge area extending from East Africa to Arabia and on to China, bridging a region that transcended cultures and kingdoms and regions of distinct sovereignty. What is the advantage to the sea? Imagine taking goods overland, even on well-established routes. Traders would have needed many pack animals, a very large herd of them, to take the same weight or volume of goods that can be carried on a single boat; a single ship's cargo of 500 tons would have been enough to provide every inhabitant of Rome with one pound of pepper per year,[3] probably an exaggeration but nonetheless a useful figure in visualizing the impact of sea trade. A mule can carry about 100 kilograms and travel only about 25 kilometres in a day, so it would take about 4,500 pack animals to carry the amount that could be loaded on one ship. Michael Pearson puts the contrast even more powerfully, noting that a dhow can travel the same distance as a camel caravan in one-third of the time and that a boat can carry the equivalent of 1,000 camel loads.[4] Even before deep keels were invented, the monsoon winds understood, and the direct 12 degree north latitude route was recognized, boats could go directly from point A to point B, where there were probably members of their own community at what Philip Curtin calls trade diasporas[5] who could assist with local negotiations over price and provide a reasonably familiar environment in which to rest before returning home with locally acquired goods for trade. I do not mean to suggest that trade systems were constant, unchanging through time. We have relatively scant records of the changes except for the goods themselves found at places distant from the site of their origin, a few inscriptions, and one trader's account, the *Periplus of the Erythrean Sea*. None of these documents the beginnings of Monsoon Asia trade, however. That we get from some Harappan representations of a boat[6] and the great dock at the site of Lothal[7] as well as some objects found at sites distant from the Indus, for example, Harappan seals at Ur and Mesopotamian cylinder seals found at Harappa. Evidence that they were transported via the ocean comes from Rafiq Mughal's discovery of Harappan seals at two sites on Bahrain, possibly a transit point in trade between South Asia and the Arabian Peninsula.[8]

By the first century BCE, perhaps the first century of the Common Era, the evidence expands. A potsherd discovered at the Egyptian port of Quseir-al-Qadim, on the Red Sea, bears a fragmentary Tamil inscription, as does a potsherd discovered on Thailand's Andaman coast.[9] An Indian ivory from Pompeii has a date before the year 79, and the site of Begram, alas today the site of a U.S. airbase in Afghanistan, yielded first-century BCE ivories from India, glass from Syria, and images from Alexandria.[10] Unless they were there because an individual collected these objects, they are more testament to overland trade than to the water. On the import side, the sites of Arikamedu and Alagankulam, both in Tamilnadu, show ample evidence of trade with Rome and north Africa during the first century.

But just a bit later, about the second or third century, we have the Stele from Vocañh, near Nha Trang on the coast in present-day Vietnam.[11] It bears a Sanskrit inscription written in Brahmi script that refers to a king who had the distinctively Indian name Srimara-raja. That means, of course, that someone in the region that today comprises Vietnam knew enough Sanskrit to compose the inscription and knew Brahmi well enough to write it. Even if we speculate that there was an Indian there who could do this, we still have to be reasonably confident that someone — perhaps all the people to whom the inscription was addressed — knew Sanskrit even if they could not read the script. A great many other early Sanskrit inscriptions found across Southeast Asia attest to the widespread use of the language, perhaps transmitted by mariners such as Buddhagupta, an Indian ship captain who left an inscription found at Seberang Perai in the Kedah region of Malaysia.[12]

This, of course, is just one of a great many aspects of culture across Southeast Asia, that is, the eastern part of the Indian Ocean, that might be described — though not without many caveats — as Indian in origin. We need to recognize the adoption of Buddhism, Vaishnavism and Saivism, Sanskrit language and the widespread use of Brahmi across Southeast Asia as Indian exports. And we might add the style of architecture and sculpture that many have seen as based on Indian models. I confess to difficulty understanding how some of these features of Indian culture were absorbed by cultures distant from India. While it is safe to imagine relatively small communities of Indians functioning as a trade diaspora across coastal Southeast Asia, these alone would be insufficient to explain the adoption of religion, language and script, particularly since there were also almost surely trade diasporas to the west, for example, in Aden and Roman Egypt, where Indian culture was not absorbed. But I wonder about the extent to which these were implements of power. If there was no pre-contact writing system — and there is no evidence across Southeast Asia that there was, though there were writing systems in Aden and Roman Egypt — then the ability to maintain written records of trade might be seen as authoritative and powerful, something well worth adopting. Transliteration was only rarely used, for example, a few Malay inscriptions in Brahmi and Arabic scripts and in several inscriptions discovered in Cambodia that have the initial portion in Sanskrit and the subsequent portion in Khmer written in Brahmi script, so the language was generally maintained with the script. As for religion, Buddhism was a proselytizing faith from the time of the Buddha himself, who sought converts from among those who listened to his sermons. The adoption of Vaishnavism, Saivism and other Hindu religions may be harder to explain, though I am taken by Michael Pearson's proposal that, quite the opposite of proselytizing, Hindu religions were adopted as a result of initiative that came from Southeast Asian monarchs, who had heard about south Indian notions of kingship and so imported Brahmins to raise their own status and legitimacy.[13] I further assume that the monarchs' interest in the community and its culture was stimulated by the tax revenue it generated and the concern for and about foreigners who operated with their own legal and cultural institutions within the king's territory.

Architecture must be considered somewhat more carefully, because I think it offers an important cultural clue to the adoption of foreign media (Figure 3.1). One clue to the spread of temple architecture comes from the remains of a stone temple erected in 1281 by an Indian merchant guild in Quanzhou, in coastal China, one elegantly and intelligently examined by Dr Risha Lee in her dissertation.[14] The remains so closely resemble Indian Chola-style sculpture and temple components that there is reasonable debate among scholars as to the authorship of the temple: was it the work of Indian architects and sculptors, or was it a product of Chinese sculptors working under the supervision of an Indian master? In either case, it served the needs of an Indian trade diaspora resident in Quanzhou, a diaspora that must have included a whole system of support beyond the traders themselves. Priests and artists certainly would have been among the members of this diaspora community much as the Tamil communities in Singapore and Malaysia still today import their priests from India and use jet-setting *stapatis* who have developed an international reputation.

But in other parts of Monsoon Asia — in Cambodia, Vietnam, Java and Burma — the styles of architecture and sculpture, however much they may be indebted to Indian models, are largely local products, perhaps with some modest collaboration by Indian architects and sculptors (Figure 3.2). How do we explain that? Of course, we can only guess, but I would suggest that long prior to Angkor in Cambodia, My Son in Vietnam, Prambanan in Indonesia, and Pagan in Burma, there were earlier monuments that no longer remain. The earliest of these likely were constructed by Indian trade diasporas, perhaps in non-durable materials, although we can imagine that indigenous artists who participated in the production of these monuments gradually developed independent styles, particularly as these artists served indigenous patrons such as royalty who had recently converted to Buddhism, Shaivism or Vaishnavism and would have vastly preferred an indigenous visual cultural marker to one that expressed a link to an alien culture such as Tamil India. Why is there no evidence of these earlier structures? One guess might be that the trade diasporas were settled at seaports. That is a very harsh climate under any circumstance, and if we add rising sea levels, we might imagine the trade

FIGURE 3.1
Pillar with Narasimha, from Hindu Temple dated 1281, now built into the Kaiyuan Temple, Quanzhou

Source: All photographs in this chapter taken by the author.

diaspora communities moving somewhat inland, to the new coast, and the monuments on the sea falling victim to the ocean. But the surviving temples of Cambodia, Vietnam, Java and Burma are not the only or earliest sculptural or architectural evidence of a trade diaspora. The explorations of H.G. Quaritch Wales in the Kedah region of Malaysia have revealed a

FIGURE 3.2
Ashram Maha Rosei, Phnom Da, Cambodia, c. 7th–8th Century

great many material connections with India including Sanskrit inscriptions dating as early as the fourth century and written in Pallava-style script and even a stone statue datable to about the seventh century and said to come from a Pallava temple[15] and a stupa that I am certain comes from the Pala realm of eastern India (Figure 3.3).

The extensive remains at sites in Kedah, the Quanzhou temple, and the widespread use of Pallava script across Southeast Asia as well as the prevalence of Roman trade works at Arikamedu and Alangkulam all point to the importance of south India in premodern world trade. But why south India, rather than the north? First, it had the advantage of a great many possible ports, more than the north, which was largely dependent

FIGURE 3.3
Stupa, Bujang Valley, Kedah, Malaysia, probably imported from Eastern India, c. 8th Century

on overland and riverine routes for trade. And for trade with Rome or Roman Alexandria, ships sailing along the 12 degree north latitude could head directly from the Horn of Africa to the Kerala coast or head around the tip of India to either Sri Lanka or the Coromandel coast. Finally, south India produced commodities such as pepper, gold and diamonds, all small in size and so economically transported, all highly prized in Rome. With the decline of Rome, it was a relatively easy task to turn the maritime trade towards Southeast Asia and China, perhaps providing the financial capital that propelled the ascent of the Pallava dynasty. Nonetheless, western India continued to play a role in maritime trade as clearly indicated by the western Indian Brahmi inscriptions of the second through fourth centuries discovered in the Hoq Cave on Socotra Island, today part of Yemen.[16] Western India could provide textiles and copper as export items. And Tamralipta, in Bengal, was a major port, the one from which Faxian sailed on his return to China in the fifth century. But the coastal area of north India is significantly more limited than that of the south, and so it is not surprising to see landlocked ruling houses in the north, the Guptas, for example, who proclaimed their alliance with the relatively unimportant Licchavis rather than with the greater world. In fact, Samudragupta's *digvijaya*, proclaimed on the Allahabad pillar initially erected by Ashoka, covers almost exclusively kingdoms within South Asia,[17] reflecting a more insular world view than might be expected from a south Indian contemporary.

But there were things a landlocked power such as the Guptas and their contemporaries, the Vakatakas, or somewhat later Harshavardhana, could do to foster an international profile, and high among those things was support for Buddhists and Buddhist institutions such as Nalanda or Ajanta, in the case of the Vakatakas. In other words, it was not just great benevolence that led these dynastic powers to promote places for Buddhist learning. It was, rather, considerable pragmatism. Buddhism had a pan-Indian footprint and regular traffic in both directions between India and East Asia.

Following the time of the Guptas and Vakatakas, we see a major shift in regional power as documented by both inscriptions and material evidence such as surviving temples. That is, northern India became a land of relatively insignificant dynastic authority, while major dynasties rose to great power in the south. We lack evidence for the changes except in very broad terms, although I cannot help but wonder whether shifts in global trade were at least partly responsible for these major movements of power. Following the period of Gupta sovereignty and its landlocked dominion, prosperity seems to have shifted to coastal regions, marked by temple building in Orissa, in the Pallava realm at Mamallapuram, and off the coast of Mumbai at Elephanta, which may have served sailing merchants as they set off on long, treacherous voyages and again as a place of thanksgiving upon their return. It is with the rise of these coastal regions, particularly in Tamil Nadu, which had a long history of maritime trade, that we see well-established diaspora communities across Southeast Asia. I cannot help but wonder about the extent to which the rise of the Tang Dynasty in China and, soon after that, the Shailendra Dynasty on Java, facilitated a maritime trading network that generated a period of prosperity for all these regions, or did the trade network facilitate the power of these dynasties?

How, though, do we understand the cultural implications of this? I worry that academic terms such as Indian Asia or Greater India give an unwarranted role to India and suggest a kind of cultural imperialism that was never intended in the past. I far prefer the term Monsoon Asia to describe the regions and cultures involved in the economic and cultural exchanges, and I think it important to contemplate the pragmatic reasons for the adoption of many aspects of Indian culture across this region and to ask ourselves why Buddhism and the Hindu faiths, as well as Sanskrit language and Brahmi script, moved eastward, not west of the Indian subcontinent, even though the evidence for trade and the associated diaspora communities is just about as clear and well-documented west of India as it is to the east. I wonder if well-established indigenous religions (Judaism, Christianity and Islam), writing systems that were very long in use, and a trade network that extended still farther west, first to Rome, then to Byzantium, made the adoption of Indian cultural features, as opposed to Indian goods, unnecessary or unappealing.

With the rise of Islam and its superior navigational techniques as well as markets in Byzantium that hungered for Asian goods, contact became much more direct as very long sea voyages, rather than relay trade, were often used to exclude the middle-man in intermediate ports. Many of these suggest a Hadrami diaspora long before the period studied by Enseng Ho in his important contribution to diaspora and Indian Ocean studies.[18] For example, I might note the large number of grave markers in Quanzhou written in Arabic and Persian, the earliest dating 1171,[19] (Figure 3.4) all indicating direct maritime contact between China and the Hadramaut and possibly other parts of the Arab and Persian world. Still earlier there is ample evidence of direct maritime contact between Arabia and ports east of India. The earliest Muslim tombstone in Southeast Asia is probably one dated equivalent to 910 CE in a mausoleum in Alor Setar in Kedah, Malaysia as well as one found at Leran in East Java dating to 1082. These tombstones, suggest that someone, probably part of a trade diaspora, spoke Arabic and could instruct a stone carver in the production of the inscription.[20]

I also think about events, both political and ecological, that might have impacted sea trade or, more likely, fostered it. First, of course, we might recognize growing understandings, for example, navigational expertise and instrumentation, and an understanding of the regularity of the monsoon with its shifting winds that facilitated both outward and return voyages. And the invention of the deep keel that could keep ships both upright and on course in the middle of the ocean, not necessitating travel that hugged the

FIGURE 3.4
Muslim Graves, now Preserved in the Maritime Museum, Quanzhou

shore and thus permitting longer voyages. Political and ecological events likely impacted overland trade and thus made maritime trade voyages still more attractive. On the political side, we might think about the Sassanian relations with Tang Dynasty China,[21] very good indeed, that must have so dominated the Silk Route that Indian traders were disadvantaged and could, instead, turn attention to sea trade with Southeast Asia and East Asia. And, finally, we have evidence of significant climatic changes along the overland Silk Route. Aurel Stein, for example, reports major shifts in the water supply to the Tarim Basin, forcing the abandonment of the Dandān-oilik Oasis by the eighth century and, in turn, a redirection of the overland route,[22] perhaps even necessitating a large-scale abandonment of the route in favour of sea routes.

A very recent areal study of Angkor Wat using airborne laser-scanning technology called LIDAR (Light Detection and Ranging) discovered an extraordinary buried city around the great temple, one involving a network of roads and a water management system that allowed a dense, formally planned downtown core to thrive. The archaeologists from Australia who conducted this study have speculated that, to quote the *New York Times* article on this study, "the intensity of these developments may have contributed to the Khmer Empire's undoing in the 15th century. The LIDAR suggests that deforestation accompanied urban growth, perhaps increasing the civilization's vulnerability to the elements."[23] And that leads me to think about ecological factors in the making and eventual undoing of Magadha, essentially the area of Bihar state south of the Ganges and once India's premier region. It was hugely wealthy and fostered some of India's most extraordinary political and religious developments. Regardless where the Buddha actually was born, his life as teacher and leader of the *sangha* occurred largely in Magadha. The last Jain saviour, Mahavira, was born in Magadha, possibly at Nalanda, and not far from Nalanda, at Pawapuri, he attained nirvana. Something extraordinary must have stimulated the rise of these remarkable teachers in about the fifth century BCE, the very time that Confucius lived in China, as well as the time of the later Jewish prophets in Babylon and Judea, and the great philosophers of Attica. There may have been a global stimulus for these transformative figures, perhaps a climatic one. India's most extensive empire ever, the third century BCE Maurya empire, ruled from Pataliputra, present-day Patna. Surely a strong local economy bolstered by a climate that supported both the agricultural component of the economy and the water routes — the Ganges and other rivers — to develop extensive and highly profitable trade networks that supported the prosperity of the capital. Nalanda was established in Magadha, not only because Magadha was the homeland of Buddhism — after all, Nalanda was not a site associated with the life of the Buddha, although nearby Rajgir was. But there was also the economic infrastructure to support an enormous monastic establishment, and that required a sort of climatic benevolence, that is a climate that could support cultivation sufficiently well that there would always be an agricultural excess sufficient to generate profit and give to the maintenance of the monastery. Finally, we might ask why the Afghan armies of Bhaktiyar Khalji were attracted to Magadha at the end of the twelfth century. Surely, they did not come as iconoclastic marauders, as most commonly they are depicted. Even though they very likely did destroy Nalanda and other monasteries in the vicinity, it is hard to believe that iconoclasm alone was the impetus for soldiers to risk their lives. They had to be attracted by the prospect of financial gain, a gain they could not achieve elsewhere in India. Part of Magadha's attraction must have been stimulated by a climate that allowed up to three crops a year. Part may have been the rich natural resources such as copper, still today a major asset, though today in Jharkand, no longer Bihar. But the very success of Magadha may have contributed to its downfall as a centre of prosperity, as was the case with Angkor. Not only did it attract invaders who wanted a share of its riches, but the increased population that urban centres attracted very likely contributed to ever-heavier deforestation to provide more agricultural land and also to fuel the kilns used in brick-manufacture, the primary construction material at Nalanda and almost every other site in Magadha, upsetting an ecology in place for millennia.

So, what does that say about the environment around Nalanda? Except for Rajgir, much of Magadha is today a plain and not an especially attractive one. I have long imagined that as Aryans, that is, speakers of Indo-European languages, moved eastward along the Jamuna and Ganges Rivers, they deforested an area that both powerfully impacted the course of the rivers and also made flooding part of the culture requiring brick, not timber, to serve as a major building material, as it was at Nalanda. But increasingly, after reading the Angkor Wat study, I wonder about the extent to which temple cities such as Khajuraho or Badami, to take examples from north and south India, involved massive deforestation, which dramatically altered the ecology of the sites and the capital cities associated with them, leaving only stone monuments devoid of traces of the residential and commercial structures occupied by people who, directly or indirectly, supported the religious monuments. Did the population so transform the places that they no longer served as a proper *tirtha*, a place where the gods might love to sport?

What then about ancient Nalanda? (See Figure 3.5.) The monastery must have had a dynamic relationship with the surrounding region, not just with towns such as Rajgir and Bihar Sharif but also with the agricultural lands outside of the towns. While the region may have prospered from the endowment wealth of Nalanda, the great monastery in turn was heavily dependent on goods and services from the region. Food alone would have been a major enterprise. The average American eats approximately two pounds of food a day, way more than we need. So let us assume the monks ate just half that amount, probably not far from accurate given the fact that temples today, for example the Golden Temple in Amritsar, provides a bit more than a half kilogram of food per person. If Yijing's estimate that there were 3,000 monks at Nalanda[24] — let us forget Xuanzang's assertion reported by Hwui Li that there were 10,000 monks at Nalanda[25] — It still means that to feed a population of 3,000, Nalanda would have required 1.5 tons of food every day, almost 550 tons a year. That is a huge amount, far more than the community immediately surrounding Nalanda could provide. But we might recall that Magadha could produce as much as three

FIGURE 3.5
Nalanda, Stucco Images on Great Monument of Site 3

crops per year, reducing the distance from which food would have to be brought to the monastery. In fact, one explanation for the concentration of Buddhist monasteries in Magadha might be the ability to supply food for large concentrated populations of monks who provided neither goods nor services to the community but rather were exclusively consumers.

How could Nalanda accommodate a huge number of monks? (See Figure 3.6.) The ancient site within the present walls of Nalanda measures 488 × 244 metres. Therefore, if there were 3,000 monks at the monastery, as Yijing asserts, that would allow 39 square metres per monk, about the size of a generous hotel room. But that is using every square metre of the site, including the area comprising temples and the present grassy area. If Xuanzang's report that there were 10,000 monks at Nalanda is anywhere near accurate, then the monks would have had only 11.9 square metres each, about the size of a typical monk's cell at Nalanda. That would be impossible unless monks were sleeping in temples and all the grassy area around the temples and monastic dwellings, or if the ten monasteries at the site had an enormous number of stories. Even for 3,000 monks, it would have been hugely crowded. Here is another way of thinking about the capacity of ancient Nalanda monastery. The typical monastic dwelling at Nalanda has approximately 30 monk's

FIGURE 3.6
Nalanda, Monastery 6

cells each around a central courtyard, a total of 300 cells among the ten dwellings that remain. To accommodate 3,000 monks, each monastic dwelling would need to have been more than 11 storeys high, a sort of premodern skyscraper without the lifts that made skyscrapers possible. To accommodate 10,000 monks, each dwelling would have needed to be 37 storeys high, even less likely.

Then we need to think about monks listening to discourses from the learned masters. (See Figure 3.7.) I estimate that no more than 100 monks could actually hear a master without modern electronic amplification unless there were acoustics as fine as those of La Scala and the learned masters could project like Enrico Caruso or Nellie Melba, whose early careers and fame predated electronic amplification. More likely only 50 monks gathered around a master could actually hear him. But even with 100 in rapt attention, that assumes 30 masters if there were 3,000 monks at Nalanda and 100 masters if there were 10,000 monks. If we assume, on the other hand, that one master held forth in each of the monastic dwellings, as Xuanzang implies, that the specific master was a reason the monks chose one monastic dwelling over another, and there are the remains of only ten monastic dwellings, then it is hard to imagine how and where so many masters could expound on the texts.

FIGURE 3.7
Nalanda, Temple of Sarai Mound

As we read Xuanzang's account of Nalanda, I think it is important to remember that he wrote it after his return to Xian and that he had a target audience. On one hand, he needed to make Nalanda comprehensible to his audience, and so casting it in the guise of a Confucian centre of study makes very good sense. He wanted to demonstrate his own erudition by describing both the difficulty of entry into Nalanda and the shame of those — not him, of course — who could not adequately discuss the *Tripitaka*. As for the enumeration of Nalanda's monuments and their royal patrons, was he trying to make a case that the Tang emperor ought to consider comparable largesse? I doubt that this was his only reason, for throughout his account of travelling in India, monuments, as we might call them today, are consistently featured, as if his description of them marked his actual visit to those places, serving as evidence that he really did travel there.

A great deal of energy has been committed to fashioning and presenting ancient Nalanda as a university despite the fact that all of the seals unearthed at Nalanda describe the place as a *mahavihara*, a great monastery, not a *vidyalaya* or school.[26] It is imagined to have had a curriculum rather than diverse subjects on which masters expounded. According to Huili, Xuanzang's biographer, the monks of Nalanda studied more than just exegesis of Buddhist texts, evidence, many believe, of a broad range of learning.[27] And it is imagined to have had a library because Taranatha, writing in the seventeenth century, describes a fire that almost completely destroyed a structure — maybe three structures; his text is ambiguous — that housed scriptural works, as if these manuscripts were collected in one library-like building. Many assert that the fire was set by Muslim invaders, though Taranatha quite clearly states that the fire was created by a beggar who had attained *siddhi* and performed a sacrifice that miraculously produced a fire. Some even go so far as to identify a specific building as the remains of Nalanda's library.[28] So the logic must be: if Nalanda had a broad curriculum, if it had a library, if it had students and teachers, then it must have been a university. Needless to say, there is a great deal of fantasy at play here, but recognizing that there are real parallels to other premodern universities, for example, Bologna and Oxford, which also have origins in religious institutions, it is not entirely far-fetched to think of Nalanda, like Bologna and Oxford at their beginnings in the eleventh and twelfth centuries respectively, as a proto-university. Even Minhaj al-Siraj, describing Bhaktiyar Khalji's attack on the fortified city of Bihar, says that the Afghan invader learned that a *vihara* is a college.[29] So sweeping aside all the fantasy used to present ancient Nalanda as a university — and, quite to the contrary of Taranatha,[30] to attribute the destruction of the library, which may or may not have existed, to Muslim invaders — we at the very least can think of Nalanda as a major seat of learning. And we can add that it attracted monks from abroad, though it is certainly an exaggeration to imagine Nalanda as an institution with an international student body. It even received international patronage. In 860, the king of Suvarnadvipa, Balaputradeva of the Shailendra Dynasty, provided funds via his contemporary, the Pala dynasty monarch, Devalapa, to build a monastery at Nalanda.[31]

Without that sense of Nalanda as a university and pride in its establishment long before European and North African religious institutions that eventually fostered university-like learning, without the foreign monks who studied there and copied Buddhist texts, I doubt that Nalanda University, the modern institution, would have been conceived and realized. Nonetheless, Nalanda University should not be imagined as a revival of the ancient Nalanda. First, of course, it is not a Buddhist institution, and intimate knowledge of the *Tripitika* is not expected of admitted students. Second, and clearly related to the first, it will have a diversified secular curriculum. But related to Nalanda in antiquity, it will have international students and international financial support. It will, in other words, not revive ancient Nalanda, as too often asserted, but will, as the new institution's prospectus indicates, "contain within it a memory of the ancient Nalanda University".

The new university's international character cements cooperation on a much wider scale in the region, and the possibilities open for this university, like any extremely well-endowed new university, are enormous and, if allowed to develop in ways led by intellectually committed administrators, enormously exciting. There are ample examples of foreign universities operating abroad, for example the Yale-NUS campus, New York University's campus in Abu Dhabi, and the Birla Institute of Technology and Science Pillani's Dubai campus. But the notion of an international cooperative venture, as the Nalanda University is, will be unique in higher education, I believe, creating a system within the present-day world system, one connected more by air and the Internet than by maritime routes and more by a quest to teach and learn and conduct research than by a quest for specific and narrowly defined truths.

Notes

1. I write this brief article with special recognition the wonderful and tireless work of Gopa Sabharwal and Anjana Sharma, whose leadership of Nalanda University had the potential to make it a world class institution, one that should have given India great pride.
2. William D. Phillips, Jr. and Carla Rahn Philips, *The Worlds of Christopher Columbus* (New York: Cambridge University Press, 1992), p. 20.
3. C.R. Whittaker, *Rome and its Frontiers: The Dynamics of Empire* (London: Routledge, 2004), p. 171.
4. Michael Pearson, *The Indian Ocean* (London & New York: Routledge, 2003), p. 29.
5. Philip Curtin, *Cross Cultural Trade in World History* (Cambridge: Cambridge University Press, 1984).
6. Moti Chandra, *Trade and Trade Routes in Ancient India* (New Delhi: Abhinav Publications, 1977), p. 34.
7. Lawrence Leshnik, "The Harappan 'Port' at Lothal: Another View", *American Anthropologist*, N.S. 70, no. 5 (October 1968), pp. 911–22, argues that Lothal was not a port and not an entrepôt for trade.
8. Cited in Jagat Pati Joshi, "India and Bahrain: A Survey of Culture Interaction in the Third and Second Millennia", in *Bahrain Through The Ages; the Archaeology*, edited by Shaikha Haya Ali Khalifa and Michael Rice (New York: Routledge, 2010), p. 74.
9. Richard Salomon, "Epigraphic Remains of Indian Traders in Egypt", *Journal of the American Oriental Society* 111, no. 4 (1991): 731–36; and

P. Shanmugam, "India and Southeast Asia: South Indian Cultural Links with Indonesia", in *Nagapattinam to Suvarnadwipa: Reflections on the Chola Naval Expeditions to Southeast Asia*, edited by Hermann Kulke, K. Kesavapany and Vijay Sakhuja (Singapore: Institute of Southeast Asian Studies, 2009), pp. 208–26.

10. Mirella Levi D'Ancona, "An Indian Statuette from Pompeii", *Artibus Asiae* 13, no. 3 (1950): 166–80; and Joseph Hackin, *Recherches archéologiques à Begram* (Paris: Les Éditions d'art et d'histoire, 1939).
11. Anton O. Zakharov, "A Note on the Date of the Vo-Canh Stele", *South East Asian Review* XXXV (2010): 17–21.
12. The inscription, datable to about the fifth century, is today in the Indian Museum, Kolkata. A replica of the inscription is housed in the Bujang Valley Archaeological Museum.
13. Pearson, *The Indian Ocean*, p. 59.
14. Risha Lee, "Constructing Community: Tamil Merchant Temples in India and China, 850–1281", PhD dissertation, Columbia University, 2012. Columbia University Academic Commons, accessed 1 January 2017.
15. H.G. Quaritch Wales, *Archaeological Researches on Ancient Indian Colonization in Malaya* (Singapore: Printers Limited, 1940). Photographs of the statue show it so abraded that I wonder if Quaritch Wales assumed, rather than determined, Pallava workmanship for the piece.
16. Ingo Strauch, ed., *Foreign Sailors on Socotra: The Inscriptions and Drawings from the Cave Hoq* (Bremen: Hempen Verlag, 2012).
17. John Faithful Fleet, *Inscriptions of the Early Gupta Kings and Their Successors* (Calcutta: Superintendent of Government Printing, 1888).
18. Enseng Ho, *The Graves of Tarim: Genealogy and Mobility Across the Indian Ocean* (Los Angeles: University of California Press, 2006).
19. No Author, "The Stones of Zayton Speak", *China Heritage Newsletter* (Australian National University), No. 5 (2006). A Review of three books in Chinese: Wu Wenliang, revised by Wu Youxiong, *Quanzhou zongjiao shike* [Religious inscriptions of Quanzhou] (Beijing: Kexue Chubanshe, 2005); Wu Wenliang, *Quanzhou zongjiao shike* [Religious inscriptions of Quanzhou] (Beijing: Kexue Chubanshe, 1957); and Chen Dasheng, *Quanzhou Yisilanjiao shike* [Islamic inscriptions of Quanzhou] (Yinchuan: Ningxia Renmin Chubanshe, 1984).
20. G.W.J. Drewes, "New Light on the Coming of Islam to Indonesia?", *Bijdragen tot de Taal-, Land- en Volkenkunde* 124 (1968): 433–59.
21. David Whitehouse and Andrew Williamson, "Sasanian Maritime Trade", *Iran*, vol. 11 (1973): 29–49.
22. Marc Aurel Stein, *Ruins of Desert Cathay* (Cambridge: Cambridge University Press, 1912), p. 257.
23. Rachel Nuwer, "Angkor's Urban Environs, Mapped from Above", *New York Times*, 1 July 2013. See also Damien Evans et al., "Uncovering Archaeological

Landscapes at Angkor Using Lidar", *Proceedings of the National Academy of Sciences* 110, no. 31 (2013): 12595–600.

24. J. Takakusu, trans. I-Tsing, *The Buddhist Religion as Practices in India and the Malay Archipelego (AD 671–695)* (Oxford: Clarendon Press, 1896), p. 65.
25. Samuel Beal, trans. Hwui Li, *The Life of Hiuen-Tsiang* (London: Kegan Paul, Trench, Trubner, 1911), p. 112.
26. H.D. Sankalia, *The University of Nalanda* (Madras: B.G. Paul & Co., 1934); and Sukumar Dutt, *Buddhist Monks and Monasteries of India* (London: George Allen and Unwin, 1962), especially part 5, ch. 2.
27. Beal, *The Life of Hiuen-Tsiang*, p. 112.
28. Rakesh Kumar Bhatt, *History and Development of Libraries in India* (Delhi: Mittal Publications, 1997), pp. 21–22, for one example of an entirely uncritical presentation.
29. H.G. Raverty, trans., *Tabakat-i-Nasiri: A General History of the Muhammadan Dynasties of Asia, Including Hindustan, from A.H. 194 (810 A.D.), to A.H. 658 (1260 A.D.), and the Irruption of the Infidel Mughals into Islam* (London: printed by Gilbert & Rivington, 1881).
30. Debiprasad Chattopadhyaya, *Tāranātha's History of Buddhism in India* (Simla: Indian Institute of Advanced Study, 1970).
31. Hirananda Sastri, "The Nalanda Copper-Plate of Devapaladeva", *Epigraphia Indica* XVII (1923–24): 310–27.

4

COLLECTING THE REGION
Configuring Bihar in the Space of Museums

Sraman Mukherjee

"TURK, TELI, TAR, WEH TINO HAIN BIHAR"[1]

Writing in 1870s Alexander Meyrick Broadley, an official of the colonial bureaucracy and an avid antiquarian, thus rounded up his account of exploits in Bihar — "Turks (Muhammadans), Telis (oil pressers), and Tar (Tar-palms), these three make up Bihar."[2] This configuration of Bihar, as Broadley persuasively argued, was a common parlance of the late nineteenth century. The choice of this particular phrase as the concluding sentence of his long essay on ancient Buddhist remains of the region, however, served a more crucial function than adding a bit of local colour to a standard nineteenth century regional history. It sought to bring out the labours of a colonial administrator and antiquarian in reclaiming the glorious pasts of a land now lost to vagaries of time, and to the all too familiar colonial charges against "uninformed native vandalism", and "misappropriation".

Framing nineteenth century Bihar as a land of wilderness, a region wrecked by lawlessness, and inhabited by natives with a disregard for their own past, enabled the colonial narratives of discovery of Bihar's ancient history. It is against these narratives of loss that colonial officials, archaeologists, and antiquarians like Broadley would stage their labours of recovering ancient pasts. In his capacity as the Assistant Magistrate of

Bihar, Broadley conducted surveys, excavations, and built up a substantial antiquarian collection which found their way into the Bihar Museum established in the town of Bihar Sharif. As the earliest museum collection of nineteenth century colonial Bihar, the Broadley Collection emerged during 1870s and 1880s as the site of rediscovered ancient Buddhist Bihar protected from the ravages of "nature" and "natives". However, this museum had a short life, spanning only some two decades.

In 1890s the Government of Bengal disbanded the Bihar Sharif Museum and transferred the antiquities to Calcutta to add to the imperial collection in the Indian Museum. In 1917, five years after the creation of the new province of Bihar and Orissa, a provincial museum was established in Patna, the new provincial capital. Citing instances of earlier carting away of antiquities outside the territorial limits of province, in which the disbanding of the Bihar Museum featured as a major grudge, the Patna Museum projected itself as the sole rightful repository of Bihar's antiquarian heritage. The institution emerged as a potent ground for the fashioning of a new provincial identity predicated on the reclamation of the province's history and antiquities.

In colonial South Asia, museums and the associated fields of antiquarian and archaeological studies sought to provide linear histories connecting the colony's pasts to its present and thereby trying to naturalize modern administrative divisions as ancient historical territories. In their self-projected image as safe houses of antiquities, as institutions of specialized research and general public instructions, museums along with other public pedagogic institutions — schools, colleges, and universities, emerged as important markers of the sites of political power.

Taking up these specific moments of building, disbanding and rebuilding of museum collections, this paper explores the changing the configurations of Bihar in the space of museums. Instead of treating Bihar as a pre-given physically available space whose ancient pasts lay waiting to be unearthed, this paper argues for a colonial production of ancient Bihar though certain ways of framing and mapping the region. The actors we encounter range from colonial surveyors, archaeologists, museum curators, and amateur antiquarians. It is across these dispersed worlds of antiquarian scholarship, covering fields of surveys and excavations, and sites of collection and display, Bihar emerged as a specific place-name signifying a particular region in the colony. During the late nineteenth century and opening decades of the twentieth century, Bihar evolved from being an administrative division of the old Bengal Presidency to a separate provincial entity. The paper tries to map this journey of the region through the prism of the changing discourse about local, regional and provincial heritage.

WHICH BIHAR? LOCATING A.M. BROADLEY AND THE BIHAR MUSEUM

> The word Bihar has ... served to designate several artificial divisions in this part of India. The name originally belonged to the ancient city, which from its far famed seat of Buddhistic learning was distinguished by the name "Bihar" [Sanskrit *Vihar*]. The Muhammadan conquerors of the city extended its name to the surrounding country, of which it became the capital; and at the time of Akbar it came to signify that important portion of Eastern India comprised in the seven *sirkars* of Munger, Champaran, Hajipur, Saran, Tirhut, Rohtas, and Bihar. This was *Subah* Bihar. Under, British rule, *Subah* Bihar and *Subah* Bengal were united under a joint government, while the *Zil'ah*, surrounding the capital and which bore its name, was divided into *Zil'ah* Patna and *Zil'ah* Gaya. In 1864, the important *parganahs* of Bihar and Rajgir were detached from the jurisdiction of Gaya, and, together with the *parganahs* of Tillarah, Pillich, and Biswak, formed into a subdivision, bearing the name of Bihar, and within the jurisdiction of *Zil'ah* Patna. *Subah* Bihar, for more than a century, has ceased to exist except in name. *Zil'ah* Bihar has now disappeared from the map of India; *the name can now only as a matter of fact be properly applied to the ancient Muhammadan capital*, founded by Bakhtyar Khilji, and the five surrounding *parganahs* of which it is still the chief town ...
>
> A.M. Broadley[3]

Tracing the etymology of the term "Bihar" in the late nineteenth century, Broadley was perhaps the first colonial official to engage most extensively with the different and shifting territorial registers along which the term had moved from its precolonial roots. By the nineteenth century while "Bihar" as a toponym/place-name was generally taken to connote certain territorial units in eastern India, there was no consensus whether the term referred to a particular town, or an entire region. As the region came to be configured and reconfigured in different ways in the colonial archives, archaeology produced an antiquarian map of Bihar around three spatial clusters — the town Gaya and the neighbouring remains of Bodh Gaya, city of Patna, and the town of Bihar Sharif and the neighbouring sites of Rajgir and Baragaon (Nalanda). So where was Broadley's Bihar? Broadley's map of Bihar was an antiquarian map, a map that charted the region in its ancient Buddhist remains amongst ruins of monasteries, universities, and temples, in sculptures and architectural fragments. In his map, Bihar was configured around the town of Bihar Sharif and the ruins of Rajgir, and Nalanda. Revisiting this particular configuration of Bihar, one is struck by the remarkable overlaps between the antiquarian map prepared by the officially instituted Archaeological Survey of India, and the one drawn up by Broadley in his "amateur" pursuit, the major point of similarity in both cases being the tropes of loss and colonial recovery of Bihar as the seat of ancient Buddhist civilization.

This Buddhist antiquarian map of Bihar was a product of a particular Orientalist framing, of colonial archaeology's reading of selective histories into sites and movable antiquities. The Buddhist focus of Bihar's ancient cartography was something that the Archaeological Survey directly inherited from the early topographic surveys of the region like the ones conducted by Francis Buchanan Hamilton in the early nineteenth century. These surveys set precedence for the colonial practice of marginalizing local narratives and traditions and the selective reading of *a priori* histories of Buddhism into Hindu Brahminical, Jain, and Islamic structures.[4] By the middle decades of the nineteenth century this became the dominant preoccupation of colonial archaeology. The refiguring of South Asia's Buddhist past can be located within the larger contemporary Orientalist engagement with Buddhism. Philip C. Almond and Tapati Guha-Thakurta have argued that the Western fascination with Buddhism, with its scriptures and doctrines of faith and persona of its founder, had specifically British and Victorian connotations.[5] The "discovery", "critical editing" and "reprinting" of precolonial Sinhalese and Chinese Buddhist texts, especially the pilgrimage itineraries of the Chinese pilgrims Faxian and Xuanzang, who had visited India during the fifth and seventh centuries, led to the creation of Buddhism as a distinctly Orientalist textual object.[6]

Two of these nineteenth century Orientalist texts on Buddhism, the translations of Faxian's and Xuanzang's accounts by Stanislas Julien and Samuel Beal, attained a Biblical status in the colonial archaeological project.[7] These nineteenth century translations provided early archaeologists like Alexander Cunningham the grounds to discover an "authentic" Buddhist landscape of ancient India. In the high noon of empirical positivism, these premodern texts were read as physical maps and geographical nodes often overlooking the political, cultural, literary ideations, norms, and contexts of their productions and the intended audience of these textual narratives.[8] It is this quest for an empirically verifiable ancient Buddhist topography of India, as commemorated in Buddhist canonical texts and chronicles, such as the Chinese pilgrim itineraries, that several Buddhist sites, structural remains, and movable antiquities now emerged as the major focus for enacting the curatorial drive of the colonial state.

Colonial archaeology in South Asia thus moved Buddhism beyond its Orientalist textual archives in Europe to the physical landscape of the colony and made it available as new "... architectural and artistic entity".[9] As the first field to be subjected to organized archaeological surveys, the ancient sites and monuments of Bihar "... became meaningful to the Western eye only through a textual filter ... as illustrations of Buddhist legends and history."[10] The Buddhist lens provided the Western scholar the frame to unearth the "earliest" "authentic" history of the colony, stripped off the later "excesses" of Hindu Brahmanism and "Muslim iconoclasm". As in the official archaeological cartography, in Broadley's configuration too material remains, structures and movable antiquities emerged as the prime repository of authentic ancient histories of the region, specifically Buddhist histories. The process involved the same trajectories of text-aided toponymic identifications, surveys, excavations, and building up of antiquarian collections. Taking over the administrative charge of the Sub-Division of Bihar, Broadley devoted his "leisure" from official duties to rescue these antiquities. Using the same textual sources, the nineteenth century translations of Chinese pilgrimage accounts, Broadley's accounts of the Buddhist antiquities in and around Bihar Sharif soon turned its focus from ancient histories of sites and monuments, to the remains as he encountered them in the late nineteenth century, their present ruined state legitimizing the intervention of the Western scholar who, in addition to his amateur antiquarian interests, was in official administrative charge of this landscape of ruins.

In October 1871, Broadley began his private excavations at Baragaon, identified in the nineteenth century as the ancient Buddhist university of Nalanda without the official consent of the government-instituted Archaeological Survey. Conducted at a rapid pace the excavations yielded a number of antiquities — votive *stupas*, Buddhist sculptures and architectural fragments and inscriptions all of which found their way into his private collection. In forming this collection Broadley displayed a remarkable sense of unapologetic propriety over the antiquities discovered during the course of his excavations. Like official Archaeological Survey Reports, Broadley's excavation report is replete with instances of contemporary uninformed native vandalism, "industrious" *ryots* (peasants) ploughing the landscape of ruined mounds to unrecoverable destruction, and local *zamindars* (landlords), recycling the old building materials from the ruins, blissfully unaware of their artistic or evidentiary values. As in accounts of officially designated archaeologists, in Broadley's reports the Muslims were specifically singled out as the destroyers of Bihar's ancient Buddhist pasts. The town of Bihar Sharif with its numerous "Islamic" structures now appeared before his eyes as the irrefutable proof of medieval Islamic iconoclasm, pillage, and misappropriation of ancient Buddhist antiquities.[11]

This whole range of colonial charge about the natives' disregard for their own past and uninformed vandalism of the antiquarian remains, which had provided the legitimacy in the organization of the government-instituted Archaeological Surveys, also provided the justification for private antiquarians like Broadley to embark on a career of excavations and antiquarian collections outside the official purview of the Survey. The lines demarcating the professional from the amateurs in field of antiquarian researches in the colony were still very fluid and in the late nineteenth century, the officials in charge of the administrative duties of the districts, with a passion for antiquities and a definitive sense of propriety over the remains of the lands under their official jurisdiction, could very well challenge their "professional archaeologist" peers in their own field. In Broadley's case this carried a step further.

In his reports and accounts Broadley produced a history of the region that re-inscribed the town of his official posting and the entire the entire administrative division of Bihar Sharif, as the political, religious, and cultural hub of Bihar's and India's Buddhist civilization. To this end, he moved the historical narrative from earlier sites of political and cultural power like Pataliputra (recognized by the late nineteenth century as representing the site of the modern city of Patna) to a period dating from the ninth to the twelfth century AD when Bihar, Bihar Sharif emerged as the locus of power under the Pala and Sena dynasties of eastern India, before Buddhism's final wipe-out in face of "iconoclastic Islamic invasions". It now rested with the Western scholar administrator to redress this historic injustice. The town of Bihar Sharif and its "Islamic" monuments — tombs, mosques, and forts — the glaring sites of this Islamic vandalism now emerged as the locale of the Bihar Museum. The antiquities sourced from the field, often by violently knocking down structures during his hurried excavations and exploratory tours in Baragaon and Rajgir, now found their way into this museum collection safe from the numerous forces threatening to wipe them out forever.[12]

The stress on this selective spatial cluster of Bihar Sharif, Rajgir and Nalanda in Broadley's antiquarian map thus had its clear political underpinnings. Bihar in Broadley's map came to be configured around the town of Bihar Sharif through the rhetoric of custody and possession, which derived its legitimacy as much from the politics of affect for and identification with the land, his private interest in antiquarianism, as from the official administrative charge over this landscape of ruins. In Broadley's map the town of Bihar Sharif with its very own museum — the Bihar Museum — housing the huge Broadley collection of sculptures, architectural pieces and inscriptions, and under the proprietary control of the "Collector", now emerged as the locus of local heritage. The Buddhist focus of Broadley's map now came to be physically recreated in the museum which itself emerged as the centre of this cartography. This centre of Bihar's nineteenth century antiquarian cartography, however, remained fragile, completely susceptible to the pulls of the colony's capital and the contesting prerogatives of the Indian Museum in Calcutta. The Bihar Museum now resurfaces in the colonial archives at the moment of its dissolution in the 1890s.

FROM BIHAR IN BIHAR SHARIF TO BIHAR IN CALCUTTA: THE "TRANSFER" OF THE BROADLEY COLLECTION

In the 1880s, the officials in charge of the Indian Museum lodged a complaint with the Government of India highlighting the singular absence of transfer of archaeological finds to the Museum. Originating in 1814 from the collections of antiquities and curiosities housed in the premises of the Asiatic Society, this Museum was designed over the course of the nineteenth century as the imperial material archive gathering, under one roof and classified into specialized galleries, all that the colony had to offer in city of Calcutta, the political capital of the Empire. Along with private spoliation of antiquities, the museum authorities marked out the local museums in various parts of the colony as major hindrances to the building of a complete, comprehensive archaeological collection in the Indian Museum.[13] As the grievances of the museum authorities were forwarded to Alexander Cunningham, the Director General of Archaeological Survey of India, he selected the Bihar Sharif Museum as the most potential collection of antiquities which could be transferred to Calcutta to fill in the void of the archaeological galleries of the Indian Museum. Why did the axe of dissolution fall on the Bihar Museum at the first go?

Cunningham argued that this extensive collection of early medieval Buddhist sculptures was exquisite from the artistic and historic points of view. As it would be difficult to ensure that another collection of sculptures of equal extent and value could be located again, he pressed, that the most valuable of such sculptures should be transferred out of this little provincial town to the colonial capital where they could be seen and appreciated by specialist scholars and general public at large.[14] Alongside arguments of the collection's historic and artistic uniqueness, the remoteness of Bihar Sharif as against the accessibility of Calcutta, it was pushed that antiquities in the Bihar Museum were singularly bereft of expert ordering, classification, and preservation. Sculptures and architectural fragments, it was argued, lay out in the open grounds susceptible to weather, and without any protection from illegal antiquarian trafficking.[15] Interests of scholarship and general public good and utility now demanded their transfer out of Bihar Sharif to the Indian Museum in Calcutta.

As persuasive as these arguments would appear, reasons behind Cunningham's selection of the Bihar Museum as the first institution to be disbanded also lay somewhere else. By the late 1870s and early 1880s Cunningham had already emerged as a trenchant critique of Broadley. His charges against the amateur antiquarian ranged from faulty scholarship, to private spoliation and amassing of antiquities.[16] The issues at stake here were more than those of sheer disciplinary expertise. As a nascent discipline in colonial South Asia, the consolidation of the emerging domain of archaeology depended to a great extent on its official institutionalization. In embarking on a career of "amateur antiquarianism" people like Broadley threatened both this institutional and disciplinary expertise that early archaeologists like Cunningham claimed as their exclusive niche. For Cunningham the proposed disbanding of the Bihar Museum presented a rare opportunity to push out "amateur antiquarianism", particularly one who had deprived the first director general of archaeology of his chances of epoch making discoveries in the earliest field of operation, Bihar.

Faced with this threat of dissolution, the trustees of the Bihar Museum now sought to defend the institution's existence precisely in the terms of deployed by the pro-dissolution lobby — the historic and artistic uniqueness of the collection, interest of scholarship, and general public good and utility. As the demands of this transfer were forwarded to the Bihar Museum, the managing body of Bihar Sharif countered Cunningham's classification of the Bihar Museum as a "private antiquarian collection", and sought to establish its legitimacy as a "Local Museum". Babu Bemola Churn Bhuttacharjee, Broadley's successor in Bihar Sub-Division and the inheritor of his collection of antiquities, argued that "as the images belonged to Behar, they should remain there. There is ... no other place in India where so many specimens of Hindu and

Buddhist sculptures could be seen and studied by Buddhist scholars and archaeologists at one place. It is desirable that they should be preserved carefully ... the sculptures are now public property and should be preserved at public interest."[17] Bhuttacharjee had moved the Broadley collection way beyond the scope of a private local antiquarian compilation. Not only did he invest his time and energy in preserving and rearranging the collection while in Bihar, he had also paved the way for the local museum that was to arise out of this collection. Drawing up a legal deed of gift to the public in Bihar, Bihar Sharif, Bemola Churn Bhuttacharjee had allied it to the local administration — the Collector, Magistrate and the Commissioner. More importantly he had allied the principal *zamindars* of the locality to this project, the *zamindars*, who had been actively involved in Broadley's building of this collection, his cringing about native vandalism of antiquarian remains notwithstanding.[18] The commissioner of Patna supported the move in the name of local heritage, public good and utility.[19] In no uncertain terms the Broadley collection now came to be defended as a "local museum" with an equal right to existence for "public benefit" in a distant Sub-Divisional town of the colony as the imperial material archive in the colony's capital.

Such concerted protests from the "trustees" of the "local museum" were not received favourably at the imperial level. By the early 1890s fate of the Bihar Museum was sealed completely. The Government decided finally to transfer all antiquities from Bihar Sharif to Calcutta. So, how was this move officially justified? In the official archives the trail now ran completely cold. In the complete silence of the colonial archives, we may never know, but can only speculate on what ultimately legitimized this transfer. By the closing decades of the nineteenth century there was a greater drive for centralization of antiquarian researches in the colony. In this scheme the Archaeological Survey of India was envisioned as the only legitimate body to carry surveys and excavations, and the primacy of the rights to house, order, classify and exhibit the antiquities of the colony in the imperial material archive in the colony's capital, the Indian Museum, was driven more forcefully than before. The passing of the Treasure Trove Act of 1878 had already upheld the proprietary rights of the colonial state over the individual collectors. While the Act did not delegitimize local museums but it definitely marginalized the right of the individual and the private collector vis-à-vis centralized government institutions like the Archaeological Survey or the Indian Museum.

It is probably something more than sheer coincidence that in the Annual Reports of the Indian Museum dating back to the early 1890s, the years of its dissolution, the Bihar Museum is only referred to as the "Broadley Collection". Probably the Trustees of the Indian Museum ultimately found a way out to declassify the collection in Bihar Sharif as a local museum and project it only as a private individual's collection which could be safely disbanded and transferred to the colony's capital for greater public benefit. Transferred to Calcutta the collections assumed a completely new life far from what Broadley or Mr. Bhuttacharjee had conceived. More importantly, Bihar now came to denote a different spatial unit than it did in Bihar Sharif.

In 1891, the Government of Bengal finally decided to transfer the contents of the Bihar Museum to the imperial material archive in the colony's capital. Baboo P.C. Mukharji, the newly appointed temporary archaeologist to the Indian Museum was sent to Bihar with precise directions "to remove the 'Broadley Collection' of ancient sculptures from Behar to Calcutta and to assist... in their arrangement in the [Indian] Museum ..."[20] Poorno Chunder Mukharji was one of the early Indian entrants in the colonial Archaeological Department. In the early decades of colonial archaeology when Indians were mostly employed in the subordinate posts of draftsmen, peons and clerks, Mukharji was one of those few who had the opportunity to carry out independent work. Like several early "native" entrants in the field Mukharji's career was rife with narratives of discrimination. The reports of the Indian Museum show that there was constant strife between Mukharji and the Museum Trustees which led to his eventual dismissal in 1894 on official grounds of incompetence.[21] What did this mean for the Bihar Sharif collection?

At the time of his removal Mukharji was still working on the detailed reports of lists, and provenance of sculptures in the Bihar Museum. These reports were never subsequently published by the museum authorities in Calcutta and soon became completely untraceable in the museum's archives. When Theodor Bloch assumed the newly created post of First Assistant to the Superintendent of the Indian Museum in November 1896, in the absence of Mukharji's report, he was left without any information about the Bihar Sharif collection and perhaps to order this vast collection, Bloch simply catalogued the provenance of the sculptures as Bihar.[22] Frederick M. Asher suggests that Bloch was probably using Bihar in the late nineteenth century as Bihar Sharif.[23] However, in subsequent museum registers, reports and publications, provenance of the sculptures continued to be catalogued and indexed as "Bihar", notwithstanding that the late nineteenth century specific spatial association of the word with Bihar Sharif and the Broadley collection of sculptures had been metamorphosed to imply a different spatial, territorial unit, the post-1912 province of Bihar. And the Bihar Sharif collection in the Indian Museum, now disassociated from its specific spatial implications, represented the supreme will of the imperial archaeological collection in Calcutta to frame "Bihar" offsite for "greater benefits" of the specialist scholars and the non-specialist public.

However, the Indian Museum's monopoly over the colony's movable antiquities would not go unchallenged. By the turn of the century, several local and provincial museums would back their claims and right to collect, classify and exhibit with equal veracity. The particular context in Bihar would be provided by the provincial redistribution of territories across the old Bengal Presidency in 1911–12 and the emergence of Bihar and Orissa as a separate province with its capital at Patna.

OF NEW PROVINCE AND ANCIENT HISTORIES: STAGING BIHAR IN PATNA

In the Delhi Durbar of 1911 George V, the King-Emperor, announced the separation of Bihar and Orissa from Bengal. On 1 April 1912, Bihar and Orissa was carved out as a separate Province with its capital at Patna. The configuration of the new province fuelled an antiquarian drive to unearth an ancient historical lineage for the modern administrative unit. The drive for historicization, as I have argued elsewhere, was concentrated on the new provincial capital of Patna. Parallel to the archaeological reinscription of modern Patna as the ancient metropolis of Pataliputra, a process where the key players remained the extra-provincial forces — the Archaeological Survey of India and the private patron of archaeological research, the Parsi millionaire, Mr Ratan Tata — there started a movement for the making of the new Provincial Capital the sole legitimate seat of antiquarian researches in the new province.[24] In less than five years of the configuration of the new province, the Bihar and Orissa Research Society (1915) and the Patna Museum (1917) came into being. The new provincial museum would now take local heritage to a different register. The "local" now came to be configured as the Provincial, especially around the provincial capital.

The Bihar and Orissa Research Society and the Patna Museum were designed to encourage researches into the history and ethnography of the newly created province. The Society, like many other antiquarian societies of colonial India, invited the equal participation of professional and amateur scholars, interested in unearthing the history and ethnography of the province. Local scholars and British administrators posted in the province worked to make this Society a centre of research activities in the new province. The *Journal of the Bihar and Orissa Research Society*, published from 1915 onwards, emerged as the mouthpiece of the Society. In his presidential address Sir Edward Gait, the Lieutenant Governor of Bihar and Orissa and the President of the Society, lamented:

> Many of our most interesting remains have already left the Province ... Very great harm was done many years ago by an amateur enthusiast who made a large collection of the remains without keeping any record of the places from which they were taken... I hope it will soon be possible to take steps to remove to the Museum some of the ancient carvings which lie scattered throughout the province, but this is a matter in which we must proceed warily, and only in accordance with the advice of experts...[25]

In the sense of loss invoked in Gait's opening speech, the dismantling and transfer of the Broadley collection to Calcutta, outside the present provincial territorial boundaries of Bihar and Orissa, featured as a major grudge. However, neither Broadley himself nor his collection of antiquities would feature as self-projected moment of origin of this new museumizing drive and the new provincial heritage discourse. In fact, Gait's Presidential Address sought to distance this new heritage movement and the demand for a provincial museum from what he would label as the antiquarian relic hunting of self-trained amateur antiquarians like Broadley. The province was to retain its fair share of antiquities and the establishment of a new Provincial Museum was to serve as the cultural signifier of a distinct historicist heritage of the new Province. However, everything was to be done within the larger disciplinary parameters of scientific archaeological research.

Exploring the spaces of the Research Society and the Museum as the sites of congealing of a new Bihari identity throws up interesting problems. The most intriguing problem is perhaps posed by the Bengali linguistic identities of majority of its members and functionaries. Why did these Bengali antiquarians and historians participate in this project of self-fashioning, particularly after the separation of Bihar from Bengal? We are dealing here with the making of a provincial identity which cohabited and did not challenge the overarching Indian national identity. What difference would it make to Bengali scholars in Patna whether antiquities would remain in the city or travel to Calcutta? Both these sites were well incorporated in the emerging national, Indian landscape. Could we then argue for a community of interests forged between the Bengali scholars and the land of their inhabitation, the newly configured province of Bihar, or write it off simply as a case of Bengali domination and colonization of research societies and histories outside the territorial limits of early twentieth century, particularly post 1912 Bengal?

At the same time, we cannot fail to overlook the clashes between the linguistic Bengali and Bihari intelligentsia of Patna, particularly over the demand of creation of a separate Bihar during the late nineteenth and early twentieth century. Pitched battles were fought in courts of law, legal councils and newspapers with two prominent factions — the pro-separation *Behar Times* (later the *Beharee*) group led by prominent linguistic Bihari leaders like Sachchidananda Sinha and Mahesh Narayan and the anti-separation lobby of the *Behar Herald* led by the prominent Bengali residents of Patna like Gurupada Sen. While the domination of the middle-class English-educated Bengalis in the new Western professions of legal and medical practice and teaching jobs in the colleges and universities had been one of the major grievances of the pro-separation lobby, the movement did not unfold across purely linguistic lines and was often marked by negotiations and clashes of material interest groups. Revisiting the nuanced histories of provincial reconfigurations and self fashioning in colonial Bihar lie beyond the limited scope of this paper:[26] to end let me just turn back briefly to the antiquarian publications of the Bihar and Orissa Research Society.

The writings in the *Journal of the Bihar and Orissa Research Society*, the works on regional history of Bihar produced by the (linguistic) Bengali members of the society and the museum reflect their deep sense of identification with the land. Affect and claims to habitation unfolded as patrimony and propriety over the over antiquities of the new province for the Bengali scholars of Patna. In reclaiming the site and the antiquities of province as the domain of Bihar's ancient heritage, contemporary linguistic Bengali scholars of Patna, were attesting their sense of identification with the land. Their engagement with recovery and reclamation of ancient Bihar reflects the Bengali scholars' renewed urgency of being and becoming Bihari in post-1912 Patna. The physical territory of the province had been configured outside Bengal. The Bengali scholars, however, retained self-projected, monopolistic authorial rights over the production of provincial histories.

Notes

1. A.M. Broadley, "The Buddhistic Remains of Bihar", *Journal of the Asiatic Society*, Part I, No. III (1872): 209–312, quoted from p. 312.

2. Ibid., p. 312, translation Broadley.
3. Ibid., pp. 209–10, italics mine.
4. Sraman Mukherjee, "Unearthing the Pasts of Bengal, Bihar and Orissa: Archaeology, Museums and History Writing in the Making of Ancient Eastern India, 1862–1936" (PhD dissertation, University of Calcutta, 2010).
5. See Philip C. Almond, *The British Discovery of Buddhism* (Cambridge: Cambridge University Press, 1988); Tapati Guha-Thakurta, *Monuments, Objects, Histories: Institutions of Art in Colonial and Postcolonial India* (New Delhi: Permanent Black, 2004).
6. Drawing on Edward Said's formulation about the Orient, Almond persuasively argues that by the mid-nineteenth century, the "essence of Buddhism came to be seen as expressed not 'out there' in the Orient, but in the West through the West's control of Buddhism's own textual past." See Almond, *The British Discovery of Buddhism*, p. 13.
7. See Stanislas Julien's *Historie de la Vie de Hiouen-Thsang et de ses voyage dans l'Inde, depuis l'an 629 jusqu'en 645* (Paris, 1853), and Julien's *Mémoires sur les Contrées Occidentales teaduits du Sanscrit en Chinois, en l'an 648, par Hiouen-Thsang, et du Chinois en Francais* (Paris, 2 vols., 1857–58) and Samuel Beal's *Si-Yu-Ki: Buddhist Records of the Western World: Translated from the Chinese of Hiuen Tsiang A.D. 629* (London: 1884, revised reprint New Delhi: Motilal Banarsidass, 2004) and Beal's *Buddhism in China* (London: S.P.C.K., 1884).
8. Frederick M. Asher has pointed out that Xuanzang's *Xiyu ji* (*Si-Yu-Ki*), for instance, was written from memory after his return to China from India and was not a modern survey field-note taken on the spot. See Frederick M. Asher, "Travels of a Reliquary, Its Contents Separated at Birth", *South Asian Studies* 28, no. 2 (2012): 147–56. Max Deeg's work on *Xiyu ji* has also pointed out the fallacies of relocating a seventh-century Chinese text, intended primarily for an audience in a royal court in China, in an essentially Indic context See Max Deeg, " 'Show Me the Land Where the Buddha Dwelled…' Xuanzang's 'Record of the Western Regions' (Xiyu ji): A Misunderstood Text?", *China Report* 48, nos. 1 & 2 (2012): 89–113.
9. Guha-Thakurta, *Monuments, Objects, Histories*, p. 36.
10. Ibid.
11. On Broadley's own accounts of the antiquarian configuration of Bihar and Bihar Sharif Museum, see Broadley, "The Buddhistic Remains of Bihar", *JASB*, Part I, No. 3 (1872): 209–312; Broadley, *Ruins of the Nalanda Monasteries at Burg'aon, Sub-Division Bihár, Zillah Patna* (Calcutta: Bengal Secretariat Press, 1872); *Photographs of the Buddhist Sculptures Discovered in Bihar (Zillah Patna) by A.M. Broadley, Esq., c.s.* (Calcutta: Thomas S. Smith, 1872). Besides these materials all published in 1872, there are three existing archival files — two in the National Archives of India, New Delhi and one in the West Bengal State Archives, Calcutta, which deal with the Bihar Museum established by Broadley. In addition to the published photographic

album accessed at the National Library, Calcutta, photographs of the Bihar Museum has been traced to the Oriental and India Office Collections of the British Library, London.

12. See Broadley, "The Buddhistic Remains of Bihar"; Broadley, *Ruins of the Nalanda Monasteries at Burg'aon.*
13. Letter from Major J. Waterhouse, Officiating Honorary Secretary to the Trustees, Indian Museum, to the Secretary to the Government of India, dated 23 August 1882, Pro. No. 3, Home Department/Archaeology and the Conservation of Ancient Monuments, December 1882; Memorandum on the Scope and Management of the Indian Museum by John Anderson, August 1882, Pro. No. 4, Home Department/Archaeology and Conservation of Ancient Monuments, December 1882 National Archives of India (henceforth NAI).
14. Memorandum by Major-General Alexander Cunningham, dated Simla, 11 October 1882, Notes, Pro. Nos. 3–7, Home Department/ Archaeology and the Conservation of Ancient Monuments, December 1882, NAI.
15. Ibid.
16. Alexander Cunningham, *Report of Tours in the Gangetic Provinces from Badaon to Bihar in 1875–76 and 1877–78*, Archaeological Survey of India, Cunningham Report, Vol. XI, 1880 (Reprint, New Delhi: ASI, 2000, pp. 190–93).
17. Letter from Babu Bemola Churn Bhattacharjee, Deputy Collector of Hooghly, to The Magistrate of Hooghly, dated Hooghly, 3 April 1883, Pro. No. 23, Home Department/Archaeology and Conservation of Ancient Monuments, October 1883, NAI.
18. In *Ruins of the Nalanda Monasteries at Burgaon*, Broadley closes by fondly recounting the cooperation of the local *zamindars* of Bihar, "Babu Byjnath Sing, Babu Shivdiyal Sing, Choudhuri Wahid Ali (zamindar of Burgaon), and Moulvie Abdul Aziz…", who had been active partners in his excavation of Nalanda. See Broadley, *Ruins of the Nalanda Monasteries at Burgaon*, pp. 10–11.
19. Letter from F.M. Halliday, Esq., Commissioner of Patna, to The Secretary to the Government of Bengal, Revenue Department, Pro. No. 24, Home Department/Archaeology and Conservation of Ancient Monuments, October 1883, NAI.
20. *Indian Museum Annual Report* (henceforth *IMAR*), *April 1891 to March 1892* (Calcutta, 1892), p. 13.
21. For a detailed biography of P. C. Mukharji, see Ramananda Chattopadhyay, "*Poorno Chandra Mukhopadhyay*", *Prabashi*, Vol. 3, No. 5 (1904), pp. 168–72, and Upinder Singh, *The Discovery of Ancient India*, pp. 316–22.
22. See Bloch, *Supplementary Catalogue of the Archaeological Collection of the Indian Museum* (Calcutta: Baptist Mission Press, 1911).
23. Frederick M. Asher, "The Former Broadley Collection, Bihar Sharif", *Artibus Asiae* XXXII, no. 2/3 (1970): 105–24.

24. Sraman Mukherjee, “New province, old capital: Making Patna Pataliputra”, *Indian Economic and Social History Review* 46, no. 2 (2009): 241–79.
25. “The Annual Presidential Address”, *Journal of the Bihar and Orissa Research Society* (henceforth *JBORS*) II, part I (1916): 1–13, quoted from p. 4.
26. See Mukherjee, “Unearthing the Pasts of Bengal, Bihar and Orissa: Archaeology, Museums and History Writing in the Making of Ancient Eastern India, 1862–1936” (PhD dissertation, University of Calcutta, 2010).

5

HERITAGE PRESERVATION IN THE GAYA REGION

Abhishek S. Amar

Being the home of two prominent UNESCO World Heritage sites of Bodhgaya and Nalanda, South Bihar region has a rich historical past. The region also witnessed the emergence of important urban and political centres of Rajgir and Pataliputra in ancient India. In early medieval India, the region was known as the centre of Buddhism because of the prominent Buddhist monasteries and their religious and political influence over the region. In this period, there also emerged a distinct tradition of stone and metal sculptural production, enriching the material assemblage of the region. The expansive material assemblage of this period can be encountered in almost every district of the South Bihar region including the Gaya district. Though the historical and religious prominence of this district is evident at the sites of Bodhgaya and Gaya, the district also has several smaller sites and villages with impressive material remains that have been documented in the last two hundred years and will be examined in this chapter.

Because of the historical and sacred importance of Gaya and Bodhgaya, the district began to attract scholarly attention from the nineteenth century onwards. This is illustrated by the surveys of numerous colonial surveyors and archaeologists. Colonial surveys began with Francis Buchanan-Hamilton, who surveyed this district in 1811–12. Along with the sites of Bodhgaya and Gaya, he also surveyed several villages that contained historical remains or older temples and shrines.[1] Following on from this initial foray, in the second half of the nineteenth century, Alexander Cunningham, the first director-general of the Archaeological Survey of India (ASI, hereafter), and J.D. Beglar also explored the district and documented several villages of historic importance and their significant remains.[2] In the last ten years, new surveys have been conducted, which resulted in the documentation of more than 350 sites with historical remains including mounds, sculptures, inscriptions, architectural elements, and shrines/temples from the ancient and early medieval periods. All of these documentations have revealed resituated contexts of several early medieval images and temples, which indicate a complex and disparate history of the district.

Colonial surveys, conducted in the second half of the nineteenth century, led to the movement of objects, images, and architectural materials into newly built colonial museums. Several scholars, such as Richard Davis and Bernard Cohn, have discussed how the movement of sculptures to the museums resulted in the loss of original meanings, where they were viewed merely as historical artifacts, to be studied, examined, and exhibited to reconstruct India's past in the colonial period.[3] Cohn has argued that the goal of the colonial state was to develop a linear history of India on the pattern of nineteenth century positivist historiography. This could be accomplished through dating ruins, reading inscriptions and texts to reveal political history and other dimensions of the past. This invigorated them to collect and classify umpteen numbers of specimens, which were used to build vast repositories.[4] As a result, the first large-scale museum was built in erstwhile Calcutta (now Kolkata), which developed into the "Indian museum" with a large collection of archaeological, natural, historical, and ethnographic specimens.[5] This trend has continued in postcolonial India, as the ASI became responsible for the preservation of historical sites. The ASI began to develop on-site museums to preserve sculptures and other remains. Though several of these collections have been examined to produce a positivist and descriptive history, the majority of these collections are yet to be studied critically. In addition, the contexts of most of these collections have hardly been investigated, because of the undue emphasis on the primary period of their production and usage. Why and how these materials were reused and preserved by later generations, including secondary and tertiary users, is yet to be investigated.

In contrast to museum collections, many Buddhist and Brāhmaṇical sculptures, architectural elements, and temples continue to be used by the local communities in the villages of Gaya. These remains were either appropriated or resituated in new socio-religious contexts at their site of discovery or in proximate distance, which indicates an ongoing dialogue between the extant communities and the past. This chapter will analyse the reuse of these material remains, specifically the early medieval images and shrines/temple, and their resituated socio-religious contexts. Consequentially, this will facilitate an understanding of how these practices led to the preservation of the historical heritage within the Gaya district. It was this assimilative practice, as the chapter argues — based on the interaction between extant communities, local knowledge, and material remains (sculptures and temples/shrines) — that resulted in their reuse and their subsequent preservation. Hence, it also illustrates an awareness of the historic potential and heritage value of material remains amongst the local inhabitants. Such a study of material remains, based on the interrogation of colonial records and recent documentation, also contributes to the study of religious history by adding new data that may not be adequately represented in the colonial documentation or archives. The new data, therefore, enriches the existing archive by explaining their current context and reuse in a variety of ways.

THE HISTORY OF GAYA DISTRICT

The district has a long illustrious history that goes as far back as the second millennium BCE. Bodhgaya and the town of Gaya, being the place of Buddha's enlightenment and an eminent Hindu centre for performing funerary rituals (*śrāddha*) respectively, are two prominent sites within the district. Both have been studied for a long time because of their long-cherished histories. In fact, UNESCO declared Bodhgaya a world heritage site in 2001. However, several other places of religious, archaeological, and historical importance including Sonpur, Konch, Taradeeh, Kurkihar, Hasra Kol, and Konch have also been known for a long time because of prior documentations, excavations, and researches. Sonpur was excavated between 1956 and 1962 and a report was published in 1977.[6] Taradeeh and Bakror, in the vicinity of Bodhgaya, have been excavated in the last three decades. The recent documentation of more than 350 sites of historical significance in the rural and urban areas of Gaya has been facilitated through my own survey as well as the survey of the Kashi Prasad Jayaswal research Institute, Patna.[7] Based on this recent survey, I will scrutinize two distinct types of heritage — sculptures and temples/shrines — to demonstrate the role of reuse in their preservation within the district of Gaya. Additionally, the paper will study the sites of Kespa, Kurkihar, Chonvar, and Main, as shown in Figure 5.1.

FIGURE 5.1
Map of Gaya (1. Bodhgaya, 2. Gaya, 3. Kespa, 4. Kurkihar, 5. Chonvar, and 6. Main)

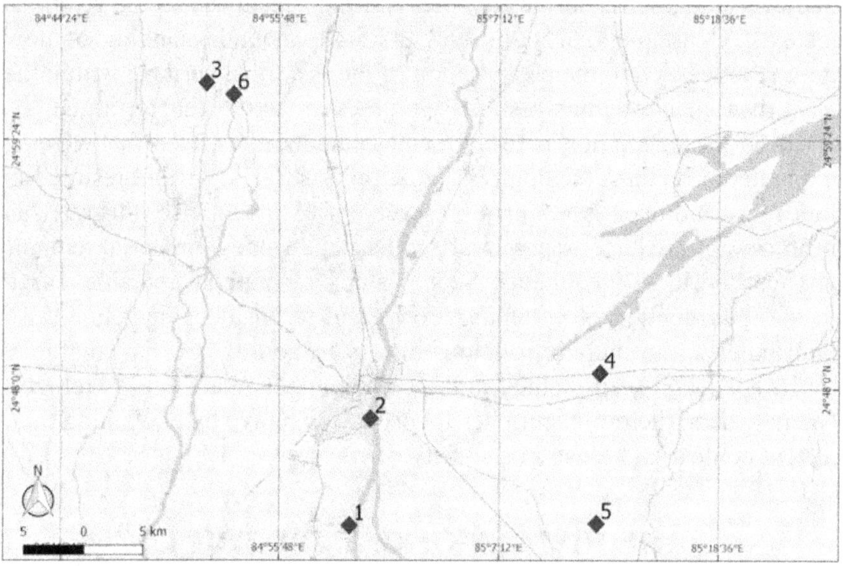

REUSE AND HERITAGE PRESERVATION

Sculptures of Village Shrines

Several older sculptures were documented in their new religious contexts in the villages of the district, where they were ritually organized and utilized on a daily basis. Almost every village in the district has *grāma-sthānas* (village spot of worship), the *dihwar-sthānas*, *devi-sthāna* (goddess-shrine), and *goraiya-sthānas* (shrines constituted mostly of fragments). *Dihwar* is the protective deity of a village and is located at the boundary of the village. *Dihwar-sthāna* may have a raised platform with either one or multiple sculptures. Very often, they are broken and fragments of images or votive *stūpas*. *Goraiya-sthānas* are shrines of low caste people, who may not have access to the village shrine or temple. *Goraiya-sthānas* (Figure 5.2) are generally a collection of broken images, architectural fragments, and other remains on a plastered platform, kept near or within the settlement of low caste people in villages. All these above listed are treated as tutelary deities. They are worshipped cyclically and on special occasions to protect villages from diseases, epidemics, and other ill effects, and also to ensure agricultural productivity and rains.

FIGURE 5.2
Goraiya Sthāna, Village-Taroa

Several texts within the Hindu tradition including *Pratimanalaksanam* warn worshippers that the "image of a burnt, worn out, broken deity after its establishment or at the time of enshrinement brings forth drought, loss of wealth, death to family members".[8] However, the villagers disregard these textual injunctions and place these fragments and broken images at their shrines to worship them. This practice is informed by a sense of belonging that people have for these sculptures that were unearthed from their land accidently. Often, the local inhabitants install these images at the find-spot, which eventually becomes *dihwar* or *goraiya-sthāna* over time. At several places, people have also installed these images within the main village temple or their houses even if these are broken and fragmentary. To protect them, they dedicate a part of their house, which doubles up as a new shrine.

Sculptures in Village Temples

The ritual usage of older Buddhist sculptures as Hindu gods and goddesses signifies "reuse" and its role in the development of a distinct local history. In my survey, I have found at least four Hindu temples — Dulhin temple in Sherghati, Devī temples in Konchi and Vishnupur, and Ugratārā temple at Kespa — in the district, where Buddhist figures are currently being worshipped as Brāhmaṇical female goddesses in a Hindu setting. Of these temples, the Ugratārā temple of Kespa village has emerged as a locally important sacred centre.

Located in the Tikari block of Gaya, Kespa is an early medieval religious site with multiple Buddhist and Brāhmaṇical images. Most of these images are now kept in and around the Ugratārā temple (Figure 5.3) on the southern boundary of this village, which is located on an older mound. Several other images are housed in two other shrines of the village. The central deity within the Ugratārā temple is a Hindu goddess, who is named as Ugratāra. Close examination suggests that this is a Buddhist image, which is currently being worshipped as a female goddess. This image and its associated legend were reported in the colonial surveys of the nineteenth century.

The history of the Ugratārā temple of Kespa raises several questions about its origin and the associated narrative. The temple was first reported by Buchanan and was also examined later by Beglar.[9] Buchanan mentioned that the Gayāwāla Brāhmaṇas of Gaya informed him about the antiquity of this temple. They informed him that the temple was at least 200 years

FIGURE 5.3
Ugratāra Temple, Village-Kespa

old. However, his visit and reconnaissance suggested otherwise. He noted that the temple, a small building of mud and brick, was of recent origin. It was situated near the ruins of bricks and stones, which indicated the existence of a temple at the site in the past.[10] The image inside was large and covered with a cotton cloth. Buchanan spoke with the priests to inquire about the origin story of this temple. He was told that:

> the image being worshipped inside the sanctum was a certain Tārādevī, who was a virtuous woman and married to an oilman. The local king Bala attempted to control Tārādevī to satisfy his sexual desire. Tārādevī, in order to protect her dignity, prayed to her protecting goddess. As a result, both she and rājā were converted into stone. The virtuous Tārādevī is now in the temple, whereas the Bala Rājā stood in a Mango grove at some distance.[11]

The narrative prompted Buchanan to see the sculpture of Bala, which was placed in the mango grove shrine along with several other images and fragments. The Bala sculpture was found from the digging of the area in the mango grove, which may have been remains of an older temple. Buchanan found the image of Bala to be that of the historical Buddha.[12] Buchanan found the narrative to be interesting enough to document in his report. However, he dismissed this narrative as a legendary account that was also unreasonable. For him, what mattered was the textual interpretation of Tārā as an incarnation of goddess Kālī, which was a standard narrative or legend. This local narrative had no historical veracity since the temple was relatively new, whereas the images were much older. Similarly, the story had characters that did not conform to the standard narrative which he may have heard from Brāhmaṇas or read from texts. Buchanan's report also manifests his scepticism and suspicion, revealed in his description of the temple goddess as a form of Gadādhar.

Buchanan's description reflects his obtuseness with regard to the current history of the Kespa village. This may also have been informed by the colonial agenda of discovering an ancient past, which was glorious unlike the current one. The Tārā Bala story was predicated on the availability of older sculptures, which illustrates the ingenuity of the local community. They wove a narrative around the existing sculptural heritage, for which there was no scriptural basis. The local inhabitants certainly were not aware of the past identities of these sculptures. In contrast, they are aware of the Buddhist nature of these sculptures now. However, they have disregarded the sectarian affiliations of these sculptures and continue to worship them.

The Ugratāra temple has become a locally important sacred centre, where villagers from the region gather for the performance of *pūjā* and other celebrations from time to time. On these occasions, the Tārādevī narrative is recounted. Local priests also worship the Tārā image on these occasions, which reinforces this version of the past amongst local inhabitants. While tracing the sacred geography of Ballabhgarh, Nayanjot Lahiri has argued, "that micro-level religious geography cannot be textually constituted and religious texts cannot always be the source and signifier of a place of religious importance."[13] This process is also evident at Kespa. There exists no scriptural basis for the Tārā Bala story. This example, therefore, illuminates the ways in which the extant communities developed a meaningful link with the past through the pre-existing material assemblage. This also facilitated the production of a distinct "timeless" history of the place that informed their sense of the past and continue to shape their present.

In fact, Buchanan himself got a taste of this "history" when he tried to inquire about the date of construction of this temple. After the refusal of the local Brāhmaṇa priests, a villager told him that, "it was needless to ask when a temple was built as the Gods are not the work of men." For the local inhabitants, what really mattered was that this temple of goddess had been worshipped for a long time. The sculptures inside the sanctum and scattered around the village were anchors of the "timeless" past. What also supported their contention was the fact that these sculptures were constructed hundreds of years ago and were not made anymore. Given the gap between the early medieval period and nineteenth century, the date of construction of these images may not have survived in the local memory. This also explains why the dialogue between the villagers and Buchanan emphasized the different understandings of history that they each harboured. For Buchanan, what mattered was the origin and primary identity of sculptures, whereas the local inhabitants were not interested in configuring these questions. For them, the temple constituted a part of their daily experience as well as a living reminder of their past. Other images in and around the temple, irrespective of their condition, were equally important and conveyed the connection with the past.

As a result, several other sculptures, irrespective of their Buddhist and Brāhmaṇical nature, were placed inside the sanctum of the temple. Several others were plastered outside in the niches. Many broken sculptures and fragments were also kept on a platform under the *pipal* tree outside.[14] All these images were — and continue to be — ritually worshipped even today. The Ugratārā temple complex almost seems like a museum now but the non-museum setting can be easily discerned here. Unlike museums, these images are not organized in accordance to their religious affiliations or chronological development. Instead, the local inhabitants interpret each image as a specific deity, *dikpāla*/protector, or some other figure of significance. Their identification and ritual usage depends on the specific contexts and order in which the locals have placed them. Each of them also evokes emotional and religious connections for the local inhabitants since their parents, grandparents, and ancestors worshipped them. In fact, the locals are aware of past sectarian identities of these sculptures, but that has not affected their religiosity or nature of ritual usage of these sculptures. They continue to be part of a lived history.

An important example of this lived history is a Viṣṇu-Garuḍa image, which was described by Buchanan as a *Mama-Bhanja* (Uncle-nephew) story.[15] According to his account, women pelted stones onto this image since the *mama*/uncle was considered to be sitting on the shoulder of *Bhanja*/ nephew. Irrespective of its identification, the sculpture is still located at the eastern boundary of the village and villagers still call it by the name of *Mama-Bhanja*. The villagers are currently constructing a shrine for this sculpture in order to protect and preserve it.

The resituated contexts of these sculptures, as illustrated in their incorporation into the local ritual-practices and religious life, have resulted in their survival, protection, and preservation in their place of origin generally. Richard Davis and Catherine Becker have argued that the prioritization of any one moment from the multiple lives of historic images and artifacts needs to be avoided. They both suggest that the meanings are made and remade continually through interactions with the communities.[16] The Kespa example indicates this process where the local inhabitants carved new meanings of these older sculptures, which has provided a distinct identity to the village and local inhabitants. The new meanings also signify the role of local inhabitants in constructing their own past imaginatively, which may have been informed by their concerns at the time of construction of this temple. As a result, the extant community engaged with the past through their reinterpretation of the material remains. This engagement has been crucial in protecting and preserving the material assemblage from this village.

GAYA TEMPLES

Several newly constructed temples and shrines significantly impacted the ritual landscape of Gaya in the nineteenth century. The analysis of colonial accounts and my survey of Gaya indicate that many new temples possess sculptures, images, and inscriptions from an earlier period. Additionally, several older temples were reconstructed in the colonial period and now contain sculptures, images, and inscriptions acquired from other places. This section will investigate these two patterns to understand the motives and refashioning of Gaya's landscape.[17]

The Viṣṇupada temple complex currently consists of multiple shrines, and contains a significant number of sculptures and inscriptions within those shrines. This temple has a long history and probably dates from the early medieval period.[18] However, the current temple was constructed through the patronage of the Holkar queen of Indore, Ahilyabai, in the second half of the eighteenth century.[19] A shrine dedicated to her (Figure 5.4) in the vicinity of the temple complex demonstrates her status as an important patron. An analysis of colonial accounts reflects the growth of the Viṣṇupada temple into a massive complex with the addition of several smaller shrines, temples, sculptures, and rest houses. My own survey of the temple complex and its surrounding shrines and areas in 2011 and 2014 revealed at least two hundred other images, architectural elements, and several inscriptions. All of these are currently housed in the smaller temples and shrines such

FIGURE 5.4
Ahilya Bai shrine, Gaya

as the Mahādeva temple, Indra temple, Radha Krishna temple, and several others within the complex.[20]

Many sculptures in these subsidiary shrines are not in active worship and are plastered in the wall haphazardly along with the inscriptions. An excellent example of this pattern is an early medieval inscription (Figure 5.5) that is plastered near the Nṛsiṃha temple along with several sculptures. Many of these sculptures are also plastered in the alleys and pathways and remain almost invisible to the visiting pilgrims. Both, Buchanan and Cunningham, emphasized in their accounts that these images were not found locally, but brought from different parts of the district, including Bodhgaya, to be placed in the temple complex. The question then is: why were these images brought from elsewhere and plastered at places where they cannot be viewed or actively worshipped?

There are two plausible explanations. A key motive may have been to preserve the rich sculptural and architectural assemblage of the district. Their placement within a temple complex ensured their protection and simultaneously led to their ritual usage. A second motive may have been to invoke the authority of the past, which could be presented through the scattered placement of sculptures and inscriptions. This was an emphatic

FIGURE 5.5
Inscription near the Nṛsiṃha temple within Viṣṇupada complex, Gaya

way to demonstrate the sacrality of Gaya to the visitors. Most pilgrims to Gaya had some familiarity with the *Gayāsura* legend. This legend is repeatedly recounted during the performance of rituals to the pilgrims, who may not have time to read the legendary history of the place as narrated in the *Gayā-Māhātmya* of the *Vāyu Purāṇa*.[21] However, the placement and ritual usage of these sculptures reminded visitors of the historicity of the temple and its surrounding area. Even if they cannot be seen or ritually engaged with, their mere presence confirmed the historicity and sacred status of the temple complex and its surrounding area for the *śrāddha* and other rituals.

Irrespective of its sacred status, there has been a legal wrangle over the control and management of the Viṣṇupada temple between the Bihar State Religious Trust Board and *Chaudhasaiya Gayāpal Samity*.[22] This *Samity* is an elected body of the Gayāwāla Brāhmaṇas, which controls and regulates this temple. The major issue remains the private versus public nature of this temple. The Gayāwāla's argument has been that the temple is a *vedī* since it contains the footprints of Viṣṇu. A *vedī* is a place within the Gaya, which is linked to the mythology of Gayāsura and is meant exclusively for the performance of *śrāddha* rituals. In contrast, a temple is a place for *darśana* and offering worship to the deity. It is widely known that the Hindu temples have often combined multiple roles, and that the Viṣṇupada temple is no different. In addition to the *piṇḍa* offerings, the footprints of Viṣṇu have to be ritually worshipped daily in accordance to the normative practice of worshipping gods and goddesses in Hindu temples. The Gayāwāla Brāhmaṇas actually perform the temple rituals here on a daily basis, a fact which they claimed in their appeal to the court.

The case is still in the Patna High Court, and hence cannot be commented upon here extensively. However, it shows the attitudes that state institutions such as the Religious Trust Board have inherited from the colonial modes of governance, which imagines a taxonomic category of "public temple" merely on a functionalist understanding of the temple. This functionalist reading disregards the entanglements between the Gayāwāla Brāhmaṇas and multi-layered histories of this temple complex over a period of time. Even though the Gayāwāla's argument that their right over the temple is predicated on the authority of "*ancient śāstras*" (scriptures such as *Gayā-Māhātmya* of *Vāyu-Purāṇa*) may not stand the scrutiny of time and scholarship, their multipronged engagements with the temple over centuries have left an enduring imprint on this temple and its subsequent blooming into a complex. They have played a significant role in preserving local heritage through their ritual actions and daily worship of older sculptures. In doing so, they did not confine themselves to the Viṣṇupada temple itself, which is the ritual centre of Gaya *śrāddha* but also included other sculptures, architectural elements, and inscriptions.

A better approach to examine the Viṣṇupada temple complex, thus, would be to move away from the debate over temple versus *vedī* or private versus public, and focus instead on its importance as a repository of local material heritage. Despite being the most important centre to perform *śrāddha* rituals historically, the local Gayāwālas did not see any problem in installing older images within the sanctum of the Viṣṇupada temple. This illustrates that even within the temple of the Viṣṇu, it was not considered inappropriate to install images of other gods and goddesses despite the textual proscriptions against it. The Gayāwālas did not see any contradiction in the *vedī* also functioning as a temple. This demonstrates a certain understanding of the historical sculptures and its appreciation amongst the Gayāwālas, and their active role in transforming the temple into a local repository. They pasted sculptures into the walls of this complex to preserve and protect them through active ritual usage. Similarly, they plastered inscriptions along with the sculptures, which were unreadable at the time. Through their actions, they challenged and transcended the binary of either preservation in the museums or mere ritual usage in a religious setting. Their actions demonstrate the simultaneous processes of ritual reuse and preservation.

RURAL TEMPLES

Several early medieval temples, of both Buddhist and Brāhmaṇical traditions, are currently reinterpreted and reused in the district. Three *in situ* temples from the early medieval period have been documented within the villages of Kurkihar, Chonvar, and Main respectively. The study of material remains from Kurkihar has proved beyond doubt that it was an early medieval Buddhist monastic site.[23] The *devī-sthāna* shrine (Figure 5.6) of the village probably was a Buddhist temple, which now has been transformed into a Hindu temple. The sanctum of the temple contains a Durgā sculpture. Most sculptures within this temple are Buddhist though they are currently being worshipped as Hindu gods and goddesses. Most local inhabitants are now aware of the Buddhist history of the place and identify Buddhist figures within the temple. However, this has not deterred the local communities from worshipping and ritual usage of these sculptures.

FIGURE 5.6
Devī-sthān Temple, Village-Kurkihar

Chonvar temple also contains stone pillars, lintels, and doorjamb that indicate its early medieval origin. The temple currently has mixed image collections including the Viṣṇu, Bodhisattva, Tāra and several votive *stūpas*. However, the temple has a *Śiva liṅga* in the sanctum, which has been repaired recently. Even though it is difficult to indicate the specific sectarian affiliation of the temple in the past, the presence of Buddhist sculptures and fragments, including *votive stūpas*, suggests a strong Buddhist link. The *votive stūpas* and other fragments are currently placed in the *maṇḍapa*, and at the entrance of the temple. Both these examples — Kurkihar and Chonvar — indicate the reuse of the older temples, which motivated the local communities to diligently preserve the architectural elements and sculptures, irrespective of past religious affiliations.

The third example of Main village denotes how the active engagement of the local inhabitants can transform an older temple into a place of religious worship and tourism. A significant collection of Brāhmaṇical sculptures is kept in Koteśvaranāth Mahādeva temple and two other shrines within this village. Koteśvaranāth Mahādeva is an older temple (Figure 5.7), which is now enveloped by a new temple. This new temple, made in *śikhara* style, could have either replaced the older shrine or may have been constructed besides the older one. However, the villager's decision to construct the new temple right over the older one showcases the importance placed on the historic and heritage value of the older shrine, which dates from the early medieval period.[24]

More recently, the village has received attention from the ASI and the Ministry of Tourism, Government of Bihar. The Bihar circle of ASI has published a catalogue cum brochure, which provides a historical and chronological description of the temple and sculptures from this village. The brochure also contains messages from eminent political and administrative figures including the current Chief Minister, and the then Ministers of Tourism, and Art and Culture. All these messages emphasize the importance of protecting and generating awareness about the temple amongst the people of Bihar. The Chief Minister's letter especially emphasizes the rich historical heritage of Bihar, which includes places like the village of Main. More recently, the Bihar Government decided to dedicate a special celebration designated as *Baba Koteśvara Mahādeva*

FIGURE 5.7
Koteśwaranath Mahādeva Temple, Village-Main

Mahōtsava to disseminate its importance as a place of remarkable heritage. Local government attempts to promote this place may be reflected in its listing as a site of historical importance on the website of the Ministry of Tourism, Government of Bihar.

The local inhabitants have also attempted consciously to engage with the new media to promote this place. They developed a temple website, which lists celebrations and cultural activities organized at the site in the last few years.[25] The website also contained information about its history, the ASI brochure, and messages by important political figures. A link to the website of this temple can be found on the Government of Bihar website. The temple website, developed by the local inhabitants, is no longer working, unfortunately.[26]

The website also provides the historical narrative of the temple. According to this narrative, Usha, who supposedly constructed this temple, was the daughter of the demon Bāṇāsura. She desired to marry Kriṣṇa's grandson Aniruddha, for which she invoked lord Śiva. Śiva instructed her to construct this temple, which led to the fulfilment of her desire to marry Aniruddha. This legendary account, with its origins in the Purāṇic and epic texts, has become the official narrative of the place, which is also affirmed in the ASI brochure. The brochure and website also claim that the village was called Śivanagari in earlier times.

The above account demonstrates the transformation of this early medieval temple site into a place of tourist and religious importance. Local initiatives to protect, preserve, and promote the temple and sculptures have been instrumental in attracting the attention of ASI and subsequently the state government. These efforts have transformed the place, as the temple has become a vehicle of growth and development. While organizing the festivities, the state government also decided to develop adequate infrastructure for facilitating travel, which is located in the interiors of the district. When inquired, local inhabitants expressed happiness over these recent developments since the "heritage tag" has resulted in the construction of new roads, a new police post (since the village was previously affected by Maoist violence in 1980s and 1990s), and brought prestige and attention to the village. This is in sharp contrast to several other sites that have similar history and heritage, but no such development.

CONCLUSION

The examples discussed above demonstrate how local inhabitants of this district have engaged with the historical material remains, which culminated in their ritual reuses and preservation. In his study of Abrahamic scriptures, David Nirenberg has argued that, "a historicist approach facilitates understanding of multiple meanings produced by myriad communities at diverse moments in time, rather than treating the religion or culture as essential and unchanging."[27] Adopting this historicist method to study reuse of material remains opens up the possibilities of multiple interpretations that the local communities of Gaya district produced at diverse moments. These interpretations were predicated on the understanding of the material remains as anchors of the past, which shaped the ritual practices and a certain understanding of the past among them.

An interesting corollary here is to think about the shrines and temples of this district as museums. As discussed previously, most museums of India emerged as a by-product of antiquarian research and collections that began in the colonial period. They aimed to study the collection through taxonomic organizations and subsequently preserved them for their "heritage value." The "heritage value," as noted in the catalogues and museum displays, was imagined as an exclusive category that emphasized their period of origin and primary usage. Their subsequent reutilizations and resituated contexts were often ignored or dismissed as the "legends" or "superstitions" by ignorant people. In most cases, the sculptures and architectural materials were picked up without any discussion of their context or how the local communities used them. This has often resulted in a dry and meaningless display of myriad objects in various museums of India, where we often encounter the name, sectarian affiliations, and the period of origin/ construction. In contrast, the extant resituated sculptures and temples of Gaya district convey multiple meanings rather than prioritizing any one moment. Even if many of these images and temples have lost their primary contexts, and are currently in their secondary or tertiary contexts, they continue to provide enough clues for the reconstruction of earlier pasts and modern use. Museums often emphasize the binary of preservation verses reuse of sculptures and architectural elements. In contrast, the temples of Gaya illustrate that this binary can be transcended since the reuse can also facilitate preservation or vice-versa. The lived experiences of these remains within temples and shrines continue to inspire people of Gaya to preserve and protect them.

Notes

1. Francis Buchanan, *An Account of the Districts of Bihar and Patna in 1811–12*, vol. I (1936; rpr., Patna: Department of Art, Culture & Youth, 2013), pp. 135–37 & 142–45.

2. See Alexander Cunningham, *Four Reports Made During the Years 1862–63–64–65*, vol. I, (1871; rpr., New Delhi: Archaeological Survey of India, 2000); Alexander Cunningham, *Report of the Year 1871–72*, vol. III (1873; rpr., New Delhi: Archaeological Survey of India, 2000); and J.D. Beglar, *Report of a Tour Through the Bengal Provinces*, vol. VIII (1878; rpr., New Delhi: Archaeological Survey of India, 2000).
3. See Bernard Cohn, *Colonialism and Its Forms of Knowledge* (Princeton: Princeton University Press, 1996), p. 97; and Richard Davis, *Lives of Indian Images* (Princeton: Princeton University Press, 1999), p. 4.
4. Cohn, *Colonialism and Knowledge*, p. 80.
5. Ibid., p. 9.
6. B.P. Sinha and B.S. Verma, *Sonpur Excavations 1956 and 1959–1962* (Patna: Directorate of Archaeology and Museum of Bihar, 1977), pp. 3–4.
7. Abishek S. Amar and Bijoy K. Chaudhary, *Archaeological Gazetteer of Gaya District* (Patna: K.P.J. Research Institute, 2017).
8. Cited in N. Lahiri, *Marshalling the Past: Ancient India and its Modern Histories* (New Delhi: Permanent Black, 2012), p. 282.
9. Buchanan, *Account of Bihar & Patna*, p. 143. see also Beglar, *Tour Through the Bengal Provinces*, p. 54.
10. Buchanan, *Account of Bihar & Patna*, p. 142.
11. Ibid., p. 143.
12. Buchanan noted that the sculpture was of human size and surrounded by heaps of bricks. He correctly identified the sculpture as a Buddha since it also contained a short Buddhist inscription on the stele. The sculpture is still located at the same shrine, though new houses have been constructed around the shrine.
13. Lahiri, *Marshalling the Past*, p. 285.
14. Many images were built into the wall and many broken ones were lying near the door, and all occasionally are marked with red lead/*ṭīkā* as a mark of respect/active worship. See Buchanan, *Account of Bihar & Patna*, pp. 142–43.
15. Ibid., p. 144.
16. See Richard Davis, *Lives of Indian Images*, pp. 5–6; and Catherine Becker, *Shifting Stones, Shaping the Past* (New York: Oxford University Press, 2015), p. 15.
17. The results of my survey and documentation are also available on the website of my digital humanities project titled "Sacred centers in India." The website link is <http://sci.dhinitiative.org/>. For analysis of colonial accounts, see Abhishek S. Amar, "Re-inventing Hindu Gaya: Shrines, Images, and Gayāwāla Brāhmaṇas," Paper presented at the Annual Meeting of American Academy of Religion, Chicago, Illinois, November 2012.
18. For a detailed history of the temple, see Abhishek S. Amar, "Buddhist Responses to Brāhmaṇa Challenges in Medieval India: Bodhgayā and Gayā," *Journal of the Royal Asiatic Society* 22, no. 1 (January 2012): 164–68.

19. Both Buchanan and Cunningham provide a detailed account of the construction of this temple through the patronage of queen Ahilyabai. For details, see Buchanan, *Account of Bihar & Patna*, pp. 115–16; and Cunningham, *Report of the Year 1871–72*, p. 108.
20. See, Amar, digital humanities project titled "Sacred centers in India".
21. They invoke the account of *Gayā-Māhātmya*, whose composition has been dated to the eleventh century. The text was subsequently added to multiple Purāṇas including the *Garuḍa* and *Vāyu Purāṇas*. For details, see Amar, *Buddhist Responses to Brāhmaṇa Challenges*, pp. 164–68.
22. Ashok Mishra, "Gaya's Vishnupad temple under spotlight after Padmanabhaswamy", *Hindustan Times*, 10 July 2011 <http://www.hindustantimes.com/patna/gaya-s-vishnupad-temple-under-spotlight-after-padmanabhaswamy/story-dM4g6VzPA28THWxu0TfL.html> (accessed 17 January 2017).
23. Claudine Bautze-Picron, *The Forgotten Place: Stone Images From Kurkihar* (New Delhi: Archaeological Survey of India, 2014), p. 3.
24. S.K. Manjul, D.N. Sinha, S. Sinha, and S.K. Tiwary, *Koteshwar Nath Dham Village Main Gaya: An Archaeological Survey* (Patna: Archaeological Survey of India, 2013).
25. For more information, see weblink, <http://www.pinddaangaya.in/english%20version%20website/index.php?pg=koteshwar> (accessed 22 January 2017).
26. Koteshwarnath Mahadeva (accessed 20 August 2016).
27. D. Nirenberg, "Sibling Rivalries, Scriptural Communities: What Medieval History Can and Cannot Teach Us about Relations between Judaism, Christianity, and Islam," in *Faithful Narratives*, edited by Andrea Sterk and Nina Caputo (Ithaca: Cornell University Press, 2014).

6

SETTING THE "RECORDS" STRAIGHT
Textual Sources on Nālandā and Their Historical Value[1]

Max Deeg

INTRODUCTION

Since its inscription into the UNESCO's list of world heritage sites in July 2016 the ruins of Nālandā will certainly attract more attention through the Indian and global public than hitherto. The most recent or forthcoming publications on Nālandā by Frederick Asher and Mary Stewart critically assess the archaeological and art-historical evidence, and for this purpose they constantly refer to textual sources. These references are made on the basis of the old nineteenh century translations of the most extensive texts on Nālandā, the Chinese records, and of the Middle-Indic (Pāli, Prākṛt) and Tibetan sources. It seems therefore appropriate that a volume on Nālandā also contains a contribution from the textual-philological point of view, not only, as the title implies, to set the records straight, but also to give contextually informed translations and discussions of the relevant textual sources. I do not claim at all that these are the final words on all the issues addressed here, but would rather like to open a critical discourse on and about some of these sources.

The textual sources referring to Nālandā are threefold: inscriptions, Buddhist and Jain "canonical" texts in Indic languages, and passages in and from the travelogues of Chinese visitors or residents of the monastery and relatively late Tibetan historiographical writings. Among these sources the ones deemed to be most informative and reliable are the Chinese records of Xuanzang 玄奘 (600/602–664), of his biographer(s), and of Yijing 義淨 (635–713), because both monks resided and studied in Nālandā for several years. Information extracted from these sources, digested mostly from the nineteenth century translations by Beal and others, feed rather uncritically into the major historical narrative of the monastery, pushing its existence even back to the time of the Buddha.[2] The article has a focus on the Chinese texts and their translations and the Pāli and Jain sources while neglecting other sources like inscriptions. As a natural consequence of this, I will not discuss the *paraṃparā* of kings given by Xuanzang,[3] since relation cannot be done without the evidence from royal inscriptions and other historical sources, as important as this is for the reconstruction of the history of the monastery. Due to restriction of space such an analysis has to be given at another occasion.

LOCATION AND NAME

Direction (north) and distance (ca. 30 Chinese miles or *li* 里) given by Xuanzang (see below) from the southern gate of Rājagṛha to the archaeological site of Nālandā near the modern villages of Bargaon and Surājpur and of other sources are approximately correct and have been the basis of the identification of the site in the second half of the nineteenth century. The archaeological site has been surveyed and excavated in several digs, starting with Francis Buchanan Hamilton in 1812 and later Alexander Cunningham in 1861ff., and others.[4] The correct identity of the site was verified by inscriptions on sealings found at Nālandā.

The most extensive name of the monastery is found in a sealing inscription in eighth century script which reads *srī-Nālandā-Mahāvihārīyāryabhikṣusaṃghasya* ("of the noble monastic community of the Great Monastery of Nālandā").[5] In the long Yaśovarmadeva inscription from Nālandā the monastery is just called Nālandā,[6] while the Devapāla and Gopāladeva inscriptions give Śrī-Nālandā.[7] In context of the "title" or status of the monastery it is striking that Xuanzang (see Appendix) does not call Nālandā *mahāvihāra* (*dasi* 大寺)[8] but Nalantuo-sengjialan 那爛陀僧伽藍/*EMC[9] *na'-lan^h-da-səŋ-gɨa-lam*, Nālandā-saṅghārāma. This may indicate that at the time of his visit the monastery had not yet received the status of a "great monastery" (*mahāvihāra*). Yijing's anthology of *dharma*-searching monks is the only Chinese source which uses the full-fledged title Shili-Nalantuo-mohepiheluo 室利那爛陀莫訶毘訶羅/

EMC **ɕit-li*^{h}*-na'-lan*^{h}*-da-mak*[10]*-xa-bji-xa-la*, Śrī-Nālandā-mahāvihāra (T.2066.6a.24), corresponding to the Nālandā sealing inscription. His explanation of a Great Monastery — that kings set up clypsedras only in *mahāvihāra*s (see below) — seems to indicate (semi-)official status of such monasteries through royal patronage[11] which is also supported by other evidence such as Xuanzang's record about the lineage of royal foundations at Nālandā. Yijing's note shows that the institutional title was already in place before the support of Nālandā and the foundation of other monastic centres also called *mahāvihāra* like Vikramaśīla, Somapura and Odantapura/Uddāṇḍapura through the Pāla dynasty (ca. 750–1161).

Yijing himself is not consistent in using the full name Śri-Nālandā-mahāvihāra: in a running note to his translation of the Mūlasarvāstivāda-vinaya (T.1453.477c.23) he calls the monastery just Shili-Nalantuo-si 室利那爛陀寺/EMC **ɕit-li*^{h}*-na'-lan*^{h}*-da-°*, Skt. Śrī-Nālandā-vihāra. This is also the title given to the monastery in the Tibetan sources, in the Mahāvyutpatti[12] and in Tārānātha's history.[13]

As can be concluded from Xuanzang's and the other Chinese records there obviously existed several etiological stories explaining why and from where the monastery had gotten its name. These stories developed only after the monastery gained importance and fame; in the fifth century, Buddhaghosa does not give any explanation of the name, and this may serve as an approximate *terminus post quem* for the coming in to existence and spread of such stories. Xuanzang (Appendix 1.a) seems to give higher authority to a narrative which links the place to a previous existence of the Buddha and is based on a learned etymology (*nirvacana*) of the name: Nālandā, Chin. Shi-wuyan 施無厭, is analysed as consisting of three elements, Skt. *na* (*wu* 無) + *alam* (*yan* 厭) + √*dā-* (*shi* 施), lit.: "not enough giving". Although this interpretation may appear a little bit over-sophisticated and artificial from a modern standpoint it reflects what at the time was thought most important for a *mahāvihāra*: to secure enough donors' support for the institution. Moreover, and one could add with Yijing, to attract donors the monastery has to observe the monastic rules (Appendix 4.b). This is also reflected in a passage in the Mūlasarvāstivāda-vinaya translated by Yijing:

> As for constructing a Great Monastery (*dasi*, *mahāvihāra*), there are two kinds of "great": 1. great [with respect] to donations, [and] 2. great [with respect] to form and size. Among these two [kinds of] "great" [the one] called [so because] of donations is [really] great.[14]

Xuanzang's also presents the reader with an alternative origin of the name that tells of a *nāga* who lived in a pond in a mango grove (*anmoluo-lin*

菴沒羅林; Skt. **āmravana*) at the place where the monastery was found. According to this old tradition (*wen zhi qijiu yue: ...* 聞之耆舊曰:...) the *nāga*'s name was transferred to the monastery after its foundation. It may well be that Xuanzang dismissed this etiology because of the predicted negative karmic effect of the violent submission of the *nāga* which will cause the monastery's scholars' heads to be split.

This story is also echoed by Yijing (T.2066.6a.26ff.): 那爛陀乃是龍名。近此有龍，名那伽爛陀，故以為號。("Nalantuo is the name of a *nāga* (*long*). Close to this [monastery] was a *nāga* called Najialantuo, and therefore this became [the monastery's] name.") This in fact may have been the more widespread explanation than the rather scholarly learned etymology ("not enough giving") obviously preferred by Xuanzang. Yijing gives a slightly different interpretation of the name (*najialantuo*) than Xuanzang's rather simplistic one to one correspondence; one may conclude from Yijing's passage that the name clearly originally was parsed as *najia* Lantuo 那伽爛陀/EMC **na'-gɨa-lan^h-da*, *nāga* *Landa/Randa (?).[15] The Tibetan name Nālendra is probably another reinterpretation — of which the etiological narrative has just not survived.

NĀLANDĀ IN CHINESE, TIBETAN AND INDIAN SOURCES

Xuanzang is the first foreign witness of Nālandā with the passage on the monastery from his Datang-Xiyu-ji, "Records of the Western Regions of the Great Tang", written by order and on behalf of the second Tang emperor Taizong 太宗 (599–649) and submitted to the throne in 646. In his description (see Appendix 1.a) Xuanzang is more interested in the royal foundation narrative of Nālandā, the sequence of kings building and supporting Nālandā, than in a description of the monastery itself. However, what he describes in great detail, after giving the lineage of the famous Buddhist masters of Nālandā, are the sites outside of and around the monastery (Appendix 1.b).

Almost twenty years later Xuanzang's biographer Huili 慧立, after reproducing Xuanzang's list of kings, gives more information retrieved and digested from Xuanzang's description of the individual sites around and inside of Nālandā (T.2053.237b.18ff.; see Appendix 2). There is a clear tendency in Huili's description to make the monastery more impressive and bigger than it could have been in reality. Although different in scope and information Huili's Nālandā resembles, in a way, Daoxuan's imagined and idealized elaborations about the Jetavana-vihāra in Śrāvastī in his Tianzhu-

Shewei-guo-Qiyunsi-tujing 中天竺舍衛國祇洹寺圖經, "Ilustrated Sūtra of the Jetavana Monastery in the Kingdom of Śrāvastī in Central India" (T.1899).[16] The tendency to make the monastery bigger than it was ("ten thousand monks") is also found in Tārānātha's history when it states that at the time of Nāgārjuna a certain "Suviṣṇu, a *brāhmaṇa* of Magadha, built one hundred and eight temples at Śrī Nalendra."[17]

Daoxuan 道宣 (596–667), in his biography of Xuanzang in the Xu-Gaoseng-zhuan, "Continued Lives of Eminent Monks", also gives a description of Nālanda. Exactly the same passage is found in Daoshi's 道世 voluminous encyclopaedia Fayuan-zhulin 法苑珠林, "Forest of Jewels from the Garden of the Dharma" from 668 (T.2122.504c.14ff.) — which is evidently drawing on the Xiyu-ji, but also contains some differing information (see Appendix 3).

In contrast to Xuanzang's brief description, Huili's aggrandizing and Daoxuan's idealizing depictions of Nālandā, the other famous Chinese traveller Yijing gives a very elaborate, in fact the longest, description of the monastery, its monastic organization and its history in his "Biographies of Eminent Monks" where he indirectly compares the architectural structure and the organization of the Indian monastery with the different layout and monastic functions of Tang monasteries (T.2066.5b.17ff.; Appendix 4.a).

It is evident that neither of the Chinese descriptions of Nālandā — Xuanzang's and Huili's — were meant to describe the monastery as it actually existed on the ground, but Yijing gives enough information to get a relatively clear picture of the monastery. And while Xuanzang and Yijing and other sources do not give concrete numbers for the area extent of the monastery, the excavated remains on the land now belonging to and administrated by the Archaeological Survey of India are certainly only a fraction of what was the monastic complex of Nālandā monastery.[18] In fact, the results of recent excavations and research[19] have demonstrated this quite clearly. Both Chinese monks support such a conclusion by the numbers of monks residing at Nālandā: Xuanzang talks of "several thousand" (*shuqian* 數千); Yijing gives the number as either 3,500 or 3,000 monks (T.2125.214a.3ff.&227a.25ff.; Appendix 4.a &4.b).

The number of eight compounds or courtyards (*yuan* 院) is confirmed in Xuanzang's Biography (Appendix 2). The number of monastic courtyards at Nālandā does, however, vary in other sources. According to Daoxuan's Shijia-fangzhi Nālandā had only seven courtyards (T.2088.964b.28f.), although the number of monks given are higher ("several thousand monks"; Appendix 5).

The biography of Muniśrī/Monishili 牟尼室利 has the monk explain in the year 806 (1st year of Yuanhe 元和) that the monastery consisted of nine courtyards which were built by nine kings and had more than 10,000 monks (T.2061.721a.8ff.; Appendix 6). In the tenth century Jiye 繼業 (10th cent.) ascribes to Nālandā even a much higher number of monastic courtyards (T.2089.982a.28ff.; Appendix 7).

Yijing mentions over ten bathing ponds (*dachi* 大池) which certainly were inside of the monastic ground (T.2125.220c.14f.). Taking into account the existing ponds or tanks outside and around the modern excavated site one can easily push the borders of the former monastery beyond these water tanks. One has to assume that the difference between the original size and the excavated part partly explains why the layout of the archaeological remains and Xuanzang's, but also that of other authors' descriptions, do not match very well.

Xuanzang agrees with Yijing that the first foundation and further development of the monastery was done by a successive line of kings most of whom have been identified as rulers of the Gupta dynasty.[20] Without being able to go into some detailed discussion of the identity of these kings the underlying time line is reasonably in accordance with the archaeological evidence: the lowest stratum being dated to the Gupta period.

Based on Indian Buddhist and Jain tradition to be discussed in the following section, some scholars pushed the date of the foundation of the monastery back and linked it to eminent personalities in Buddhist history or even went so far to claim the existence of Nālandā at the time of the Buddha (and the Jina). This is partly due to the distorted chronology of the Chinese sources: Xuanzang claims the foundation of the first monastery at a time close to the *parinirvāṇa* of the Buddha, and Huili gives the more concrete date of seven hundred years which would refer the foundation back to the Śuṅga period (2nd/1st cent. BCE).

According to the claimants of an early date for Nālandā this is then corroborated by another Chinese sources. The Chinese traveller Faxian 法顯 (early 5th century), who does not mention Nālandā, has a short note on the birth place of Śāriputra, Naluo 那羅/**na'-la*.[21] This place was then, by its assumed phonetic similarity and its vicinity to Rājagṛha identified with Nālandā,[22] despite the fact that the directions given by Faxian — Naluo is situated one *yojana* west of Indraśāila-guhā and one *yojana* east of Rājagṛha — are not compatible with the location of Nālandā at all. Furthermore Xuanzang mentions the birth place of Śāriputra south of Nālandā.

If we turn to the Pali sources, mainly later commentaries, the situation is even more complicated. Different name forms for the home village of

Śāriputra are found (Nāla, Nālaka(-gāma), Nālika, Nāḷa[23]) which are taken by some scholars as a different name form of or at least as a reference to Nālandā. However, the fact that these sources do not attempt to make a connection with (Pāli) Nāḷandā clearly shows that at least the Pāli redactors and commentators did not see a link between the two places. This is even more evident in the Saṃyutta-nikāya, where in two subsequent sections, the Buddha and Sāriputta are described as staying in the mango grove at Nāḷandā (47.12.1), and later in the text Sāriputta as "dwelling in the village Nāla in Magadha" (*Magadhesu viharati Nālagāmake*: 47.13.2), and hence these places cannot be the same. The place is considered to be identical with the place of Śāriputra's *parinirvāṇa* (Deeg 2005, p. 405). This identification seems to be relatively old since it is already found in Dharmarakṣa/Zhu Fahu's 竺法護 (fl. 265–313) Jātaka collection Shengjing 生經 (T.154.79c.225ff.). Similarly the place of Śāriputra's *parinirvāṇa* is given as Naluotuo-cun 那羅陀 (村)/EMC **na'-la-da* — Nālada in the Pravajyāvastu of the Skt. version of the same *vinaya*,[24] — and clearly distinguished from Nālandā in Yijing's translation of the Mūlasarvāstivāda-vinaya to which Yijing adds the following note: "[This is] more than twenty *li* southeast of Nālandā monastery."[25]

The Tibetan tradition links Nāgārjuna with Nālandā — frequently rendered as Nālendra (*na-len-dra*) in Tibetan. Bu-ston (1290–1364), in his "History of the Dharma" (Chos-'byuṅ) presupposes the existence of the monastery before Nāgārjuna's time.[26] But this is certainly a hagiographic tradition according to which all great Buddhist teachers had to have studied and lived in Nālandā (Bu-ston: Āryadeva, Vasubandhu, Candragomin, Śāntideva; Tārānātha: Rāhulabhadra, Mātṛceṭa, Asaṅga, Vasubandhu, Sthiramati, Jayadeva, Candrakīrti, Candragomin, Dharmapāla, Virūpa, Śāntideva, Vinītadeva). Tārānātha states that Śāriputra was born and attained *parinirvāṇa* in Nālandā (Nālendra) and ascribes the foundation of the first monastery there to Aśoka.[27] Nālandā, for the Tibetans, had become a *pīṭha*, a "power place" (Tib. *gnas*), and such a central place of Buddhist learning and practice that almost all famous Buddhist masters had to have resided, studied, taught or debated there.

NĀLANDĀ IN PĀLI AND JAIN SOURCES

The toponym Nāḷanda/ā occurs several times in the Pāli canon[28] — while it is completely and suspiciously absent in the two Pāli chronicles of Śrī Laṅkā, the Dīpavaṃsa and the Mahāvaṃsa — with a clear tendency to aggrandize the place. When in Nāḷandā, the Buddha normally dwells in the mango grove of Pāvārika (Pāvārikambavana). In the Pāli version of the Mahāparinirvāṇasūtra (Mahāparinibbānasuttanta) the Buddha delivers a sermon in this mango grove at Nāḷandā (Dīghanikāya 16.1.15ff.) from where he proceeds to Pāṭaligāma. In the Kevadhasutta Kevadha describes Nāḷandā as being "rich, with a dense population, full of people who have trust in the Venerable One".[29] In the same text Kevadha asks the Buddha to perform different miracles and charms among which a Gandhāra-charm is mentioned. In the Brahmajālasutta the Buddha is staying between Rājagṛha and Nāḷandā (Dīghanikāya 1.1). In the Upālisutta (Majjhimanikāya 1.6.56) the Buddha has an encounter with the heretic Nigaṇṭha Nātaputta — often, but not undisputedly, identified as Mahāvīra[30] — in Nāḷandā. In the Kassapa-saṃyutta of the Saṃyuttanikāya (16.11.16) the Buddha is dwelling at the Bahuputta-*cetiya* between Rājagṛha and Nāḷandā — the Chinese versions give different locations (Śrāvastī, Jetavana) — while Buddhaghosa twice mentions a *nigrodha*-tree of the Bahuputta(-cetiya?) (*bahuputtakanigrodharukkhamūla*) where the Buddha stayed (Sāratthappakāsinī, used edition Chaṭṭhasaṅgāyana: 148, on Jiṇṇasutta& 154, on Cīvarasutta). This *caitya/cetiya* is otherwise localised north of Vaisālī/Vesāli (Malalasekera 1974, p. 273, s.v.) and well linked to a series of other shrines,[31] so that the location in the Kassapa-saṃyutta may be a late interpolation based on some confusion in the geography of Magadha. One section in the Saḷāyatana-saṃyutta is even called "Nālandā" (Saṃyuttanikāya 35.126) — the Chinese translations have no correspondence (sic!) — however without giving much further detail about the place.

In the record of the first council in Rājagṛha in the Pāli Vinaya Ānanda, asked by Kassapa after the *parinirvāṇa* of the Buddha especially about where certain sermons had been delivered, answers that the Brahmajāla (*sutta*) was preached at the Ambalaṭṭhikā park between Rājagaha and Nāḷandā (Cullavagga 11.1.8). This detail is not given in the *sutta* itself which just has the Buddha stay a night in the Ambalaṭṭhikā royal park. However, according to Buddhaghosa's commentary (*rañño uyyāno*), he does not locate the park between Rajagaha and Nāḷandā (Sumaṅgalavilāsinī 1, 41f.) but in Rājagṛha (Dīghanikāya 1.2). It is therefore likely that the Vinaya passage is a relatively late addition identifying a somewhat formulaic original "between Rājagaha and Nāḷandā" as the basis for localizing the park while other reference locate it directly in Rājagṛha. In the light of such confusion a distinction between three different parks of the same name each in relatively short distance from each other as Malalasekera assumes[32] then becomes superfluous.

If we look at the Pāli commentaries (Aṭṭhakathā) on the respective passages it seems that the author, Buddhaghosa (5th cent.), did not know a big deal about the place and nothing about a monastery in Nāḷandā and, in fact, presents confused information. Only a pseudo-explanation of the Pāvārikambavana, the "mango grove of Pāvārika", is given (*Pāvārikassa ambavana*: Sumaṅgalavilāsinī 2.388 on Kevaṭṭasutta = Kevadhasutta). Most information about Nāḷanda — note the uncertainty of the gender of the place name (Nāḷanda, Nāḷandā)! — is given in Buddhaghosa's remarks about Nāḷandā and Pāvārikambavana in the commentary on the shortest *sutta*, the Upālisutta:

> What is called "in Nāḷanda" here is [referring] to a city called by that name "Nālandā", [and] this city had been made into a village for the supply of food [for the *saṅgha*]. "In the Pāvārikambavana" [means] in the mango grove of a wealthy cloth merchant. This park belonged to him. When he heard the teaching of the *dharma* of the Buddha he took trust in the Venerable One, built a residence (*vihāra*) adorned with huts, caves, open halls, etc., for the Venerable One in this park and gave [it to him]. This residence is likened to the mango grove of Jīvaka — [this] is the meaning of "[he] dwells in this Pāvārikambavana".[33]

Buddhaghosa also gives a distance of one *yojana* between Rājagṛha and Nāḷandā (Sumaṅgalavilāsinī 1, 35) which seems to be stereotypic. This distance is relatively close to Yijing's note to his translation of the Ekaśatakarman of the Vinaya of the Mūlasarvāstivādin where he gives five *krośa* (*julushe* 俱盧舍) as the distance between Nālandā and Rājagṛha which would be a little bit more than one *yojana*, one *yojana* being 4 *krośa* (T.1453.467c.13ff.).

In the Chinese parallels to the discussed Pāli passages, as far as they exist, the place name Nālandā is suspiciously absent. In the Mahāparinirvāṇasūtra it is even missing in all versions or translations of the text.[34] It should be remembered that Waldschmidt lists the Pāli as "Sondertext" ("singular text");[35] including the Sanskrit parallel which places the sermon delivered by the Buddha at a place called Veṇuyaṣṭikā[36] which is located between Pāṭaligrāma and Rājagṛha.[37] In the Brahmajāla-sūtra in the Chinese Dīrghāgama/Chang-a'han-jing 長阿含經, translated by Buddhayaśas/Fotuoyeshe 佛陀耶舍 and Zhu Fonian 竺佛念 (finished 413), the Buddha stays in a royal hall in Veṇuvana (*zhulin* 竹林[38]: T.1.88b.14[39]). The older translation ascribed to Zhi Qian 支謙 (fl. first half of 3rd cent.) places the sermon in the Jetavana in Śrāvastī (T.21.264a.29f.[40]). The Tibetan translation of the *sūtra* also does not mention Nālandā but only a place name Od-ma'i cug pran, literally "thin branch of bamboo".[41] Since the Chinese *āgama*s were translated in the first decades of the fifth century it is likely that the place name Nāḷandā was inserted into the Pāli passages not before the fourth or fifth century, i.e., at a time when the monastery had attained some status and size. The closest to the Pāli is the Upālisūtra of the Chinese Madhyamāgama where the place names Na'nantuo 那難陀 and Bopoli-nailin 波婆離棕林 (T.26.628a.19f.) are given, demonstrating that either the underlying Indic text did not have the right or a different form of the place name.

Another frequently quoted occurrence of the place name is in the Śvetāmbara Jain Sūtrakṛtāṅga/Sūyagaḍa in its last chapter, II.7.842–845, called Nālandā.[42] The chapter starts with a stereotype description of Nālandā as a highly populated and rich northern suburb (*bāhiriyā*, Skt. *bāhīrika*) of Rājagṛha where the *gaṇadhara* Gotama convinces the rich layman Udaka to abandon the teaching of Pārśva and convert to the teaching of Mahāvīra.[43]

> At that time, at that period, there was a town of the name Rājagṛha: it was rich, stable, thriving, and also beautiful. Outside of Rājagṛha, in [its] north-eastern part, there was the suburb Nālandā, well-established with many hundreds of buildings and also beautiful. In that suburb Nālandā there was a householder called Lepa; he was prosperous, well-known, famous; rich in high and large houses, beds, seats, vehicles, and chariots, abounding in riches, gold, and silver, having income and means, wasting plenty of food and drink, owning many male and female slaves, cows, buffaloes, and sheep, superior to many people. This householder Lepa, a layman of the *śramaṇa*s, comprehended (the doctrine of) living and things without life. This householder Lepa possessed, in the north-eastern part of the suburb Nālandā, a bathing-hall called Śeṣadravyā with many hundreds of pillars, delightful and also beautiful. To the north-eastern of this bathing-hall Śeṣadravyā, there was a forest called Hastiyāma, a forest black of colour. And there in the same house the venerable Gautama was staying.[44]

Although the Sūtrakṛtāṅga is considered to be one of the oldest Jain texts preserved[45] it clearly was, as other Jain scriptures, open to interpolations and extensions. For instance, according to the Śvetāmbaras' own "canonical narrative", until the Council of Valabhī in the fifth century with the chapter II.7 being positioned at the end of the whole text, seems to be a reaction to the emerging status of a prominently (but not exclusively) Buddhist Nālandā: the Jains claimed a presence there for the time of Mahāvīra by the support of the rich merchant Lepa.[46]

In the end, all claims for an existence of Nālandā before the monastery's foundation in the Gupta era are without any archaeological basis and concluded from a superficial reading of texts which more reflect the growing prominence of the monastery at exactly that time period than prove its high antiquity.

CONCLUSION

A critical reading and interpretation of the textual sources about Nālandā may leave us with disappointingly few "hard facts" in historical terms. For the reconstruction of the history of the monastery a simplistic, naïve and positivist reading of the textual sources, applied so often and pushing back its existence to the time of the Buddha, is misleading. A cautious and contextual interpretation of the sources in combination with the archaeological evidence leads to a clear conclusion: Nālandā became prominent as a transregional centre of Buddhist monasticism and learning at a time when India was prospering under the rulership of a dynasty which presented itself officially as prominently non-Buddhist and dedicated to major Hindu deities: the imperial Guptas. What this means for our understanding of the religious history of that period needs more and careful investigation, but Nālandā and its sudden rise can be seen as an indicator for a religious situation which was more complex than it looks on the surface.

ABBREVIATIONS

EMC	Early Middle Chinese (according to Pulleyblank 1991)
HDC	Hanyu-dacidian
T	Taishō-shinshū-daizōkyō (quoted according to the CBETA database)

APPENDIX: CHINESE SOURCES ON NĀLANDĀ

1. Xuanzang 玄奘 (600/602–664), Datang-Xiyu-ji 大唐西域記, "Records of the Western Regions of the Great Tang", compiled 645–646:[47]

a. "Going more than thirty miles from there (i.e. the southern gate of Rājagṛha) in northern [direction one] arrives at the monastery of Nalantuo[48] (in the language of the Tang [this is] 'Not-Enough-Giving'). [One can] hear old people say that south of this monastery, in a mango-grove, there is a lake, and the *nāga* in it is called Nālanda, and because the monastery was built close to it, it has received his name. [But] as a matter of fact [it is because] the Tathāgata in the past, [when he] practiced the Bodhisattva path and was the king of a great kingdom, was compassionate with the living beings and found pleasure in giving generously, [so that people] praised [him] for [his] virtue and called [him] 'Not-Enough-Giving'. And from [this name] the monastery received its name. This land originally was a mango-garden [which] five hundred merchants bought for one billion gold coins in order to donate it to the Buddha. There the Buddha preached the *dharma* for [a period] of three months, and all the merchants realized the fruit of sainthood. Not long after the *nirvāṇa* of the Buddha, the former king of this kingdom, Shuojialuoadieduo[49] (in the language of the Tang [this is] 'Ruler-Sun'), honoured the One Vehicle, venerated the Three Jewels, formally declared [this] a site of merit[50] and built this monastery. [When] the construction work was begun, the body of the *nāga* was pierced. A *niqian*-heretic,[51] skilled in divination, saw [this] and prophesized: "This is a sacred place, [and] the monastery built [here] will certainly be prospering and will become a model for [all the other] monasteries in the Five Indias. It will be thriving more than one thousand years. Scholars joining it in the future will easily succeed in [their] work, but [they] often will spit blood, because the *nāga* has been damaged." His son Fotuojuduo[52] (in the language of the Tang [this is] 'Awakened-Protection') followed [him] on the throne and continued [his] superb work, and built [another] monastery further to the south of the [former] one. King Datajieduojuduo[53] (in the language of the Tang [this is] 'Thus-Come') seriously practiced [like his] predecessors, and built [another] monastery further to the east of the [former] one. When king Poluoadieduo[54] (in the language of the Tang [this is] 'Infant-Sun') ascended the throne, [he] built [another] monastery further to the northeast of the [former] one. After these matters were achieved, [the king summoned] an assembly of merit[55] to offer congratulations, showed sincerity to this world and to the yonder world, and invited commoners and saints. For this assembly monks from the Five Indias, ten thousands of miles [away], flocked together like clouds. When the community was finally seated, two arrived late, and were led to the third floor of a pagoda. Some [of the others] asked: "[When] the king wanted to set up the assembly, [he] first invited commoners and saints; where are [you] *bhandanta*s from [that you] arrived as the latest?" [They said]: "We [are from] the kingdom of Zhina.[56] [Our] master[57] [is suffering] from infant measles;[58] when [he] just had eaten [his] meal, [he] received the king's invitation from afar; therefore [we] came to attend the assembly." The ones [who] had asked were shocked and quickly told the king [about this]. In [his] mind the king knew that [they] were saints, and [he] went himself to ask them. [But since he] went up to the pagoda too late, nobody knew where [they] had left to. The king gained deep faith, gave up [his] kingdom and left the household.[59] After [he] had left the household, [he] was positioned at the [lower] end of the monks' community,[60] was constantly in a disgruntled state of mind and felt not very happy [saying]: "Formerly I was the king and [held] the most respected and highest position, [but] now [that I] have left the household [I] am the [most] inferior at the lower [end] of the monks' community!" [He] went to the community [of monks] and told [them the] situation [he was in]. Thereupon the community agreed that those who had not taken the [full] precepts[61] could establish [their] position according to [their] age. Therefore only this monastery has this regulation. After the son of this king, Fasheluo[62] (in the language of the Tang [this is] 'Diamond Bolt'), had ascended the throne, [his] faith was really strong, and [he] also built a monastery to the east of the [former]. Later again [another] king of Central India built [another] monastery to the north of the [former]. Then [he] encompassed [everything] by a strong wall [with] one and the same gate [for all the monasteries]. Since continuous generations of rulers were [involved] in constructing activities and employed [all their] efforts in carving [stones for the buildings], [this] really is a magnificent view. A statue of the Buddha is nowadays placed in the first great monastery of 'Ruler-Sun', and each day forty different monks from the community go there and take [their] meal to pay back the favour of the donors[63]."

T.2087.923b.13ff. 從此北行三十餘里，至那爛陀(唐言施無厭)僧伽藍。聞之耆舊曰:此伽藍南菴沒羅林中有池，其龍名那爛陀，傍建伽藍，因取為稱。從其實議，是如來在昔修菩薩行，為大國王，建都此地，悲愍眾生，好樂周給，時美其德，號施無厭。由是伽藍因以為稱。其地本菴沒羅園，五百商人以十億金錢買以施佛。佛於此處三月說法，諸商人等亦證聖果。佛涅槃後未久，此國先王鑠迦羅阿迭[T. 逸]多(唐言帝日)敬重一乘，遵崇三寶，式占福地，建此伽藍。初興功也，穿傷龍身。時有善占尼乾外道見而記曰:"斯勝地也，建立伽藍，當必昌盛，為五印度之軌則，逾千載而彌隆。後進學人，易以成業，然多歐血，傷龍故也。"其子佛陀毱多王(唐言覺護)繼體承統，聿遵勝業，次此之南又建伽藍。

呾他揭多毱多王(唐言如來)篤修前緒，次此之東又建伽藍。婆羅阿迭多(唐言幼日)王之嗣位也，次此東北又建伽藍。功成事畢，福會稱慶，輸誠幽顯，延請凡聖。其會也，五印度僧萬里雲集。眾坐已定，二僧後至，引上第三重閣。或有問曰:"王將設會，先請凡聖，大德何方，最後而至？"曰:"我至那國也。和上嬰疹，飯已方行，受王遠請，故來赴會。"問者驚駭[T. 骸]，遽以白王。王心知聖也，躬往問焉。遲上重閣，莫知所去。王更深信，捨國出家。出家既已，位居僧末，心常怏怏，懷不自安:"我昔為王，尊居最上，今者出家，卑在眾末！"尋往白僧，自述情事。於是眾僧和合，令未受戒者以年齒為次。故此伽藍獨有斯制。其王之子伐[T. 代]闍羅(唐言金剛)嗣位之後，信心貞固，復於此西建立伽藍。其後中印度王此北復建大伽藍。於是周垣峻峙，同為一門。既歷代君王繼世興建，窮諸剞劂，誠壯觀也。帝日[T. 曰]本大伽藍者，今置佛像，眾中日差四十僧就此而食，以報施主之恩。

b."On all sides around the monastery are several hundreds of sacred traces, [but only] two or three of them will be presented and [this] can be done in an abridged form. To the west of the monastery, not far away, is a temple[64] [in which] the Tathāgata formerly stayed for three months and widely preached the *dharma* to men and gods. More than one hundred steps further in southern [direction] is a small *stūpa* [marking] the place where the foreign *bhikṣu* had seen the Buddha. Formerly there was a *bhikṣu*, [who] had come from afar to this place to see the sacred community of the Tathāgata, and with a respectful inner mind threw himself to the ground. When [he] then made a vow to strive for the status of a wheel[-turning] king, and the Tathāgata saw [this], he said to the community: "That *bhikṣu* is really pitiable! The virtue of [his] merits is far developed, [and his] faith firm and steady; had [he] strived for the fruit of Buddha[hood], [he] soon would have realized it. [But] now he has made the vow to strive [to be] a wheel [-turning] king, and in a future time [he] will certainly receive the retribution of this [vow]. The number of all the fine dust particles between the ground [to which he] has thrown himself down to the golden wheel — each of [these] dust particles is one retribution [of a life] as a wheel[-turning] king. [And] because [he will] indulge in worldly pleasures, the fruition of sainthood is [still] so far away." To its southern side is the standing statue of the Bodhisattva Avalokiteśvara [who] sometimes is seen holding an incense burner and going to the monastic compound and circumambulating [it] rightward. In a *stūpa* south of the standing statue of the Bodhisattva Avalokiteśvara are the hair and the nails which the Tathāgata cut off during the three months' period [of the summer retreat], [and if one] has an itching skin disease and circumambulates [the *stūpa*], it is mostly cured. The *stūpa* to the side of the pond outside [the monastery's] western wall [marks] the place of the event of the heretic who, holding a sparrow [in his hand], asked the Buddha about [its] life and death.[65] More than fifty steps further in south-eastern [direction], inside of the wall [of the monastery], is a peculiar tree, eight or nine feet high, its trunk split into two [halves]. Formerly the Tathāgata had chewed the branch of a poplar tree and thrown it to the ground, and subsequently [it] took roots; although this was a long time ago it has not grown nor shrunk [since] the beginning. Further to the east [is] a big temple, more than two hundred feet high, [where] the Tathāgata formerly explained all the subtle *dharma*s for [a period of] four months. More than one hundred steps further to the north, in a temple, is a statue of the Bodhisattva Avalokiteśvara; when [those] with pure faith give offerings, the places of [its] appearance is not the same, [and] nobody [can] determine its place. Sometimes it stands beside the gate, sometimes it is outside in front of the eaves. The religious and the laypeople of all the kingdoms come to give offerings [to it]. To the north of the temple of the Bodhisattva Avalokiteśvara is a big monastic structure, more than three hundred *chi* high and built by king Bālāditya. [Its] ornaments and measures and the Buddha-statue inside are the same as [in] the big temple beneath the Bodhi-tree. The *stūpa* to its northeast [marks the place] where the Tathāgata formerly expounded the subtle *dharma* for [a period] of seven days. On its north-western side is the place where the four Buddhas of the past were sitting. The temple [made] of brass to its south is being built by king "Sun of Virtue" (Śīlāditya), and although the work is not yet finished it is planned to measure ten *zhang* when it once will be finished. More than two hundred paces in eastern [direction] and outside of the wall is a standing Buddha-statue [made of] copper, more than eighty *chi* high, [which] could only be covered by a six-storeyed pavilion. It was formerly made by king "Full Armour".[66] Two or three miles north of the copper Buddha-statue of king "Full Armour", in a temple [made] of brass, is a statue of the Bodhisattva Tārā;[67] its size is really high, and its miraculous manifestations are very clear. Each year, at the first day of the lunar month, prosperous offerings are made [to it]. The kings, ministers and powerful clans of the neighbouring kingdoms present delicate incense and flowers, hold bejewelled banners and parasols [in their hands], bells and chime stones play alternatively, and string and wind [instruments] are in harmony with each other, and [they] establish a *dharma*-assembly for [a period] of seven days. Inside of the southern gate of its walls is a big well: formerly, when the Buddha was in the world, there was a big band of merchants [who], driven by [their] thirst in the heat, came to the Buddha, and the World-Honoured One pointed to the ground so that [they] could get water. And when the leader of the merchants hacked the ground with the axle of [their]

> chart, the ground caved in and water then gushed out. After [they] had drunk, [they] listened to the *dharma*, and all [of them] awoke to the fruition of sainthood."
>
> T.2087.924a.8ff. 伽藍四周，聖迹百數，舉其二三，可略言矣。伽藍西不遠有精舍，在昔如來三月止此，為諸天、人廣說妙法。次南百餘步小窣堵波，遠方比丘見佛處。昔有比丘自遠方來，至此遇見如來聖眾，內發敬心，五體投地。便即發願求輪王位，如來見已，告諸眾曰:"彼比丘者，甚可愍惜。福德深遠，信心堅固，若求佛果，不久當證。今其發願，求轉輪王，於當來世，必受此報。身體投地，下至金輪，其中所有，微塵之數，一一塵是一輪王報也。既耽世樂，聖果斯遠。"其南則有觀自在菩薩立像，或見執香爐往佛精舍，周旋右繞。觀自在菩薩像南窣堵波中，有如來三月之間剃剪髮爪，有嬰疾病，旋繞多愈。其西垣外池側窣堵波，是外道執雀，於此問佛死生之事。次東南垣內五十餘步，有奇樹，高八九尺，其幹兩披。在昔如來嚼楊枝棄地，因植根柢，歲月雖久，初無增減。次東大精舍，高二百餘尺，如來在昔於此四月說諸妙法。次北百餘步，精舍中有觀自在菩薩像，淨信之徒興供養者，所見不同，莫定其所。或立門側，或出簷前。諸國法俗，咸來供養。觀自在菩薩精舍北有大精舍，高三百餘尺，婆羅阿迭多王之所建也。莊嚴度量及中佛像，同菩提樹下大精舍。其東北窣堵波，在昔如來於此七日演說妙法。西北則有過去四佛坐處。其南鍮石精舍，戒日王之所建立，功雖未畢，然其圖量一十丈而後成之。次東二百餘步，垣外有銅立佛像，高八十餘尺，重閣六層，乃得彌覆，昔滿胄王之所作也。滿胄王銅佛像北二三里，甎精舍中有多羅菩薩像，其量既高，其靈甚察。每歲元日，盛興供養。鄰境國王、大臣、豪族。齎妙香花，持寶旛蓋，金石遞奏，絲竹相和，七日之中，建斯法會。其垣南門內有大井，昔在佛世，有大商侶，熱渴逼迫，來至佛所，世尊指其地以可得水。商主乃以車軸築地，地既為陷，水遂泉涌。飲已聞法，皆悟聖果。

2. Huili 慧立, Datang-daciensi-sanzang-fashi-zhuan 大唐大唐慈恩寺三藏法師傳, "Biography of the Tripiṭaka Dharma-master of the Great Cien Monastery of the Great Tang":

> "Courtyards are arranged separately [and] they are divided into eight complexes. Precious platforms are arrayed like the stars, magnificent buildings are towering [like] lofty peaks, temples [standing] respectful in the mist, the halls [erected as if they are] flying on rosy clouds, clouds and wind arising in [their] windows and doors [and] sun and moon alternately [shining] at the eaves of the cells; there are further clear water courses meandering, blue lotuses, water lilies and *kanaka* flower trees[68] radiating inside, [and] mango groves are scattered

outside of it. The monk cells of all the courtyards are [constructed] as four-storeyed pavilions with ridge beams [shaped like] horned dragons and roof beams [painted in the colours] of the rainbow, finely chiselled capital and vermillion red pillars, carved [lines of] columns and engraved railings, foundations [shining like] jade and patterned tips of the rafters, the ridge beams of the roofs arrayed with shining precious stones, the laths [of the roofs] lined up in the colourfulness of ropes. There are ten millions of monastery in India [but] this is the ultimate in terms of majesty and loftiness. There are always ten thousand monks, residential and visiting, [who] all study the Mahāyāna but also the eighteen *nikāya*s, and then [they] also study all kinds of secular texts like the scriptures of the Veda, [works on] logic, grammar, medicine, fortune telling. Generally speaking of those who understand the scriptures, there are more than a thousand [who have mastered] twenty, more than five hundred [who have mastered] thirty, and then ten *dharma* masters [who have mastered] fifty. Only the *dharma* master Śīlabhadra has mastered [them] completely, [and since his] virtues are excellent [and he] is of old age he is the great master of the *saṅgha*. Inside of the monastery there are more than a hundred lectures every day [where] the students learn without resting a single moment. As it is inhabited by a virtuous *saṅgha* [the monastery] is naturally a solemn [place]. During the more than seven hundred years since [the monastery's] erection there was not one [monk who committed] a crime, slandering, [or] an offense. Out of admiration the kings gave more than one hundred settlements [as fiefs] in order to [supply] full support, [each] settlement [consisting of] two hundred households, daily supplying polished non-glutinous rice [and] several hundred *dan* of ghee and milk. Therefore, although scholars do not ask for it, the four supplies are sufficiently available, so that [they could] fulfil [their] skills and studies [in which] the [monastery's] strength lies."
T.2053.237b.18ff. 庭序別開，中分八院。寶臺星列，瓊樓岳峙，觀竦烟中，殿飛霞上，生風雲於戶牖，交日月於軒簷，加以淥水逶迤，青蓮菡萏，羯尼花樹暉煥其間，菴沒羅林森竦其外。諸院僧室皆四重重閣，虬棟虹梁，繡櫨朱柱，彫楹鏤檻，玉礎文桷，甍接瑤暉，榱連繩彩。印度伽藍數乃千萬，壯麗崇高，此為其極。僧徒主客常有萬人，並學大乘兼十八部，爰至俗典《吠陀》等書，因明、聲明、醫方、術數亦俱研習。凡解經、論二十部者一千餘人，三十部者五百餘人，五十部者并法師十人。唯戒賢法師一切窮覽，德秀年耆，為眾宗匠。寺內講座日百餘所，學徒修習，無棄寸陰。德眾所居，自然嚴肅。建立已來七百餘載，未有一人犯譏過者。國王欽重，捨百餘邑充其供養，邑二百戶，日進粳米、酥乳數百石。由是學人端拱無求而四事自足，藝業成就，斯其力焉。

3. Daoxuan 道宣 (596–667), Xuanzang's biography in the Xu-Gaoseng-zhuan 續高僧傳, "Continued Lives of Eminent Monks" (= Fayuan-zhulin 法苑珠林, T.2122.504c.14ff.):

> "… the monastery of Nālandā, [which] in the language of the Tang [means] 'Not-Enough-Giving'. It is the greatest of the monasteries in Jambudvīpa, and no one is more eminent than it. All together five kings have built [it and] have made offerings with increasing generosity; from this it has received its name. This monastery has five monastic [courtyards which use] the same big gate, the whole door being four storeys [high] and having a [total] height of about eight *zhang*.[69] The whole [monastery] is built of brick, [and] its highest walls are six *chi* thick. The outer [ring] wall is three storeys [high], the walls also built of brick, with a height of about five *zhang*. Inside there are water [bodies] meandering and extremely deep lakes and trenches. [The monastery] is beautifully and impressively equipped with flowers and animals. From its foundation [the monastery] has been guarded in a pure and stern [way so that] neither women were abused nor concealed [in it]. There are more than four thousand residential monks, [and] the guest mendicants [who] come to debate about the wrong and right [points of the teachings] are beyond several ten thousands. [They] all provide robes and food [so that the stocks] are never exhausted; this is another reason that the monastery is called 'Not-Enough-Giving'. Inside [of the monastery] is a compound for the Buddha with sacred remains, the temple being more than twenty *zhang* high. In the past the Buddha preached the *dharma* in it for four months. There is another temple, more than thirty *zhang* high; inside there are miracles that cannot be imagined at all. A bronze statue has been erected [there], more than eight *zhang* high, [and] a six-storeyed pavilion, very majestic and beautifully ornamented, built by the elder brother of [king] Śīlāditya, the king 'Fully Armored'.[70] There is also a temple [built of] brass, about eight *zhang* high [and] built by Śīlāditya himself, [its] engraved form not finished yet with the service of a thousand workers. The ancient custom of that country is to respect virtuous conduct and prestige. [If] there are masters of debate [whose] knowledge is pure and broad the king endows [them] with up to ten settlements, decreasing [according to their] merit to not less than three settlements. At the moment this monastery houses more than three hundred *bhadanta*s who receive an endowment."
>
> T.2060.451c.2ff. …那爛陀寺，唐言施無厭也。贍部洲中寺之最者，匆高此矣。五王共造，供給倍隆，故因名焉。其寺都有五院，同一大門，周閭四重，高八丈許。並用甎壘，其最上壁猶厚六尺。外郭三重，牆亦甎壘，高五丈許。中間水遶，極深池塹。

備有花畜嚴麗可觀。自置已來防衛清肅，女人非濫，未曾容隱。常住僧眾四千餘人，外客道俗通及邪正乃出萬數。皆周給衣食無有窮竭，故復號寺為施無厭也。中有佛院備諸聖迹，精舍高者二十餘丈。佛昔於中四月說法。又有精舍高三十餘丈。中諸變態不可名悉。置立銅像高八丈餘，六層閣盛莊嚴綺飾，即戒日之兄滿冑王造也。又有鍮石精舍高可八丈，戒日親造，彫裝未備，日役千工。彼國常法欽敬德望。有諸論師智識清遠，王給封戶乃至十城，漸降量賞不減三城。其寺現在受封大德三百餘人。

4. Yijing 義淨 (635–713), Datang-qiufa-gaoseng-zhuan 大唐求法高僧傳, "Biographies of Eminent Monks Searching for the Dharma of the Great Tang":

a. "Going about seven stations from the 'Great-Enlightenment-Monastery' in north-eastern [direction one] arrives at the Nālandā-monastery; this was originally built by the former king Śrī Śakrāditya for the North-Indian monk Heluoshepanshe.[71] This monastery's first foundation just [consisted of] some square walls, [but] later generations of kings [and their] successors continuously built it into an imposing [monastery] so that in Jambudvīpa there is nowadays none which exceeds its [grandeur]. One cannot fully relate [its] layout but [I will] just briefly describe the area [it] encloses. So the shape of this monastery is neatly square as [the plan] of a city with straight eaves on [all] four sides [forming] covered corridors all around; all [the buildings] are brick cells, three stores high, a store more than one *zhang* high, the cross-beams covered by wooden boards; originally there were no rafters or tiles [but only] bricks were used to cover the surface. All the monastic courtyards are [outlined] straight [so that one can] move around at ease. The walls behind the cells form the outer side [of a courtyard]. The piled-up bricks are three or four *zhang* high. On top [one] has made human heads in the natural size of human [heads]. As for the cells for the monks, there are nine on each side. Each cell [measures] one square *zhang*. At the back windows open towards the eaves [of the outer wall]. Since the entries are [more] high [than wide they] are only equipped with one door. The [entries] all are faced towards each other and no curtains are allowed. [If one] goes outside and plainly looks around [one can] see to all four sides. If [one] rather watches each other, how then can [even] little privacy be kept? In one corner a planked way[72] is made to come and go [to the upper floors]. On top of each of the four corners of a monastic courtyard are brick halls which are inhabited by famous *bhadanta*s. The gates of the monastic courtyards face to the west, with lofty pavilions rising into the air, carved in delicate shapes with very fine ornaments. These gates are connected with [the compound of] cells and are originally not separately built, but two paces outside of [them] four pillars are neatly arranged. Although these gates are not excessively big [their] framework is very solid. When the time for the meal has come the heavy [door] bolts are closed again,[73] as it is the teaching of the Saint, the meaning of it being to prevent privacy. The ground inside of the monastic courtyards of about thirty square paces is all laid out with bricks. For small [spaces] of only seven or five paces [as] normally the space on top of the roofs, in front of the eaves, [and] inside of the cells fragments of bricks, as big as peaches or jujubes are used, [in the gaps of which] a mixture sticky stuff and mud is rubbed to make a smooth [surface]; lime stone is used mixed with [material] such as hemp fibre, oil, hemp dreg, rotten skin, soaked [together] for several days, [the mixture] spread as a plaster on the brick, [all of this then] covered by green grass, and after three days or so it is checked if it is about to dry, [then] repeatedly wiped with a slippery stone, whisked with a liquid of stone or cinnabar, then with an oily coating [so that it] is bright and transparent like a mirror. The flights of stairs of its halls are all [treated] like this. After this is done once it will never crack even if people trample on it for ten or twenty years. A different lime stone will become soaked by water and then break. Of this kind there are eight monastic courtyards, all [constructed] in the same way [as described] above and of a similar scheme. On the eastern side of the monastic courtyards one or three cells are selected for setting up venerated statues; or in some cases a separate platform is erected a little bit outside of this [eastern] side and made into a Buddha hall. To the southwest of this monastery, outside of a large courtyard, great *stūpa*s (formerly called *ta* [which] is erroneous and abbreviated) and *caitya*s (formerly erroneously called *zhiti*) are just standing in a line, more than a hundred in numbers. So [many] sacred traces are next to each other that [one] cannot record them. [Embellishments of] gold and jade-like gems really make [these] unusual. The etiquette of the disciplinary path and manners [of speech or gesture][74] of the monks in this [monastery] is as reported in the 'Records of the Middle Region' and in the 'Report Sent Back'.[75] Although the oldest *sthavira* is made respected master[76] inside of the monastery [his] virtues are not disputed. Every night whoever has a key for the gates hands it over to the *sthavira* [after] having sealed [the] gates [but] no specific master of the monastery or *weina* is appointed [from the monastic ranks]. But those who build the monastery are called masters of the monastery, in Sanskrit *piheluosuomi*.[77] If [they] deal [with the things] directly, are in charge of the gates of the monastery and tell the *saṅgha* the [different] monastic procedures (*karman*) [they] are called *piheluoboluo*,[78] translated as 'protecting the monastery'. If [they] ring the *jianzhi*[79] and supervise the meals [they] are called *jiemotuona*,[80] translated as 'giving monastic procedures'. [When] this is called *weina*,[81] then it is an abbreviation [of *karmadāna*]. [If] the *saṅgha* has [to deal with] monastic procedures the *saṅgha* gathers on a regular basis [and] orders the protector of the monastery (*vihārapāla*) to walk around and to announce [this] in front of each [monk who] has to perform *añjalī*, and each of them comments on the procedure. If one does not accept then this procedure will not be imposed, [and] there is no way at all to enforce [the matter like] striking a hammer. If the matter is not accepted [they] try to convince by reason, [but] there is no coercion and also no force is executed. [In the case] of the 'protector of storehouse' pursuing business, even [if there] are two or three people [involved in it they] still have to dispatch laypeople in charge of the storehouse [who] perform *añjalī* and tell [the assembly], and if there is overall consent [one] can pursue the business, [and then] there is really no fault in performing the duty alone. If, [however], [someone] uses [the monastic property] alone without having announced [it] — and even if it is only half a *sheng* of grain — then [he] is expelled. If one person is self-assuming and uses the property of the *saṅgha*, decides on principal tasks and does not tell [it] the great *saṅgha*, [he] is called *juluobodi*,[82] translated as 'master of the household'. Such [behaviour] is a great excess[83] [against] the *dharma* of the Buddha, resented by men and gods, and even if it is for the benefit of the monastery it is a very severe offense [which] a wise person does not commit. Then formerly there were ninety-six groups of heretics, but now there are only more than ten. When there are gatherings for feasts [they] each reside in a [different] place, and [they] do not compete with the [Buddhist] monks and nuns for [hierarchical] order. Since their *dharma* is different [and their] principles are not practiced in the same way, each [of them] studies [their] tradition [and they] do not sit mingled with each other. The regulations in this monastery [Nālandā] are extremely strict; every half-month the assistant clerk[84] of regulations and monastic procedures is made to go around the monastic cells and to read the regulations. The names of the monks are not listed on the royal registry, and those who commit a crime are punished by the *saṅgha* accordingly, in its own right, and because of this the monks respect and fear each other. Although this monastery is [always] in need [its] benefits are very extensive. [When I] formerly was in the capital [I] saw a man drawing the model of Jetavanavihāra, [but it] was completely based on empty phantasy.[85] According to [my] comprehensive and different information [I] briefly outline it as it is. Furthermore, in the lands of the Five Indias only in the great monasteries (*mahāvihāra*) the sovereigns have clypsedras installed so that [the measuring] of the time at day and night is not difficult. Exactly as the *vinaya* teaches, the night is divided into three watches, and the first and the last are destined for meditation and recitation [while] the middle [watch] is for rest as one pleases. The method of the clepsydra is as is broadly explained in the (Nanhai-)jigui-(neifa-) zhuan. Although [I] have explained the arrangement of the monastery [I] fear that it is in the end still misleading, and therefore [I] painted this map and hope that this will [let it] appear before [one's] eyes without diversion. If this is able to cause the erection of it according to this plan [then this] will be indeed Rājagṛha [in] China [and] then it will be arranged without difference. Therefore [I] exclaim: The beauty of the *saṅgha* is still spread out, the assembly of heroes was in the past and is in the present as well. [If one then] also knows the difference between life and death, then there will be not suffering! Model of the monastery.[86] This is the model of Srī Nālandā-mahāvihāra, [in the language of] the Tang translated as 'Ominous Great Residence of the Divine Nāga'. In the western countries [they] first call sovereigns and great officials, but also great monasteries Srī which has the meaning of 'ominous [and] respectable'. Nālandā just is the name of a *nāga*. In the [monastery's] vicinity there was a *nāga* called ... [see above]. *Vihāra* means residence [which] is in comparison [with its Chinese equivalent] called 'temple' (*si*) [in Chinese, but] this is not translated correctly. If [one] has looked at one monastery the other seven look the same. [They] are straight on the back [so that] people passing through [can] come and go.[87] Normally, [if one] looks at a monastery's scheme [one] should face west to look at it, [and if one] is about to leave its gate on the west [one] can perceive its straight layout. [At a distance of] about twenty paces from the gate, on the southern side, there is a *stūpa*, about a hundred *chi* high, [which marks] the place where the World-Honoured One formerly spent the summer retreat of three months. In Sanskrit it is called Muluojiantuojuzhi [which] means 'Original Fragrance Hall'[88] [in the language] of the Tang. [At a distance of] about fifty paces from the gate, on the northern side, there is another great *stūpa*, even higher than the [Mūlagandhakūṭī], built by king 'Youthful Sun'[89] [and] completely made of bricks, exquisitely decorated and with flat areas [made] of gold [and] levels [made] of precious stones, [as such] a rare offering; inside is a statue of the Tathāgata turning the *dharma*-wheel. Next to it, in southwestern [direction], is a small *caitya*, more than one *zhang* high, [which marks] the place where a *brāhmaṇa* held a sparrow and asked [the Buddha], [and what] is called Queli-futu [in the language of] the Tang is exactly this one.[90] To the west of the 'Original Fragrance Hall' is a tooth

[-cleaning] tree of the Buddha, and it is not a poplar. On the western side next to it is the ordination platform[91] of the [monastery which] has more than one *zhang* and one *chi* side length and consists of a brick wall covering the whole ground of about two *chi* height. The foundations to sit upon on the wall [structure][92] are about five *cun* high and at its centre is a small *caitya*. To the east of the platform, at the corner of a hall, are the foundations of the *caṅkramana* [path] of the Buddha, consisting of piled-up bricks, about two cubits wide and about fourteen or fifteen cubits long, [and] a little bit more than two cubits high. The top [of it] is white-washed, [and] lotus-flowers in opened shape were made, about two *cun* high [and] about one *cun* wide, [of which] there are fourteen or fifteen, indicating the traces of the Buddha's feet. [If one] looks in southern direction from the monastery the royal city (Rājagṛha) is only thirty miles away. The Vulture Peak [and] the Bamboo Grove are both near the city. In southwestern direction is the Mahābodhi, in straight southern direction [lies] the 'Cock-Foot' mountain (Kukkuṭapada-giri), all about seven stations [away]. In northern direction is Vaisālī,[93] twenty-five stations [away]. In western direction [Nālandā] looks at the Deer Park [which is] more than twenty stations [away]. In eastern direction [lies] the kingdom of Tāmralipti,[94] sixty or seventy stations [away].[95] This is the seaport where [one] enters the ships returning to [the land] of the Tang. The *saṅgha* in the monastery [consists] of three thousand five hundred [monks]; there are two hundred and one villages belonging to the monastery which were given, with their population, by successive generations of rulers as eternal offerings [to the monastery]. ([Yijing's comment:] what is called station (*yi*) is equivalent to one *yojana*)."

T.2066.5b.17ff. 大覺寺東北行七驛許，至那爛陀寺，乃是古王室利鑠羯羅昳底為北天苾芻曷羅社槃社所造。此寺初基纔餘方堵，其後代國王苗裔相承，造製宏壯，則贍部洲中當今無以加也。軌模不可具述，但且略敘區寰耳。然其寺形，叕方如城，四面直簷，長廊遍匝，皆是塼室，重疊三層，層高丈餘，橫梁板闐，本無椽瓦，用塼平覆。寺皆正直隨意旋往。其房後壁即為外面也。疊塼峻峭，高三四丈。上作人頭，高共人等。其僧房也，面有九焉。一一房中可方丈許，後面通窓戶向簷矣。其門既高，唯安一扇，皆相瞻望，不許安簾。出外平觀，四面皆覩，互相檢察，寧容片私？於一角頭作閣道還往。寺上四角，各為塼堂，多聞大德而住於此。寺門西向，飛閣凌虛，雕刻奇形，妙盡工飾。其門乃與房相連，元不別作，但前出兩步，齊安四柱。其門雖非過大，實乃裝架彌堅。每至食時，重關返閉，既是聖教，意在防私。寺內之地方三十步許，皆以塼砌。小者或七步，或五步耳。凡所覆屋脊上簷前房內之地，並用塼糈如桃棗大，和雜粘泥，以杵平築，用彊石灰，雜以麻筋并油及麻滓爛皮之屬，浸漬多日，泥於墫地之上，覆以青草，經三數日，看其欲乾，重以滑石揩拭，拂赤土汁或丹朱之類，後以油塗，鮮澄若鏡。其堂殿階陛，悉皆如此。一作已後，縱人踐蹋，動經一二十載，曾不圮坼。不同石灰，水沾便脫。如斯等類，乃有八寺，上皆平通，規矩相似。於寺東面取房或一或三，用安尊像，或可即於此面前出多少，別起臺觀，為佛殿矣。此寺西南大院之外，方列大窣覩波(舊云塔者訛略)及諸制底(舊云支提者訛)數乃盈百。聖跡相連，不可稱記。金寶瑩飾，實成希有。其間僧徒綱軌出納之儀，具如《中方錄》及《寄歸傳》所述。寺內但以最老上座而為尊主，不論其德。諸有門鑰，每宵封印，將付上座，更無別置寺主、維那。但造寺之人，名為寺主，梵云毘訶羅莎弭。若作番直，典掌寺門，及和僧白事者，名毘訶羅波羅，譯為護寺。若鳴健稚及監食者，名為羯磨陀那，譯為授事。言維那者略也。眾僧有事，集眾平章，令其護寺。巡行告白，一一人前，皆須合掌，各伸其事。若一人不許，則事不得成，全無眾前打槌秉白之法。若見不許，以理喻之，未有挾強便加壓伏。其守庫當莊之流，雖三二人，亦遣典庫家人合掌為白，若和方可費用，誠無獨任之咎。若不白而獨用者，下至半升之粟，即交被驅擯。若一人稱豪，獨用僧物，處斷綱務，不白大眾者，名為俱攞鉢底，譯為家主。斯乃佛法之大疣，人神所共怨，雖復於寺有益，而終獲罪彌深，智者必不為也。又諸外道先有九十六部，今但十餘。若有齋會聚集，各各自居一處，並與僧尼無競先後。既其法別，理不同行，各習所宗，坐無交雜。此之寺制，理極嚴峻，每半月令典事佐史巡房讀制。眾僧名字不貫王籍，其有犯者，眾自治罰，為此僧徒咸相敬懼。其寺受用雖迮，而益利彌寬。曾憶在京見人畫出祇洹寺樣，咸是憑虛。為廣異聞，略陳梗概云爾。又五天之地，但是大寺，君王悉皆令置漏水，為此晝夜期候不難。准如律教，夜分三分，初後制令禪誦，中間隨意消息。其漏水法廣如《寄歸傳》中所述。雖復言陳寺樣，終恐在事還迷，為此畫出其圖，冀令目擊無滯。如能奏請依樣造之，即王舍支那，理成無別耳。乃歎曰:眾美仍羅列，群英已古今。也知生死分，那得不傷心！寺樣。此是室利那爛陀莫訶毘訶羅樣，唐譯云吉祥神龍大住處也。西國凡喚君王及大官屬并大寺舍，皆先云室利，意取吉祥尊貴之義。那爛陀乃是龍名。近此有龍，名那伽爛陀，故以為號。毘訶羅是住處義，比云寺者，不是正翻。如觀一寺，餘七同然。背上平直，通人還往。凡觀寺樣者，須面西看之，欲使西出其門，方得直勢。於門南畔可二十步，有窣堵波，高百尺許，是世尊昔日夏三月安居處。梵名慕攞健陀俱胝，唐云根本香殿矣。門北畔五十步許，復有大窣堵波，更高於此，是幼日王所造，皆並墫作，裝飾精妙，金床寶地，供養希有，中有如來轉法輪像。次此西南有小制底，高一丈餘，是婆羅門執雀請問處，唐云雀離浮圖，此即是也。根本殿西有佛齒木樹，非是楊柳。其次西畔，有其戒壇，方可大尺一丈餘，即於平地周疊塼牆，可高二尺許。牆內坐基可高五寸，中有小制底。壇東殿角有佛經行之基，疊塼為之，寬可二肘，長十四五肘，高可二肘餘。上乃石灰素作蓮華開勢，高可二寸，闊一尺許，有十四五，表佛足跡。此寺則南望王城，纔三十里。鷲峯、竹苑，皆在城傍。西南向大覺，正南尊足山，並可七驛。北向薛舍離，乃二十五驛。西瞻鹿苑，二十餘驛。東向耽摩立底國，有六七十驛，即是海口昇舶歸唐之處。此寺內僧眾有三千五百人，屬寺村莊二百一所，並是積代君王給其人戶，永充供養(言驛者即當一踰繕那也)。[96]

b.Nanhai-jigui-neifa-zhuan 南海寄歸內法傳, "Record of the Inner Dharma Sent Back From the Southern Sea":

"These [monastic rules] are even stricter at Nālandā monastery [than in Tāmralipta]. Even though the number of monks exceeds [just] three thousand [the monastery] is enfiefed with over two hundred villages which were all donated by rulers of successive generations [so that it will] flourish continuously — how could this be other than [because of the strict] *vinaya* [rules]!"
T.2125.214a.3ff.其那爛陀寺，法乃更嚴。遂使僧徒數出三千，封邑則村餘二百，並是積代君王之所奉施，紹隆不絕，非律而誰者哉。[97]
"In the case of Nālandā monastery the people there are numerous and the number of monks exceeds three thousand [so that] it is difficult to gather them quickly. The monastery has eight compounds and has three hundred rooms."
T.2125.227a.25ff.至如那爛陀寺，人眾殷繁，僧徒數出三千，造次難為翔集。寺有八院、房有三百，...[98]

5. Daoxuan, Shijia-fangzhi 釋迦方志, "Record of the Regions of the Śākya" (T.2088.964c.1ff.):

"The monastery has established strict rules. Since the foundation of the monastery no woman has come there. The ten monastic administrators are on inspection tours every evening. The rank of those who have not received ordination is determined by their [real] age. There are several thousand monks, [and] eminent travelling scholar monks are coming through in their ten thousands, all of them brilliant and of excellent learning. There are several hundred [monks] whose fame has quickly spread to foreign regions, [and] therefore all monks in India look up to them as their authority."
T.2088.964c.1ff. 寺立嚴制。立寺已來女人不至。知事十人每夕巡檢。未具受者齒敘為次。僧徒數千，遊學名僧通數將萬，多是俊才通學。聲馳異域者，其人數百，故印度諸僧皆仰則焉。

6. Biography of Muniśrī/Monishili 牟尼室利 (?-806), Song-Gaosengzhuan 宋高僧傳 (comp. 988 by Zanning 贊寧) (T.2061.721a.8ff.):

"First Muni[śrī] explained that Nālandā-monastery in Magadha, Central India, had a circumference of forty-eight miles, [consisted of] nine monasteries [and had] one gate, [and] that these [monasteries] were built by nine Indian kings. The days when Muni[śrī] was in the monastery [it] had more than ten thousand residents, with a great *dharma* master in charge of all the [monastic] administrators. There is no [other] monastery in the Western Regions as big as this one." T.2061.721a.8ff. 初默說中天竺摩伽陀國那爛陀寺周圍四十八里，九寺一門，是九天王所造。默在寺日住者萬餘，以大法師處量綱任。西域伽藍無如其高廣矣。

7. Jiye 繼業 (2nd half of 10th cent.) (T.2089.982a.28ff.):

"Fifteen miles further to the north [of Rājagṛha] is the monastery of Nālandā. Each to the north and the south of the monastery there are several tens of monastic [courtyards] with all their gates facing west. North of it there are the seats of the four Buddhas. [Going] fifteen miles further in north-eastern [direction], [one] arrives at the monastery of Wudiantou.[99] Five miles [from Nālandā], in south-eastern [direction] there is a statue of the noble Avalokiteśvara. [Going] ten miles further in north-eastern [direction one] arrives at the Kaśmīran monastery.[100] About eight miles south of the monastery is the Chinese monastery." T.2089.982a.28ff. 又北十五里有那爛陀寺。寺之南北各有數十寺，門皆西向。其北有四佛座。又東北十五里至烏巔頭寺。東南五里有聖觀自在像。又東北十里至伽濕彌羅寺。寺南距漢寺八里許。

Chinese Measurements

1 *cun* 寸	ca. 30 cm
1 *chi* 尺	ca. 30 cm (10 *cun*)
1 *zhou* 肘	45–60 cm (1.5–2 *chi*)
1 *bu* 步	ca. 150 cm (5 *chi*)
1 *zhang* 丈	ca. 300 cm (10 *chi*)
1 *li* 里	400–440 m (shorter *li*)
1 *yi* 驛	ca. 10 km (≈ 1 *yojana*)
1 *sheng* 升	ca. 600 ml
1 *dan* 石	ca. 60 l (100 *sheng*)

Notes

1. This paper is an extended and altered version of the presentation which I gave in the seminar series "*Entre Nous*" in January 2016 at Nālandā University when I had the honour to be the first invited Scholar in Residence. I would like to thank all the students and my colleagues at Nālandā University who attended the presentation and got involved in a lively discussion from which this paper benefitted a lot.
2. See, e.g., N. Sastri (1941), pp. 1ff.; H. Sastri (1942), pp. 1ff., esp. 19f.
3. On another example and analysis of Xuanzang's representation of Indian royal lineages, see Deeg (2016).
4. For an overview, see Asher (2015), and Stewart (2016), particularly pp. 73ff.
5. Sastri (1931–32), p. 72; Tsukamoto (1996): 198, Nālandā no.4.
6. Tsukamoto (1996), p. 195, verse 5, Nālandā no.9.
7. Ibid., p. 203, verse 38, Nālandā nos.10 & 204, Nālandā no.11.
8. On *mahavihāra*s in India, see Durt (1983).
9. EMC reconstructions are all given according to Pulleyblank (1991).
10. The guttural final of this syllable together with the initial *x* of the following one may indicate a fricative pronunciation of the *h* in Skt. *mahā*-. Another possibility is that the EMC **mɔʰ* (modern pronunciation *mu*).
11. It is difficult to determine how far these *mahāvihāra*s were regulated and institutionalized as their correspondent *dasi* 大寺 were in China (see Forte 1983).
12. Sakaki (1916): no. 4120: *dpal* Na-lan-da/Na-landa.
13. Chattopadhyaya (1990), p. 106.
14. T.1442.691a.24ff.
15. Or with "dittological" repetition of the syllable *nā*: **nāga Nālanda*(?); see Chavannes (1894), pp. 84f., note 2. Lahiri (1995), p. 58, without any further explanation, gives Nāgananda (Chin. *n* = *l*?). As far as I know, no *nāga* of such a name is known; closest comes the singular name Luotuo(-long) 羅陀(龍)/EMC **la-da-*° in Amoghavajra's collection of *mantra*s (T.1092.332c.25).
16. See Tan (2002).
17. Chattopadhyaya (1990), p. 109.
18. Asher (2015), pp. 43 & 69.
19. See especially the survey by Rajani (2016).
20. Kuwayama (1988), pp. 9ff.
21. Deeg (2005), pp. 405f.
22. Kuwayama (1988), pp. 7ff.
23. Malalasekara (1974), pp. 2, 55, s.v. Nāla, etc.
24. Bagchi (1970), pp. 2, 80ff.
25. T.1451.289a.7 在那爛陀寺東南二十餘里許。
26. Obermiller (1932), pp. 122ff.; see also in Tāranātha, Chattopadhyaya (1990), pp. 106ff.

27. Chattopadhyaya (1990), p. 101.
28. Malalasekera (1974), pp. 2, 56f., s.v. If not noted otherwise I quote all Pāli texts according to the Pali Text Society's editions.
29. Dīghanikāya 11.1: *phītā ca bahujanā ākiṇṇa-manussā Bhagavati abhippasannā.*
30. See, e.g., Dundas (2002), p. 31.
31. Deeg (2004), pp. 119f.
32. Malalasekera (1974), pp. 1, 158f. s.vv. Ambalaṭṭhikā 1, 2, 4.
33. Papañcasūdanī (Majjhimanikāyaṭṭhakathā) 3, 52. *Tattha Nāḷandāyan ti Nālandā ti evaṃnāmake nāgare taṃ nagaraṃ gocaragāmaṃ katvā. "Pāvārikambavane ti dussapāvārikaseṭṭhino ambavane." Taṃ kira tassa uyyānaṃ ahosi. So Bhagavato dhammadesanaṃ sutvā Bhagavati pasanno tasmiṃ uyyāne kuṭilenamaṇḍapādipatimaṇḍitaṃ Bhagavato vihāraṃ katvā niyyādesi. So vihāro Jīvakambavanaṃ viya Pāvārikambavanant' eva saṅkhaṅgato tasmiṃ "Pāvārikambavane viharatī" ti attho.*
34. Waldschmidt (1944), pp. 47ff.
35. Ibid., p. 18.
36. See Tibetan *'od-ma'i dbyug-pa-can*: Waldschmidt (1950), p. 135 and Waldschmidt (1944), p. 48, note 63.
37. Waldschmidt (1950), p. 134.
38. Variant reading *zhucun* 竹村.
39. See Weller (1971), p. 207.
40. Ibid., p. 203.
41. Weller (1935–36), pp. 1 & 39, note 8.
42. Jacobi (1895), pp. 419ff.
43. The narrative has a parallel in the dispute between Gotama (Skt. Gautama Indrabhūti) and Keśin, another follower of Pārśva, in the Uttarādhyayanasūtra 23; see Dundas (2002), p. 31.
44. *842. Teṇaṃ kāleṇaṃ teṇaṃ sama'eṇam Rāyagihe nāmaṃ nagare hotthā, riddhitthimitasamiddhe jāva paḍirūve. Tassa ṇaṃ Rāyagihassa nagarassa bahiyā uttarapuratthime disībhā'e, ettha ṇaṃ Nālandā nāmaṃ bāhiriyā hotthā aṇegabhavaṇasayasanniviṭṭhā jāva paḍirūvā. 843. Tattha ṇaṃ nālaṃdā'e bāhiriyā'e le'e nāmaṃ gāhāvatī hotthā, aḍḍhe ditte vitte vitthiṇṇavipula-bhavaṇasayaṇāsaṇajāṇavāhaṇā'iṇṇe bahughaṇa-bahujātarūvarajate ā'oga-pa'ogasaṃpa'utte vicchaḍḍitapa'uramatapāṇe bahudāsī-dāsa-go-mahisa-ga-velagappabhūte bahujaṇassa aparibhūte yāvi hotthā. Se ṇaṃ leha gāhāvatī samaṇovāsa'e yāvi hotthā abhigatajīvā-'jīve jāva viharati. 844. Tassa ṇaṃ leyassa gāhāvatissa Nālaṃdā'e bāhiriyā'e bahiyā uttarapuratthime disībhā'e ettha ṇaṃ Sesadaviyā nāma udagasālā hotthā aṇegakhaṃbhasayasanniviṭṭhā pāsādīyā jāva paḍirūvā. Tīse ṇaṃ sesadaviyā'e udagasālā'e uttarapuratthime disībhā'e, ettha ṇaṃ Hatthijāme nāmaṃ vaṇasaṃḍe hotthā kinhe, vaṇṇa'o vaṇasaṇḍassa. 845. Tassiṃ ca ṇaṃ gihapadesaṃsi bhagavaṃ Gotame viharati* ... translation slightly changed from Jacobi 1895: 419ff., with modernized romanization of Jacobi's Skt. renderings of the names.

45. Schubring (2000), p. 87; Dundas (2002), pp. 22f.
46. In this context of "competition" there may have been more behind the fact that the *gaṇadhara* Gautama who converts Udaka has the same name as the Buddha.
47. All translations from Chinese are my own.
48. 那爛陀/ EMC **na'-lanʰ-da*, Skt. Nālanda, Chin. Shi-wuyan 施無厭. All EMC reconstructions follow Pulleyblank (1991).
49. 鑠迦羅阿迭多/EMC **ɕiak-kɨa-la-ʔa-dɛt-ta*, Skt. Śakrāditya, Chin. Diri 帝日. The transliteration of the names of the king displays some deficiencies, as here and in Bālāditya (see also Sīlāditya) the two *akṣara*s/syllables *-ditya* are rendered as if the pronunciation of the underlying name had been **-ditta*, as reconstructed by Mizutani (1999), vol. 3, p. 163, note 2. I have no philological explanation for this form. The underlying Indic cannot be a Prakrit form of *-ditya* which would be **-dic(c)a* (Pāli *ādicca*, or Ārdhamāgadhī *ā'icca*: Ratnacandraji (1977), p. 3b): see von Hinüber (2001), p. 192, §247.
50. *fudi* 福地 here probably has a double connotation, the concrete one of the place and another one of "field of merit" (Skt. *puṇyakṣetra*).
51. *niqian-waidao* 尼乾外道: *niqian* 尼乾/EMC **nri-gian*, stands for *ni(r) graṇ(ṭha)*; the term normally refers to the Jains.
52. 佛陀毱多/EMC **but-da-kuwk-ta*, Skt. Bu(d)dhagupta, Chin. Juehu 覺護. The name *Buddhagupta seems to be a "buddhisized" form for the Gupta king Budhagupta of the inscriptions. There is no need to correct the inscriptional name on the basis of Xuanzang. The transliteration of the name element *-gupta* as EMC **kuwk-ta* with a final guttural of the first syllable is odd. Older, phonetically more suitable transliterations of the name element *-gupta* were well known: e.g. Dharmagupta/Tanmojueduo 曇摩崛多/EMC **dam-ma-gut-ta* (probably Pkt. Dhammagutta) (fl. 384–417), Dharmagupta/Damojiduo 達摩笈多/EMC **dat-ma-gɨap-ta* (fl. ca. 590–619). Other characters/syllables would have been more suited to represent the final *-p* of *gupta*: e.g. *jia* 莢, 頰, 鋏, et al./EMC **kɛp*, *jie* 劫/**kɨap*, etc.
53. 呾他揭多毱多/EMC **tat-tʰa-kiat-ta-kuwk-ta*, Skt. Tathāgatagupta, Chin. Rulai 如來: the Chinese translation of the name is incomplete and should rather be Rulaihu 如來護 (Mizutani 1999, vol. 3, p. 164, note 5; Ji 1985, p. 755, note 4).
54. 婆羅阿迭多/EMC **ba-la-ʔa-dɛt-ta*, Skt. Bālāditya, Chin. Youri 幼日.
55. *fuhui* 福會, Skt. **puṇyapariṣad*.
56. 至那/EMC **tɕiʰ-na'*, Skt. Cīna.
57. *heshang* 和上/EMC **ɣwa-dʑiaŋ'*, originally a transliteration of *ācārya* and here used in this sense.
58. *yingzhen* 嬰疹; or, with the variant reading *yingji* 嬰疾, some skin disease (s. HDC, s.v. *yingji*).
59. *chujia* 出家, i.e. he became a novice (took the *pravrajanā*).
60. *seng* 僧, corresponding to Skt. *saṅgha*. The full term used here is *sengmo*

僧末 which only occurs twice elsewhere in the canon (T.2043.141a.12; T.2121.252a.10).

61. *weishoujie-zhe* 未受戒者, lit.: "who has not yet taken the precepts (*sīla*)", Skt. *anupasaṃpada*.
62. 伐闍羅/EMC **buat-dẓia-la*, Skt. Vajra, Chin. Jin'gang 金剛; could this be an abbreviated form of an unattested *Vajragupta or *Vajrāditya? Xuanzang uses the same transliteration for Vajra in a short text (T.2030.13a.12f.) for an *arhat* called Vajraputra/Fasheluofuduoluo 伐闍羅弗多羅. Nothing is known of a Gupta or later king bearing this. The identification of Vajra with the ruler *va-kārākhya*, "[king whose] name [starts] with *va-*", in the Mañjuśrīmūlakalpa 53.779 (Jayaswal 1934, pp. 55f. & 67; Raychaudhuri 1957, p. 525, note 2; Mizutani 1999, vol. 3, p. 164f., note 7; Ji 1985, p. 756, note 7), is at best hypothetical. According to the Mañjuśrīmūlakalpa this king is the successor (*anuja*) of Prakaṭāditya (*pa-kārākhya*) and is ruling at the beginning of the *kāliyuga* as one of the last of his lineage.
63. *shizhu-zhi-en* 施主之恩.
64. *jingshe* 精舍, lit.: "perfect, pure abode"; Skt. *pariveṇa* or *prāsāda* (Hirakawa 1997, p. 924b, s.v. *jing* 精). The word is used by Xuanzang, particularly in his description of Nālandā, for structures of considerable size containing statues.
65. There is, as far as I know, no trace of this legend in Buddhist literature, but Yijing mentions the *stūpa* as well (T.2066.6b.7f.; see below). The story must have been known in China, since it is alluded to, with a little bit more details, in different texts related to Xuanzang's translation activity, e.g. in his disciple Puguang's 普光 (fl. 650–63) Jushe-lun-ji 倶舍論記 (T.1821.446a.1f.): 如外道離繫子以手執雀問佛死．生。佛知彼心不為定。若答言死。彼便放活。若答言生。彼便捨殺。故佛不答。 ("Like [when] the heretic *nirgranthika-putra* held a sparrow in his hand and asked the Buddha about [its] death or life. The Buddha knew that his mind was not concentrated, and if he would answer "[Let it] die!" [he] immediately would release it alive, [but] if [he] answered: "[Let it] live!", [he] immediately would throw [it to the ground] and kill it. Therefore the Buddha did not answer.")
66. Manzhou 滿冑, lit.: "Fully Helmeted", Skt. Pūrṇavarma(n).
67. Duoluo 多羅/**ta-la*.
68. *jieni-hua-shu* 羯尼花樹: *jieni* is an abbreviation of *jienijia* 羯尼迦, Skt. *kanaka* which is used for a variety of plants (PW, s.v.), but it very probably refers to the Michelia/Magnolia champaca, a large tree with very prominent yellow flowers. The yellowness of the flowers is used metaphorically several times in the Abhidharma texts translated by Xuanzang (T.1536.445c.5f.; T.1542.713a.14; T.1545.440b.3, etc.).
69. I am not sure if this is the right translation but I take the phrase *zhoulüsichong* 周閭四重 as specifying the one great gate (*yidamen* 一大門). 8 *zhang* would make the gate approximately 30 metres high.

70. Manzhou 滿胄.
71. 曷羅社槃社/EMC **ɣat-la-dʑia'-ban-dʑia'*; several identifications have been proposed. Chavannes' (1894, p. 84), reconstruction Rājavaṃśa (see also Mizutani 1999, vol. 3, p. 163, note 2) and Adachi's *granthavatsa* as a reference to a Jain (*nirgrantha – nir-*) are certainly wrong (Wang 2009, p. 119: note 2). A tentative, phonetically sound reconstruction of the name would be *Rājabhañja (or *Rājavañja), but this name would be odd for a monk, is not documented anywhere and is speculative at best.
72. This seems to be the meaning of the term *gedao* 閣道 as explained in Yiqiejing-yinyi (T.2128.839a.24): 木於危險處為路名閣道也。("Wooden [plank used] as a pathway in dangerous places is called *gedao*."). Chavannes (1894), p. 86, translates "chemin suspendu".
73. Chavannes (1894), p. 86 translates exactly the opposite: "on enlève les barres de fermeture à toutes les portes." What is meant is obviously that the main gates of the monastic courtyards were closed during mealtimes when monks had to assemble in the refectory and were not supposed to be in their cells but should gather to have their meal: see Pravajyāvastu of the Mūlasarvāstivādavinaya (T.1444.1035c.11f.), and also the Abhisāmācārikā on common meals of the *saṅgha* in the refectory (*bhaktāgra*) (Karashima 2012, pp. 21ff.).
74. *chu'na* 出納 is a technical translation for Skt. *vyavahāra* and in this context clearly has the translated meaning (see Edgerton 1953, p. 516a, s.v.).
75. The Jigui-zhuan 寄歸傳 is Yijing's Nanhai-jigui-neifa-zhuan while the Zhongfang-lu 中方錄 is not known from any other source. Since this passage is particularly dealing with monastic regulation and discipline I am tempted to interpret this as an otherwise unknown name used by Yijing for the Mūlasarvāstivāda-vinaya: "the records [of the discipline] in the Middle Region (*zhongfang* = *madhyadeśa*)" as practised in an ideal way at Nālandā.
76. Chavannes (1894), p. 88, note 2, takes *zunzhu* 尊主 as a Chinese translation of *sthavira*, but the preceding *shangzuo* 上座 already has this meaning. For an English translation of this passage on monastic functionaries see Silk (2008), p. 130.
77. 毘訶羅莎弭/EMC **bji-xa-la-swa-mji'*, Skt. *vihārasvāmin*.
78. 毘訶羅波羅/EMC **bji-xa-la-pa-la*, Skt. *vihārapāla*; on the role of the *vihārapāla*, see Silk (2008), p. 137ff.
79. 健稚/EMC **gɨan*^{h}*-drɨ*^{h}, Skt. *gaṇḍī*, the monastic semetron.
80. 羯磨陀那/EMC **kɨat-ma-da-na'*, Skt. *karmadāna*; on *karmadāna* (*karmādāna*), see Silk (2008), p. 127ff.
81. 維那/EMC **jwi-na'*: Yijing here refers to the old translation term the Indic equivalent of which is, however, not clear: see Silk (2008), pp. 128ff.
82. 俱攞鉢底/EMC **kuə́-la-pa-tɛj'*, Skt. *kulapati*. This is certainly an ironic nickname for a monk who is self-assuming.
83. *dayou* 大疣, literally: "big wart".

84. I suspect that *zuoshi* 佐史 should be read *zuoli* 佐吏 here which, from the Han period to the Tang, refers to a clerk of lower rank; see Hucker (1985), pp. 523b, no. 697a, s.v. *tsŏ-lì*.
85. This probably refers to a model or plan of Jetavana made on the basis of Daoxuan's work (see my essay in this volume) which was without any doubt circulating in China during this period.
86. Unfortunately this map is not preserved in any version or edition of the text or elsewhere.
87. I am not sure what the sentence *beishangpingzhi, tongrenhuan-wang* 背上平直，通人還往。 exactly means. Chavannes (1894), p. 94 translates: "En haut ils (les temples) offrent une terrasse plane où les passants peuvent aller et venir."
88. 慕攞健陀俱胝/EMC **mɔʰ-la-gɨanʰ-da-kuə́-tri*, Skt. Mūlagandhakūṭī, Chin. Genben-xiang-dian 根本香殿. On the Mūlagandhakūṭī, see Strong (1977).
89. Youri 幼日, Skt. Bālāditya, identified as Narasiṃhagupta, a late Gupta-ruler of the 6th cent.: Wang (2009), p. 128, note 40.
90. *queli-futu* 雀離浮圖/EMC **tsɨak-liʰ-buw-dɔ*.Yijing identifies the *stūpa* of the *brāhmaṇa* holding the sparrow (Chin. *que* 雀) with the *queli-stūpa* in the Northwest of India well known from other Chinese sources: see Deeg (2004), pp. 27ff.
91. *jietan* 戒壇: while we do not know much about ordination platforms in India, these became very important in East Asian Buddhism from the first half of the Tang period onwards; see MacRae (2005).
92. The text has *qiangnei* 牆內, literally: "inside of the wall", which implies a wall around the platform, either demarcating the ordination area or serving as a railing around the elevated platform. My translation assumes a platform of two *chi* high and takes *nei* 內 in a more open sense of "on the space formed by the brick structure".
93. Xuesheli 薛舍離; the first character is a mistake for 薜: Bisheli 薜舍離/EMC **bεjʰ-ɕiaʰ-liʰ*, used by Yijing in his translation of the Mūlasarvāstivāda-vinaya.
94. Danmolidi 耽摩立底/EMC **tam-ma-lip-tεjʰ*; the seaport at the mouth of the Gaṅgā through which most trade and sea-travel passed from Southeast Asia and East Asia, and through which Yijing himself entered India.
95. It seems that the purpose of this positioning of Nālandā in relation to other places, most important Buddhist sites — the only not specifically Buddhist place being Tāmralipti which also is much more distant than the other places — is to put the monastery in a central position.
96. The text is following the punctuation and emendations in Wang (2009), pp. 112ff.
97. Text and punctuation in Wang (2000), p. 88.
98. Text and punctuation in Wang (2000), p. 176f.
99. 烏巔頭/EMC **ʔɔ-tεn-dəw*; reading 巔 with the Yuan edition for T.嶺. Chavannes (1904), p. 80, stated that the name cannot be identified, but despite

of some phonetic difficulties — Skt. reconstructions would be *Utanda/Utaṇḍa or *Otanda/Otaṇḍa — and according to the indicated location near today's Bihār Sharif this transliteration seems to be rendering an abridged form of (inscriptional) Uddāṇḍa(pura).

100. Jiashimiluo-si 伽濕彌羅寺. Already Chavannes (1904), p. 81, pointed out that the reading, accepted by T., is a mistake; see also the translation by Huber (1902), p. 259.

Bibliography

Asher, Frederick M. *Nalanda: Situating the Great Monastery*. Mumbai: The Marg Foundation, 2015 (Marg, Vol. 66, No. 33, March 2015).

Bagchi, S. *Mūlasarvāstivadavinayavastu*. 2 vols. Darbhanga: Mithila Institute of Post-Graduate Studies and Research in Sanskrit Learning, 1967 & 1970 (Buddhist Sanskrit Texts 16).

Chattopadhyaya, Lama Chimpa Alaka (Chattopadhyaya Debiprasad, ed.). *Tārānātha's History of Buddhism in India*. Delhi: Motilal Banarsidass, 1990.

Chavannes, Édouard. *Mémoire composé à l'époque de la grande dynastie T'ang sur les religieux éminents que allèrent chercher la loi dans les pays d'occident par I-Tsing*. Paris: Ernest Leroux, 1894.

———. "Notes sinologiques: l'itinéraire de Ki-ye". *Bulletin de l'École Française de l'Extrême Orient* 4 (1904): 75–82.

Deeg, Max. "Legend and Cult — Contributions to the History of Indian Buddhist Stūpas — Part 2: the 'Stūpa of Laying Down the Bows'". *Buddhist Studies Review* 21 (2004.2): 119–49.

———. *Das Gaoseng-Faxian-zhuan als religionsgeschichtliche Quelle. Der älteste Bericht eines chinesischen buddhistischen Pilgermönchs über seine Reise nach Indien mit Übersetzung des Textes*. Studies in Oriental Religions 52. Wiesbaden: Harrassowitz, 2005.

———. "The Political Position of Xuanzang: The Didactic Creation of an Indian Dynasty in the Xiyuji". In *The Middle Kingdom and the Dharma Wheel: Aspects of the Relationship between the Buddhist Saṃgha and the State in Chinese History*, edited by Thomas Jülch, pp. 94–139. Leiden, Boston: Brill, 2016.

Dundas, Paul. *The Jains*. 2nd ed. London, New York: Routledge, 2002.

Durt, Hubert. "Daiji (Inde)". In *Hōbōgirin* 法寶義林, *Dictionnaire encyclopédique du Bouddhisme d'après les sources chinoises et japonaises, Sixième Fascicule: Da-Daijizaite*, pp. 679–81. Paris, Tōkyō: Librairied'Amériqueetd'Orient, Maison Franco-Japonaise, 1983.

Edgerton, Franklin. *Buddhist Hybrid Sanskrit Grammar and Dictionary, Vol. II: Dictionary*. New Haven: Yale University Press, 1953.

Forte, Antonino. "Daiji (Chine)". In *Hōbōgirin* 法寶義林, *Dictionnaire encyclopédique du Bouddhisme d'après les sources chinoises et japonaises, Sixième Fascicule: Da*-Daijizaiten, pp. 682–704. Paris, Tōkyō: Librairied'Amériqueetd'Orient, Maison Franco-Japonaise, 1983.

Hinüber, Oskar von. *Das ältere Mittelindisch im Überblick.* Wien: Verlag der Österreichischen Akadamie der Wissenschaften, 2001. (Österreichische Akademie der Wissenschaften, Phil.-Hist. Kl., Sitzungsberichte 467.Band, 2., erweiterte Auflage).

Hirakawa Akira 平川彰. *Bukkyō-kanbon-daijiten* 佛教漢梵大辭典/*Buddhist Chinese-Sanskrit Dictionary*. Tokyo: The Reiyukai, 1997.

Huber, Édouard. "Itinéraire du Pèlerin Ki Ye dans l'Inde". *Bulletin de l'École Française de l'Extrême Orient* 2 (1902): 256–59.

Hucker, Charles O. *A Dictionary of Official Titles in Imperial China.* Stanford: Stanford University Press, 1985.

Jacobi, Hermann. *Gaina Sûtras (Translated from Prakrit). Part II: The Uttarâdhyayana Sûtra — The Sûtrakritâṅgasûtra.* Oxford: Clarendon Press, 1895 (Sacred Books of the East XLV).

Jayaswal, K.P. *An Imperial History of India in a Sanskrit Text [c. 700 B.C. – c. 770 A.D.] With a Special Commentary on Later Gupta Period.* Lahore: Motilal BanarsiDass, 1934.

Ji Xianlin 季羡林, et. al. *Datang-xiyuji-xiaozhu* 大唐西域記校注. Beijing: Zhonghua-shuju 中華書局, 1985.

Karashima Seishi 辛嶋靜志. *Die Abhisamācārikā Dharmāḥ. Verhaltensregeln für buddhistische Mönche der Mahāsāṃghika-Lokottaravādins (herausgegeben, mit der chinesischen Parallelversion verglichen, übersetzt und kommentiert).* 3 vols. Tokyo: The International Research Institute for Advanced Buddhology, Soka University, 2012 (Bibliotheca Philologica et Philosophica Buddhica XIII, 1–3; plus corrigenda).

Kuwayama Shōshin. "How Xuanzang Learnt About Nālandā". In *Tang China and Beyond (Studies on East Asia from the Seventh to the Tenth Century)*, edited by Antonino Forte, pp. 1–33. Kyoto: Italian School of East Asian Studies, 1988.

Malalasekara, Gunapala Piyasena. *Dictionary of Pali Proper Names.* 2 vols. London: The Pali Text Society, 1974 (repr. of 1937).

McRae, John. "Daoxuan's Vision of Jetavana: The Ordination Platform Movement in Medieval Chinese Buddhism". In *Going Forth. Visions of Buddhist Vinaya: Essays Presented in Honor of Professor Stanley Weinstein*, edited by William M. Bodiford, pp. 68–100 (Kuroda Institute Studies in East Asian Buddhism 18). Honolulu: University of Hawai'i Press, 2005.

Mizutani Shinjō 水谷真成. *Daitō-saiiki-ki* 大唐西域記. 3 vols. (Tōyō-bunko, vols. 653, 655, 657). Tokyo: Tōyō-Bunko 東洋文庫, 1999.

Obermiller, Evgenyevich. *History of Buddhism (Chos-ḥbyung) by Bu-ston. II. Part: The History of Buddhism in India and Tibet.* Heidelberg: O. Harrassowitz, Leipzig, 1932.

Pulleyblank, Edwin G. *Lexicon of Reconstructed Pronunciation in Early Middle*

Chinese, Late Middle Chinese, and Early Mandarin. Vancouver: UBC Press, 1991.

Rajani, M.B. "The Expanse of Archaeological Remains at Nalanda: A Study Using Remote Sensing and GIS". *Archives of Asian Art* 66, no. 1 (2016): 1–23.

Ratnacandrajī, Jaina Muni Shri. *An Illustrated Ardha-Magadhi Dictionary, Literary, Philosophic and Scientific With Sanskrit, Gujrati, Hindi and English Equivalents, References to the Texts & Copious Quotations*. 2 vols. Tokyo: Meicho-Fukyū-Kai, 1977 (originally published 1923).

Raychaudhuri, Hemchandra. *Political History of Ancient India. From the Accession of Parikshit to the Extinction of the Gupta Dynasty*. 7th ed. Calcutta: University of Calcutta, 1957.

Sakaki Ryōsaburō 榊亮三郎. *Honyaku-meigi-daishō – Bonzōkanwa-shiyaku-taikō* 翻譯名義大集梵藏漢和四譯對校. 2 vols. Kyoto: Bunka-daigaku-zōhan 文科大學藏版, 1916 (repr. Tokyo, 1982).

Sastri, Hirananda. "The Clay Seals at Nalanda". *Epigraphia Indica* 21 (1931–32): 72–77.

———. *Nalanda and its Epigraphic Material*. New Delhi: Archaeological Survey of India, 1942 (Memoirs of the Archaeological Survey of India No. 66).

Sastri, K.A. Nilakanta. *Nālandā*. Bombay, 1941.

Schubring, Walther. *The Doctrine of the Jainas. Described after the Old Sources*. Rev. ed. Delhi: Motilal Banarsidass, 2000.

Silk, Jonathan A. *Managing Monks: Administrators and Administrative Roles in Indian Buddhist Monasticism*. Oxford, New York: Oxford University Press, 2008.

Stewart, Mary L. *Nālandā Mahāvihāra: A Critical Analysis of the Archaeology of an Indian Buddhist Site*. Delhi: Manohar, 2016 (revised version of *Nālandā Mahāvihāra. A Study of an Indian Pāla Period Buddhist Site and British historical archaeology, 1861–1938*. Oxford, 1989, BAR International Series 529).

Strong, John S. " 'Gandhakuṭī': The Perfumed Chamber of the Buddha". *History of Religions* 16, no. 4 (1977): 390–406.

Tan Zhihui. *Daoxuan's Vision of Jetavana: Imagining a Utopian Monastery in Early Tang*. Ann Arbor: UMI, 2002. Unpublished PhD thesis, University of Arizona.

Tsukamoto Keishō 塚本啓祥. *Indo-bukkyō-himei no kenkyū* インド佛教碑銘の研究. 3 vols. Kyōto: Heirakuji-shoten 平樂寺書店, 1996, 1998, 2003.

Waldschmidt, Ernst. *Die Überlieferungvom Lebensende des Buddha. Eine vergleichende Analyse des Mahāparinirvāṇasūtra und seiner Textentsprechungen*: Göttingen: Vandenhoeck & Ruprecht, 1944 & 1948 (Abhandlungen der Akademie der Wissenschaften in Göttingen, Philologisch-Historische Klasse, Dritte Folge, Nr.29+30).

———. *Das Mahāparinirvāṇasūtra: Text in Sanskrit und Tibetisch, verglichen mit dem Pāli nebst einer Übersetzung der chinesischen Entsprechung im*

Vinaya der Mūlasarvāstivādins aufgrund der Turfan Handschriften. Berlin: Verlag der Akademie der Wissenschaften, 1950 & 1951 (Abhandlungen der Deutschen Akademie der Wissenschaften zu Berlin, Klasse für Sprachen, Literatur und Kunst, Nr.1–3).

Weller, Friedrich. "Dastibetische Brahmajālasūtra". *Zeitschrift für Indologie und Iranistik* 10 (1935–36): 1–60.

———. "Das Brahmajālasūtra des chinesischen Dīrghāgama". *Asiatische Studien* 28 (1971): 202–64.

Wang Bangwei 王邦維. *Datang-xiyu-qiufa-gaoseng-zhuan-xiaozhu* 大唐西域求法高僧傳. Beijing: Zhonghua-shuju 中華書局, 2009 (Zhongwai-jiaotong-shiji-congkan 中外交通史籍叢刊).

———. *Nanhai-jigui-neifa-zhuan-xiaozhu* 南海寄歸內法傳校注. Beijing: Zhonghua-shuju 中華書局, 2000 (Zhongwai-jiaotong-shiji-congkan 中外交通史籍叢刊).

7

"CENTRAL INDIA IS WHAT IS CALLED THE MIDDLE KINGDOM"

Anne Cheng

I come into the discussion on the intersection of history, culture and heritage and its ecological and environmental connections from a position that may seem to be a non-specialist one: I am not an art historian, nor an archaeologist, nor a specialist of environmental or social studies. However, what I most certainly am is someone who has been working for some forty years now in the field of Chinese intellectual history (this is the title of my Chair at Collège de France in Paris), and who has been since long developing a growing interest in intercultural studies, more specifically between India and China. I therefore feel tremendously privileged to have been given the opportunity to come to Nâlandâ as a pilgrim, right in the heart of a land which has witnessed not only cross-cultural exchanges between India and China but also a space that is redolent with the memory of the historic endeavour of members of the Chinese elites to leave behind their heritage in their quest for something other than what had so far constituted the civilizational centrality and self-proclaimed superiority.

This historic movement outwards is even more critical to recall in the present day: a time when China's official discourse is entirely geared towards the Chinese rise to power and recovery of its imperial centrality in the East Asian region. To my mind, more than ever, it is timely and salutary to remind ourselves of the periods in the past when the Chinese themselves did not necessarily perceive themselves as *the* centre of the world (the "Middle Kingdom", *zhongguo* 中國), or even more simply as *the world* ("all under Heaven", *tianxia* 天下).

My starting point will be a sentence which sounds rather intriguing to me, as it has done so far for a good number of scholars, from Faxian 法顯's *Foguo ji* 佛國記 (*Notes on the Country of the Buddha*), which was first translated about two centuries ago into a European language, namely French, by Jean-Pierre Abel-Rémusat (1788–1832).[1] This self-taught Sinologist was elected to the very first Chair dedicated to Chinese Studies ever created in Europe in 1814 at the Collège de France (then called the Collège Royal) in Paris. As it happens, the *Foguo ji* has recently been translated afresh into French by Jean-Pierre Drège, as the first volume dedicated to Buddhist studies within a bilingual Chinese–French collection that I have contributed to create with a well-known publishing house in Paris.[2]

The *Foguo ji* is the narrative assigned to the Chinese Buddhist monk Faxian (ca. 340–ca. 420) who, with a few other monks, embarked on what would turn out to be a fifteen-year pilgrimage (or rather quest[3]) to India between 399 and 414 CE, with a view to bringing back to China some manuscript versions of Vinaya texts (that is, texts on the Buddhist monks' discipline) in the Hinayana tradition. This is the opening sentence (§1):

> 法顯昔在長安, 慨律藏殘缺. 於是遂以弘始一年歲在己亥, 與慧景、道整、慧應、慧嵬 等, 同契至天竺尋求戒律.
>
> Faxian was living of old in Chang'an.[4] Deploring the lacunae and imperfections of the collection of texts on Discipline (*Vinaya*, Chinese *lü* 律),[5] in the 1st year of the Hongshi era, which was the cyclical year *yihai* (i.e. 399 CE), he, together with Huijing, Daozheng, Huiying, Huiwei and others, took the joint engagement to go to India (*Tianzhu*)[6] and seek for the precepts[7] and the discipline.[8]

The sentence which caught my attention in Faxian's narrative runs as follows in the original Chinese (§8):

> 度河便到烏萇國. 其烏萇國是正北天竺也. 盡作中天竺語, 中天竺所謂中國. 俗人衣 服、飲食, 亦與中國同. 佛法甚盛.[9]
>
> After crossing the river, [Faxian and his companions] came to the country of Wuchang (Udyāna).[10] Udyāna is really in North India (*bei Tianzhu* 北天竺). The people all use the language of Central India.

> Central India (*zhong Tianzhu* 中天竺) is what is called the "Central country" (*Zhongguo* 中國). The food and clothes of the common lay people are the same as in the Central country (*Zhongguo* 中國). The Law of the Buddha there is most flourishing.

The term Central India (Chinese *zhong Tianzhu*) was premised upon the spatial construction that divided India into five regions, the northern, southern, eastern, western, and middle; the middle being where the Buddha was born. The whole question revolves around the meaning of the Chinese expression *Zhongguo* 中國 which literally means "middle or central country", but which in a Chinese context would automatically be taken to mean "the Middle Kingdom", that is, China. The question is therefore whether the Chinese designation *Zhongguo* here refers to China, or whether it simply means a "central country", in which case it would have to be understood as a literal translation of the Sanskrit *Madhya-deśa* (Pâli *Majjhima-desa*).

In her discussion of this question, Janine Nicol[11] definitely opts for the latter reading and for the following translation:

> Udyāna is truly in North India. All the [people of this place] use the language of Central India. Central India is that which is called the Central State (*Zhongguo* = *Madhyadeśa*). The dress and food and drink of the ordinary people [in Udyāna in North India] are the same as those in the Central State (*Zhongguo* = *Madhyadeśa*).

According to Janine Nicol, "this section has been misinterpreted by some (Sen, Deeg and Felt) to suggest that the people of the *Madhyadeśa* had the same habits as those of China (*Zhongguo*). This can probably be traced back to James Legge's ambiguous translation", which is: "Central India being what we should call the Middle Kingdom. The food and clothes of the common people are the same as in that Central Kingdom."[12]

For instance, David Jonathan Felt writes: "From Faxian's account of India, China first became aware that the Indian subcontinent had a land called Madhyadeśa, meaning 'middle kingdom' (*zhongguo*), the very same name China had used for itself." In a note, he adds:

> Faxian stated in this passage that the dress and food of Madhyadeśa were like that of China (Faxian 法顯, Gaoseng Faxian zhuan 高僧法顯傳 [*Biography of the Eminent Monk Faxian*], T. 2085.858a18–20). Li Daoyuan in the *Shuijing zhu* took this statement and claimed that it was because of this that central India was called the Middle Kingdom

(*Shuijing zhu xiaozheng* 水經注校證, by Li Daoyuan 酈道元, ed. Chen Qiaoyi 陳橋驛 (Beijing: Zhonghua shuju, 2007), 1.4).[13]

Janine Nicol goes on to explain: "Other translators have hedged their bets by using a literal translation without explanation (for example, Beal). Only Abel-Rémusat, and recently Haiyan Hu-von Hinüber[14] treat the second instance of *Zhongguo* in this passage as referring to *Madhyadeśa*. Given the context (the author has just mentioned the language of Udyāna and the habits of the people of *Madhyadeśa* are discussed in a later passage and sound nothing like those of China) I follow Rémusat and Hu-von Hinüber." It may be useful to be reminded of Abel-Rémusat's French translation, the first, as we have seen, in a European language:

> Quand on a passé le fleuve, on est dans le royaume d'Ou tchang [Wuchang]. Ce royaume d'Ou tchang forme précisément la partie septentrionale de l'Inde. On y fait absolument usage de la langue de l'Inde centrale. L'Inde centrale est ce qu'on nomme royaume du Milieu. Les habillements du peuple et sa manière de se nourrir sont aussi semblables à ceux du royaume du Milieu.

In a footnote, Abel-Rémusat makes the following comment:

> Le royaume du Milieu, dans le texte, Tchoung kouë [Zhongguo]. Comme c'est précisément l'expression dont on se sert pour désigner communément la Chine, il faut prendre garde, dans les relations bouddhiques, à ne pas confondre les passages qui se rapportent à la Chine avec ceux qui sont relatifs aux contrées de Matoura [Mathurā], de Magadha, et autres royaumes situés dans l'Inde centrale. Cette confusion ne peut avoir lieu dans le livre de Chy Fâ Hian [Shi Faxian], qui, en parlant de son pays natal, le désigne toujours par les noms de dynasties Han, Thsin [Qin], etc. Sur le mot de royaume du Milieu, voyez le chap. XVI.[15]

In a similar fashion, Jean-Pierre Drège translates *Zhongguo* as "le Royaume du Milieu", but without making any explicit comment: "L'Inde centrale est ce que l'on appelle le Royaume du milieu. Les vêtements des laïcs et la nourriture [et la boisson] sont les mêmes que dans le Royaume du milieu".[16]

The gist of the matter is therefore a highly controversial with a contested notion of centrality. Whereas, by the fourth century CE, *Zhongguo* would unequivocally designate the Chinese idea of its own centrality, be it geographical, political or cosmological,[17] it appears that in Faxian's narrative the expression would be used to translate the Sanskrit term for central Northern India (*Madhyadeśa*), the sphere of operation of the Buddha. Ancient Indian sources seem to offer varying definitions of *Madhyadeśa*. In a "Note on the Middle Country of Ancient India" dated 1904,[18] T.W. Rhys Davids starts by observing that any place in the world tends to consider itself as the centre of the world. Thus,

> the Chinese are often reported habitually to speak of China as "the Middle Country". It is difficult to say whether this last is a designation merely geographical, or whether it also connotes that the people outside are outsiders, barbarians. And I do not know if any Chinese scholar has adequately discussed the history and full bearing of the term. But it is interesting to notice that certain writers in India made use of a similar expression.

Rhys Davids then traces "the oldest use of the phrase in the brahmin books in *Manu* (2.21), which says: "That (country) which (lies) between the Himâlaya and Vindhya mountains, to the east of the Destruction and to the west of Prâyâga, is called the Middle Country (*Madhyadeśa*)."[19]

Three decades later, Bimala Churn Law, the author of a *Historical Geography of Ancient India*,[20] examines the notion of *Madhyadeśa* in Sanskrit Buddhist sources: "As in the Pali texts, so in the Sanskrit Buddhist texts as well, Madhyadeśa is the country that is elaborately noticed. Its towns and cities, parks and gardens, lakes and rivers have been mentioned time and again. Its villages have not also been neglected. It seems, therefore, that the Middle country was exclusively the world in which the early Buddhists confined themselves. It was in an eastern district of the Madhyadeśa that Gotama became the Buddha, and the drama of his whole life was staged on the plains of the Middle country. He travelled independently or with his disciples from city to city, and village to village moving as it were within a circumscribed area. The demand near home was so great and insistent that he had no occasion during his lifetime to stir outside the limits of the Middle country. And as early Buddhism is mainly concerned with his life and the propagation of his teaching, Buddhist literature that speaks of the times, therefore, abounds with geographical information mainly of the Madhyadeśa within the limits of which the first converts to the religion confined themselves. The border countries and kingdoms were undoubtedly known and were often visited by Buddhist monks, but those of the distant south or north or north-west seem to have been known only by names handed down to them by traditions."[21]

It would seem therefore that, in Indian Buddhist sources, *Madhyadeśa* would be tantamount to the country where the Buddha was born, lived and attained *parinirvāṇa*. This "Central country" is often described in highly favourable terms. According to Bimala Churn Law, this is how some prominent places in *Madhyadeśa* (which are still identifiable in present day Bihar) are characterized:

> In the Divyâvadâna (p. 545), Râjagrha [present day Rajgir] is described as a rich, prosperous and populous city at the time of Bimbisâra and Ajâtasatru. [...] It is interesting to note that Râjagrha was an important centre of inland trade where merchants flocked from different quarters (Div. p. 307) to buy and sell their merchandise. At Râjagrha there used to be held a festival known as Giriagrasamâja when thousands of people assembled in hundreds of gardens. Songs were sung, musical instruments were played and theatrical performances were held with great pomp (Mahâvastu, Vol. Ill, p. 57).[22]
>
> Vaisâli was a great city of the Madhyadeśa and is identical with modern Besarh in the Muzaffarpur district of Bihar. The city which resembled the city of the gods was at the time of the Buddha, happy, proud, prosperous and rich with abundant food, charming and delightful, crowded with many and various people, adorned with buildings of various descriptions, storied mansions, buildings and palaces with towers, noble gateways, triumphal arches, covered courtyards, and charming with beds of flowers, in her numerous gardens and groves.[23]
>
> The rich village of Nâlandâ is stated in the Mahâvastu (Vol. III. p. 56) to have been situated at a distance of half a yojana from Râjagrha. Nâlandâ is identified with modern Baragaon, seven miles to the north-west of Rajgir in the district of Patna.[24]

These distinctively laudatory descriptions are corroborated by Faxian's testimony, unless it is to be assumed that he was under the total influence of the rhetoric inherited from the Indian traditions. In the *Foguo ji*, the "Central country" (*Zhongguo*, i.e. *Madhyadeśa*) is repeatedly described as an ideal kingdom (§16):

> 從是以南, 名為中國. 中國寒暑調和, 無霜雪. 人民殷樂, 無戶籍官法, 唯耕王地者乃 輸地利. 欲去便去, 欲住便住. 王治不用刑罔, 有罪者但罰其錢, 隨事輕重, 雖復謀為 惡逆, 不過截右手而已. 王之侍衛、左右皆有供祿. 舉國人民悉不殺生, 不飲酒, 不食 蔥蒜, 唯除旃荼羅. 旃荼羅名為惡人, 與人別居, 若入城市則擊木以自異, 人則識而 避之, 不相唐突. 國中不養豬、雞, 不賣生口, 市無屠、酤及估酒者, 貨易則用貝齒, 唯 旃荼羅, 漁、獵師賣肉耳.[25]

> South from this, it is called the Central country (*Zhongguo*, *Madhyadeśa*). In the Central country, the cold and heat are in harmony, there being neither frost nor snow. The people are numerous and happy. There is neither household registration nor the laws of officials. Only those who plough the lands of the King need hand over part of their profits [in tax]. If one wishes to go, one can go; if one wishes to stay, one can stay. The King governs without having to resort to decapitation. Criminals are only punished with a fine, which will be light or heavy depending on the offence. Even in the case of repeatedly planning wicked rebellion, the offender will only have his right hand cut off, no more. The King's attendants and guards of his entourage all have a salary. Throughout the whole country the people do not kill any living being, nor do they drink alcohol, nor eat onions or garlic. The sole exception is the *caṇḍāla. Caṇḍāla* is the name for bad people, they live apart from others. Whenever they enter a city or a market-place, they strike a piece of wood to mark their difference, people then know and avoid them so as not to come into contact with them. In that country they do not raise pigs nor poultry, and animals are not sold while alive. In the markets there are no butchers or alcohol dealers. In buying and selling they use cowrie shells. Only the *caṇḍāla* fish, hunt and sell meat.

In her discussion of this passage, Janine Nicol quotes from a book by Tian Xiaofei:[26]

> Xiaofei Tian has analysed this "idealised account" of central India. Noting that all trace of hardship and danger disappear once Faxian had reached central India (*Zhongguo*), Tian argues that the journey to central India should be seen as a journey through hell ending in the earthly paradise described above. She argues that, "in many ways, Faxian's portrayal of central India ... serves as a reversed mirror image of the Chinese regimes at the time. Corporal punishment was an important part of punitive law; ... Household registers were another important issue, because registered households were the taxpayers on whom the state relied for income and corvée labour. Many people tried to evade being registered by secretly moving to another place ... the state fought constantly against such practices, and the freedom of going or staying at will, enjoyed by the people of central India was quite unimaginable.

In a jocular way, we could even remark that this contrasting between India and China sounds strangely relevant to our contemporary situation! One should observe, however, that Faxian, in what looks like an uncritical approach to a modern mind, does not even raise an eyebrow on the discrimination of the low caste of the *caṇḍāla*. Quite to the contrary, he describes Pāṭaliputra (present day Patna) as an absolutely ideal kingdom, the depiction of which would even go beyond anything imaginable in the mind of the wisest Confucian sage (§86):

> 凡諸中國, 唯此國城邑為大. 民人富盛, 競行仁義. 年年常以建卯月八日行像. 作四 輪車, 縛竹作五層, 有承櫨、榎戟, 高二疋餘許, 其狀如塔. 以白氎纏上, 然後彩畫, 作 諸天形像. 以金, 銀, 琉璃莊校其上, 懸繒幡蓋. 四邊作龕, 皆有坐佛, 菩薩立侍. 可有 二十車, 車車莊嚴各異. 當此日, 境內道俗皆集, 作倡伎樂, 華香供養. 婆羅門子來請 佛, 佛次第入城, 入城內再宿. 通夜然燈, 伎樂供養. 國國皆爾. 其國長者、居士各於 城中立福德醫藥舍, 凡國中貧窮、孤獨、殘跛、一切病人, 皆詣此舍, 種種供給. 醫師 看病隨宜, 飲食及湯藥皆令得安, 差者自去.
>
> The cities and towns of this kingdom are the greatest of all in the Central country (*Zhongguo*, *Madhyadeśa*). The inhabitants are rich and prosperous, and vie with one another in the practice of benevolence and righteousness [Note that the terms used in Chinese, *ren yi* 仁義, are two of the cardinal Confucian virtues]. Every year on the eighth day of the second month they celebrate a procession of images. They make a four-wheeled car, and on it erect a structure of four storeys by means of bamboos tied together. This is supported by a king-post, with poles and lances slanting from it, and is rather more than twenty cubits high, having the shape of a tope. White and silk-like cloth of hair is wrapped all round it, which is then painted in various colours. They make figures of devas, with gold, silver, and lapis lazuli grandly blended and having silken streamers and canopies hung out over them. On the four sides are niches, with a Buddha seated in each, and a Bodhisattva standing in attendance on him. There may be twenty cars, all grand and imposing, but each one different from the others. On the day mentioned, the monks and laity within the borders all come together; they have singers and skillful musicians; they pay their devotion with flowers and incense. The Brahmans come and invite the Buddhas to enter the city. These do so in order, and remain two nights in it. All through the night they keep lamps burning, have skillful music, and present offerings. This is the practice in all the other kingdoms as well. The Heads of the Vaisya families in them establish in the cities houses for dispensing charity and medicines. All the poor and destitute in the country, orphans, widowers, and childless men, maimed people and cripples, and all who are diseased, go to those houses, and are provided with every kind of help, and doctors

examine their diseases. They get the food and medicines which their cases require, and are made to feel at ease; and when they are better, they go away of themselves.

As was noted by Abel-Rémusat, Faxian seems to consider as a matter of fact that the Chinese designation *Zhongguo* can only refer to *Madhyadeśa*, which is confirmed by the fact that he and his fellow-monks consistently refer to themselves as coming from the "borderlands" (*biandi* 邊地, literally "lands on the margins"), implicitly designating *Madhyadeśa* as the only possible "Central country or kingdom" (*Zhongguo*). And as Abel-Rémusat specified in his footnote, the Chinese monks never use *Zhongguo* to refer to their homeland, but persistently identify themselves as coming from the land of such and such a dynasty, e.g., "the land of Qin" (Qindi 秦地) , "the land of Han" (Handi 漢地), or "the land of Jin" (Jindi 晋地, Jin being the Chinese reigning dynasty at the time of Faxian). See for instance §37:

從此東行三日, 復渡新頭河, 兩岸皆平地. 過河有國, 名毘荼. 佛法興盛, 兼大小乘學. 見秦道人往, 乃大憐愍, 作是言: "如何邊地人, 能知出家為道, 遠求佛法?" 悉供給 所須, 待之如法.

From there [Faxian] walked eastwards for three days, and across the River Sind (Indus). The ground is flat on either side. After crossing the river, there was a country called Pitu. The Law of the Buddha was very flourishing, and both the Mahayana and the Hinayana were studied [by the monks]. When they saw the monks from Qin walking by, they were moved with great pity and compassion, and proferred these words: "How is it that these men from a borderland (*biandi*) could have learned to become monks (literally: to leave their families) and to practice the Way, and travel such a long distance to seek for the Law of the Buddha?" They supplied them with what they needed, and treated them in accordance with the rules of the Law.

In this passage, Faxian and his companions are identified, or identify themselves, as coming from Qin which refers to both the short-lived dynasty which founded the first centralized Chinese empire in 221 BCE, and to the Later Qin dynasty under which Faxian was born. It is worth noting that Qin is probably the origin of the Sanskrit transliteration Cīna which in turn was transliterated as China in a number of European languages. Janine Nicol here comments:[27] "The text records that on more than one occasion Faxian meets with monks who express astonishment: how can men of a borderland have been able to understand about leaving the household to pursue the Buddhist way and come such a great distance in search of the law? 如何邊地人能知出家為道遠求佛法. It is possible to read into their reaction not only surprise that Buddhism had spread to China, and that Chinese Buddhists had made this incredibly arduous journey, but also that Chinese people, being from a borderland and *mleccha*, should have been able to practice Buddhism in the first place. When Faxian and Daozheng arrived at Jetavana, where the Buddha had lived for so long, they keenly felt their borderland status, which was undoubtedly exacerbated by the reaction of the local monks" (§59):

> 法顯、道整初到祇洹精舍, 念昔世尊住此二十五年, 自傷生在邊地, 共諸同志遊歷諸 國, 而或有還者, 或有無常者, 今日乃見佛空處, 愴然心悲. 彼眾僧出, 問顯等言: "汝 從何國來?" 答云: "從漢地來." 彼眾僧歎曰: "奇哉! 邊地之人乃能求法至此!" 自 相謂言: "我等諸師和上相承以來, 未見漢道人來到此也."[28]

> When Faxian and Daozheng first arrived at the Jetavana Vihāra (monastery), they reminisced how in the past the World-honoured one (*shizun* 世尊, i.e. the Buddha) had resided there for twenty-five years. They reproached themselves for being born in a borderland (*biandi*). Along with their like-minded companions, they had travelled through so many countries; some had returned home, and some were no more; and here they were, contemplating the Buddha's place left vacant, and feeling inexpressibly sad at heart. At that moment a crowd of monks came out and asked Faxian and the others,
> 'What country have you come from?' They replied, 'From the land of Han (*Handi*).' The monks exclaimed with a sigh, 'How strange that men of a borderland should come as far as here to seek the Law.' They said to one another: 'In the whole succession of our teachers and fellow-monks, we have never seen any monks from Han coming here'.

The text here specifies that Faxian and Daozheng "reproached themselves for being born in a borderland". As T.H. Barrett explains:

> For, flying in the face of a predominant Chinese cultural chauvinism, these men insisted on accepting Indian rather than Chinese claims to the title of "Central Kingdom". This was no easy transfer of allegiance: as one of Hsüan-tsang's (Xuanzang) contemporaries makes clear in discussing the controversial question (to the true Buddhist) of the peripheral position of Chinese civilization, it entailed an acceptance

> of an implicit spiritual inferiority for all Chinese since personal karmic forces were held to determine not only one's own station in life but also the whole environment in which one found oneself. To have witnessed the Buddha's own preaching in India was a sure sign of past spiritual effort; to live in China a millennium later...was itself an indictment for past failings.[29]

Janine Nicol adds this comment:[30] "It is not just geography that presented a problem, but time itself. Faxian's account repeatedly remarked on the temporal links between the places he visited and the Buddha, recording several times that the various rites being performed or customs followed had been passed down since the time of the Buddha. It is as if Faxian felt that in India, and in particular in *Madhyadeśa*, one could overcome the temporal issue by these links with the time of the Buddha. Not so for those born outside India. Faxian's lament when he reached Vulture Peak (*Gṛdhrakūṭa*) near the ancient city of Rājagṛha (present day Rajgir in Bihar) where the Buddha often gave teachings, is one of the few parts of the record that gives the impression of a personal account." T.H. Barrett reminds us that the hill known as Vulture Peak was so called because "… Ānanda was sitting in meditation when the deva Māra Piśuna, having assumed the form of a large vulture, took his place in the front of the cavern where he was, and frightened the disciple. Then the Buddha, by his mysterious, supernatural power, made a cleft in the rock, introduced his hand, and stroked Ānanda's shoulder, so that his fear immediately passed away. The footprints of the bird and the cleft for the Buddha's hand are still there, and hence comes the name." We read of Faxian preparing for the ascent by purchasing incense, flowers, oil and lamps, and arranging for guides to assist him. After toiling up to this place, made his offerings and lit his lamps, he found little else besides these marks: "The hall where the Buddha preached his dharma has been destroyed, and only the foundations of the brick walls remain. On this hill the peak is beautifully green, and rises grandly up; it is the highest of all the five hills…" He was overcome with sadness; holding back his tears he said "Here the Buddha delivered the Śūraṃgama-sūtra. I, Fa-hsien, was born at a time when I could not meet the Buddha; and now I can only see the footprints which he has left, and the place where he lived, and nothing more."

The "Central country" is so idealized and the despair of being born elsewhere is such that Faxian's fellow pilgrim Daozheng decides not to return to "the land of Han" (*Handi*), that wretched "borderland" (*biandi*), and to remain in India (§113–14):

故法顯住此三年, 學梵書, 梵語, 寫律.
道整既到中國, 見沙門法則, 眾僧威儀, 觸事可觀, 乃追歎秦土邊地, 眾僧戒律殘缺. 誓言: "自今已去至得佛, 願不生邊地." 故遂停不歸. 法顯本心欲令戒律流通漢地, 於是獨還.[31]

[Having found a number of texts on the Discipline in Pāṭaliputra (present-day Patna)], Faxian stayed there for three years, learning Indian writing and language (presumably Brahmi and Sanskrit) and copying the Vinaya.

When Daozheng arrived in the Central country (*Zhongguo*, i.e., *Madhyadeśa*) and saw for himself the rules of the Law of the *śramaṇa* and the dignified demeanour of the monks which he could observe in all circumstances, he deploringly recalled the borderland of Qin, with the lacunary and faulty precepts and discipline (Sanskrit *śīla* and *vinaya*, Chinese *jielü* 戒律) practised by the monks there. He thereupon took the oath: "From this time forth until I reach the state of Buddha, I vow not to be reborn in a borderland." He consequently remained (in India) and never returned (to China). As to Faxian, whose original intention it was to make the precepts and the Discipline widely available in the land of Han, he went back there alone.

We witness here a radical parting of the ways between the two monks from "the land of Han". Daozheng was convinced that central Northern India, the very place where the Buddha had lived, was the only place where one could stand a chance of achieving Buddhahood, or at least of accumulating merit in that respect through successive rebirths. On the other hand, Faxian did not deviate from his initial purpose, the one for which he had set out on that long and perilous journey, namely bring back the authentic texts and rituals of the Vinaya from the land of Buddha to the "borderland' that was China, and thereby provide a chance for awakening and enlightenment to the Chinese who were not lucky enough to be born in the right place.

As was remarked above, the narratives of Faxian and other Chinese pilgrims are usually quite matter-of-fact and down-to-earth, on extremely rare occasions does one encounter gushes of emotion that convey their personal feelings. Nevertheless, however strong and all-enduring Faxian's sense of his mission might have been, he is at least in one instance shown to shed tears out of homesickness. This occurs when he reached Ceylon which he wanted to visit in order to pay homage to the jade statue of Buddha and to the relic of Buddha's tooth. From there, he was to make his way back to China by sea (§120):

> 法顯去漢地積年, 所與交接悉異域人, 山川草木, 舉目無舊, 又同行分披, 或流或亡, 顧影唯己, 心常懷悲. 忽於此玉像邊見商人以晉地一白絹扇供養, 不覺悽然, 淚下滿 目.
>
> Several years had now elapsed since Faxian left the land of Han; the men with whom he had been in contact had all been of regions strange to him; his eyes had not rested on an old and familiar hill or river, plant or tree; his fellow-travellers, moreover, had been separated from him, some by death, and others drifting off in different directions; turning back he could only see his own shadow, and a constant sadness was in his heart. Suddenly (one day), by the side of this jade statue of Buddha, he saw a merchant presenting as his offering a fan of white silk from the land of Jin; and tears of sorrow involuntarily filled his eyes and ran down his face.

In Faxian's narrative as well as in many other texts associated with Chinese Buddhist monks, the repeated references to central India as being the land of the Buddha, and as being consequently the only possible Central Country, pushing China very far on the margins, have led to the celebrated diagnosis by Antonino Forte of a "borderland complex"[32] of which Faxian was by no means the first representative, but by all means a particularly acute case. As recalled by Janine Nicol: "During the latter part of the fourth century increasing numbers of Buddhist texts found their way to China, and Chinese Buddhists began to suspect there was much they did not understand about their religion. Men like Shi Dao'an 釋道安 (312–385), struggling to make sense of this partial picture complicated by the simultaneous arrival of texts from rival Buddhist schools, began to feel that China was not the best place to be for a Buddhist and it is in his writings that the first traces of the Borderland Complex are to be found. In the *Preface to the Sūtra of the Skandha-dhatū-āyatana* (*Yinchiru jing xu* 陰持入經 序), Dao'an laments that he was born at the wrong time and in the wrong place: 世不值佛又 處邊國. (T2145, 45 a11) 'The age has not encountered a Buddha and I dwell in a border country.'" And again in the *Preface to the Sūtra on the Twelve Gates* (*Shi'ermen jing xu*, 十二門經序), Dao'an decries the legacy of his former existences: 安宿不敏、生值佛後又處異國. (T2145, 46 a8–9) "My karmic residue has left me slow-witted, born after a time I could encounter a Buddha and dwelling in a different country." To Dao'an, it is India (*Tianzhu* 天竺) that is central and China, merely a borderland. In his *Preface to the Sūtra of the Stages of the Path* (*Daodi jing xu* 道地經序), in the context of a discussion on the challenges of translating the teachings into Chinese, he provides us with a vivid glimpse into his feelings about being so far from India: 然天竺聖邦，道岨遼遠。幽見硯儒，少來周化。先哲既逝來聖未至。進退狼跋咨嗟涕洟。(T 2145, 69 c15–17) "The road to *Tianzhu* (India), state of sages, is uneven and long, from our remote situation we are aware of the great erudition there, but few come to complete our conversion. The Wise One of old has departed, and the future sage has not yet arrived. [All we can do] is pace back and forth like wild beasts, sighing and weeping."

Dao'an is not alone in lamenting his geographical position. Shi Huiyuan 釋慧遠 (334–416 CE), his pupil, also talks of India as superior. Another of Dao'an's pupils who was particularly affected by his plight is Shi Sengrui 釋僧叡 (c. 352–436), also a leading disciple of the great Indo-Scythian translator and exegete Kumārajīva (Jiumoluoshi 鳩摩羅什 355/60–413), whose arrival in Chang'an in 402 CE marked a turning point in the history of Chinese Buddhism. Sengrui talks of his "border situation" (*bianqing* 邊情), which was offset by the wisdom his foreign master brought to China.

In sum, Faxian's case of the "borderland complex", once placed in its context, appears to represent one particular stage in a long-evolving process which was still to reach a climax with the subsequent "batch" of famous Chinese monks who took the road to India over two hundred years later, and also visited "the Central country" and stayed at Nālanda: Xuanzang 玄奘 (602–664 CE) and Yijing 義淨 (635–713 CE). After a prolonged stay at Nālanda, Xuanzang announced his intention to return to China. The Indian monks there attempted to persuade him to remain, like Daozheng, in India:

> 法師即作還意，莊嚴經像。諸德聞之，咸來勸住，曰：「印度者，佛生之處。大 聖雖遷，遺蹤具在，巡遊禮讚，足豫平生，何為至斯而更捨也？又支那國者，蔑戾車地，輕人賤法，諸佛所以不生，志狹垢深，聖賢由茲弗往，氣寒土嶮，亦焉足念哉！」法師報曰：「法王立教，義尚流通，豈有自得霑心而遺未悟。且彼國衣冠濟濟，法度可遵，君聖臣忠，父慈子孝，貴仁貴義，尚齒尚賢。加以識洞幽微，智與神契。體天作則，七耀無以隱其文；設器分時，六律不能韜其管。故能驅役飛走，感致鬼神，消息陰陽，利安萬物。自遺法東被，咸重大乘，定水澄明，戒香芬馥。發心造行，願與十地齊功，斂掌熏修，以至三身為極。向蒙大聖降靈，親麾法化，耳承妙說，目擊金容，並轡長途，未可知也，豈得稱佛不往，遂可輕哉！」[33]
>
> India (*Yindu*) is the land of Buddha's birth, and though he has left the world, there are still many traces of him. What greater happiness could there be than to visit them in turn, to adore him and chant his

> praises? Why then do you wish to leave, having come so far? Moreover, China (*Zhina guo* 支那國) is a country of *mlecchas*, who despise the religious and the Faith. That is why Buddha was not born there. The mind of the people is narrow, and their coarseness profound, hence neither saints nor sages go there. The climate is cold and the country rugged — you must think again![34]

As noted by Janine Nicol, the word *mleccha*, here used by the Indian monks to talk about China (again deliberately not referred to as *Zhongguo* "the middle country", but as *Zhina guo* "the country of Zhina", a phonetic transliteration of the Sanskrit Cīna which itself, as noted above, is a transliteration of Qin), "frequently translated as 'barbarian', has many connotations and is certainly no synonym for foreigner. In Brahmanical thought *mleccha* was a term encompassing all the 'uncultured' including indigenous non-Aryan tribes and foreigners; those outside of the ritual, religious, social and linguistic community of the Aryans. They were regarded as beneath even the category of *caṇḍālas*[35] (indigenous outcastes, who are part of the karmic system whereas *mlecchas* are not). For Buddhists, '*mleccha* as a term of exclusion also carried within it the possibility of assimilation ...' (Romila Thapar, "The Image of the Barbarian in Early India", *Comparative Studies in Society and History* 13 no. 4 (1971): 157). This was not readily appreciated by the Chinese who felt they were at a severe spiritual disadvantage having been born in China."[36]

Whatever be the case, the use of that particular term applied to China elicited a polite but firm reaction from Xuanzang who had to oppose a rejoinder to the disdainful words used by his Indian fellow-monks, in defense of China's age-old civilization which could not possibly be dismissed as a mere "country of *mlecchas*", even by a staunch Buddhist believer:

> The Master of the Law (i.e. Xuanzang) replied, "Buddha established his doctrine so that it might be diffused to all lands. Who would wish to enjoy it alone, and to forget those who are not yet enlightened? Besides, in my country the magistrates are clothed with dignity, and the laws are everywhere respected. The emperor is virtuous and the subjects loyal, parents are loving and sons obedient, humanity and justice are highly esteemed, and old men and sages are held in honour. Moreover, how deep and mysterious is their knowledge; their wisdom equals that of spirits. They have taken the Heavens as their model, and they know how to calculate the movements of the Seven Luminaries; they have invented all kinds of instruments, fixed the seasons of the

> year, and discovered the hidden properties of the six tones and of music. This is why they have been able to tame or to drive away all wild animals, to subdue the demons and spirits to their will, and to calm the contrary influences of the Yin and the Yang, thus procuring peace and happiness for all beings ... How then can you say that Buddha did not go to my country because of its insignificance ?"[37]

As Antonino Forte remarks, "whether it be true or imaginary, this episode is a perfect expression of the feeling of uneasiness and the state of dilemma which could only be solved by showing that China, too, was a sacred land of Buddhism, that is, by overcoming the 'borderland complex.'"[38] It was a task which China would undertake in the centuries following Xuanzang's quest and which would be tantamount to a massive overhaul of Buddhism from its original land to new "borderlands". David Jonathan Felt aptly concludes: "An effort to recreate China into a sacred Buddhist realm in its own right was not the only consequence of the argument for an Indic-centered model of the world. The long-existing discourse on China's place in the world had been forever altered. A new voice had been added to the conversation, to which all other voices now had to accommodate. Even outside of Buddhist circles, some Chinese began to understand the world not as a Chinese/center and barbarian/periphery construct, but as a polarity of civilization between a Chinese East and an Indian West."[39]

In 1882, Friedrich Maximilian Müller, the renowned Sanskritist of German origin, gave a famous series of lectures at the University of Cambridge entitled "What can India teach us?", and proceeded to show in detail in what way India was at the source of numerous aspects of European languages, cultures, religious beliefs, etc. In that respect, Max Müller's question was raised from a European point of view. Being born and bred in France, but of Chinese ancestry, I would personally raise the question both from a European and a Chinese viewpoint. What I have just expounded was meant to remind us that India had something to teach to China in the early first millennium of the Christian era, but it is my profound and intimate conviction that it still has something to teach to China in our early third millennium. I would here borrow the words of Vikram Seth, an Indian writer who once travelled mostly by road from Nanjing to Delhi, but unlike Faxian and the other Chinese pilgrims, he was on his way *back* to India: "If India and China were amicable towards each other, almost half the world would be at peace. [...] The best that can be hoped for on a national level is a respectful patience on either side [...]. But on a personal level, to learn about another great culture is to enrich one's life, to understand one's own country better, to feel more at home in the world, and indirectly to add to that reservoir of individual goodwill that may, generations from now, temper the cynical use of national power."[40] What words could better convey the mindset of one who, like me and many others, came to Nâlandâ as a pilgrim?

Notes

1. Jean-Pierre Abel-Rémusat, translator, *Foe-koue-ki ou relation des royaumes bouddhiques, voyage dans la Tartarie, dans l'Afghanistan et dans l'Inde, exécuté à la fin du IVe siècle par Chy Fa Hian* (Paris: Imprimerie royale, 1836).
2. Jean-Pierre Drège, translator, *Faxian, Mémoire sur les pays bouddhiques* (Paris: Les Belles Lettres, collection "Bibliothèque chinoise", 2013).
3. For a discussion of the appropriate use of the term "pilgrimage" in the Chinese context, see Timothy H. Barrett, "Exploratory Observations on Some Weeping Pilgrims", in *The Buddhist Studies Forum, vol. I: Seminar Papers 1987–1988*, edited by Tadeusz Skorupski (London: London School of Oriental and African Studies, University of London, 1990), p. 101.
4. Chang'an, which had been the capital of the Former Han dynasty, was the capital of the Later Qin whose king was then Yao Xing (r. 394–416) who had converted to Buddhism.
5. The Buddhist Canon was traditionally composed of three "baskets" (*Tripitaka*, Chinese *san zang*): the *Sūtra*, the *Vinaya* and the *Abhidharma.*
6. *Tianzhu* was then a common designation in Chinese for the Indian subcontinent.
7. The Chinese term *jie* 戒 is for *śīla* which concerns the rules of moral conduct to be practised by lay Buddhists as well as monks.
8. The translations from the original Chinese into English are mine, unless otherwise stated.
9. T2085, 858a19–20. All references in this form refer to the *Taishō Shinshū Daizōkyō* 大正新脩大藏經 edition of Buddhist texts.
10. Wuchang is Udyâna, which, according to James Legge, is just north of modern day Punjab, "the country along the Subhavastu, now called the Swat, noted for its forests, flowers, and fruits."
11. Janine Nicol, "Outsiders: Medieval Chinese Buddhists and the 'Borderland Complex' — An Exploration of the Eight Difficulties", *SOAS Journal of Postgraduate Research* 6 (2014): 27–48.
12. James Legge, translator, *A Record of Buddhistic Kingdoms: Being an Account by the Chinese Monk Fa-Hien of his Travels in India and Ceylon (A.D. 399–414) in Search of the Buddhist Books of Discipline* (1886, reprint, New York: Dover Publications, 1965).
13. David Jonathan Felt, "De-Centering the Middle Kingdom: The Argument for Indian Centrality within Chinese Discourses from the 3rd to the 7th Century",

Beyond Borders: Selected Proceedings of the 2010 Ancient Borderlands International Graduate Student Conference (2010), p. 2.

14. Haiyan Hu-von Hinüber, "Faxian's (法顯 342–423) Perception of India — Some New Interpretations of His *Foguoji* 佛國記", *Annual Report of The International Research Institute for Advanced Buddhology at Soka University for the Academic Year 2010* XI (2011), pp. 223–47.
15. Abel-Rémusat, *Foe-koue-ki ou relation des royaumes bouddhiques*, p. 45 and note 3 on p. 60.
16. Drège, *Faxian, Mémoire sur les pays bouddhiques.*
17. There is a great deal of scholarship on the importance of centrality in Chinese thought. For a useful synthesis, see Mark Edward Lewis, *The Construction of Space in Early China* (New York: State University of New York Press, 2006).
18. T.W. Rhys Davids, "Note on the Middle Country of Ancient India", *Journal of the Royal Asiatic Society of Great Britain and Ireland* (January 1904): 83–93.
19. Ibid., p. 92.
20. *Historical Geography of Ancient India*, Kegan Paul, Trench, Trubner & Co., Ltd., 1932.
21. Bimala Churn Law, "Geographical Data from Sanskrit Buddhist Literature", *Annals of the Bhandarkar Oriental Research Institute* 15, no. 1/2 (1933–34): 1–38 (quotation from p. 7). I am grateful to Dr Samuel Wright for providing me with this reference.
22. Law, "Geographical Data from Sanskrit Buddhist Literature", pp. 11–12.
23. Ibid., p. 13.
24. Ibid., p. 27.
25. T51 No 2085 859 b2–14.
26. Tian Xiaofei, *Visionary Journeys: Travel writings from early medieval and nineteenth-century China* (Cambridge, Mass.: Harvard University Asia Center: Distributed by Harvard University Press, 2011), p. 102.
27. Nicol, "Outsiders: Medieval Chinese Buddhists and the 'Borderland Complex'", p. 32.
28. T. 2085.860c1–8.
29. Barrett, "Exploratory Observations on Some Weeping Pilgrims", pp. 99–100.
30. Nicol, "Outsiders: Medieval Chinese Buddhists and the 'Borderland Complex'", p. 33.
31. T. 2085.864b28–c4.
32. Antonino Forte, "Hui-chih (fl. 676–703 A.D.), A Brahmin Born in China", *Estratto da Annali dell'Instituto Universitario Orientale* 45 (1985).
33. T. 2053.246a12–18.
34. *Da Tang da Ci'en si sanzang fashi zhuan* 大唐大慈恩寺三藏法師傳 (A Biography of the Tripitaka Master of the Great Ci'en Monastery of the Great Tang Dynasty); translation from Joseph Needham, *Science and Civilisation,*

volume 1: Introductory Orientations (Cambridge, UK: Cambridge University Press, 1956), pp. 209–10. Alternate translation in Li Rongxi, *A Biography of the Tripiṭaka Master of the Great Ci'en Monastery of the Great Tang Dynasty* (Berkeley: Numata Center for Buddhist Translation and Research, 1995), pp. 138–39.

35. Mentioned in Faxian's *Foguo ji* (see above).
36. For a detailed study on the concept of *mleccha*, see Aloka Parasher, *Mlecchas in Early India: A Study in Attitudes towards Outsiders up to A.D. 600* (Delhi: Munshiram Manoharlal Publishers Pvt. Ltd., 1991). For more on Indian and Chinese concepts of barbarians, see Richard B. Mather, "Chinese and Indian Perceptions of Each Other between the First and Seventh Centuries", *Journal of the American Oriental Society* 112, no. 1 (Jan–Mar 1992): 1–8.
37. Translation from Joseph Needham (see note 34 above).
38. Forte, "Hui-chih (fl. 676–703 A.D.), A Brahmin Born in China", p. 127.
39. Felt, "De-Centering the Middle Kingdom", p. 11.
40. Vikram Seth, *From Heaven Lake*, 1st ed. (London, Chatto & Windus, reed, 1983; New York, Vintage Departures, 1987), pp. 177–78.

8

THE OBJECT | THE TREE
Emissaries of Buddhist Ground

Padma D. Maitland

The story of the Buddha's enlightenment is one of complete transformation, of the world shaking, and of universal paradigms being broken. It was, in all senses of the word, cataclysmic. The story goes that after practising asceticism for many years, the Buddha ate some rice and milk before discerning a new path to liberation. Looking for a place to realize his new vision, the Buddha set his eyes on a small spot of ground below a *pipal* tree. He prepared his seat by laying a woven mat of grass and vowed never to rise before achieving total enlightenment. The climax of the dawn of enlightenment is when Mara, the God of Illusion, appears before Siddhartha demanding that he support his claim to defeat all delusion. In response, Siddhartha reaches his right hand down, touching the earth as witness to the magnitude of the merit of his acts up to that moment. The earth trembled and Siddhartha became a Buddha, realizing the truth of liberation from the cycle of death and rebirth.

There is something about the composition of ground, tree, and figure that creates a poignant scene for the great conflict of the Buddha's liberation. In many representations, the Buddha is shown serenely seated under a tree as demons attack, beautiful ladies tempt, and Mara provokes. In some depictions, the arching bows of the tree begin to trace a circle around the Buddha, defining an entire microcosm — a vision of reality or an ecosystem — that frames the moment of liberation. Like the transformation of the

Sakya Prince into the Lord Buddha, the ground the Buddha sat upon and the tree he sat beneath were remade. The spot became the *bodhimanda*, or seat of enlightenment, and the tree the Buddha sat beneath became the *bodhi* tree, or tree of enlightenment. While both demand further consideration, this paper will focus on the bodhi tree as a liminal object between the figure of the Buddha and the ground of his enlightenment. It is, in fact, the tree's liminality that has made it an important living symbol of Buddhism. While iconographically rich with a history that extends from early depictions in the third century to countless iterations around the world, *bodhi* trees also occupy a central place in ritual engagements with Buddhism, especially around the making of sacred space[1] and a modern history of Buddhism in India.

Despite the common use of the term, bodhi trees are not technically "bodhi trees". They are a variant of the fig tree known as the *ficus religiosa*, and sometimes known as a *pipal* tree, *bo* tree, or *ashtvatta*. The term "bodhi" — wisdom, knowledge, insight — is not even specific to the type of *pipal* tree that the Buddha Shakyamuni sat under. Instead, the appellation defines a general class of trees associated more broadly with enlightenment itself. While the Buddhist *bo* tree of today is one such bodhi tree, according to Buddhist texts there are several specific bodhi trees, each unique, and each associated with a different Buddha. Related to the four major Buddha's of the past, they are: The *ficus religiosa* of Sakya Muni, the *ficus bengalensis* of Kasyapa, the *ficus glomerata* of Kanaka Muni, the *albizzia lebbek* of Krakuchhanda, and the *shorea robusta* of Vipaswi.[2]

While it is possible to talk of one Bodhi Tree, it is more correct to talk of many bodhi trees. While the bodhi tree that the Buddha Sakya Muni is said to have sat beneath died many years ago, saplings and cuttings of the original — or of its decedents — have been planted in Sri Lanka, Japan, India, Europe, and the United States. The current tree that stands at Bodh Gaya (Figure 8.1) is said to be a cutting of the tree planted in Sri Lanka, which is said to have been a cutting of the original bodhi tree gifted by the Emperor Asoka in the third century BCE.[3] An account of the tree's journey to Sri Lanka is recorded in the *Mahavamsa*, or "Great Chronicle", as part of a history of the spread of Buddhism to Sri Lanka.

Despite the numerous transplantations and roving depictions of bodhi trees over the centuries, bodhi trees have managed to remain incredible indexes of place. Bodhi trees serve as symbols of the *dharma*, of Buddhist teachings and culture. They define a narrative around the spread of

FIGURE 8.1
The bodhi tree at Bodh Gaya.

Source: Photography by Patma D. Maitland, 2017.

Buddhism, emphasizing Bodh Gaya's spot at the centre of an expansive Buddhist cosmology. As bodhi trees take root in each locale, they help represent Buddhism's own process of taking root there.

In modern times, bodhi trees have become important objects in the establishment of new Buddhist centres. After discussing some of the various ways bodhi trees have figured in South Asia, I will transition to a modern history of bodhi trees in India and their use for reimagining the subcontinent as a Buddhist holy land. Rather than considering the tree as part of the tradition itself, I would like to suggest that bodhi trees have come to stand for a particular relationship to place, fostering a sense of Buddhism's changing grounds and traditions.

There is more than an easy confusion between the Buddha and bodhi trees. Overlaid one onto the other, the tree and the body, begin to express the many forms Buddhism can take, evoking both the ancient tradition and its founder, as well as a more material engagement with spaces of Buddhist practice and dissemination. The conflation of the tree with multiple narratives — historical, botanical, religious — and with figure and ground, make it a prime object for considering the ways Buddhism spread around the world and its modern return to India. Just as Buddhism experienced periods of transformation at the hands of new ways of seeing and studying, bodhi trees have been caught up in multiple discourses and modes of figurations related to efforts to conceptualize India as a Buddhist territory. In particular, the continued presence of bodhi trees at Bodh Gaya has been vital to arguments about Buddhism's enduring connection to its original landscape.

Reading the Buddha's figure against the ground may run contrary to common readings of figure-ground relationship, but it situates the tree quite accurately between the two. If we allow for a more expanded reading of these terms, it is even possible to suggest that the "enlightenment" of the *pipal* tree confuses common figure-ground relationships, requiring a new way of analysing Buddhist art and architecture. The application of the term "bodhi" onto the *pipal* tree includes the tree in the Buddha's realization. Alternating between the roles of figure and ground, bodhi trees act as ambassadors of the Buddha and his teachings and the landscapes they traverse.

We might consider bodhi trees as a kind of *cargo*, a foreign object brought into new systems of exchange and value. As Simon Schaffer explains in his essay "Instruments of Cargo in the China Trade", cargo has served as an important instrument of cultural exchange. As he writes, "*Cargo* entered English from Spanish during the period of early modern imperial and commercial expansion, then shifted in the China-Pacific trade to become a name for more potent objects supposed to embody the culture and the economy of which they were components."[4] While Schaffer's article is focused on the introduction of mechanical devices, he ascribes a vibrancy to them that seems pertinent to a discussion of bodhi trees. Bodhi trees express an incredible ability to travel — to be shipped, carried, transplanted, and grafted — while still evoking a sense of place and a connection to a longer history of Buddhism.

I begin this paper by situating bodhi trees within a class of objects that I am calling "Buddhist objects", considering them as "potent objects" within systems of knowledge and exchange vital to the spread of Buddhism.[5] Attempting to discern any differences between how bodhi trees are incorporated into Buddhist accounts and how they appear once they are depicted or sown in new Buddhist lands, I will consider how the bodhi tree appears in the life story of the Buddha and subsequently in the legend of Asoka and in early Buddhist Art. A history of Asoka's legacy in India and the various figurations of bodhi trees leads to a discussion of the spread of Buddhism to Sri Lanka. As narrated by the *Mahavamsa*, the delivery of a bodhi tree to Sri Lanka suggests something about the ways bodhi trees mediate the conversion of territory, marking and defining new Buddhist ground. Jumping forward in time, I will proceed to consider how debates over the bodhi trees at Bodh Gaya informed the colonial curation of the site, and later post-colonial and more modern engagements with the *pipal* tree. Bodhi trees have played an important role in mediating debates over existing sites like Bodh Gaya, while also helping to legitimize new Buddhist sites like the conversion ground of Nagpur, Diksha Bhumi.[6] In their role as ambassadors of Buddhism, bodhi trees speak to both the lingering presence of Buddhism in India —Buddhism's connections to its homeland — and the process of reviving Buddhism in the subcontinent.

Cutting across vast stretches of time and space, various histories and figurations of bodhi trees remain surprisingly constant emblems of Buddhism, suggesting an enduring relationship to India: the delicate foliage of bodhi trees and their rampant branches offer a powerful symbol of Buddhism's spread and growth around the world.[7] Much as each bodhi tree maintains a sense of connection to the very tree the Buddha sat beneath, multiple accounts of different bodhi trees similarly build off of one another to create a much more entangled narrative of Buddhist transmission. It is precisely this point that I wish to emphasize: when planted as part of the creation of new Buddhist landscapes, bodhi trees legitimize each new locality as sacred space, invoking the Buddha and fostering an equivalence between that spot and the ground where the Buddha achieved enlightenment. Through the planting of bodhi trees, sites become linked to much longer histories of Buddhism. They become part of a network of Buddhist sites and cultures, each unique, yet linked by a common invocation of the Buddha as a teacher and Bodh Gaya as his seat of liberation.

BUDDHIST OBJECTS

The history of Buddhist objects from South Asia is a complex one. It cuts across thousands of years in a narrative that links current practices and cultural appreciation with ancient rituals, colonial appropriations, and modern day reappropriations of Buddhism. Premised on the idea that contemporary engagements with Buddhism are a means to connect to a legacy of a Buddhist past, certain material objects negotiate the exchange between the personal and the institutional, the religious and the secular, the past and the present, one place and another place.

The *objecthood* of Buddhist objects relates them to expansive discourses around the study of culture, politics, and religion.[8] These discourses define intellectual and physical terrains within which Buddhist objects act as guiding and interpretive nodes. Buddhist texts describe such systems as a cosmology, an ordering of things and experiences within an organized depiction of the universe. Colonial studies refer to a process of mapping, which leads to the inclusion of objects within an archive as part of larger taxonomies. In post-colonial theories, Buddhist objects are read as points within an expanded network leading to current notions of nationalism or transnationalism.[9] Within such mobility, Buddhist objects invariably appear multifaceted or, when a tree, as having many limbs.

There is a reflexive relationship between Buddhist objects and ritual. Objects and ritual help inform and legitimate each other. Whether it is the small piece of fruit left before a statue in a gallery, elaborate displays at major religious sites, or the consecration of structures through the internment of relics, acts of devotion impress personal and collective notions of religious worth onto objects and into space. They reaffirm religious import through a dialectic process that reifies objects by affirming their potency through a recourse to a specific relationship to a place or person. As Jonathan Smith notes in his work on ritual, the inconsistencies, or lack of "truth", of rituals are less important than the ideals they project: rituals are not so much about how things really are, but rather about how we might want them to be.[10] For objects, it is often the associative value that matters most. Whether it is a presumed relationship to divine bodies — saints, heroes, and gods — or through associations with sites of religious significance, objects often gain greater potency through a presumed connection to people, places, and things. Other objects become "sacred" or "holy" simply through their presence, or their unusual qualities, often resulting in the sanctification of the place where they sit. This is particularly true of bodhi trees and their relationship to place. The small leaves and seeds that pilgrims in Bodh Gaya collect and take home are sacred because they speak to a connection to the seat of the Buddha's enlightenment. They also testify to the experience of pilgrims travelling there, and the ongoing connection of Buddhist communities and religious centres to the site of the Buddha's enlightenment. If, as Smith continues, presence is a fundamental part of things becoming sacred — "The ordinary (which remains, to the observer's eye, wholly ordinary) becomes significant, becomes sacred, simply by being there",[11] — then the reduplication of bodhi trees in other places suggests the ability to make Buddhism feel present in other grounds. In Smith's words, a site can act as a "focusing lens", defining relationships as we would like them to be or as we understand them ideally. Following this metaphor, bodhi trees act as prisms, refracting relationships to rituals and places onto other lands and other people.

Formal and material resemblance can also be enough to evoke a sense of devotion. Consider, for example, the story of the Sandalwood Buddha. The Sandalwood Buddha was created when the Buddha ascended to Tushita Heaven so that there would be a way to worship him while he was away. Imbued with the vivacity of the Buddha himself, the legend of the Sandalwood Buddha spread. Accounts map out various journeys of the Sandalwood Buddha from modern day Afghanistan to China and even Tibet. In her article "From Magadha to Buryatia: The 'Sandalwood Buddha' from the Mongol's perspective", Isabelle Charleux explains how the Sandalwood Buddha acted as a "palladium", the material qualities of which were central to defining and affirming political and religious claims to power. As Charleux writes, "Ming dynasty observers noted some miraculous particularities of the icon, that clearly belongs to the category of 'living image': its color subtly changed with the seasons and with the temperature and hour of the day."[12] Special materials and the unique materiality convey sacrality. Charleux's emphasis on the "living" qualities of the Sandalwood Buddha speaks to the power of materials to evoke a sense of vibrancy essential to an object's role in religious and political economies. In the case of the Sandalwood Buddha, the choice of sandalwood was not accidental. The fragrance of the material was said to mimic the smell of the Buddha, helping to revive a sense of him even in his absence.[13] A history of bodhi trees similarly capitalizes on the materiality and animacy of trees in order to legitimize their use as symbols of Buddhism.

Over time, material properties give way to associative properties. Originals are copied, trees are grafted and transplanted, and yet their significance is allowed to carry over into new objects and copies because of the historical or physical connections they embody. Relics are the best example of this. When the Chinese tooth relic was brought to Burma (present-day Myanmar) in 1994, copies of it were made and also toured along with it. After the original relic was returned to China, the copies that were made were installed in new stupas built for the occasion.[14] While clearly duplicates, the associative power of the original was enough to allow the duplicates to serve as potent objects within their new context. How much greater is a copy that is split from the original, as is the case with bodhi trees, especially given that each cutting and sapling is imbued with the same genetic qualities of the original? The bodhi tree at Anuradhapura, for example, has been used on multiple occasions as the source of new bodhi trees in Bodh Gaya. Each bodhi tree's sanctity is validated or heightened through the ability to claim a direct link back to the original bodhi tree the Buddha sat beneath, and the processes of cutting and nurturing that has enabled such continuity.

Scholars like Tapati Guha-Takurta, Toni Huber, and H.R. Ray have written about the ways in which copies of historical monuments have become part of efforts to evoke a Buddhist past for India.[15] A longer historical view suggests that such copies and reinterpretations are in fact part of an ongoing pattern of recontextualizing and framing Buddhism according to local context. Bodhi trees are a great example of this process. They have been transmitted and depicted in various forms over centuries as part of the maintenance of Buddhist ground. They also speak to the power of bodhi trees as living objects, able to suggest a continuity even in the absence of a vibrant community to tend to them directly. As we will see below, this has been particularly true in modern debates over Bodh Gaya, in which the tree features as an important linchpin in arguments over the continued ritual practice of Buddhism at the site.

The Emperor Asoka is heralded as the great promoter of early Buddhism, creating an expansive empire that spread across much of South Asia. He initiated an extensive building campaign to help unify his empire, constructing hundreds, if not thousands, of new sites and structures. It is no surprise that bodhi trees feature prominently in accounts of his reign and the expansion of his influence. In his translation of the *Asokavadana, The Legend of King Asoka*, John Strong explains that the worship of bodhi trees by Asoka has three parts: worship of the bodhi tree itself, veneration towards the bodhi of the Buddha through worship of the tree, and finally in a more humorous moment, as a point of misunderstanding when Asoka's queen, Tisyaraksita, becomes jealous of Asoka's devotion to the tree, believing "bodhi" to be Asoka's mistress.[16] This last point, with all its sexual allusions, has some precedence in accounts of Asoka's own tree, the Asoka tree, which is said to only bear fruit after being kicked by a young maiden.[17] More pertinent to our discussion here is the constant pairing of Asoka's life story and the trees that frame major events.

Within the life story of Asoka, the body and the tree, as well as the Buddha and the emperor, are constantly conflated, resulting in a reading of the ground as a sacred Buddhist empire and Asoka as its royal and religious monarch. In a particularly telling passage of the *Asokavadana*, while on the way to Bodh Gaya, Asoka encounters a *naga* (a mythic creature in the form of a serpent) on the road. During their encounter, the naga takes on the form of the Buddha, but "before the naga is experienced as the Buddha, he also becomes the king: Asoka sits him on the throne, pays homage to him, and surrounds him with the women of his harem."[18] Nagas are complex figures, featuring prominently in Buddhist text and imagery. They are great snakes that can be understood as earth spirits or mythic animals. Taming them through the projection of an image, first royal, then sacred, suggests a process of controlling the land and the "untamed" wilderness of India. In the *Asokavadana*, this conversion is enacted through a performance of devotion by Asoka towards the figure that has assumed the form of a Buddha. His reverence is thus applied to the ground, his devotion mapped out onto the terrain, uniting his kingdom with a Buddhist cosmology. If we consider the empire as a kind of geo-body,[19] then the act of projecting the king's body onto the body of the Buddha, or vice versa, can be read as a process of mapping, a process which is further sanctioned through the planting and transplanting of trees. In the *Asokavadana*, trees become an index of religious and political power. Comparisons linking the health of trees to the health of a religious or political systems only further emphasize the ability of trees to serve as objects in the dissemination of ideas and policies.

Each tree begins to suggest its own cultural, historical, and environmental ecology. As John Strong writes: "In the *Asokavadana* ... Asoka's pilgrimage goes beyond a simple retracing of the Buddha's career; it is, like the building of the eighty-four thousand stupas, the establishment of a mesocosm where Asoka himself can experience the presence of the Buddha." A mesocosm is when a section or contained amount of a natural environment is brought into a controlled setting.[20] While Strong emphasizes the role of pilgrimage in carrying ideas, environments, and ambiances to new places, objects are similarly able to carry with them a sense of the sacred, serving as the mesocosm of each new sacred site. While relics traditionally sit at the centre of stupas — making them sites where one can experience the presence of the Buddha — bodhi trees have a more affective impact on the landscape itself. Bodhi trees serve as a Buddhist mesocosm, helping to transform their environment into Buddhist ground or sacred space.

If a parallel is suggested between Asoka's empire and a Buddhist empire, there is also a comparison to be made between the geo-body of the emperor and the geo-body of the Buddha, embodied in bodhi trees understood as potent object. This is particularly poignant in moments when bodhi trees serve as ambassadors of both political and religious authority. The story of Buddhism's spread to Sri Lanka provides a wonderful case study in how bodhi trees acts as emissaries in the conversion of land and people. The Buddha foretold of the spread of Buddhism to Sri Lanka, saying that when the time came, the southern branch of the bodhi tree should be taken to Sri Lanka to establish a base for Buddhism there. The alignment of the bodhi tree at Bodh Gaya with the cardinal directions — the southern branch of the tree is sent south, to Sri Lanka — situates Bodh Gaya, and the tree that stands there, at the centre of the Buddhist world. When the cutting of the bodhi tree at Bodh Gaya reached Sri Lanka, it immediately produced a number of major and minor sites. Accounts relate how the branch sprouted a single fruit, which then yielded eight "bodhi" saplings. These were planted around Sri Lanka. The original branch then sprouted four more fruits, each yielding eight more saplings for a total of thirty-two trees with the potential to "transform" thirty-two sites into new Buddhist ground.[21] This is the same pattern of eight and thirty-two that underlies the major and minor marks of the Buddha, as well as the eight major and minor pilgrimage sites of India. These accounts reveal the importance of bodhi trees as symbols and living objects related to the spread of Buddhism. Furthermore, they draw parallels between ground and body, identifying the tree as a mediating object able to act as an ambassador of Buddhism, making the Buddha and the ground of his enlightenment present in each new locale.

According to Christophe Jaffrelot, religion asserts itself over land and people much in the same way that a royal realm does.[22] Both conflate the divine body of the ruler or saint with the landscapes they move through, inhabit, or control. Tracing various systems of state machinery that have come to define India — first the Mughal Empire, and then the British — Jaffrelot looks at how Hindu nationalists in India recently sought to return to the more antiquated notions of a ground as a realm understood both as territory and community: the kingdom as composed of property and persons. Aligning *bhumi* with territory, in his chapter "From Indian Territory to Hindu Bhoomi the Ethnicization of Nation-state mapping in India", Jaffrelot argues that in Indian political traditions, territory and people come together within a more general idea of "a country" (*janapada*) or "realm". However, in modern times, India became the *bhumi* of religious claims to the nation. More than just a geo-political designation, *bhumi* can be read as territory and realm, a sacred landscape sanctified through ritual, potent objects, and religious associations.

The remnants of Asoka's empire have become important markers for defining a modern and historical Buddhist landscape in India.[23] His legacy is evoked in state iconography, linking modern politics with social, religious, and historical conceptions of Buddhism as an Indian religion.[24] The Lion Capital on Indian currency and the presence of the Asokan *chakra* on the national flag are two prominent examples. Bodhi trees are caught up in a similar process of legitimization. However, as living objects, bodhi trees suggest a more sensual relationship to place. They also offer a more nuanced sense of the movement of people and ideas across Asia and within the subcontinent. The planting of bodhi trees across India over the last century has been one more way of making India a Buddhist landscape, a *diksha bhumi*, linking it to conceptions of India's Buddhist past and the continuation of Buddhism abroad.

As an object that stands for Buddhist ground, bodhi trees take on heightened importance within ritual readings of site. In early stupa reliefs, such as those at the Bharhut or Sanchi, a bodhi tree frames an empty platform. In such friezes, the bodhi tree clearly refers back to the site of the Buddha's enlightenment and the Buddha himself, alluding to him in his absence. But, what is the basis for the religious significance of bodhi trees? Many refer to the fact that the Buddha touched the bodhi tree at the moment of liberation, including it in a class of relics known as relics of touch. The prominence of bodhi trees in images, texts, and practices though suggests a more unique status to bodhi trees, one that transcends the sense of a single tree that the Buddha touched. In the *Kalingabodhi-jataka*, Ananda asks the Buddha about the different types of *caityas* — shrine or objects of veneration after the Buddha's passing — and relics that there are in the world.[25] The Buddha responds that there are three types: relics of body, relics of use, and relics of memory. The bodhi tree embodies all three. It is a relic of the body because the Buddha declared that seeing the bodhi tree was like seeing him.[26] It is a relic of use because the Buddha touched it. And, it is a relic of memory because it brings to mind the Buddha's presence and enlightenment, reminding visitors of the moment the Buddha sat under the bodhi tree in Bodh Gaya. To demonstrate this further, consider the following line from the *Kalingabodhi-jataka*: "But the great bodhi [tree] delighted in by the buddhas is indeed a *caitya* that exists while [the buddhas] are alive and after they have passed into *nibbana*."[27] Unlike traditional stupas and *caityas*, which are only constructed after the passing of the Buddha, bodhi trees are unique as objects of devotion because they suggest a living continuity between the moment of the Buddha's enlightenment and the present. It is surprising that the passing of the original bodhi tree has not lessened the value of the tree that stands in Bodh Gaya today. Instead, it seems that the process of cutting and maintaining multiple bodhi trees in multiple localities has allowed them to remain vibrant embodiments of the Buddha's continued presence in the world.

ROOTS OF THE DHARMA

Trees mark key moments in the Buddha Shakyamuni's life story: There is the tree his mother held during childbirth, the pair of *sal* trees that frame the Buddha's *paranirvana* at Kushinagar, the famous *pipal* tree at Bodh Gaya (in modern times there were in fact two), not to mention the banyan tree the Buddha sat beneath for seven days after his great realization, gazing unblinkingly at the bodhi tree that sheltered him. While several different trees continue to perform important roles in marking the holy places of the Buddha, bodhi trees maintain an understandably elevated status among them. More than any other tree, they mark Buddhist ground in India and abroad. Most of the eight major pilgrimage sites of the Buddha's life story prominently feature bodhi trees, often framed by bricked walls, gilt fences, and other forms of ornamentation that call the tree out as an object of reverence.

The bodhi tree at Sarnath, for example, is planted next to the Mulagandhakuti Vihara, a new temple built by the Maha Bodhi Society in the first part of the twentieth century to house a relic of the Buddha. Around the tree is an elevated wall, with Buddha statues set into niches around the base. A few paces out from the tree, another ring is made by a series of large marble slabs supported by concrete bases. In front of the bodhi tree, there is a small pavilion featuring a life size statue of the Buddha turning the wheel of the dharma — giving his first teaching — with a set of monks devoutly folding their hands and listening to the Buddha's sermon. The scene created by this life size diorama, with the bodhi tree at its centre, conflates the spaces of the first sermon and the Buddha's enlightenment. While the two sites are separated by hundreds of miles, the inclusion of a bodhi tree draws a parallel between the Buddha's first teaching and the insight he gained at Bodh Gaya. It also gives the scene a strangely timeless quality. It is easy to imagine the Buddha giving similar talks throughout his life, harboured under similar trees, and to interpret that first teaching as the outpouring of the insights the Buddha gained seated below a bodhi tree at the moment of his liberation.

Bodhi trees are also surprisingly international. Wherever Buddhism has spread, bodhi trees have become popular motifs in art and literature. In the last two hundred years, as Buddhism has returned to India, the foreign conceptions of Buddhism fostered over centuries abroad have also returned. Bodhi trees have featured prominently as part of this renaissance. In his work *The Holy Land Reborn*, Toni Huber presents a history of the shifting terrain of major and minor Buddhist sites in India. His poignant analysis argues for a connection between culture and doctrine in defining sacred landscapes. The main thrust of Huber's work is the ways in which Tibetan's imagined India as a Buddhist land from afar. Their distant appraisals often resulted in multiple misconceptions about the subcontinent that then came to be manifested through the construction of new sites and new terrains for pilgrimage and acts of devotion. Only in the twentieth century, when Tibetans began to return to India in greater numbers, were the previous conceptions of India that had been held in Tibet brought into contact with the living condition of Buddhism in India. With the Tibetan diaspora at the end of the 1950s, Buddhist pilgrimage sites in India saw an even further surge of development as they were reimagined as sites of a shared and common history; the basis for a holy land in exile. This provided a moment to reassess long held perceptions of Buddhism in India and to help build new visions of what India's Buddhist landscape could or should be. The bodhi tree emerges in Huber's account as a powerful symbol of continuity, and related to that, a budding icon of Buddhism's global presence.

Huber's work cleverly shows how it is not only the act of seeing a bodhi tree, but specific ways of seeing such trees, that are important. As he highlights in his study, accounts often build on and reproduce understandings of bodhi trees and Buddhism over centuries. Because most Tibetans were unable to travel to India, they relied on written accounts to furnish their imagination. For example, the Tibetan scholar Ra Lotsawa relied on the account of Xuanzang from five hundred years prior rather than any first-hand evidence for his own discussion of India. As Huber writes: "This particular examples is enough to point out here the remarkably artificial and concocted or even falsified nature of early Tibetan *namthar* (hagiographic) accounts of India as a holy land of Buddhism."[28] The same account by Xuanzang, which was repeated by Ra Lotsawa, also informed the expeditions of colonial surveyors like Alexander Cunningham. When Anagarika Dharmapala, the great Sinhalese Buddhist reformer came to India and began his fight for control of the Mahabodhi Temple, Xuanzang's account again, this time his focus on ritual around the bodhi tree at Bodh Gaya, was referenced as part of debates over the control and use of Bodh Gaya by different religious communities.

Modern debates over the use of Bodh Gaya by Hindus and Buddhists have focused on two things: the Buddha statue in the centre of the shrine room, and the bodhi trees at the site.[29] Some accounts refer to Hindu pilgrims giving offerings to the bodhi tree there, suggesting ongoing use of the site by Hindus for religious purposes. Others, such as Xuanzang's report, offer conflicting evidence, suggesting that in the past the bodhi tree at Bodh Gaya had actually been "anathema to Hindus, the emperor Sasanka having dug it up and burned it around 600 CE".[30] It was only in the sixth century, he suggests, that a bodhi tree became incorporated into Hindu rituals at Bodh Gaya.[31] As Steven Kemper writes in his account of Bodh Gaya and the life of Anagarika Dharmapala:

> Whatever their attitudes toward the temple in earlier days, at the time of Dharmapala's intervention Hindus were not reluctant to come near the temple to offer pindas at the bodhi tree. Colonial officials made a distinction between the mahant's conducting worship in the Maha Bodhi temple and his right to the offerings pilgrims left there — whether he conducted worship or not. It is possible to dismiss arguments about who worshipped where as "derisive comments of orientalist experts" and thus more of an essentializing effect than a reliable picture of what went on at Maha Bodhi temple. But there is an easier reading that avoids the interpretive questions: the temple itself was on the margins of the practices that counted at Bodh Gaya during most of the nineteenth century (and perhaps earlier) and became central only when Dharmapala made it so. Before that, whether the image in the temple stood for the Buddha, the ninth avatar of Visnu or Siva in heroic form, was not of much consequence. Hindu pilgrims assumed the image was powerful and auspicious. They had their eyes

> fixed on the bodhi tree where they made offerings to their ancestors. Not all pilgrims visited Bodh Gaya or all forty-five vedis, but those who had wealth and took orthodoxy seriously tried to visit them all. At Bodh Gaya what was important was the tree, not the temple. For the mahant the tree was important for the "substantial income from the offerings made by Hindu pilgrims at the sacred pipal-tree.[32]

Regardless of its history, by the nineteenth century, the bodhi tree of Bodh Gaya had become an important object in debates over ritual, rights, and space. Legal battles over Bodh Gaya continued for years until finally the Mahabodhi Temple was entrusted to a committee of both Hindu and Buddhist representatives. Bodhi trees were at the centre of such debates, providing a pivot for historical, religious, and social discourses. As part of historical accounts, bodhi trees offered one way to assess continuity, while evidence of ritual observances around them offered another. Today, a bodhi tree stands on the west side of the Mahabodhi Temple, a clear focus of devotion and contemplation by pilgrims from around the world.

TREES, TREES, AND MORE TREES

Studies that specify and identify bodhi trees and their botanical equivalent assume an easy parallel between religious text, art, and nature.[33] The stone reliefs of the Bharhut stupa are most commonly used as corroborative evidence for the identification of trees associated with the Buddhas of the past. For example, Kasyapa Muni's bodhi tree has been identified as a *ficus bengalensis* by comparing artistic representations of it against living specimens.[34] In *Bodhi Tree Worship in Theravada*, Yohei Shimizu uses descriptive accounts and historical word of mouth to identify bodhi trees in their natural environment today. Going beyond normative descriptions of four trees and four Buddhas, Shimizu even describes a grove of twenty-eight different kinds of "bodhi" trees, all planted in a single grove in Myanmar, each one distinct from the other and each associated with a different Buddha.

Rather than affirm or deny any legitimacy to these studies, what I hope to highlight is how they engage botanical, religious, and historical studies of Buddhism. The "scientific" name of bodhi trees, for example, as *ficus religiosa* attests to the connection between the botanical system of naming plants and cultural observation of the trees' religious status. Can such associations allow us to study bodhi trees within botanical and art historical classifications? Colonial texts provide a wealth of material through which to consider this point. As a case study, James Fergusson begins his text *Tree and Serpent Worship or Illustrations of Mythology and Art in India* with a survey of the ancient worship of trees around the world. Dividing the text into the "Western World" and "Eastern Asia," Fergusson offers a quick account of the similarities and differences between these cultures as a way to "explain" or introduce European artists to the art and culture of India. As Fergusson writes:

> Where we miss the point of contact with our own religious notion, is when we ask how anyone could hope that a prayer addressed to a Tree was likely to be responded to, or how an offering presented to such an object could be appreciated. Originally it may have been that a divinity was supposed to reside among the branches, and it was to this spirit that the prayer was first addressed; but anyone who has watched the progress of idolatry must have observed how rapidly minds, at a certain state of enlightenment, weary of the unseen, and how willingly they transfer their worship to any tangible or visible object. An image, a temple, a stone or a tree may thus become an object of adoration or of pilgrimage, and when sanctified by time the indolence of the human mind too gladly contents itself with any idol which previous generations have been content to venerate. It is so much easier than to strive actively to realize an invisible ideal which even the highest intellects too often fail to reach.[35]

While we should be wary of drawing parallels between the Buddha's enlightenment and Europe's Enlightenment, the ready comparison is in fact a by-product of how Buddhism entered into academic discourses in the nineteenth century. The tree's status in this process is a compelling point for further research. In his insightful article "Trading Knowledge: The East India Company's Elephants in India and Britain", Sujit Sivasundaram discusses how objects facilitated colonial encounters across cultures, leading to new forms of knowledge. He takes as his case study the elephant, which was the focus of intense cultural, religious, scientific and popular interest in the eighteenth and nineteenth century. The elephant is in fact analogous to the bodhi tree in terms of its status in colonial and precolonial studies of India, not to mention the highly prominent role of both bodhi trees and elephants in early Buddhist art. As important cultural symbols, they feature in religious, political, and historical narratives, offering multiple points for inquiry and discovery. The point that Sivasundaram makes is that all of these different avenues for figuring an object — elephant, tree, or otherwise — lead to novel understandings of objects and their role in global systems of exchange and knowledge production. As a case study, Sivasundaram focuses on the famous shooting of the elephant Cluny in the early part of the nineteenth century. Causing a stir in London's popular culture, the event also involved surgeons who were brought in to consult on how best to kill the elephant.[36] The coming together of so many perspectives around a single event and object resulted in multiple misunderstandings around the elephant, as well as a heightened imagination around the animal as a cultural object. It is possible to read bodhi trees as being similarly caught up in multiple, cross-cultural exchanges, providing a point of entry through which to consider alternative approaches to religion, culture, and science.

Not isolated to colonial surveyors, pilgrims from around the world have come to Bodh Gaya, seen the bodhi tree there, and carried back with them pictures, drawings, leaves, and other tokens as souvenirs of their journey. These objects speak to a direct connection to the place, realized through travel, heightening the sanctity of the material objects they bring with them. These material things further inspire alternative visions of India and the site of the Buddha's enlightenment. John Guy picks up this theme in his article "The Mahabodhi Temple: Pilgrim souvenirs of Buddhist India". In it, Guy explains the important role small models of the Mahabodhi Temple at Bodh Gaya had in disseminating perceptions of Buddhism across Asia. Later, when the Mahabodhi Temple was restored by colonial surveyors, these same tokens guided the sites restoration.[37]

While visitors today might imagine that the Mahabodhi Temple has always looked as it does now, it has in fact evolved and changed over time. At first, it was likely just a bodhi tree surrounded by some columns with a stone slab representing the Buddha's seat beneath it.[38] Later a temple was constructed to mark the site, but this too morphed and evolved over time, often to accommodate the growing bodhi tree next to it, or to make room for a new one. A striking image by Charles D'Oyly from 1824, featured in Guy's article, illustrates this point. The focus of the image is a bodhi tree elevated almost half way up the Mahabodhi Temple, surrounded by a plinth of concentric rings. D'Oyly's painting offers a very different image of the site than as it exists today. The raised plinth that supported the tree is gone, as is the structure around the base of the Mahabodhi Temple. The tree from D'Oyly's image is also not the tree that presently stands at Bodh Gaya. According to the accounts of Alexander Cunningham in his survey of Bodh Gaya, the tree died over the course of several years.[39] It was eventually replaced with a cutting from the bodhi tree in Sri Lanka.

The excavation of the bodhi tree and seat of enlightenment at Bodh Gaya went hand in hand. Such excavations stimulated new and alternative histories of the site, remaking its physical form in the process. It is hard to say how much the peculiar aspects of Cunningham or other colonial officers altered the development of Bodh Gaya. What is clear though is that the site of the Buddha's enlightenment, as it stands now, is not the product of a single vision. Rather, it is a product of multiple perceptions of what Bodh Gaya is or should be. At the centre of all of these visions, its branches broad over the ground below, is the bodhi tree, a vibrant and enduring Buddhist object.

CONCLUSION

Today the seat of enlightenment is marked by the Mahabodhi Temple, in the town of Bodh Gaya in the northeast state of India known as Bihar. In 2002 Bodh Gaya was declared a UNESCO World Heritage site. Classified as a "living heritage site", the prime directive of Bodh Gaya's preservation is predicated upon attempts to facilitate rather than dampen acts of devotion.[40] An object that clearly embodies the sense of a "living history" at Bodh Gaya is the bodhi tree. Towering above a stone plinth said to mark the spot where the Buddha sat over two thousand years ago, the tree is not the original, but a relative of the one that stood there many years before. A cutting of the original was taken to Sri Lanka where it matured into an old and large tree. When the tree at Bodh Gaya died, a cutting from the Sri Lankan tree was taken back to Bodh Gaya. This process has happened several times, perpetuating a metaphoric and literal process of decay and renewal that mirrors the history of Buddhism itself through the preservation of successive generations of the historic *ficus religiosa*.

This paper is an attempt to consider what the transformation of the *pipal* tree into the bodhi tree meant for the making of Buddhist ground. Reading figure, ground, and tree comparatively as a system that informs basic principles of Buddhist history and practice, it traces an expanded ecology of place centred on the bodhi tree at Bodh Gaya. Beyond the natural systems of a given local, ecologies of place implicate the movement of people and things in order to define a cultural field around a site or object. The movement of bodhi trees has played a crucial role in the preservation of Bodh Gaya and in perpetuating conceptions of India as a Buddhist holy land. They have acted as ambassadors, helping to instill Buddhist ideals and a sense of community, *sangha*, abroad. More recently, bodhi trees have been used to revive notions of Buddhist ground and sangha in India, redefining cultural and ecological landscapes in South Asia.

When Ananda Coomaraswamy begins his work "The Nature of Buddhist Art" with a call to "reconstruct the environment", it is a twofold proposition: We must reconstruct the environment from which a specific work of art emerges, but we must also adjust ourselves to it, taking into account the new contexts in which we view a piece of work from another time or a distant place.[41] The environment here is both literal and figurative. Each artwork is a kind of mesocosm, an ambassador of the time and place it came from. The "adjustment" Coomaraswamy demands of viewers is that we attempt to imagine the place and time of each object. This "reconstruction" is a basic principle of ritual, but also the appreciation of art and culture. It points to the power of ritual and religious objects to help facilitate the imagination around sacred spaces, and to our ability to trace differences and similarities between one place and another, one culture and another, the past and the present. Today we can find ample reproductions of bodhi trees. Their leaves feature on new and old publications, artwork, and as a prominent symbol of Buddhism around the world. We can also choose to travel to Bodh Gaya, and sit beneath the tree that is there now, imagining our own connection to that spot, to the Buddha who sat there, and the incredible history of Buddhism as it travelled from that place. For a moment, we might enjoy a sense of continuity evoked through the presence of the tree, planted above the *vajrasana*. It is possible that, many years ago, the leaves of a bodhi tree shimmered in the sunlight just as they do now.

Notes

1. For more on the use of bodhi trees in Buddhist rituals around the consecration of space, see: A.G.S. Kariyawasam, *Buddhist ceremonies and rituals of Sri Lanka* (Kandy, Sri Lanka: Buddhist Publication Society, 1995); Petra Kieffer-Pülz, "Rules for the sīmā Regulation in the Vinaya and its Commentaries and their Application in Thailand", *Journal of the International Association of Buddhist Studies* 20, no. 2 (1997): 141–53.
2. For a more detailed discussion of each, see M.S. Randhawa, *The Cult of Trees and Tree Worship in Buddhist–Hindu Scripture* (New Delhi: All-India Arts and Crafts Society, 1964).
3. <http://srimahabodhi.org/> (accessed 22 January 2017). The website opens with a quote from H.G. Wells: "In Sri Lanka, there grows to this day, a tree, the oldest historical tree in the world which we know certainly to have been planted as a cutting from the Bodhi tree in the year 245 B.C."

4. Simon Schaffer, "Instruments and Cargo in the China Trade", *History of Science* 44 (2006): 218.
5. "Potent objects" is beginning to gain more currency as a term. We see it in Schaffer's study, but also in Peter H. Welsh's "Repatriation and Cultural Preservation: Potent Objects, Potent Pasts", *University of Michigan Journal of Law Reform* 25 (1992): 837.
6. Dr. B.R. Ambedkar lead a mass conversion to Buddhism in Nagpur in 1956. The site is today known as Diksha Bhumi, or conversion ground.
7. For example, Susan L. Huntington and John C. Huntington. *Leaves from the Bodhi Tree: The Art of Pāla India (8th–12th Centuries) and Its International Legacy* (Dayton, Ohio: Dayton Art Institute in association with the University of Washington Press, 1990); Harsha V. Dehejia, *Leaves of a Pipal Tree: Aesthetic Reflections on Some Hindu Myths and Symbols* (Motilal Banarasidass Publishers, 2005).
8. For more on materiality, see Daniel Miller, *Materiality* (Durham: Duke University Press, 2005).
9. Tapati Guha-Thakurta, *Monuments, Objects, Histories: Institutions of Art in Colonial and Post-colonial India* (Columbia University Press, 2004).
10. Jonathan Z. Smith, *Map Is Not Territory: Studies in the History of Religions* (Leiden: Brill, 1978).
11. Jonathan Z. Smith, "The Bare Facts of Ritual", *History of Religions* 20, no. 1/2 (1 August 1980): 115.
12. Isabelle Charleux, "From Magadha to Buryatia: The 'Sandalwood Buddha' from the Mongol's perspective", paper given at the Fourth International Conference on Tibetan Archaeology and Arts. Beijing, 17–20 October 2009.
13. Benjamin Rowland, "A Note on the Invention of the Buddha Image", *Harvard Journal of Asiatic Studies* 11, no. ½ (1948): 181–86.
14. For a longer discussion of the Chinese tooth relics tour of Myanmar, see: Juliane Schober, "Buddhist just rule and Burmese national culture: state patronage of the Chinese Tooth Relic in Myanmar", *History of Religions* 36, no. 3 (1997): 218–43.
15. Tapati Guha-Thakurta, "The Production and Reproduction of a Monument: The Many Lives of the Sanchi Stupa", *South Asian Studies* 29, no. 1 (2013): 77–109; Toni Huber, *The Holy Land Reborn: Pilgrimage and the Tibetan Reinvention of Buddhist India* (Chicago: University of Chicago Press, 2008); Himanshu Prabha Ray, *The Return of the Buddha: Ancient Symbols for a New Nation* (Routledge, 2014).
16. J.S. Strong, *The Legend of King Asoka* (Princeton: Princeton University Press, 1983).
17. Ibid.
18. Ibid., p. 123.
19. To use the term of Sumathi Ramaswamy. For a discussion of the formation

of the geo-body in colonial and postcolonial India, see his text: Sumathi Ramaswamy, "Visualising India's Geo-Body Globes, Maps, Bodyscapes", *Contributions to Indian Sociology* 36, no. 1–2 (1 February 2002): 151–89.

20. *Oxford English Dictionary*, online.
21. There are many accounts of the travel of the Bodhi Tree's branch journey to Sri Lanka. The most famous is the *Mahavamsa*, which continues to be a defining text for practice in Sri Lanka. For a more general recounting of the myths and rituals around the Bodhi Tree in Sri Lanka see K.M.I. Swarnasinghe's *Worlds' Oldest Historical Sacred Bodhi Tree at Anuradhapura* (Chaga Publications, 2005).
22. Christophe Jaffrelot, "From Indian Territory to Hindu Bhoomi: The Ethnicization of Nation-State Mapping in India", in *The Politics of Cultural Mobilization in India*, edited by John Zavos, Andrew Wyatt and Vernon Hewitt (Oxford and New York: Oxford University Press, 2004), pp. 197–215.
23. Himanshu Prabha Ray, *The Return of the Buddha.*
24. Ananda Kentish Coomaraswamy, *Hinduism and Buddhism* (Golden Elixir Press, 2011).
25. Yuvraj Krishan, *The Buddha Image: Its Origin and Revelopment* (Bharatiya Vidya Bhavan, 1996), 14.
26. There are several *sutra* passages in which the Buddha says venerating the tree is the same as venerating him. This includes the tree as part of a category of "sacred objects" imbued with special properties because they have been identified to be "like" the saint or holy person. Known affectionately as "like me" objects, these mostly include statues that the subject happens to see and exclaim, "That looks like me."
27. Translation and account of the *Kalingabodhi-jataka* from Yohei Shimizu, Nagoya Daigaku and Indogaku Bukkyōgaku Kenkyūkai, *Bodhi Tree Worship in Theravāda Buddhism* (Nagoya: Nagoya University Association of Indian and Buddhist Studies, 2010).
28. Toni Huber, *The Holy Land Reborn: Pilgrimage & the Tibetan Reinvention of Buddhist India* (Chicago: University of Chicago Press, 2008), p. 66.
29. Steven Kemper, *Rescued from the Nation: Anagarika Dharmapala and the Buddhist World* (Chicago: University of Chicago Press, 2016), pp. 246–47.
30. Ibid., p. 247.
31. Ibid.
32. Ibid., p. 250.
33. Shimizu, Daigaku and Kenkyūkai. *Bodhi Tree Worship in Theravāda Buddhism.*
34. Ibid., p. 27.
35. James Fergusson, *Tree and Serpent Worship: Or, Illustrations of Mythology and Art in India in the First and Fourth Centuries after Christ, from the Sculptures of the Buddhist Topes at Sanchi and Amravati.* Delhi: Oriental Publishers, 1971 (1st published 1873), p. 2.

36. For more on this, see Sujit Sivasundaram's article "Trading Knowledge: The East India Company's Elephants in India and Britain", *The Historical Journal* 48, no. 1 (2005): 27–63.
37. John Guy, "The Mahābodhi Temple: Pilgrim Souvenirs of Buddhist India", *The Burlington Magazine* 133, no. 1059 (1 June 1991): 356–67.
38. Albertina Nugteren, "Rituals around the bodhi-tree in Bodhgaya, India", in *Pluralism and Identity: Studies in Ritual Behavior*, edited by J. Platvoet and K. van der Toorn (Leiden: EJ Brill, 1995), pp. 145–65; Lahiri Nayanjot, "Bodh-Gaya: An Ancient Buddhist Shrine and its Modern History (1891–1904)", in *Case Studies in Archaeology and World Religion* (Oxford: Archaeopress, 1999), pp. 33–41.
39. Sir Alexander Cunningham, *Mahâbodhi or the Great Buddhist Temple under the Bodhi Tree at Buddha-Gaya* (London: W.H. Allen & Co, 1892), p. 31.
40. "While management of a World Heritage property normally calls for the highest possible protection at national level, in the present case the ASI feels strongly that national designation involving 'monument protection' would be counterproductive, given the importance of the property as living religious heritage." World Heritage Centre: UNESCO, Mahabodhi Temple Complex at Bodh Gaya (India) (C 1056rev).
41. Ananda Kentish Coomaraswamy, *The Origin of The Buddha Image & Elements of Buddhist Iconography* (Louisville: Fons Vitae, 2006; 1st published 1938), p. 3.

Bibliography

Cunningham, Alexander. *Mahâbodhi or the Great Buddhist Temple under the Bodhi Tree at Buddha-Gaya.* London: WH Allen & Co, 1892.

Coomaraswamy, Ananda K. *The Transformation of Nature in Art.* New York: Dover, 1956.

———. *The Origin of The Buddha Image and Elements of Buddhist Iconography.* Louisville: Fons Vitae, 2006.

Dhar, Parul Pandya and National Museum Institute. *Cultural Interface of India with Asia: Religion, Art and Architecture.* D.K. Printworld & National Museum Institute, 2004.

Dharmapala, Anagarika, Lakshman Jayawardane and Maha Bodhi Society of Sri Lanka. *"From a Tiny Seed to a Healthy Tree": The Story of Mahabodhi: Reminiscences of Anagarika Dharmapala.* Colombo: Mahabodhi Society of Sri Lanka, 2001.

Fergusson, James. *Tree and Serpent Worship: Or, Illustrations of Mythology and Art in India in the First and Fourth Centuries after Christ, from the Sculptures of the Buddhist Topes at Sanchi and Amravati.* Delhi: Oriental Publishers, 1971 (1st published 1873).

Geary, David, Matthew R. Sayers and Abhishek Singh Amar. *Cross-Disciplinary*

Perspectives on a Contested Buddhist Site: Bodh Gaya Jataka. Routledge, 2012.

Griswold, Alexander B. *The Holy Land Transported: Replicas of the Mahābodhi Shrine in Siam and Elsewhere*. Colombo: M.D. Gunasena, 1965.

Guy, John. "The Mahābodhi Temple: Pilgrim Souvenirs of Buddhist India". *The Burlington Magazine* 133, no. 1059 (1 June 1991): 356–67.

Huber, Toni. *The Holy Land Reborn: Pilgrimage and the Tibetan Reinvention of Buddhist India*. Chicago: University of Chicago Press, 2008.

Huntington, Susan L. and John C. Huntington. *Leaves from the Bodhi Tree: The Art of Pāla India (8th–12th Centuries) and Its International Legacy*. Dayton, Ohio: Dayton Art Institute in association with the University of Washington Press, 1990.

Irwin, John. "The 'Tree-of-Life' in Indian Sculpture". *South Asian Studies* 6, no. 1 (1990): 27–37.

Irwin, John C. "The Sacred Anthill and the Cult of the Primordial Mound". *History of Religions* 21, no. 4 (1 May 1982): 339–60.

Kemper, Steven. *Rescued from the Nation: Anagarika Dharmapala and the Buddhist World.* Chicago: University of Chicago Press, 2016.

Krishan, Yuvraj. *The Buddha Image: Its Origin and Revelopment*. Delhi: Bharatiya Vidya Bhavan, 1996.

Leoshko, Janice. *Sacred Traces: British Exploration of Buddhism in South Asia*. Aldershot, Hants, England; Burlington, VT: Ashgate Publisher, 2003.

Miller, Daniel. *Materiality*. Durham: Duke University Press, 2005.

Nugteren, A. "Rituals around the Bodhi-Tree in Bodhgaya, India". *Studies in the History of Religions* 67 (1995): 145.

Platvoet, Jan G. and Karel Van Der Toorn. *Pluralism and Identity: Studies in Ritual Behaviour*. Leiden: Brill, 1995.

Ray, Himanshu Prabha. *Sacred Landscapes in Asia: Shared Traditions, Multiple Histories*. New Delhi: Manohar Publishers & Distributors, 2007.

———. *The Return of the Buddha: Ancient Symbols for a New Nation*. Routledge, 2014.

Schaffer, Simon. "Instruments and Cargo in the China Trade". *History of Science* 44 (2006): 217.

Schober, Juliane. "Buddhist Just Rule and Burmese National Culture: State Patronage of the Chinese Tooth Relic in Myanmar". *History of Religions* 36, no. 3 (1997): 218–43.

Shimizu, Yohei, Nagoya Daigaku and Indogaku Bukkyōgaku Kenkyūkai. *Bodhi Tree Worship in Theravāda Buddhism*. Nagoya: Nagoya University Association of Indian and Buddhist Studies, 2010.

Sivasundaram, Sujit. "Trading Knowledge: The East India Company's Elephants in India and Britain". *The Historical Journal* 48, no. 1 (2005): 27–63.

Smith, Jonathan Z. "The Bare Facts of Ritual". *History of Religions* 20, nos. 1/2 (1 August 1980): 112–27.

Strong, John. *The Legend of King Aśoka: A Study and Translation of the Aśokāvadāna*. Princeton Library of Asian Translations. Princeton, N.J: Princeton University Press, 1983.

Swarnasinghe, K.M.I. *Worlds' Oldest Historical Sacred Bodhi Tree at Anuradhapura*. Chaga Publications, 2005.

Tapati Guha-Thakurta. "The Production and Reproduction of a Monument: The Many Lives of the Sanchi Stupa". *South Asian Studies* 29, no. 1 (2013): 77–109.

Vatsyayan, Kapila. *Concepts of Space: Ancient and Modern*. New Delhi: Abhinav Publications, 1991.

W. Cole (William Owen). *The Buddha and the Bodhi Tree/Retold by Owen Cole and Judith Lowndes; Illustrated by Tony Morris*. Oxford: Heinemann Educational, 1995.

Welsh, Peter H. "Repatriation and Cultural Preservation: Potent Objects, Potent Pasts". *University of Michigan Journal of Law Reform* 25 (1991): 837.

9

TRACING TRANSREGIONAL NETWORKS AND CONNECTIONS ACROSS THE INDIC MANUSCRIPT CULTURES OF NUSANTARA (AD 1400–1600)

Andrea Acri

It is truly not easy to write a "well integrated" history of Southeast Asia.... The main difficulty is in fact to transcend the heaviness of regional, colonial and then nationalistic histories which have strongly partitioned off the historical space. (Lombard 1995, p. 10)

1. INTRODUCTION

Disparate areas of Nusantara experienced a religious and socio-political "paradigm shift" during the period of AD 1400–1600, which here I call "early modern" for the sake of convenience.[1] The Indic-influenced polities of Java and Sumatra, where Hinduism and Buddhism had been prevalent for nearly a thousand years, began to succumb to the advance of Islam and the Islamicate social paradigm. Yet, in spite of — or perhaps thanks to — political instabilities, the disruption (or reconfiguration) of patterns of international trade and diplomacy, and the emergence of new literary genres, religio-ritual paradigms, and social orders, those regions appear to have maintained a vigorous activity of preservation, transformation, and circulation of knowledge based on Indic paradigms.

Victor Lieberman (2009, p. 10) describes a process of cultural integration in Southeast Asia from the fifteenth century onwards, an example of which is what he calls the "demoticisation" of "textually based Indic religions [that] once had been the more or less exclusive preserve of capital-based elites". (Lieberman here refers to western and central mainland Southeast Asia, and does not look further into the insular region.) Following this lead, in this paper I explore the "parallelisms" that seem to have existed across the mosaic of literary and manuscript cultures of Western Nusantara — i.e., Sumatra, Java, and Bali — in the early modern period. Those locales witnessed the flourishing of vernacular text-manuscript cultures that shared religious ideas, literary conventions, and text-building practices stemming from the heyday of the Sanskrit Cosmopolis and the ensuing Vernacular Millennium (Pollock 1996, 2006). Rather than being separate and delinked peripheries, I suggest that these locales partook, through religious and cultural networks, of a translocal textual tradition of ultimately Indic origin. Although their textual documents were produced in different local contexts characterized by different histories of reception, socio-cultural specificities, and religious contingencies, they appear to have developed in parallel, as it were, from what must once have been a shared Sanskritic tradition.

Here I will approach the literary cultures of early modern Malay and Javano-Balinese spheres by focusing on what Pollock (2007, p. 83) calls the "materiality of manuscript culture", and elaborate on historical evidence that linked their social and religious contexts. I will first describe the networks of manuscripts and literati in the Javano-Balinese sphere from the late fourteenth to the sixteenth century. Then I will pinpoint some parallels between the Sanskrit colophon of the late fourteenth/early fifteenth-century Malay Tanjung Tanah codex from the highlands of Sumatra and nearly contemporary Old Javano-Balinese sources. Those parallels, which extend to earlier South Asian Sanskrit sources, carry some implications for the history of early modern literary cultures of Nusantara as they support the view that the Malay-Sumatran and Javano-Balinese sources, although originating from distant geographical areas, stemmed from a common Indic (and Śaiva-influenced) supralocal tradition of text-building and exegetical practices.

Paraphrasing Lieberman's (2009, p. 10) question on premodern Eurasia, I ask: in what ways and to what extent can we regard the literary high-cultures of both premodern and early modern Nusantara as part of a coherent, integrated Ecumene? And further, who were the transmitters of (manu)scripts and ideas? Given the sheer amount of untapped manuscript sources, such wide-ranging question is bound to remain unanswered for the time being. However, by tracing ancient connections and contextualizing them against the background of historical facts that are part of an Indic-derived continuum, this chapter will advance a perspective that tries to transcend the narrowly-constructed and parochialized divisions of local literatures and histories that were formulated through the lens of modern conceptions of nation-states, ethnicity, and academic disciplines.

2. APPROACHING THE INDIC MANUSCRIPT CULTURES OF EARLY MODERN WESTERN NUSANTARA

In his epoch-making contribution to the study of premodern Southeast Asia, Oliver Wolters (1999 [1982]) regarded the Southeast Asian region as a coherent cultural and geographical whole, which constituted a " 'mosaic of literary cultures' characterized by foreign and local features fitting into various text-like wholes" (ibid., p. 65). His comparative approach, the pivot of which is the idea of "localization"[2] of Indic cultural motifs, has contributed to reorient historical studies towards a literary dimension, basing itself upon the Structuralist and Post-Structuralist assumption that cultural tracts may be regarded as "texts" to be read.

While looking for "synchronisms" in Southeast Asian history, Lombard (1995, p. 15) pointed at first at the Dongsonian period and its bronze drums, and then at the "so-called 'Indianized' period, characterized by state formation and dissemination of both the Indian alphabet and of Sanskrit". Following Lombard, we may call "synchronisms" the transregional cultural phenomena of the Sanskrit Cosmopolis and Vernacular Millenium, which impacted much of Asia in the medieval or Post-Gupta period of Indic history. Restricting our domain of enquiry to insular Southeast Asia, we could ask, with Pollock (2001, p. 393),

> whether, and if so, when, Sanskrit culture ceased to make history; whether, and if so, why, it proved incapable of preserving into the present the creative vitality it displayed in earlier epochs, and what this loss of effectivity might reveal about those factors within the wider world of society and polity that had kept it vital.

Granting that "there exist no good accounts or theorizations of the end of the cultural order that for two millennia exerted a transregional influence across Asia — South, Southeast, Inner, and even East Asia — that was unparalleled until the rise of Americanism and global English" (ibid.), one may still try to find vestiges of Indic Cosmopolitan culture in the vernacular cultures that, according to Pollock, were the regional polities of maritime Southeast Asia after the tenth century. In the present enquiry I will extend the chronological boundaries well beyond the watershed event that Pollock has defined as "death of Sanskrit", which according to him gradually takes place in Java after the ninth-century emergence of highly perfected specimens of Sanskritic poetry in the Old Javanese vernacular, namely *kakavins*.[3]

Our investigation is hampered by the relative paucity of accessible written records — not that the records do not exist, but they have not been surveyed, catalogued, edited, and translated, let alone studied. Yet, by just paying attention to the material aspects of manuscript cultures, i.e., not uniquely to "abstract 'literature' but… concrete 'sub-texts' in the form of physical 'manuscripts' or 'books'" (Kragh 2013, p. 1), one may be able to gather a wealth of historical information that would help us to transcend preconceived and essentializing historical narratives (including "literary histories") and do justice to the complexity of the past.[4] For instance, by asking questions concerning "the time-space matrix of text diffusion, that is, how quickly, how far and along what routes a text was circulated, and what relationship the resultant spatio-temporal map bears to the genre in question and its language" (Pollock 2007, p. 78),[5] and also by considering the dynamics at play behind manuscript production, the milieux of the scribes-intellectuals, and the "philological practices" that they applied to the texts, we may gain precious insights into the socio-political contexts of the "local" and "cosmopolitan" Indic cultures of western Nusantara in the early modern period.

Preliminary evidence drawn from the rare manuscript archives that have survived the ravages of time reflects rich and complex networks of scholarly exchanges (of book-manuscripts, and ideas) and centres of learning stretching eastwards from Sumatra to Java, Bali, and Lombok. With the exception of Bali and some areas of Lombok — where the activity of Old Javanese textual (re)production, and the Indic-derived ideology that supported it, have continued to exist down to the present day — we are left with a handful of "time capsules" spread across mountainous areas of Java and Sumatra. No manuscript written on palm-leaf or other perishable material earlier than the fourteenth century has survived to us from the Indonesian archipelago;[6] whereas the overwhelming majority of the manuscripts from Bali and Lombok are recent (e.g., last copied in the twentieth or, more rarely, nineteenth century), most of the rare palm-leaf manuscripts that have survived in the Javanese archives, as well as in Sumatra, date back to the period from the late fifteenth to the early seventeenth century.[7] Hence, many of these archives may be regarded as time capsules "photographing" a situation — with respect to linguistic, literary, and even socio-political factors — going back to that period. Whereas the manuscripts existing in Bali and Lombok have been subjected to a continuous activity of copying, and have continued to be a medium for the circulation of knowledge up to nowadays, their counterparts from Java and Sumatra represent the last concrete instances of (re)production of knowledge through the Indic-derived technology of palm-leaf book-manuscripts before the "epistemic break" was complete. These manuscripts represent epigones bearing witness to a period in which new technologies (i.e., paper), languages (i.e., Modern Javanese, Classical Malay, Arabic), scripts (i.e., Jawi, Pegon, etc.), and religions (i.e., Islam) were starting to supplant the earlier paradigm.[8] It is perhaps during that period that Indic manuscripts started to be perceived, and used, mainly as *pusaka* or sacred heirlooms, and regarded as supernaturally powerful (ritual) objects inherited from the ancestors rather than *books*, i.e., vehicles of knowledge that could be read, apprehended, improved upon, and shared. Since those artifacts were no longer used for the purpose they had been designed, and were ceased to be given proper care (i.e., fumigation, cleaning, lubrication, etc.), let alone recopied, by the specialists, most of them eventually disintegrated. In contrast to the several thousands of palm-leaf manuscripts that have been recovered in Bali alone — the actual extent of which is still unknown — only a few hundreds are known from Javanese collections. This figure undoubtedly represents a tiny fraction of what must have been extant in the fifteenth century, not to speak about earlier periods.

3. INDIC CONTINUITIES AND TRANSREGIONAL NETWORKS

3.1 The Javano-Balinese Sphere

Lieberman (2009, p. 795), on the basis of epigraphic and textual evidence discussed by Noorduyn (1978, pp. 255–56), argued that in Java "religious patronage, Sanskrit scholarship, and Old Javanese belles-lettres flourished for most of the 15th century as they had in the 14th". As noted by Hunter (2007), political devolution favoured the emergence and spread of such new vernacular genres as the Middle Javanese *kiduṅ*, which flourished in East Java during and after the collapse of cosmopolitan kingdom of Majapahit, and in Bali for a few centuries thereafter. The literary vestiges recovered from Javanese manuscript repositories confirm the views that an Indic-derived tradition of knowledge production and transfer was still alive in certain areas of Java by the late sixteenth century.

Manuscript repositories have been found in the Sundanese-speaking region of West Java (i.e., the scriptorium or *kabuyutan* of Ciburuy),[9] in Central Java (i.e., the Merapi-Merbabu repository),[10] and in East Java (i.e., the "Puger" collection).[11] The most part of the rare manuscripts recovered from these repositories are written in Old Javanese, Middle Javanese (with occasional, usually remarkably corrupt, Sanskrit excerpts), and Old Sundanese languages in related (yet distinct) regional varieties of Indic scripts on different material supports. The scripts include Old Sundanese script (referred to as *ka-ga-nga* by modern Sundanese people), West Old Javanese "quadratic" script, related varieties of Central Javanese "Buda" or "Gunung" script, and East Javanese scripts (that have much in common with Balinese script); the supports are either ink-written leaves of the *talipot* palm or *Corypha umbraculifera*, which have survived uniquely in West Java, or stylus-engraved leaves of the Palmyra or *lontar* palm, i.e., *Borassus flabellifer*, which are prevalent in Central and East Java, Bali, and Lombok. The first variety of manuscripts, which scholars (including myself) have hitherto incorrectly referred to as Nipah (thatch-palm, i.e., *Nypa fructicans*), has been shown to derive from the leaves of the *talipot* palm by Aditia Gunawan (2015); this support, referred to in some Old Javanese and Old Sundanese texts as *gebang*, corresponds to what the Sanskritic tradition called *śrītala* (as opposed to *tala*, i.e., *lontar* [*ron* + *tal*]). The ecological considerations by van Lennep (1969, pp. 16–17) and van der Molen (1983, p. 88) contrasting the thatch-palm, generally growing only in a humid climate along muddy coasts, beaches and lagoons (West Java), to the *lontar* palm, thriving in drier climates (Central and East Java, Bali, Lombok), appear to be still valid with respect to the *talipot* and *lontar* palms.[12] These ecological considerations may explain why the number of *gebang* or *śrītala* manuscripts that have survived until today is very small compared to the number of *lontar*s, and none of them has been recovered from East Javanese or Balinese collections. Similar considerations could be applied to Sumatra, where the *daluang* or tree-bark is the commonest writing material while the *lontar* palm is unknown except in the dry part of Aceh (Kozok 2004, p. 37).

That manuscripts circulated through cultural brokers who travelled across and beyond Java is suggested by the existence of codices belonging to different scribal traditions than that of the collection where they have been found: for instance, if we are to believe to the report by Friederich, the fifteenth-century *codex unicus* of the Old Javanese Śaiva text *Dharma*

Pātañjala, written (with ink) in a West Javanese variety of "quadratic" script on the leaves of *gebang* palm, was found in the Merapi-Merbabu collection in Central Java (Acri 2011*a*, pp. 43–45).[13] The circulation of texts is also proved by the existence of multiple copies of certain literary texts (*kakavin* and *kiduṅ*),[14] as well as Śaiva religious treatises known as *tutur*s and *tattva*s, in Javanese and Balinese manuscript collections. To the latter category of texts belong, for instance, the *Tattvajñāna*,[15] which was regarded to have come down to us only on Bali, but which is in fact also extant in three manuscripts from West, Central, and East Java (Acri 2011*b*; Ricklefs and Gallop 2014, p. 328; Figure 9.1). As documented by the *Tattvajñāna* and the *Dharma Pātañjala*, the Javanese tradition is clearly related to the Balinese one, whose most representative text of the *tattva* genre is the Sanskrit-Old Javanese *Vṛhaspatitattva*. All the three texts share the same substantial number of doctrinal parallels and stylistic features with the Śaiva literature in Sanskrit from South Asia.[16] The discovery of three manuscripts containing related Javanese versions of the *Tattvajñāna* strengthens the likelihood, already assumed by earlier generations of Old Javanese scholars and — not less important — by the Balinese themselves, that a not insignificant part of the Śaiva literature that has come down to us on Bali may be of Javanese provenance. This, of course, does not in any way diminish the originality and antiquity of the Balinese literary culture; rather, it shows that the *tutur* and *tattva* literature, far from being a purely "indigenous" and "embedded" Balinese product, represents a transregional Indic Cosmopolitan phenomenon. The *Dharma Pātañjala*, the *Tattvajñāna*, and the *Vṛhaspatitattva* thus belong to a scriptural corpus representing the relic of what might have once been a widespread canon that, just as happened with the canon of Śaiva scriptures in the Indian Subcontinent, has suffered major losses from the sixteenth century onwards. Just as the early Śaiva scriptures in Sanskrit referred to as Siddhāntatantras, once spread over the whole Indian Subcontinent, have survived in manuscripts from Nepal and/or South India only, so Old Javanese scriptures like the three *tattvas* mentioned above have survived only in a handful of remote Javanese locations and/or in Bali and Lombok.

Similar considerations can be made with respect to the Old Sundanese textual tradition documented from West Javanese manuscripts. That this is not uniquely an isolated, "rustic" or "demotic" tradition developed in mountainous enclave (*gunung*), but a transregional/cosmopolitan one, is suggested by the fact that an important Old Sundanese source, the *Siksa Kandaṅ Karəsian*, lists a series of Old Javanese major *kakavin*s, *parva*s,

FIGURE 9.1
Four manuscripts of the *Tattvajñāna*: (1) Ciburuy, (2) Merapi-Merbabu, (3) Puger, (4) Bali (not on scale).

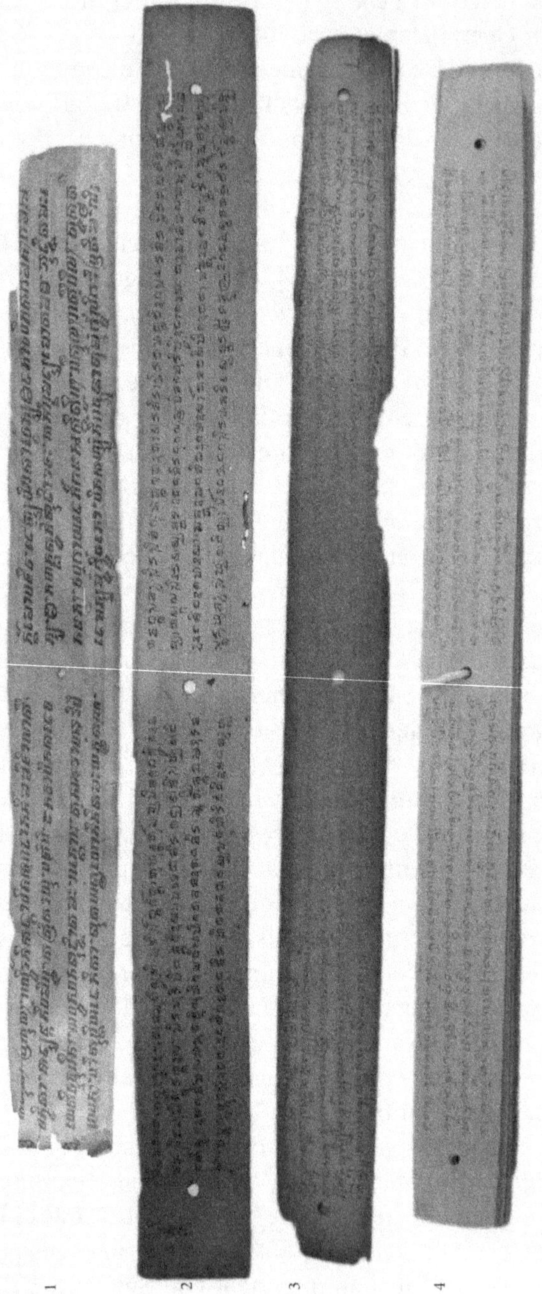

Source: Author.

and other prose works.[17] From these references we may infer that a transregional, Indic-derived, and diglossic literary tradition was shared by the Sundanese- and Javanese-speaking areas of Java. Furthermore, some of the sources in the Old Sundanese corpus mention a series of geographical names that show an awareness of Islamicate networks and locales, e.g., Mecca, Madinah, and Mesir (cf. Noorduyn and Teeuw 2006, pp. 142–43), as well as other Asian locales (e.g., Cina, Cham, Negara Deccan). Commercial, political, and cultural contacts between the cosmopolitan South Indian kingdoms and Nusantara flourished during the heyday of Majapahit as a result of the rapid growth of international trade, but were seemingly maintained well into the sixteenth century, during the period of its decadence. The existence of cultural ties between Majapahit and Vijayanagara in the Telegu country of southern India may be evinced on the basis of data mined from the Classical Malay texts *Sejarah Melayu* and *Hikayat Hang Tuah* (see Teeuw et al. 1969),[18] as well as Old Javanese *kakavin*s, such as Mpu Tanakuṅ's *Śivarātrikalpa*, which attests to the introduction of new doctrines into Javanese Śaivism from India (Nihom 1997, pp. 104, 108–109).[19] According to de Casparis (1997, p. 308), a revival of "Hinduism" took place simultaneously in Vijayanagara and Majapahit in the early sixteenth century, suggesting "a direct relation between the developments in South India and eastern Java at a time when both were confronted with the expansion of Islam".

In spite of the situation outlined above, one has to reckon with the fact that the majority of the Old Javanese and Old Sundanese *tutur*s that have been recovered from the Javanese scriptoria[20] bear witness to a "popular" and localized variety of Śaivism that is the expression of non-courtly cultural milieux far removed from those of the earlier cosmopolitan courts of Central and East Java. Witness the considerations made by Noorduyn and Teeuw (2000, p. 296) with respect to the Old Sundanese "pseudo-Śaiva" poem *Sri Ajnyana*, which

> indeed is a far cry from the systematic philosophical and theological Old Javanese texts which were the main topic of Dr. Sudarshana's researches [i.e., the *Vṛhaspatitattva* and *Tattvajñāna*]. It is an expression of popular religion as it developed in Java in the Middle Ages in *patapan*s and *mandala*s, hermitages and abodes of religious community, which were widespread especially in the mountainous areas of Java.

As to the issue of the "local" character of this literature, the two scholars formulated the following, to my mind pertinent, reflections (ibid., p. 295):

> The word local ... refers to non-Indian cultural elements, words and concepts. In some cases these may be typically Sundanese, in others they may be common to the medieval Javanese and Sundanese cultural heritage. Often it is difficult to decide whether we have to do with the former or the latter, as insufficient information is available for such a distinction.

An interesting process of "demoticization" or, more exactly, "narrativization" of the earlier Śaiva scriptures appears to have been at play in Javanese milieux from the sixteenth century. Witness, for example, the transformation undergone by the *Tattvajñāna* into narrative texts, or rather, the insertion of the philosophical parts of the *Tattvajñāna* within the narrative framework of texts such as the *Navaruci*[21] and *Bhīmasvarga*. These relatively late Old/Middle Javanese texts, along with the *Koravāśrama* and *Tantu Paṅgəlaran*,[22] also display a degree of linguistic and doctrinal "localization". Similar features are also detectable in Balinese *tutur*s, whether the ones which were arguably compiled during (and even well after) the period of cultural influence from East Java (late thirteenth to early sixteenth century) on the basis of older textual materials. Although further research in this direction is required before making any informed statement as to whether the two traditions developed in an independent way along similar lines or mutually influenced each other (at least until the sixteenth century, as in the case of West Java),[23] it may be assumed — and this is indeed the assumption underlying this chapter — that some among the elements that appear to us as "local" may in fact be reconfigurations stemming from a translocal tradition.[24] (The case studies discussed below will provide examples of this perspective). It seems to me that the most important distinction at play here is that between the cosmopolitan urban centres in the plains, which were the seats of centralized political power, and the non-courtly milieux of the *kabuyutan*s ("place of the elder") on the mountains, where relative isolation and regional political devolution played a role in shaping the literary and religious paradigms. It is probably in the isolated milieux of mountainous Java that a sort of Śaiva-Bauddha "mystic synthesis" was developed, as the theological and ritual boundaries between the various orientations of those Indic religions became blurred (Acri 2015, pp. 272, 275). At the same time, the influence of Islam started to be felt, which would eventually lead to the Javanese-Islamic "mystic synthesis" discussed by Ricklefs (2006), or to the "cultural compromises" between Islamic religion and the earlier tradition embodied in such figures as the hereditary *juru kunci* (or *kuncen* in West Java), the custodian of village spirit-shrines, sacred graveyards, or *kabuyutan*s (Hefner 1985, pp. 108–109).

The bearing of the above findings from the realm of textual studies and codicology on the cultural, religious and literary history of pre-Islamic Java is significant, for they provide evidence for links existing among West and Central Javanese scriptoria, locally called *kabuyutan* or *maṇḍala* ("sacred rings"). Those *kabuyutan*s, which may represent the historical continuations of earlier *pāśraman* ("hermitages"), *patapan*s ("penance groves"), and *kaṛṣyan* ("places of the ascetics of the Ṛṣi class"), were usually set along mountain slopes, and populated by communities of scholars who studied the texts at a "comfortable distance", but by no means isolated, from the outside world and the cosmopolitan cities in the plains, where Islam was becoming dominant. Furthermore, those centres might have been tied in some ways to the courts, even though "kings had circumscribed authority over these, as evidenced by their limited reference in royal charters" (Hall 1996, p. 96):

> While the leaders of the favored Śaivite and Buddhist religious sects resided within the walled compound, where they performed ritual on the king's behalf, important communities of religious specialists lay beyond the king's residence and all major temples (*dharma*), including royal ancestral temples and state temples that were dedicated to specific deities, were also dispersed. (ibid.)

Indeed, those centres of knowledge and religio-ritual praxis were integrated in the political and administrative network: for instance, Hunter (in Worsley et al. 2013, pp. 577–78) describes the networks of courtly and rural centres in East Java, as well as the local vs. cosmopolitan dynamics that shaped their literary cultures from the eleventh to the early sixteenth century, as natural by-products of the Javanese tax transfer system. On the basis of the consistent occurrence of fixed codicological features during a period of over two centuries, Van Lennep (1969, pp. 29–38) has argued that the West Javanese *gebang* manuscripts are likely to have been produced by one and the same school sustained by a central political authority, i.e., the late kingdom of Padjadjaran (ca. AD 1333–1579).[25]

The existence of scriptoria-cum-hermitages in the Sundanese region of Java is confirmed by the survival of one such sites up to the present, i.e., the Ciburuy repository, where some thirty Old Sundanese and Old Javanese manuscripts plus some ancient metal artifacts, such as scribal implements and ritual objects, can be found (Figures 9.2 and 9.3). Furthermore, the report of Pleyte (1914, pp. 66–374) documents the figure of Kai Raga, a teacher and ascetic living in a hermitage near Gunung Larang Srimanganti (now Gunung Cikurai) in the beginning of the eighteenth century (cf. van

FIGURE 9.2
***Juru kunci* at *kabuyutan* Ciburuy displaying palm-leaf manuscripts.**

Source: Author.

der Molen 1983, p. 113). The existence of contacts among *kabuyutans* at an even earlier time is supported by the early sixteenth-century Old Sundanese chronicle (or travelogue) of Bhujaṅga Manik. In this text the main character, a "Hindu" hermit, describes his journey throughout Java (Figure 9.4), and especially the peripheral and hard-to-access mountainous areas, in search of Śaiva vestiges and centres of learning. He also mentions to have visited the scriptorium of Pamrihan near Gunung Damalung, which has been identified as the Merbabu mountain in Central Java.[26]

FIGURE 9.3
Ritual and scribal implements at *kabuyutan* Ciburuy.

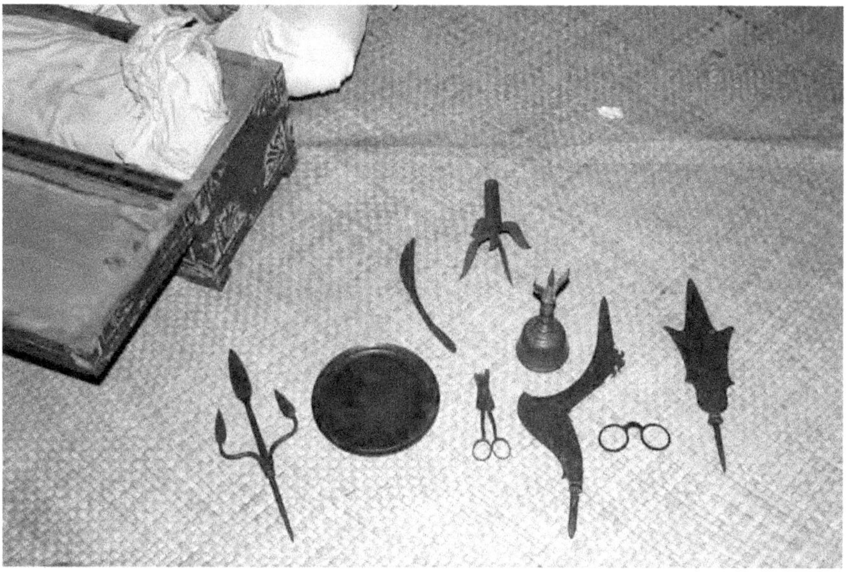

Source: Author.

The figure of the travelling cleric (scholars-cum-ascetics, or people of noble descent) or *bhujaṅga*[27] seems to have been the cultural broker or mediator — between different regional scripts, languages, and literary traditions — to which the production, preservation, and circulation of knowledge and religious lore was entrusted throughout the early modern period. The *bhujaṅga*, who bears many of the tracts of the shaman or wandering wizard/"exorcist", may be seen as a nexus between the central state and the populace, or between the "inner circle" and "outer circle" of Nusantarian societies, also in Islamic times (Hooykaas 1964*a*). Hall (1996, p. 108) sees an opposition between the *ṛṣi*s, "rural priests" or "local religious specialists" who were active beyond the court's direct religious sphere, masters of a "parochial religious tradition" and heirs to traditional knowledge, and the *(bhu)jaṅga*s, "local" shamans involved with the rituals dealing with chthonic forces, deceased ancestors, and purification of demonic entities. While the *ṛṣi*s were incorporated into the royal ritual hierarchy in Majapahit times, the *(bhu)jaṅga*s were not. Thus, Hall sees a "dichotomy between court-based and countryside ritual performance",

FIGURE 9.4
Topography of Java reconstructed on the basis of the *Bhujanga Manik.*

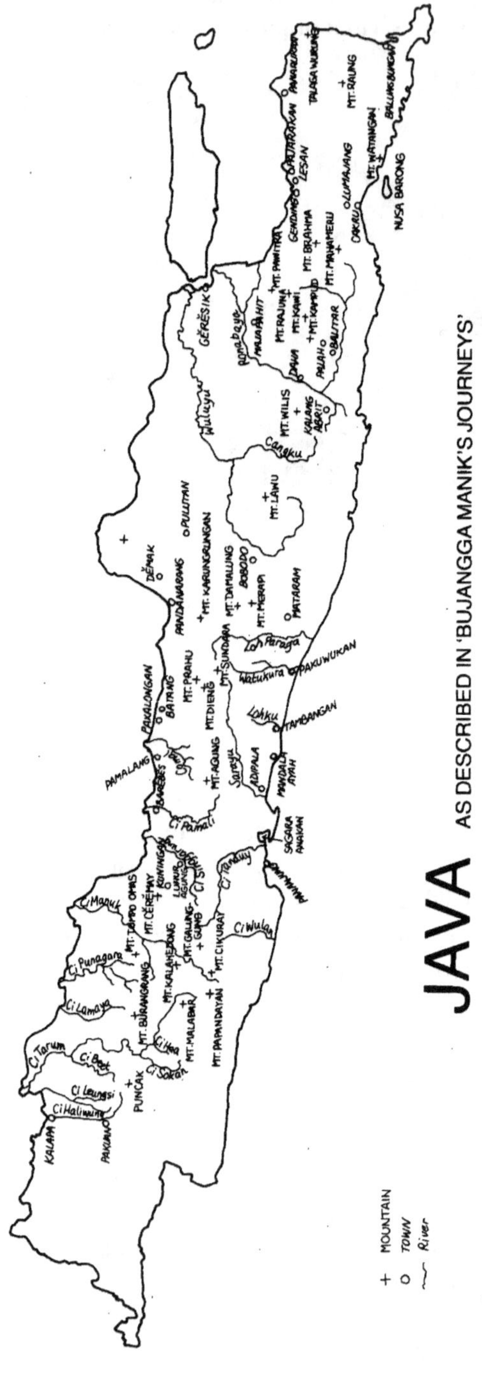

Source: Adapted from Noorduyn (1982).

whereby the *maṇḍala*s "are associated with mysterious and magical rural tantric fire-based worship of indigenous spirits; these rites were performed well outside what is considered to be the appropriate concern of the court" (Hall 1996, p. 108). The descendants of the *bhujaṅga*s may have survived until the early nineteenth century later Mataram kingdom as *pujaṅga*s or "priestly court-writers" (Moertono 1981, p. 22); compare the Modern Javanese term *pujangga*, denoting a "master of the literary art, poet".[28] It is, therefore, the *kabuyutan*s that provided an umbilical cord connecting the premodern/Indic with the modern/Islamic Javanese literary culture, for the works preserved there inspired the production of the literary treasures of the *kraton*s of Surakarta and Yogyakarta. A class of low-status *śudra* priests called (Rṣi) Bhujaṅga may be found in present-day Bali, where they retain a ritually subordinated position with respect to the Brahmanical Pedanda Śiva. It is interesting to note that among the palm-leaf manuscripts used by the ritual specialists of the prevalently Hindu Tengger community, inhabiting a remote mountainous area of East Java, we find the *Pūrvaka Bhūmi*, a remarkably old Śaiva cosmogonic text that has also survived on Bali as the exclusive preserve of the priestly class of the Ṛṣi Bhujaṅga (Hooykaas 1974). These textual and codicological data speak about a shared Javano-Balinese priestly, literary, and religio-ritual tradition, and casts some doubt on the purely "local" ritual and religious character of the Javanese *bhujaṅga*s and their Balinese counterparts.

Indeed, it is the above-discussed category of clerics who travelled far and wide across Java and Bali that may have inspired the Balinese narratives around the semi-legendary figures of "powerful strangers" that contributed significantly to the creation of the current religious and ritual order of the island. For instance, the important character of the ritual *topeng* mask-dance Sidha Karya is regarded as a filthy, ash-covered — yet supernaturally endowed — Brahmin coming from Java, while the Brahman-ascetic Daṅ Hyaṅ Nirartha (also referred to as Mpu Dvijendra) is believed to have travelled to Bali from the decayed kingdom of Majapahit in the sixteenth century, bringing with him a body of Old Javanese texts that are still considered by the contemporary Balinese as the basis of their religious canon. The historicity of the latter figure, which has hitherto been called into question by Western scholarship, would appear to be confirmed by the colophon of a remarkably old Balinese manuscript dated AD 1537, which is declared to have been copied by one whose (nick-)name (*parab*) is Nirartha; to the same figure is attributed the copying of a manuscript of the *kakavin Bhomāntaka* (see Worsley et al. 2013, p. 31).

3.2 The Malay Sphere of Sumatra

Textual evidence suggests the existence of intra-regional contacts between Sumatra and the Javano-Balinese sphere throughout the early modern period, as well as a shared Indic tradition that might have stemmed from Buddhist Śrīvijaya.[29] Yet, scholarship on early modern Sumatra has often tended to downplay the Indic elements characterizing its regional literary cultures, anachronistically studying them in the light of the contemporary Islamized Malay cultural sphere.

Griffiths (2011), advocating a "corpus approach" to the study of the extant Old Malay inscriptions, adopts a working definition of Old Malay as "the variant of the Malay language found in documents written in an Indic system of writing … before it [e.g., the Malay language] had undergone any influence from Arabic", that is from the seventh to ca. the fifteenth century. The cosmopolitan dimension of "Old Malay" results clearly from the geographical extent of the attestations — almost exclusively in inscriptions — of this language, nearly all of which are from what is now Indonesia, including both Sumatra (25) and Java (7), but also the present-day Philippines (1), Singapore (1), and peninsular Malaysia (1). Griffiths further speaks of a "commonality of religious culture between 8th c. Java and contemporary Sumatra" on the basis of a comparison of the Buddhist themes featuring in the Mañjuśrīgṛha and Talang Tuwo inscriptions on the one hand, and in contemporary South Asian inscriptions in Sanskrit on the other. In a previous study, Griffiths (2012, pp. 201–209) drew attention to two stone *makara*s from Candi *kedaton* (Muara Jambi, Sumatra) bearing short Old Javanese inscriptions that can be palaeographically dated to the period 950–1050 CE. The dating is on the ground that the form of writing is virtually identical to the "quadratic" script found engraved on contemporary monuments of East and also West Java.

Direct contacts between Sumatra and East Java are attested throughout the thirteenth and fourteenth centuries. For instance, an inscribed statue of the Tantric icon Amoghapāśa Lokeśvara was sent by Kṛtanagara to Dharmāśraya in the Kerinci regency of Sumatra — where the Tanjung Tanah codex originates from (see below) — in AD 1286, and reconsecrated by Ādityavarman in AD 1347 (Reichle 2007, pp. 127–32).[30] In general, the wild, ferocious character displayed by the iconography found in Biaro Bahal and Muara Takus in Sumatra, and in the colossal Mahākāla statue from Padang Roco, attributed to Ādityavarman, share common features with the Buddhist and Śaiva Tantric imagery developed in East Java during the reign of Kṛtanagara at Siṅhasāri. Ādityavarman, born in East Java between the end of the thirteenth and the beginning of the fourteenth century, was a grandson of Tribhuvanarāja, king of Malāyu (Dharmāśraya),[31] and cousin of king Jayanagara of Majapahit; he became the senior minister of Majapahit (*vṛddhamantri*) and set for Sumatra, where he eventually re-established the kingdom of Malayapura in the central Sumatran highland region of Dharmāśraya. He was a follower of Tantric Buddhist cults that were prevalent in East Java and much of Buddhist Asia by that time, and issued several eulogistic inscriptions — in fact, among the last pieces of *praśāsti* to be composed in the Archipelago — written in a kind of "localized" Sanskrit. Ādityavarman himself may have followed the same ideology and ritual technology adopted earlier by Kṛtanagara and his rival Kublai Khan, who equated themselves to the central deity of the *maṇḍala*s of the *Guhyasamājatantra* or the *Hevajratantra* (see Hunter 2015, pp. 324–27; Bautze-Picron 2014, pp. 107, 123; Reichle 2007, p. 139). The fourteenth-century inscription of Saruaso II, which praises the crown prince Anaṅgavarman, son of Ādityavarman, still mentions his "daily meditation on Hevajra" (*hevajranityāsmṛtiḥ*). This shows a continuity with the earlier centuries, which attest to a vigorous Buddhist activity on the island: images found at the Sumatran sites of Padang Lawas are integrated in a network that connects them to South Asia, East Java, Central Sumatra, Cambodia and Campā in the eleventh and thirteenth centuries, "when esoteric Buddhism was tightly intertwined with politics and when fierce characters like Mahākāla or Heruka/Hevajra were made the protectors of various kingdoms" (Bautze-Picron 2014, p. 123).[32]

Echoes of the Sanskrit, and specifically Buddhist, Cosmopolis that we find in Sumatra from the early fourteenth to the early sixteenth century are found in the straits region. Miksic (2010, p. 31) notes that "one of the last Buddhist Malay kingdoms was located in Singapore" around the fourteenth century, and that "the first ruler of the Malays according to the *Sejarah Melayu* was named Sri Tri Buana, Sanskrit for 'Lord of the Three Worlds', an allusion to the belief that the universe was divided into a heaven of gods, a world of humans, and a hell for demons". Miksic notes that some Southeast Asian kings used this phrase as their title, and indeed we find it in the name of Ādityavarman's grandfather Tribhuvanarāja,[33] and, as we will see below, in the Trailokyādhipati mentioned in the Sanskrit colophon of the Tanjung Tanah codex (*tr[a]ilok[y]a* = *tribhuvana*). Originally known as Sang Utama, Sri Tri Buana magically appeared on the Seguntang Hill in Palembang (Sumatra), and was proclaimed to be "his Highness, the Sri Maharaja, ruler of the whole of Suvarna-bhumi"; to Miksic (ibid.), this title "strongly implies a tradition handed down from Srivijaya".

The study of vernacular primary sources and accounts of travellers suggests that the Islamization of Sumatra and Java was a long and complex process. For instance, the early-sixteeenth-century Portuguese visitor to the north coast of Java, Tome Pires,

> reported that there were still about fifty thousand non-Muslim ascetics (*tapas*) in Java. "And these men are also worshipped by the Moors, and they believe in them greatly; they give them alms; they rejoice when such men come to their houses" (Ricklefs 2006, p. 11).

Interesting data are yielded by the Malay works of Islamic scholars who polemically write against certain non-Islamic practices. These are, for instance, the influential eighteenth-century South Sumatran scholar 'Abd as-Samad al-Palimbani (Drewes 1976), and especially the Muslim mystic Hamzah Fansuri, who lived in North Sumatra between the end of the sixteenth and the beginning of the seventeenth century. As shown by Brakel (1979, 2004, pp. 10–11; cf. Al-Attas 1972, pp. 17–20), in a poem[34] Fansuri attacks surviving "yoga" practices, contrasting "the jungles of the interior, where such practices frequently occur, with the sea and the Islamized coasts which are open to the world". To Brakel (ibid.), the division between the highlands in the interior and the plains on the coasts "corresponds almost exactly with the geographic expansion of Islam in Indonesia".

Fansuri's critique of the ascetic practices carried out in seclusion by spiritual seekers contain clear echoes of yogic techniques known in the Javano-Balinese tradition; for instance, the clause "They draw their breath into the brain, Lest their fluids get in commotion" reminds us of the technique of retention of the breath (*prāṇāyāma*), which is described in the Sanskrit-Old Javanese *Vṛhaspatitattva* precisely as the closing of the bodily apertures and the breaking through of the breath from the cranial vault (*śloka* 56 and Old Javanese commentary, see Sudarshana Devi 1957, p. 105). In a passage of his prose *Asrār al-Ārifin* (Brakel 1979, pp. 74–75), Hamzah admonishes his reader not to localize God in the fontanel (*ubun-ubun*) or on the tip of the nose (*dipucuk hiduṅ*) or between the eyebrows (*di antara keniṅ*) or in the heart (*didalam jantuṅ*), all of which correspond to the classical loci or *sthāna*s of the human body described in yogic texts from both the Sanskrit and Javano-Balinese tradition, in which the practitioner should imagine Śiva to reside (e.g., *śivadvāra* = fontanel, *nāsāgra* = tip of the nose, *lalāṭa* = space between the eyebrows, *hṛdaya* = heart). Brakel (1979, p. 76) concluded that yogic techniques were still current in sixteenth-century Aceh; this finding complements his earlier appreciation of "Hindu" cultural elements in seventeenth-century Aceh sultanate, the study of which, according to him, was hampered by Snouk Hurgronje's overemphasis on the Muslim factor, but which "can best be understood within the general context of the 'Hinduised States of Southeast Asia'" (Brakel 1975, p. 66). It is tempting to link the ascetics practising a form of Śaiva yoga in the seclusion of the Sumatran forests to those who populated the "isolated communities" of the *kabuyutan*s in fifteenth and sixteenth century Java. Two articles by Braginsky (2004, forthcoming) shed light on the syncretic Sufi-Tantric mystical literature in Malay from Sumatra, which contains element of sexual yoga representing the continuation of a pre-Islamic Indic heritage.

Whereas I must leave the study of the many textual documents recovered from the Kerinci highlands[35] to the specialists of Old and Classical Malay, here I shall draw attention to the Sanskrit verse forming the colophon of the Tanjung Tanah codex, a manuscript containing a legal text written in a form of Indic script and pre-Classical Malay language (Kozok 2015; Figure 9.5).[36] Originating from Dharmāśraya but found in the

FIGURE 9.5
Palm-leaf from the Tanjung Tanah codex.

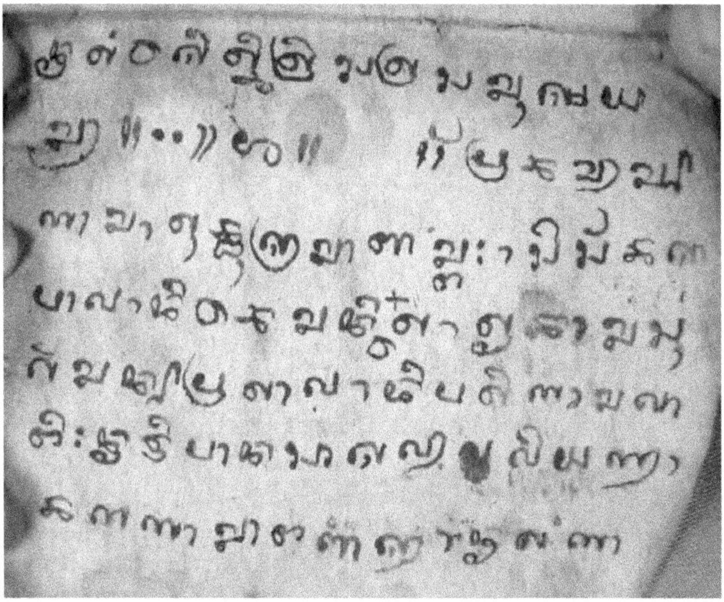

Source: Photo courtesy of Uli Kozok.

Kerinci highlands of Sumatra, it is the oldest Malay manuscript currently known, and therefore deserves to be regarded as a tremendously important document of pre-Islamic Malay literary culture. As I have argued elsewhere (Acri 2015*b*), this text attests intriguing parallels with related Sanskrit verses from Balinese and South Asian sources. These parallels suggest that, as far as the period from the late fourteenth to the early sixteenth century is concerned, the courtly milieu of Ādityavarman's scions on the one hand and the Javano-Balinese literary tradition on the other may be considered manifestations stemming from a common tradition of Indic manuscript cultures.

Griffiths (2010, p. 134) has rightly stressed the pre-Islamic element of this work, which bears no connection with Malay works transmitted in Jawi script and standing under clear Islamic influence. The *śloka* that the text calls *saluka dipati* ("the *śloka* of the *dipati* [=king, or regent?]") "clearly stands in a scribal tradition inherited from India": being a verse of praise placed at the conclusion of the Malay prose text, it constitutes the codex's colophon, and contains the original title of the text: *Nītisārasamuccaya* ("Compendium of the Essence of Policy"). Hunter (2015, p. 333) devotes a long discussion to this *śloka*, stressing that "from the point of view of locating this text in a socio-political milieu these are undoubtedly the most crucial lines in the entire TTms". The verse runs as follows:

Original version	Restored version
pranamya śrisa divam· *tṛlūkyadipāti stutim·* *ṇāṇasattrudṛtaṃ vakit* *nitrisatrasamukṣayam*	*praṇamya śirasā devaṁ* *trailokyādhipatistutam* *nānāśāstroddhṛtaṁ vakti* *nītisārasamuccayam*

Translation:
Having bowed down with the head before God, who is praised as the Lord of the Triple World, [the author] expounds the Compendium of the Essence of Policy, extracted from various authoritative sources.

This is obviously a eulogy to Śiva, and confirms the fundamentally Indic nature of the scribal and text-building tradition from which it stems. Building on the work by Griffiths and Hunter on this colophon, I have proposed to restore the corrupt first quarter to *praṇamya śirasā devaṁ* on the basis of a parallel in Old Javanese texts that I will discuss below (Acri 2015*b*). I also pointed out that the *-sattra* occurring in two compounds in both the first and second quarters poses a philological riddle, multiple solutions of which are possible. While the emendations *-śāstra* constitutes the more natural outcome, one should also take into account, as done by Griffiths in the case of the second quarter, *-sāra*. One notes the frequent occurrence of the cliché *-sāroddhṛta* ("extracted from the essence") on the one hand, and the relative rarity of *-śāstroddhṛta* ("extracted from the treatises") on the other, in Sanskrit texts of various genres from South and Southeast Asia, as well as in Old Javanese literature.[37] Further, while the sequence *(nīti)sāra(samuccaya)* is well-attested in Javano-Balinese literature — witness the Sanskrit-Old Javanese legal code entitled *Sārasamuccaya*, which has reached us through Balinese manuscripts, and the Old Javanese *Nītisāra* — the word *nītiśāstra* is also found in Old Javanese,[38] as well as in Sanskrit.[39] Conversely, *-sattra* in the second quarter could be alternatively rendered as *śāstra*, namely *Nītiśāstrasamuccayam*. Thus, the verse-quarter could have been "recomposed" from an original **nānāśāstrasāroddhṛtam* ("the essence of which has been extracted from various treatises").[40] Whatever the original form of the half-*śloka* might have been, the idea it conveys is clear: the work in question is a synthetic compendium containing material extracted from many legal codes.

If we consider the religious aspect of the verse, i.e., the focus on the figure of Śiva as Lord of the threefold World, as well as its element of royal eulogy, we may conclude that it conveys a pun. Here the author is bowing down to a God (*deva*) and, at the same time, a King (*deva*) praised as (or by?) Trailokyādhipati, i.e., the Lord of the Threefold World that is Śiva, and a king named Trailokyādhipati. This bears the implication that the kingly figure might have been a deified king. Hunter (2015, p. 316) arrived to the same conclusion, surmising that the mantra-like formula introducing the *saluka dipati* is addressed to a deified king, and therefore be intended as an eulogy of Ādityavarman. The monarch glorified in an eulogistic section of the text (2.6–8) may have been the direct successor of Ādityavarman, either Anaṅgavarman or Bijayendravarman, and the "deity of the place of keeping watch" (*sang hyang kĕmattan*) should, therefore, be taken as the apotheosized ancestor. The "deification" of deceased kings represents a tradition attested in Java from the ninth to the fifteenth century, as well as in other locales of the Indic world, most notably the Khmer empire.

A set of Malay glosses on the *Saluka Dipati* is provided by Kuja Ali, the alleged author or recompiler of the Tanjung Tanah codex. As pointed out by Hunter (2015, p. 335), these glosses contain a number of lacunae and "imperfections", which reflect the long process of "drift" undergone by the local scribal tradition of enunciation, orthographic representation, and exegesis from the Indic tradition from which the codex and its colophon stem. He concludes that through this document we may glance Kuja Ali's access to a local scribal tradition and his role in the court that sponsored the code of laws, and pay attention

> not just to the continuing presence of elements of the Sanskrit tradition in the textual record of the Malay-Indonesian archipelago, but also to the reception of these elements in diverse cultures that were involved in processes of Sanskritization in differing ways. (ibid.)

Kuja Ali "was working with a Sanskrit original that had already gone through processes of drift in terms of both phonological shape and meaning" (ibid., p. 340);[41] at the same time, "his understanding of the local Sanskrit form of the Sanskrit original was imperfect, so that he only partially succeeded in giving an expert gloss". Nonetheless, the result pinpoints

> an unexpected link between the scribal tradition he represented with the pedagogical traditions pioneered in Sumatran Buddhist institutions of the mid-first millennium CE that set the standard for the text-building techniques of the Old Javanese didactic traditions, and live on in modern embodiments like the practice of the reading clubs of contemporary Bali (*Pesantian, Sekaha Mabasan*). (ibid., p. 354)

Hunter draws a link between the *Saluka Dipati*, the Javano-Balinese didactic tradition, and modern Balinese practices of "extemporaneous glossing", that is hermeneutical strategies that do not (primarily) involve analytical means, drawn from a systematic knowledge of morphology and grammar, or try to establish historical derivations and etymologies; they are mainly based on contemporary/popular lexical know-how, "folk etymology", and associative thinking effected through homology, metaphor, and assonance. It may be argued that these hermeneutical practices are not uniquely the expression of a "local" or "embedded" milieu, but represent a continuation, or "demoticization", of the codified norms of semantic analysis and argumentation that characterized the Sanskrit śāstric tradition, which were passed on to the Buddhist learning centres of Sumatra and the Javanese literary and religious milieux.

An occasion to connect the fourteenth-century Sanskrit-Malay codex to Javano-Balinese text-building practices is provided by a parallel found in the Śaiva *tutur* text preserved in Balinese manuscripts, namely the *Bhuvanakośa* ("The Storehouse of Worlds").[42] This voluminous work, consisting in some

200 Sanskrit verses provided with Old Javanese glosses, is of uncertain date but likely to stem from no later than the early seventeenth century. The first verse of this text attests an identical verse-quarter to the first quarter of the *Saluka Dipati* that, insofar that it obviously represents an introductory eulogy to (various manifestations of) Śiva, mirrors it with respect to both context and function:

> *praṇamya śirasā devaṁ* | *vākya(ṁ) munir amanmathaḥ* |
> *devadeva mahādeva* | *parameśvara śaṅkara* || 1.1
>
> Having bowed down with the head before God, the sage who is free from (erotic) desire spoke: 'O God of Gods, O Great God, O Supreme Lord, O Śaṅkara!'

The two passages contain a verbal praise (*stuti*) of, and represent a physical act of worship towards, a paramount deity — that is, Śiva[43] — by either the text's author or, in the case of the *Bhuvanakośa*, the main interlocutor of Śiva and "revealer" of the text. The form *munir amanmathaḥ* is puzzling. *Manmathaḥ* in Old Javanese usually means "love or the god of love, amorous passion or desire"; however, no attestation of this form with the *alpha privans* is known to me. I take it to be a pun hiding the name of the author identified as the revealer of the text, that is Mpu Tanakuṅ — *tan akuṅ* meaning "without desire/ love", or "not enamoured/filled with amorous desire" in Old Javanese (cf. Teeuw et al. 1969, pp. 13–14). If my hypothesis is correct, we must then attribute the authorship of the *Bhuvanakośa* to the East Javanese author of the *Śivarātrikalpa* and other texts of Śaiva persuasion, and date it to the late fifteenth century — that is, not too far from the period of composition of the Tanjung Tanah codex.[44]

Additional evidence comes from the corpus of Sanskrit hymns (*stuti, stava*) handed down to us through Balinese palm-leaf manuscripts. The opening verses of several hymns attest the sequence *praṇamya śirasā* + name of the deity (e.g., *rudram, sūryam, viṣṇum*) to which the hymn is devoted.[45] The verse-quarter *praṇamya śirasā liṅgam*, found in the first stanza of the *Liṅgastava* (Stuti 670):

> *praṇamya śirasā liṅgaṁ divyaliṅgaṁ maheśvaram* |
> *sarvadevātidevanaṁ tasmai liṅgāya vai namaḥ* || 1

It is accompanied by an Old Javanese gloss (Ms. K 1843, ed. Hooykaas 1964*b*, p. 151) depicting the image of a worshiper performing a *səmbah* by literally bowing down with the head to touch the feet of the paramount Lord Maheśvara (that is, Śiva) embodied in the Liṅga, which is obviously a rendering of the Sanskrit verse-quarter *praṇamya śirasā liṅgam.* The Sanskrit-Old Javanese dyad is of a clear eulogistic nature, and features similarities with both the Tanjung Tanah codex and the *Bhuvanakośa* — witness the nearly-dentical verse-quarter, and the mention of Maheśvara, as in the introductory line to the *Saluka Dipati.*[46]

The existence of these formal as well as contextual parallels suggests that Sanskrit materials from the highlands of central Sumatra and the island of Bali, although separated by a significant geographical distance, are witness to the existence of a shared supralocal textual tradition, of ultimately South Asian origin and theistic (Śaiva) character. Although the distinct vernacular glosses discussed here were produced in different local contexts characterized by different histories of reception, socio-cultural factors, and religious contingencies, they appear to have developed in parallel from what must once have been a common tradition of text-building and exegetical practices. As argued by Hunter, contemporary Balinese *mabasan* may represent a continuation of these practices.

The *Saluka Dipati* reflects not only religious but also political overtones, being an eulogy directed towards a heir to Ādityavarman by a *dipati* who was "either his representative in Dharmāśraya, or one of a group of *dipati* in Kerinci who received copies of the TTms as a visible proof of their close relationship to the centre of political power" (Hunter 2015, p. 343). The relevant socio-political considerations drawn from this document by Hunter are that Kuja Ali, by virtue of his expertise in Sanskrit, the "specialized language that was so intimately tied to the discourse of the political centre", was acting as intermediary between this centre and local political leaders in the highlands of Kerinci. Hunter's considerations about this intellectual's role of intermediary between the centre and the periphery resonate with the analogous considerations I have made above about the figure of the *bhujaṅga*s, who represented the intellectuals to whom the preservation of the Indic cultural and religious paradigm was entrusted in fifteenth and sixteenth-century Java, and who were at the same time the cultural brokers connecting the political centres to the peripheries, where "localized" manifestations of Indic religion continued to exist well into the Islamic period alongisde the new socio-political and religious configurations.

With respect to the socio-political and religious aspects of the *Saluka Dipati* and its Malay gloss, one notes, as done by Hunter (ibid., p. 348), the "puzzling fact that a document so thoroughly embedded in a Sanskritized sociocultural milieu has been penned by someone whose title and name both suggest an Islamic hand". To Hunter, the use of *kuja* (= *khoja*)

> [p. 348] has resonance with a larger world of Islamic networks that had begun to make significant inroads into Sumatra in the later fourteenth century, thus during the same period that we can place the TTms.... [p. 352] Given the importance of the idiom of kinship for socio-political networks of highland Sumatra in later centuries, and adding to that the evidence of the inscriptions of Ādityavarman it seems certain that the issue of a "genealogically derived sacrality" must have loomed as large for Kuja Ali as much as for any member of the royal line. This would suggest that he choose to make prominent his title as a *kuja/khoja* not simply to call attention to his access to the trans-national networks that reached out to Persia through material and symbolic associations, but to underline the fact of his membership in a wider lineage network that carried with it a new form of legitimacy in terms of Islamic transnationalism.... Kuja Ali might thus represent a local Sumatran lineage whose role in the Malay society of Dharmāśraya was enhanced through a genealogical (affinal) relationship to trans-national sources beyond Sumatra that reached out to the Persianised areas of India, [p. 353] and to the Persian and Arabic heartlands of a new religion that was rapidly gaining popularity in much of Sumatra.

To Hunter, the source of legitimization for Kuja Ali as a literate and local political actor with sufficient authority to connect the royal centre in Dharmāśraya with the peripheral areas of Kerinci might be sought in "Malay foundation myths of 'stranger kings' who attain success through bringing some special new quality to a kingdom that ensures their intermarriage into a prominent local line among the nobility".

Another piquant detail of the religious nuances of both the *śloka* and its introductory line, devoted to *deva*, *trailokyādhipati* and *maheśvara* respectively, is their apparently Śaiva persuasion, which we would not expect in a setting — i.e., that of Ādityavarman and his scions, as well as of Sumatra in general — that has been linked to Buddhism on the basis of archaeological and art-historical findings as well as epigraphic documents. Similarly, in the royal title of the nobleman Sang Nila Utama from Palembang who founded Temasek (now Singapore) in the end of the thirteenth century, i.e., Sri Maharaja Sang Utama Parameswara Batara Sri Tri Buana, we note the resilience of a Śaiva nuance associated with royal ideology: Parameśvara ("the Supreme Lord"), Bhaṭāra ("the Lord") and Śrī Tribhuvana[rāja] = Trailokyādhipati, Trailokyanātha, Tribhuvaneśvara, etc.) ("Illustrious [King of] the Threefold World") are appellatives of Śiva, and apparently convey the idea of an identity (in terms of emanation) between the monarch and the deity, if not a deification tout-court (either in life or post-mortem).[47] Another "stranger king" who adopted the name Parameśvara was the Javanese nobleman of Majapahit pedigree who founded Malacca at the beginning of the fifteenth century.[48] Thus, the motif of the "stranger king" to which Hunter rightly draws atttention when discussing the figure of Kuja Ali may be equally applied to the context of the mixed Sumatran-Javanese nobleman Ādityavarman and the near-contemporary Sumatran and East Javanese noblemen who founded what are nowadays Singapore and Melaka between the end of the thirteenth and the beginning of the fifteenth century. This state of affairs suggests that intertwined political, religious, and literary networks connected Java, Sumatra, the Straits, and the Malay Peninsula in the final period of the "Indic" kingdoms of Nusantara.

4. CONCLUSION

In this chapter I have focused on manuscripts and textual practices in Java, Bali and Sumatra in the period going from the fourteenth to the sixteenth century. In taking the manuscript cultures of those areas as the basis for socio-historical analysis, I have highlighted not only their shared, Indic-derived tradition of text building, but also their common religious imaginaries. My aim has been to reconnect what are often perceived as "local" and disconnected historical developments in the Javano-Balinese world and the Sumatran highlands on the one hand, and the cosmopolitan centres and the peripheries within those regions on the other. In doing so, I have stressed the continuities and changes between the Hindu-Buddhist and Islamic epistemes in the production and consumption of knowledge during the crucial centuries that led to a religious and socio-cultural paradigm shift in Nusantara.

Notes

1. This partly coincides with the period that Anthony Reid has called the "Age of Commerce" (ca. AD 1450–1680).
2. I use the term "localized" following Wolters' (1999, p. 55) well-known definition: "Indian materials tended to be fractured and restated and therefore drained of their original significance by a process which I shall refer to as 'localization'". Cf. the quotation from Noorduyn and Teeuw (2000) below, p. 219.

3. Wrestling with Pollock's view that "Sanskrit begins to die in Java the moment Old Javanese begins to live" (Pollock 1996, p. 229), Hunter (2001, p. 90) argues that the composition, as late as the early sixteenth century, of the Old Javanese poem on metres *Vṛttasañcaya* by Mpu Tanakuṅ "suggests that for the courts of East Java the dates of the transnational phase of this 'cosmopolis' must be pushed ahead nearly two centuries". Scepticism about the alleged "death of Sanskrit" in India and other areas of the Sanskrit Cosmpolis has been voiced by Hanneder (2002).
4. Besides the excellent article by Kragh (2013) on Jain (and, in general, South Asian) literary history in the light of manuscript studies, two recent edited volumes focusing on the codicological aspects of premodern Indian textual practices are those of Colas and Gerschheimer (2009) and Saraju Rath (2012). For the Javanese sphere, see van der Molen (1983).
5. When discussing the manuscript cultures in premodern and early modern South Asia (1500–1800), Pollock (2007, p. 78) notes that "few sustained analyses are available of the core dimensions of manuscript culture in the subcontinent, aside from old-style text criticism. [...] It is not that we don't have data to get some answers to these questions; rather, the questions have simply not been raised."
6. The oldest known (Old) Javanese and (Old or Pre-Classical) Malay manuscripts are, respectively, PNRI 16 L 641, preserving a copy of the *Arjunavivāha* dated AD 1334 (from West Java), and the Tanjung Tanah codex from Kerinci (late fourteenth–early fifteenth century).
7. The dating of these manuscripts has been established via their colophons or post-colophons, or on palaeographic grounds.
8. Here a parallel may be drawn with the process called by Lombard (1995, p. 10) "graphic breaking off", i.e. the adoption of Latin scripts in Southeast Asian countries such as Malaysia, Indonesia and Vietnam during the late colonial period, which has "strongly facilitated 'westernization' and thus has given a real access to 'modernity', ... [but also] led in a few generations to an alienation with considerable effects of which people speak too little". Lombard here seems to hint at an "epistemic break" or "paradigm shift", which has been facilitated by the introduction of Western script (and technology/media, i.e. printing).
9. Set in a village on the slopes of a forested mountain in a remote area of the Garut regency, this is one of the largest West Javanese collections of palm-leaf manuscripts. The other significant amount of such texts are part of what is known as the "Bandung collection", originally found in the village of Cilegon (Netscher 1853), and the Raden Saleh legacy (*Notulen van het Bataviaasch Genootschap* 1867, p. 155). Apart from twenty-seven manuscripts (twenty-three *lontar*s and three *gebang*s) still to be found in Ciburuy, the bulk of the other West and Central Javanese collections is now kept at the National Library of Indonesia in Jakarta.

10. This collection was recovered in what might have formerly been a scriptorium in the area between the Merapi and Merbabu volcanoes in Central Java: see Wiryamartana (1993) and van der Molen and Wiryamartana (2001). A *terminus ante quem* for the dating of the manuscripts is 1759, the year of death of Windu Sona, the last keeper of the collection (see van der Molen 1983, p. 113). The problem of the real extent of this Central Javanese collection, whose manuscripts were only partly acquired after 1851 by the Batavian Society and are now kept at the National Library in Jakarta, has been tackled by van der Molen (1983, pp. 114–17); for a catalogue, see Sedyawati, Wiryamartana and van der Molen (2002).
11. A collection consisting of ca. thirty palm-leaf manuscripts was recovered by Lieutenant Colonel Colin Mackenzie during his journey through Java in 1812, and is now kept at the British Library as part of the Raffles collection of the India Office Library (IOL Jav 52: see Ricklefs and Voorhoeve 1977, pp. 65–67, and Ricklefs and Gallop 2014, pp. 65–67). As reported by Mackenzie, these manuscripts "were brought by the civility of a regent from a long deserted house in the distant forests, where they had lain neglected for years" (Hill 1834, p. 358). The regent might have been Kyahi Tumeṅgung Puger (Puger being a regency in the Eastern hook of Java), mentioned — along with the name of Mackenzie — in the sub-colophon of one of the manuscripts. The manuscripts are written in different varieties of scripts, the majority of which seem to be of East Javanese origin (and in fact very close to the Balinese variety of script), with a few specimens written in the type of Buda script characterizing most of the manuscripts originating from the Merapi-Merbabu area. My preliminary identification of some of the manuscripts, containing such important Old Javanese texts as the *Arjunavivāha*, the *Agastyaparva*, and the *Tattvajñāna*, may be found in Ricklefs and Gallop (2014), p. 328.
12. Perumal (2012, p. 159), on the authority of Murthy (1996, pp. 27–28), distinguishes three types of palm-leaves, namely *Corypha umbraculifera, Borassus flabellifer*, and *Corypha utan*, however he mistakenly describes the first as growing "in comparatively dry climates like those of Gujarat, Sindh and Rajasthan", confuses the third with the *lontar*, and incorrectly characterizes it as growing "in humid coastal areas, particularly on the west coast of India, in Burma and Thailand"; the opposite is true, namely the *Corypha umbraculifera* does not tolerate well dry climates, and in fact grows mainly on the littorals of south and eastern India, Sri Lanka, and western Java and Sumatra, whereas *lontar* (*Borassus flabellifer*) prefer relatively dry climates, such as those of East Java, Bali, and Lombok.
13. See also the remarks by Holle (1877, p. 16): "Manuscripts written with ink in Kawi-quadratic-script have come to light also from the Merbabu; however, as already said, after inspection it appeared to me that their provenance is from the Sundanese area, for in them are found not only single Sundanese words, but also whole sentences in Sundanese" (my translation from the

original Dutch). Ms. PNRI 16 L 455 (from the Merapi-Merbabu collection) is a *gebang* containing the Old Javanese *Bhimasorga*, a text which displays a marked Sundanese influence; another copy of this text has been preserved on a *lontar* written in Old Sundanese script. During one of my visits to the National Library of Indonesia, I noted an undated, apparently nineteenth-century handwritten roman transliteration (PNRI 89 no. 262) of manuscript 628 *Siksa Guru*), a *gebang* that was not described by Poerbatjaraka (1933) in his list of the manuscripts of the Batavian Society collection and that may now be traced to the Merapi-Merbabu repository thanks to a note reported in the above transliteration explicitly referring to its provenance from that collection; in the *Bhujaṅga Manik* (lines 860–68, Noorduyn and Teeuw 2006, pp. 259–60) the protagonist quotes a sentence from a text bearing the same name; however, the quoted passage is in Old Sundanese. Kropak (*gebang*) 69 L 629, to which was stuck the hand-written catalogue mark "Merbaboe 3", includes some loose fragments of several *lontar*s from the Merapi-Merbabu collection (catalogued as 30 L 501), and of two fragmentary pieces of a *gebang*. Since it appears that most of the *gebang*s that have survived to us originate from West Java, it seems safe to conclude that the above-mentioned complete codices, among which the *Dharma Pātañjala*, and presumably also the fragmentary ones, found their way from West Java to the Merapi-Merbabu scriptorium before AD 1759 (cf. van der Molen 1983, p. 113).

14. Such as the *Arjunavivāha* in the Merapi-Merbabu collection (Wiryamartana 1990, p. 16) and in the IOL Jav 52 collection now at the British Library (Gallop and Ricklefs 2014, p. 328). The latter collection has also preserved a copy of the *Agastyaparva* (see *ibid.*).
15. This is an Old Javanese prose texts with a single *śloka* and a few Sanskrit "quotes", of uncertain date. The relatively close reliance on Sanskrit models and doctrinal themes found in the speculative genre of *tattva* texts, along with relatively little localization, suggest that the earliest stratum of the text might date back to a historical period during which the socio-cultural and religious ideologies carried through Sanskrit texts were strictly adhered to in intellectual circles.
16. The parallelisms can be appreciated from the comparison of the three texts arranged in tabular form in Acri 2011*a*, pp. 619–31. It is evident that the three texts — which I shall refer to as *tattva*s rather than *tutur*s — share a similar agenda of "translation" of Sanskrit elements into a local linguistic and intellectual framework; in doing so, they display a similar degree of faithfulness to what appears to be a common and prototypical Sanskrit canon.
17. See XVI (ed. Danasasmita et al.): "*Hayaṅ nyaho di sakveh niṅ carita ma: Damarjati, Sanghyang Bayu, Jayasena, Sedamana, Pu Jayakarma, Ramayana, Adiparwa, Korawasrama, Bimasorga, Rangga Lawe, Boma, Sumana, Kala Purbaka, Jarini, Tantri; sing sawatek carita ma memen tanya*". The *Saṅ Hyaṅ Siksa Kandaṅ Karesian* has been transmitted to us through the oldest dated Old Sundanese manuscript (AD 1518).

18. The latter is an epic text in prose written in the seventeenth century but referring to events pertaining to Malacca and other countries in the fifteenth and sixteenth century, in which we find the episode of the travels of the protagonist Hang Tuah to Viajayanagara (Bijaya Nagaram) and Nāgapaṭṭiṇam (Negapatam). The mention of the king Kisna Rayan is a clear reference to the king Kṛṣṇadevarāya I who ruled Vijayanagara from 1509 to 1529, whose court Hang Tuah visited. In occasion of the display by the latter of a fluent command of the "Vijayanagaran language" (Kaṇṇaḍa or Tamil?), the king is amazed and asks him from which country does he come from. Hang Tuah replies that he is Malay but has studied the Indian language in Majapahit (Kassim 1997, p. 393), which by that time was just about to fall at the hands of Demak. While it is true that the *Hikayat*s cannot be taken as reliable historical accounts, the presence of such information, however exaggerated may it be, probably reflects a Malay popular tradition referring to Majapahit as a centre of learning that maintained links with India, and where it was even possible to study Indian languages.
19. Teeuw et al. (1969, pp. 19–26) noted that Mpu Tanakuṅ and many other literati of that period probably visited South India in order to perfect their knowledge of Indian languages and look for Śaiva scriptures. This opinion is supported by Hunter on the basis of his analysis of the treatise on prosody *Vṛttasañcaya* by the same Javanese author (Hunter 2001, p. 90).
20. These are the *Saṅ Hyaṅ Siksa Kandaṅ Karəsian*, the *Saṅ Hyaṅ Raga Devata* (coll. Museum Sri Baduga Bandung, ms. 07.106), the *Sevaka Dharma* (Kropak PNRI 16 L 408), the Sri Ajnyana (see below), and the metrical work known as *Jati Niskala* (or *Jati Raga*) (cf. Noorduyn and Teeuw 2006, pp. 2–10).
21. As I have noted elsewhere, the *Navaruci* shares several philosophical passages with the *Tattvajñāna* and other *tutur*s: see Acri 2011*a*, p. 696, s.v. *Navaruci*. Several manuscripts of this text bear the title (*Saṅ Hyaṅ*) *Tattvajñāna* (*Nirmala*) in their colophons.
22. Given the peculiarity of their language, these texts are often referred to as "Middle Javanese". It is, however, difficult to apply a clear demarcation between Old and Middle Javanese in a consistent manner: see Zoetmulder 1974, pp. 24–36.
23. Although a few titles of scriptures are identical, i.e. *Sevaka Dharma* (West Jav. PNRI 637 and 408, cf. Bal. LOr 9644, 9697, 9699), *Tiga Jñāna* (West Jav. LOr 2267, cf. Bal. LOr 9401, 10.084), *Bhimasorga/Bhīmasvarga* (West Jav. PNRI 16 L 623 and 455, cf. Bal. Lor. 3974–7, 3816, 3869, 4132–5), my preliminary readings suggest that these manuscripts contain different texts/recensions, even though they feature comparable themes. But I suspect that this picture is bound to change as soon as further codicological and philological research on these Javanese and Balinese collections is carried out.
24. For a list of such "reconfigured" elements, see Acri (2011*a*), pp. 6–7.
25. Those manuscripts appear to belong to a common tradition: apart from sharing the same support, writing technique and script, the manuscripts bear other

uniform features, such as four lines to a page, one single binding hole for which a definite space occupying two lines of text is left blank, and elaborate wooden cases (*kropak*) lacquered in red and with black and yellow floral designs — probably derived from China.

26. See Noorduyn (1982), pp. 416–18, van der Molen (1983), p. 78, Wiryamartana (1993), pp. 503–5.
27. See OJED (268): "2. *brahman* or other person of clerical rank. In older texts it often appears to be a younger *brahman* (student or disciple); later (Majapahit and after) a religious official (*śaiwa* or *boddha*, but distinct from *wipra* and *ṛṣi*)".
28. Thus implying no religious connotation; however, note the Indonesian *pujangga* "celibate", which may hint at the celibate, ascetic status of those wandering literati. Hoogervorst (2016, p. 328) outlines the "rather atypical shift in meaning" from Sanskrit *bhujaṅga* through Old Javanese to Malay *bujang* as follows: Sanskrit *bhujaṁga* "serpent, serpent-demon" > "divine helper" > "part. class of Brahmins" > "court scholar" > "literary man"; Malay *bujang*: "court scholar" > "gallant of the prince" > "young man" > "bachelor".
29. According to Hunter (2009), the sudden beginning of the Old Javanese *belles-lettres* and the coming to light of Old Javanese language in an already highly refined form suggests that a rather long "incubation period" is likely to have occurred: the most prominent antecedent of Old Javanese language is probably to be looked for in Old Malay, preceding the former by at least a few centuries, during which it received significant Sanskrit influence. On this hypothesis, see also Braginsky (1993).
30. Ādityavarman's name was engraved on the back of an earlier Arapacana Mañjuśrī image found in the thirteenth-century Candi Jago in East Java (Lunsingh Scheurleer 2008, pp. 294–96). Amoghapāśa Lokeśvara was represented prominently in East Java in the Siṅhasāri period, for instance in the thirteenth century at Candi Jago and in a series of Nāgarī-inscribed bronze plaques commissioned by East Javanese King Kṛtanagara (Reichle 2007, pp. 117–20). Many of these images attest to transregional networks of artisans moving across Asia as they may be linked to a diaspora of northeastern Indian and/or Newar Buddhist masters and artists (Lunsingh Scheurleer 2008, pp. 296–98; Reichle 2007, pp. 103–4).
31. On this figure and the historical and epigraphic evidence suggesting that the Batang Hari area constitutes the remnants of a kingdom called Dharmāśraya, see Reichle (2007), pp. 194–95.
32. The single, striking image of a dancing Hevajra/Heruka unearthed at Padang Lawas bears resemblances to two similar eleventh- or twelfth-century icons from Comilla district in modern Bangladesh (Bautze-Picron 2014, pp. 111, 125; Fig. 5). On the popularity of Hevajra and the *Hevajratantra* in Sumatra, see Griffiths (2014).

33. That is, Srimat Tribhuvanarāja Mauli Varmadeva. We also know of a queen named Tribhuvana (1329–50) who reigned in Majapahit, and of a Buddhist king of Ayutthaya named Trailokanat (r. 1431–88).
34. See Doorenbos (1933), pp. 42–43, and Drewes and Brakel (1986), pp. 110–15.
35. Kozok (2004, p. 37) reports that some 200 manuscripts were photographed and transliterated by Petrus Voorhoeve in 1941; a copy of this document (in Bahasa Indonesia), entitled *Tambo Kerinci*, is kept in the library of the KITLV in Leiden, and can now be accessed online at <http://ipll.manoa.hawaii.edu/indonesian/research/tambo-kerinci> (last accessed 13 January 2017).
36. As the form of language preserved by the text is still free of the Arabic loanwords that characterize Classical Malay, it may be concluded that Tanjung Tanah Malay is an intermediate form of Malay standing somewhere between Old and Classical Malay.
37. OJED (1697) glosses *sāroddhṛta* as: "(Skt) 'the selected essentials of the books of learning', name of a work containing rules for the conduct (policy) to be followed; cf *Sārasamuccaya*", but does not give any instance of *śāstroddhṛta.* For the sanskrit sources attesting *samuddhṛtya, sāraṃ uddhṛtya*, etc., see Acri (2015*b*), p. 60, fn. 5.
38. See OJED 1200: " '(Skt) the science of or a work on political ethics', cf. *Sutasoma* 4.5: *warahĕn riṅ nītiśāstra*; TK 34.23: *mahyun iṅ wiwāhakrama saṅke śāstrāgama mwaṅ nītiśāstra*; 16.27)". In fact the *Nītisāra* and *Nītiśāstra* are the same work (see Sternbach 1975, p. 394).
39. This may be either a general term meaning "the science of political ethics" or the title of a specific work (or class thereof). In fact several works bearing this sequence as part of their title are known to exist in the Sanskrit and Tibetan tradition (see Sternbach 1975, pp. 370–73). Monier-Williams' dictionary records a work named *Nītiśāstrasamuccaya.*
40. The resulting *pāda* would violate the rules of the standard *anuṣṭubh*, having a long fifth syllable (a minor blemish compared to a hyper- or hypo-metrical *pāda*). But the expression could have been originally found in a prose text, and adapted to a metrical form, thereby losing the *sāra* to fit the metre. For attestations of the compound *śāstrasāroddhṛta* and its variants in Old Javanese texts preserved in Balinese manuscripts, cf. Acri 2015*b*, p. 60, fn. 8.
41. On "Archipelago Sanskrit" — a "hybrid" language mixing Sanskrit and Old Javanese and/or Balinese — see Goudriaan and Hooykaas (1971), pp. 11ff. To my mind, the Sanskrit of the *Saluka Dipati* does not constitute Archipelago Sanskrit, but an instance of corrupt Sanskrit.
42. An edition (based on a single manuscript) and Indonesian translation is Mirsha et al. (1994).
43. The mention of Mahādeva in the line preceding the colophon of the Tanjung Tanah codex is mirrored in the occurrence of Mahādeva (and the other epithets Parameśvara and Śaṅkara) in the *Bhuvanakośa.*
44. Of course, it is entirely possible that the authorship was attributed post facto

by the Balinese tradition — as it happened in the case of the short poem *Udyalāka* (Teeuw et al. 1969, p. 13). Furthermore, the *Bhuvanakośa* is made of two different texts, both of which contain early Śaiva material. Therefore, Tanakuṅ might have rearranged and recompiled older texts into a single work.

45. See *Rudrakavaca* (Stuti 673 and 676), *Dvādaśādityastava* (Stuti 679), and *Viṣṇustava* (Stuti 682) in Goudriaan and Hooykaas (1971).
46. The verse-quarter *praṇamya śirasā devam* is found in the similarly eulogistic first stanza of the *Gaṇapatistava* (Stuti 667), a hymn dedicated to the elephant-headed god Gaṇapati, son of Śiva. As pointed out by Goudriaan and Hooykaas (1971, pp. 390–91), this hymn finds a close parallel in the *Saṁkaṣṭanāśanagaṇeśastotram*, a Sanskrit hymn of South Asian provenance published in the *Bṛhatstotraratnākara* collection. Besides in the Sanskrit hymn, an identical verse-quarter is also attested in a number of Sanskrit sources, spanning from the *Mahābhārata* and *Rāmāyaṇa* Epics to the *Atharvavedapariśiṣṭa*s, various Purāṇas, and Śaiva and Vaiṣṇava Tantric texts.
47. While the use of this royal title was common among Southeast Asian kings and cannot therefore be taken as uncontroversial evidence of the Śaiva affiliation of monarchs (see above, n. 32), I wonder whether in the cases discussed here it may represent a tradition derived from the Śaiva line of East Java. That is to say, Ādityavarman and the other royals of Javanese descent could have adopted Buddhism in Sumatra so as to conform to the dominant religious and ritual paradigm, yet kept their Śaiva royal names. As far as the Straits region is concerned, Miksic (2010, p. 31) notes that "Buddhism was the dominant religion in the Straits of Melaka for almost 1,000 years....", yet admits that "concrete evidence of the detailed religious beliefs of this area is scarce" (ibid., p. 35).
48. Van Stein Callenfels (1937, p. 165), on the authority of d'Albuquerque, considered Bhaṭāra Tumapel the father-in-law (or a relative) of Parameśvara, the founder of Melaka, who probably owed his position to a marriage with a royal princess who might have been the daughter of the former. This princess became known in Melaka as Queen Parameśvarī.

Bibliography

Acri, A. *Dharma Pātañjala; A Śaiva scripture from ancient Java Studied in the light of related Old Javanese and Sanskrit texts*. Groningen: Egbert Forsten Publishing, 2011*a*.

———. "Javanese Manuscripts of the Tattvajñāna". In *From Beyond the Eastern Horizon; Essays in honour of Professor Lokesh Chandra*, edited by ManjuShree, pp. 119–29. New Delhi: Aditya Prakashan, 2011*b*.

———. "Revisiting the Cult of 'Śiva-Buddha' in Java and Bali". In *Buddhist Dynamics in Premodern and Early Modern Southeast Asia*, edited by C. Lammerts, pp. 261–82. Singapore: Institute of Southeast Asian Studies, 2015*a*.

———. "The Sanskrit Colophon of the Tanjung Tanah Codex and its Malay Gloss as Illuminated Balinese and South Asian Parallels". *Bijdragen tot de Taal-, Land- en Volkenkunde/Journal of the Humanities and Social Sciences of Southeast Asia* 171 (2015*b*): 56–68.

al-Attas, Syed Muhammad Naguib. *The mysticism of Hamzah Fansuri*. Kuala Lumpur: University of Malaya Press, 1970.

Bautze-Picron, C. "Buddhist Images from Padang Lawas region and the South Asian connection". In *History of Padang Lawas, North Sumatra, II: Societies of Padang Lawas (Mid-Ninth–Thirteenth century CE)*, edited by D. Perret, pp. 107–28. Paris: Archipel, 2014.

Braginsky, V. *The System of Classical Malay Literature*. KITLV Working Papers 11. Leiden: KITLV, 1993.

———. "The science of women and the jewel: The synthesis of Tantrism and Sufism in a corpus of mystical texts from Aceh". *Indonesia and the Malay World* 32/93 (2004): 141–75.

———. "The manner of the prophet — concealed, found and regained: Revisiting the science of women". *Indonesia and the Malay World.* Forthcoming.

Brakel, L.F. "State and statecraft in seventeenth century Aceh". In *Pre-colonial state systems in Southeast Asia*, edited by A. Reid and L. Castles, pp. 56–66. Kuala Lumpur: Malaysian Branch of the Royal Asiatic Society, 1975.

———. "Hamza Fansuri, notes on Yoga practice, *lahir* dan *zahir*, the *taxallos*, a difficult passage in the Kitab al-Muntahi, Hamza's likely place of birth and Hamza's imagery". *Journal of the Malaysian Branch of the Royal Asiatic Society* 52, no. 1 (1979): 73–98.

———. "Islam and local traditions: Syncretic ideas and practices". *Indonesia and the Malay World* 32-92 (2004): 5–20.

Brown, C.C. *Sějarah Mělayu or Malay Annals.* Kuala Lumpur and Singapore: Oxford University Press, 1970.

Budha Gautama, Wayan. *Tutur Bhuwana Koṣa.* Surabaya: Paramita, 2009.

De casparis, J.G. "Hindu Revival in Fifteenth-Century Java". In *India and Beyond, Essays in Honour of F. Staal*, edited by D. van der Meij, pp. 50–54. London/Leiden: Kegan Paul/IIAS, 1997.

Colas, G. and G. Gerschheimer. *Écrire et transmettre en Inde classique*. Paris: École française d'Extrême-Orient, 2009.

Danasasmita, S., et al. *Sewaka Darma (Kropak 408), Sanghyang Siksakandang Karesian (Kropak 630), Amanat Galunggung (Kropak 632), Transkripsi dan Terjemahan.* Bagian Proyek Penelitian dan Pengkajian Kebudayaan Sunda (Sundanologi) Direktorat Jendral Kabudayaan Dep Pendidikan Dan Kebudayaan Bandung. 1987.

Doorenbos, J. *De Geschriften van Hamzah Pansoeri*. Leiden: Batteljee & Terpstra, 1933.

Drewes, G.W.J. "Further Data Concerning 'Abd as-Samad al-Palimbani". *Bijdragen tot de Taal-, Land- en Volkenkunde* 132 (1976): 267–92.

——— and L.F. Brakel. *The poems of Hamzah Fansuri*. Dordrecht: Foris, 1986.

Goudriaan, T. and C. Hooykaas. *Stuti and Stava (Bauddha, Śaiva and Vaiṣṇava) of Balinese Bauddha Brahmans*. Amsterdam/London: North Holland Publishing Company, 1971.

Griffiths, A. Review of Uli Kozok et al. (2006). *Kitab undang-undang Tanjung Tanah: Naskah Melayu yang tertua*, *Bijdragen tot de Taal-, Land- en Volkenkunde* 166 (2010): 133–38.

———. "A Corpus Approach to the Study of Inscriptions in Old Malay Language". Paper presented at SEA epigraphy conference in Kuala Lumpur, 2011.

———. "Inscriptions of Sumatra II. Short Epigraphs in Old Javanese". *Wacana* 14-2 (2012): 197–214.

———. "Inscriptions of Sumatra, III: The Padang Lawas Corpus studied along with inscriptions from Sorik Merapi (North Sumatra) and Maura Takus (Riau)". In *History of Padang Lawas, North Sumatra. II: Societies of Padang Lawas (9th c.–13th c.)*, edited by D. Perret, pp. 211–62. Paris: Archipel, 2014.

Gunawan, A. "Nipah or Gebang? A Philological and Codicological Study based on Sources from West Java". *Bijdragen tot de Taal-, Land- en Volkenkunde* 171 (2015): 249–80.

Hall. K.R. "Ritual Networks and Royal Power in Majapahit Java". *Archipel* 52 (1996): 95–118.

Hanneder, J. "On 'the death of Sanskrit'". *Indo-Iranian Journal* 45 (2002): 293–310.

Hefner, R.W. *Hindu Javanese: Tengger Tradition and Islam*. Princeton: Princeton University Press, 1985.

Hill, D. "Biographical Sketch of the Literary Career of the late Colonel Colin Mackenzie, Surveyor-General of India; comprising some particulars of his Collection of Manuscripts, Plans, Coins, Drawings, Sculptures, &c. illustrative of the Antiquities, History, Geography, Laws, Institutions, and Manners, of the Ancient Hindús; contained in a letter addressed by him to the Right Hon. Sir Alexander Johnston, V.P.R.A.S. &c. &c.". *Journal of the Royal Asiatic Society* 1/2, Art. xxix (1834): 333–64.

Hooykaas, C. "The Balinese Sengguhu priest, a Shaman, but not a Sufi, a Śaiva, and a Vaiṣṇava". In *Malayan and Indonesian Studies*, by J. Bastin and R. Roolvink, pp. 267–81. Oxford: Oxford University Press, 1964*a*.

———. *Āgama Tīrtha; Five Studies in Hindu-Balinese Religion*. Amsterdam: N.V. Noord-Hollandsche Uitgevers Maatschappij, 1964*b*.

———. *Cosmogony and Creation in Balinese Tradition*. The Hague: Nijhoff, 1974.

Holle, K.F. *Tabel van oud- en nieuw- indische alphabetten*. Buitenzorg: C. Lang, 1877.

Hoogervorst, T. "Lexical Influence from North India to Maritime Southeast Asia: Some New Directions". *Man In India* 97, no. 1 (2016): 293–334.

Hunter, T.M. "Wṛttasañcaya Reconsidered". *Bijdragen tot de Taal-, Land- en Volkenkunde* 157 (2001): 65–96.

———. "The Body of the King: Reappraising Singhasari Period Syncretism". *Journal of Southeast Asian Studies* 38 (2007): 27–53.

———. "Bahasa Sanskerta di Nusantara: Terjemahan, Pemribumian, dan Identitas Antardaerah". In *Sadur: Sejarah Terjemahan di Indonesia dan Malaysia*, edited by H. Chambert-Loir, pp. 23–47. Jakarta: Kepustakaan Populer Gramedia, 2009.

———. "Sanskrit in a Distant Land: The Sanskritized Sections". In *A 14th Century Malay Code of Laws: The Nītisārasamuccaya*, by Uli Kozok (with contributions by Thomas Hunter, Waruno Mahdi and John Miksic), pp. 281–379. Singapore: Institute of Southeast Asian Studies, 2015.

Kassim, A. *Hikayat Hang Tuah*. Kuala Lumpur: Yayasan Karyawan dan Dewan Bahasa dan Pustaka, 1997.

Kozok, U. *A 14th Century Malay Code of Laws: The Nītisārasamuccaya* (with contributions by Thomas Hunter, Waruno Mahdi and John Miksic). Singapore: Institute of Southeast Asian Studies, 2015.

Kragh, U. "Localized literary history: Sub-text and cultural heritage in the Āmer Śāstrabhaṇḍār, a Digambara manuscript repository in Jaipur". *International Journal of Jaina Studies* (Online) 9-3 (2013): 1–53.

Lieberman, V. *Strange Parallels; Southeast Asia in Global Context, c. 800–1830. Volume 2: Mainland Mirrors: Europe, Japan, China, South Asia, and the Islands*. Cambridge: Cambridge University Press, 2009.

Lombard, D. "Networks and Synchronisms in Southeast Asian History". *Journal of Southeast Asian Studies* 26, no. 1 (*Perspectives on Southeast Asian Studies*) (1995): 10–16.

Lunsingh Scheurleer, P. "The well-known Javanese Statue in the Tropenmuseum, Amsterdam, and its Place in Javanese Sculpture". *Artibus Asiae* 68, no. 2 (2008): 287–332.

Miksic, J. "The Buddhist-Hindu Divide in Premodern Southeast Asia". Nalanda-Sriwijaya Centre Working Paper No. 1 (March 2010) <http://nsc.iseas.edu.sg/documents/working_papers/nscwps001.pdf>.

Mirsha, I Gusti Ngurah Rai, et al. *Buana Kosa. Alih Aksara dan Alih Bahasa (Brahma Rahasyam)*. Denpasar: Upada Sastra, 1994.

Moertono, S. *State and Statecraft in Old Java: A Study of the Later Mataram Period, 16th to 19th Century*. Ithaca: Modern Indonesia Project, Southeast Asia program, Cornell University, 1981.

Monier-Williams, M. *Sanskrit-English Dictionary*. Oxford: Clarendon Press, 1899.

Murthy, R.S. Shivaganesha. *Introduction to manuscriptology*. Delhi: Sharada Publishing House, 1996.

Netscher, E. "Iets over eenige in de Preanger-Regentschappen gevonden Kawi-handschriften". *Tijdschrift van de Bataviaasch Genootschap* 1 (1853): 469–79.

Nihom, M. "Diksa, Kala and the Stuti of Siwaratrikalpa 33.1-2". *Bijdragen tot de Taal-, Land- en Volkenkunde* 153 (1997): 103–11.

Noorduyn, J. "Majapahit in the fifteenth century". *Bijdragen tot de Taal-, Land- en Volkenkunde* 134 (1978): 207–74.

———. "Bujangga Manik's journeys through Java: Topographical data from an

Old Sundanese source". *Bijdragen tot de Taal-, Land- en Volkenkunde* 138 (1982): 413–42.

Noorduyn, J. and A. Teeuw. "The Ascension of Sri Ajnyana; A local form of Śaivism in an Old Sundanese allegorical poem". In *Society and Culture of Southeast Asia; Continuities and Changes*, edited by Lokesh Chandra, pp. 283–98. New Delhi: IAIC/Aditya Prakashan, 2000.

———. *Three Old Sundanese poems*. Leiden: KITLV Press, 2006.

Notulen van de Bataviaasch Genootschap. Notulen van de Algemene en Bestuursvergaderingen van het Bataviaasch Genootschap. van Kunsten en Wetenschappen (published as vols. 1–59, 1862–1921). Bandung, 1867.

OJED. *Old Javanese-English Dictionary*. P.J. Zoetmulder, with the collaboration of S.O. Robson. The Hague: Nijhoff, 1982 [Two vols, KITLV.]

Perumal, P. "The Sanskrit Manuscripts in Tamilnadu". In *Aspects of Manuscript Culture in South India*, edited by Saraju Rath, pp. 157–72. Leiden and Boston: Brill, 2012.

Pleyte, C.M. "'Poernawidjaja's hellevaart, of de volledige verlossing. Vierde Bijdrage tot de kennis van het oude Soenda". *Tijdschrift van het Bataviaasch Genootschap* 56 (1914): 365–441.

Poerbatjaraka, R.M.N. "Lijst der Javaansche handschriften in de boekerij van het Kon. Bat. Genootschap". *Jaarboek van het Koninklijk Bataviaasch Genootschap* 1 (1933): 269–376.

Pollock, S. "The Sanskrit Cosmopolis, 300–1300; Transculturation, Vernacularization and the Question of Ideology". In *Ideology and the status of Sanskrit; Contributions to the history of the Sanskrit language*, edited by J.E.M. Houben, pp. 197–247. Leiden: Brill, 1996.

———. "The Death of Sanskrit". In *Comparative Studies in Society and History* 43, no. 2 (2001): 392–426.

———. *The language of the gods in the world of men; Sanskrit, culture, and power in premodern India*. Berkeley: University of California Press, 2006.

———. "Literary Culture and Manuscript Culture in Precolonial India". In *Literary Cultures and the Material Book*, edited by S. Eliot, A. Nash and I. Willison, pp. 77–94. London: The British Library, 2007.

Rath, S. *Aspects of Manuscript Culture in South India*. Leiden and Boston: Brill, 2012.

Reichle, N. *Violence and serenity: Late Buddhist sculpture from Indonesia*. Honolulu: University of Hawai'i Press, 2009.

Ricklefs, M.C. *Mystic synthesis in Java; A history of Islamization from the fourteenth to the early nineteenth centuries.* Norwalk: EastBridge, 2006.

——— and Gallop, A. *Indonesian Manuscripts in Great Britain: A Catalogue of Manuscripts in Indonesian Languages in British Public Collections (New Editions with Addenda et Corrigenda).* Jakarta: Yayasan OBOR Indonesia/ EFEO, 2014.

——— and Voorhoeve, P. *Indonesian manuscripts in Great Britain: A catalogue of manuscripts in Indonesian languages in British public collections*. Oxford: Oxford University Press, 1977.

Sedyawati, K., I.K. Wiryamartana and W. van der Molen. *Katalog Naskah Merapi-Merbabu Perpustakaan Nasional Republik Indonesia*. Leiden: Opleiding Talen en Culturen van Zuidoost-Azië en Oceanië, 2002.

Sternbach, L. "General Appeal of Subhāṣita Literature in Sanskrit". In *Proceedings of the First International Sanskrit Conference*, edited by V. Raghavan, pp. 370–97. Delhi: Rashtriya Sanskrit Sansthan, 1975.

Sudarshana Devi. *Wṛhaspati-tattwa; An Old Javanese philosophical text*. Nagpur: IAIC, 1957.

Teeuw, A., et al. *Śiwarātrikalpa of Mpu Tanakuṅ*. The Hague: M. Nijhoff, 1969.

van der Molen, W. *Javaanse Tekstkritiek; Een overzicht en een nieuwe benadering geillustreerd aan de Kunjarakarna*. Dordrecht: Foris [PhD Dissertation, Leiden University], 1983.

——— and I.K. Wiryamartana. "The Merapi-Merbabu manuscripts. A neglected collection". *Bijdragen tot de Taal-, Land- en Volkenkunde* 157 (2001): 51–64.

van Lennep, D. "Some observations on the *nipah* leaf *kropak*s from West Java, with an analysis of content and historical relevance of the *manggala* to the Old-Javanese *Amaramālā*". BA Honours Thesis, University of Sydney, 1969.

van Stein Callenfels, P.V. "The Founder of Malacca". *Journal of the Malayan Branch of the Royal Asiatic Society* 15-2 (128) (1937): 160–66.

Wiryamartana, I.K. *Arjunawiwāha; Trasformasi teks Jawa Kuno lewat tanggapan dan penciptaan di lingkungan sastra Jawa*. Yogyakarta: Duta Wacana University Press, 1990.

———. "The scriptoria in the Merbabu-Merapi area". *Bijdragen tot de Taal-, Land- en Volkenkunde* 149 (1993): 503–509.

Wolters, O.W. *History, culture, and region in Southeast Asian perspectives*. Singapore: Institute of Southeast Asian Studies, 1999 [1st ed. 1982].

Worsley, P. et al. *Mpu Monaguṇa's Sumanasāntaka; An Old Javanese Epic Poem, its Indian Source and Balinese Illustrations*. Leiden/Boston: Brill. 2013.

Zoetmulder, P.J. *Kalangwan: A survey of Old Javanese Literature*. The Hague: Nijhoff, 1974.

———. *Old Javanese-English Dictionary*. With the collaboration of S.O. Robson. The Hague: Nijhoff, 1982 [Two vols, KITLV.]

10

SEEKING A SUFI HERITAGE IN THE DECCAN

Kashshaf Ghani

In the multi-volume work *The Heritage of Sufism* covering an entire millennium of Persianate Sufism, Leonard Lewisohn recognizes the difficulty of undertaking a "comprehensive coverage of all the mystical contexts" that characterize Sufi heritage within the span of a single study. Covering the expansive idea of a "spiritual and cultural renaissance" in Persian society between 1200 and 1500 the work identifies Sufism as a major catalyst for these developments. The religious climate of Persia in the aforementioned period was intensely influenced by Sufi traditions led by masters like Jalaluddin Rumi (d. 1273), Nimatullah Wali (d. 1431), Hafez Shirazi (d. 1389), Saadi (d. 1292), and Saiyid Ali Hamadani (d. 1384) among many others. Their works and activities shaped pre-Safavid Persia in a manner which scholars have characterized as a "renaissance" — in literature, arts, Islamic sciences, philosophy, music and mystical scholarship. One can grasp Lewisohn's emphasis on the impossibility of covering comprehensively all dimensions of this Sufi tradition between the covers of a single volume. Certain important aspects remain unexplored, even though they are critical towards understanding the *heritage* of Persian Sufism.[1]

In an interesting parallel, South Asia presents before us similar difficulties of undertaking a comprehensive study of a Sufi heritage in this region. Within the same time frame, before the rise of the Mughal Empire — the South Asian equivalent of the mighty Safavids — Sufi activities spread across north India, and also the South, particularly the Deccan region. This paper will look into certain aspects connected to the rise of

Sufi networks in the Deccan in the thirteenth and fourteenth centuries, at a time when Deccan's Sanskritized cultural world experienced the coming of a north Indian Persian tradition. In spite of some obvious similarities with the Iranian situation, the focus will be less on such sweeping categories as "renaissance". Rather the article will seek to engage with a different set of questions more relevant to the idea of a Sufi heritage.

What roles did Sufi saints and, later, their shrines play in creating a heritage? Was this idea sustained only through tangible traces of their shrines? Or can it be located in the intangible idea of mystical rituals and practices, like *sama*? How did the chain of spiritual succession ensure the continuity of this heritage? These questions lead us towards an understanding of Sufism in the Deccan not as a monolithic idea that can be framed against a single set of causes. Rather, the aim is to explore the plurality of trends and tendencies that existed against the larger backdrop of a transregional Sufi world in the Deccan. The ensuing discussion will explore how varying degrees of Persianization gave rise to a multi-layered Sufi heritage in the Deccan.

FROM NORTH TO SOUTH, 1327

In 1327, after becoming the Sultan of Delhi, Muhammad bin Tughluq set up an administrative centre in the Deccan that would, in all senses, operate as the second capital. The former Yadava stronghold of Deogir or Devagiri was chosen for the purpose and renamed Daulatabad in 1328. A successful completion of this project was done through the physical transfer of the Muslim elite from Delhi to the Deccan. This involved the movement of intellectuals, scholars, clergy, administrators, warriors, revenue officers, poets and artisans to the Deccan capital, who, it was expected, would inaugurate a new era in the socio-cultural and political life of the region. Sufis formed a considerable section of this migrant population who were expected to spread the worldview of Islam in Daulatabad, and subsequently the larger Deccan region, thereby advancing the agenda of the Sultan to fuse "Islamic religious symbolism with the rhetoric of empire".[2] This transfer, Muhammad bin Tughluq hoped, would reaffirm his authority within the larger realm, and, as a result he paid little heed to the strong resentment, expressed by Sufis in Delhi, towards this imperial order.[3]

The foremost Sufi order of South Asia, the Chishtis participated in this migration under the leadership of Shaykh Burhanuddin. Entrusted with the robe of succession by his master Shaykh Nizamuddin, the aged saint set off on his long journey towards Khuldabad, few miles from the imperial capital of Daulatabad, accompanied by an assembly of Sufis and scholars such as Amir Hasan Sijzi (d. 1337), the author of *Fawaid ul Fuad*, Pir Mubarak Karwan (d. 1333), Khwaja Hasan, Khwaja Umar (d. 1349), Kamaluddin Samana, Kaka Sa'd Baksh, Shaykh Ruknuddin Kashani, Imaduddin Kashani, Khwaja Majiduddin Kashani, Khwaja Burhanuddin Kashani, Khwaja Jamaluddin Kashani, Fariduddin Adib (d. 1337) and Maulana Ruknuddin.[4] Popular legends and local hagiography would set the figure of Sufis arriving in the Deccan at 1400, commemorated by the "Mosque of Fourteen Hundred Saints". Burhanuddin's arrival continued the Chishti spiritual tradition in the Deccan, sanctified by the handing over of the sacred insignias (*tabarrukat*) of Shaykh Nizamuddin that included his staff and rosary, to be carried to Khuldabad. This transfer of spiritual authority both through training in the ethics of spirituality, moral conduct, and ritual practice, along with the possession of the sacred regalia attested the authority of the succeeding saint. This was ensured through the master-disciple (*pir-murid*) relation that bound the disciple with his master right from the days of initiation. The scope of this relation was supposed to be limitless as a master was believed to be able to guide and protect his successor even after passing away from the material world. This bond between the master and the disciple lived on through an expression of extreme devotion and utmost sincerity by the disciple.

It was perhaps keeping in mind the high standards of succession set forth by Shaykh Nizamuddin and Shaykh Burhanuddin, resting on strict adherence to codes of moral conduct and ethical practice, that their disciple Shaykh Zainuddin refrained from appointing a successor (*khalifa*). Scholars in the circle of Shaykh Burhanuddin, and even later, would recognize the end of one major branch of the Chishti tradition with Zainuddin. Hence, going by his position in the genealogical table, he is recognized as the twenty-second master (*bais khwaja*) starting from the founder of the Chishti order. All the spiritual regalia that were handed down to him from his ancestors were laid to rest with him, along with the robe of the Prophet Muhammad that passed through all the Chishti masters. It would only be with the coming of Shaykh Husayni Gesudaraz in the Deccan that a competing line of Chishti Sufism gets activated.

A TRANSREGIONAL PERSIAN CONNECTION

At the time when Shaykh Burhanuddin passed away in 1337, the experiment with the second capital in the Deccan had begun to unravel for the Tughluq's. Within a decade the political landscape of the Deccan changed dramatically in 1347 with the rise of the two powerful kingdoms of Vijayanagara established by Bukka, and the Bahmani founded by Zafar Khan, who ascended as Sultan Alauddin Hasan Bahman Shah.[5]

The rise of the Bahmanis also witnessed the consolidation of a Persianized world — in politics and culture — across the Deccan. Ancient trade and migration corridors connected South Asia to Persia through Delhi and Lahore. The region of the Deccan however had contacts with these lands through maritime networks too, which transported goods and warhorses from the Persian Gulf regularly to the Konkan and Malabar coast, through the ports of Chaul and Dabhol. Rise of the imperial Tughluqs in north India ensured the spread of a Persian political and cultural world across a vast area from Lahore to Bengal. Tughluq conquests in the south and the establishment of the new capital brought this Persianized political culture into the Deccan, through the idea of the Sultan as an absolute political authority, the place of justice in governance, land revenue assignments based on the *iqta* system, together with styles of art, architecture, music, dress, cuisine, and the use of Persian language for all practical purposes.[6]

Interestingly, these very first links that would connect the nascent Bahmani Sultanate to the Persianized north Indian empire of the Tughluqs would survive the fall of Tughluq authority in the Deccan; primarily through the Bahmani attempt at reaching out to the Perso-Islamic political world of West Asia, particularly Iran and Central Asia. This move was imperative as it ensured a continuous supply line of warhorses, precious items, luxury wares, men of letters and administrative talent. In their own backyard, however, the Bahmani Sultans would adopt a means of gaining political and social legitimacy through the patronage of eminent Sufi masters who in turn conferred their blessings on the Sultan thereby sanctifying the territory over which he ruled.[7] Perhaps the reason why, as we find later, Bahmani Sultans made it a habit of seeking blessings from Sufi shaykhs even before setting off for military campaigns. Victory over such territories would then be read as a direct consequence of the saint's blessings, legitimizing the act of conquest.

COMING OF THE WESTERNERS

It needs to be remembered however that the influx of Persian elements into the Deccan had started to gain currency from the days of Sultan Muhammad II (r. 1378–97) who aspired to host the great Persian poet

Hafiz Shirazi (d. 1390) at his court in Gulbarga. With this aim in mind he extended an invitation to the poet, who while accepting it initially travelled to the port of Hormuz to board a Bahmani ship. However alarmed by a sea storm the poet decided to retrace his steps, and as a consolation send a poem composed by himself for the Bahmani ruler.[8] On the other hand, Shia influence was steadily gaining prominence in the Bahmani kingdom with the inflow of Westerners (*afaqis*) from Iran and Iraq increasing by the day. Locals in the administration were being outnumbered by Shia immigrants. The Bahmani army at this point of time consisted of elements from Iran, Iraq, Khurasan, Transoxiana, and Turkey. In addition the Sultan recruited an elite fighting corps of 3,000 archers from the Persian Gulf and Khurasan regions.

Sultan Firoz Bahmani carried this obsession forward. One of the reasons can be located in the activities of Timur (d. 1405) throughout Central and West Asia where he had carved out a grand empire for himself. His invasion into north India in 1398–99 dealt a death blow to the Tughluq Empire centred at Delhi. Neither the city nor the empire could recover from this devastation. This left Timur as the greatest living patron of Persian culture and heritage. His magnificent capital at Samarqand stood as the epitome of all things best in the Persian world, setting standards in literature, art, architecture, and imperial ambition. Firoz Bahmani — in awe of this great conqueror — sent him lavish gifts, with a request to be counted among Timur's dependents. Timur graciously accepted the gifts and addressed the Bahmani ruler as his son. This recognition was sealed with gifts that included a belt, a gilded sword, four royal robes, a Turkish slave and four splendid horses.

This reciprocation from Timur bolstered the confidence of Firoz Bahmani by many degrees. With Delhi devastated, and only a shade of its glorious past, Firoz saw a perfect opportunity to aim for the grandeur that Delhi once displayed, for his own capital city of Gulbarga. This, he realized could only be possible by making his kingdom a satellite of Samarqand, steeped in Persian culture and aesthetics. With this aim in mind Bahmani Sultans started recruiting scholars, soldiers, merchants, poets, administrators, nobles, military commanders, and similar other talent from regions of Iran and Central Asia. These Westerners came to be known as the *afaqis*, and occupied a position of prestige compared to the older class of north Indian immigrants who had settled in the Deccan during the transfer of the capital.[9] Persian came to be aggressively patronized in the Deccani royal courts, as a language with a transregional prestige, compared to local Dakhni Urdu. Over the fifteenth and sixteenth century

Persian would achieve a degree of prestige and literary status similar to that enjoyed by Sanskrit earlier.

In the above context one can perhaps argue that the elite family lineage of Gesudaraz was not lost on Firoz Bahmani when the Sultan invited the Sufi Shaykh to his capital. Gesudaraz came from a Sayyid family of Khurasan, a thriving centre for intellectual and spiritual activities in northern Iran. As a leading centre of Islamic mysticism Khurasan stood almost parallel to the equally revered centre at Baghdad led by Shaykh Junayd. Ancestors of Gesudaraz were popularly known as *sadat i daraz gisu* (Sayyids with the long locks), the reason why the epithet *gesudaraz* stuck with his original name, Sayyid Muhammad al Husayni.[10] Apart from his impeccable spiritual lineage in the direct line of succession within the prestigious north Indian Chishti order, the saint also carried an enviable status of belonging to the descendants of the Prophet Muhammad, hence called a *sayyid.* Firoz Bahmani could not have asked for a more perfect spiritual patron for his Sultanate — one whose transregional family roots originated from the Arab Prophet, while his forefathers were trained in the Sufi culture of Khurasan, in the heart of Persia.

The Bahmani obsession with the transregional cultural world of Iran manifested itself in many ways, but also through literary productions. When Sultan Ahmad Shah shifted his capital from Gulbarga to Bidar he commissioned an epic history of his dynasty in line with the classical Persian work of *Shahnama* (Book of Kings). The work was entrusted to the court poet Shaykh Azari (d. 1463). It was titled *Bahman Nama-i Dakhni* (Book of Bahman of the Deccan), possibly to assert its Deccani character, as both the *Shahnama* and the *Bahman Nama* claimed their respective dynastic origins from the ancient Iranian ruler Bahman.

In architecture, the decoration of the new palace in Bidar on a lighter Persian style, was inspired by Timur's Aq Sarai palace in Samarqand, evident through its extensive use of glazed tiles — blue, yellow and green, with white borders — on most walls of the palace complex.[11] The fort-city in Bidar was larger in architectural style and decorative embellishment than any contemporary one in Iran and Central Asia. The outer court or the Diwan-i Aam took inspiration from the *Iwan* — a Persian equivalent of the basilica. The placement of the pool in front of the throne represented a style found frequently in Iranian and Indian painting of this time with an idea of a transregional architectural style resulting from the handiwork of Persian architects.

In the meantime Sultan Ahmad Shah succeeding his brother Firuz to the throne decided to start his reign on a fresh note. He shifted his capital to Bidar. In an attempt to project his kingdom as matching up to the Sultanate of Delhi that provided refuge to immigrants from the Persian world, Sultan Ahmad Shah distributed 3,000 *tankas* among the Syeds of Karbala. It is not difficult therefore to read into Sultan Ahmad Shah's mind when he decided not to solicit support from any of the Deccani Sufi orders — Chishti and Junaydi — for his new capital, but looked beyond the shores of his kingdom towards Iran.

Sultan Ahmad Shah had heard about the renowned Sufi saint Shah Nimatullah Wali (d. 1431) who resided in Kirman, in southeastern Iran from one of his disciples Shaykh Nizamuddin Faruqi in Gulbarga. The Sufi master was born in Aleppo from an Arab-Persian descent and was trained in Shiraz. He settled in the town of Shahr-i Sabz in Khwarazm (present-day Uzbekistan) at the heart of the Timurid Empire. Drawn into a political conspiracy, when the saint was forced to leave the city he supposedly stood up to Timur through the following verse, before his final departure

Off with you, my prince!
Don't flaunt gold and silver before me!
While your domain stretches from China to Shiraz,
Mine is a realm which has no frontier.[12]

A delegation of nobles and elders representing the Bahmani court, carrying gifts and presents was sent to Kirman to convey the regards of the Bahmani Sultan, and invite him to settle in the capital city of Bidar: much in the same way as Firoz Shah had invited Gesudaraz to bless his capital city at Gulbarga. Years ago the Chishti master conceded, but Shah Nimatullah declined the invitation, presumably due to his advanced age. Instead, one of his disciples Mulla Qutubuddin Kirmani was sent to Bidar with a green crown with twelve peaks and a letter for the Sultan. At the royal court Sultan Ahmad Shah was given the letter where Shah Nimatullah addressed him as "the greatest of the kings, Shihabuddin Ahmad Shah Wali",[13] but regretted his inability to move from Kirman. Thereafter the Sultan was offered the crown. Thus, through a single act of coronation not only was the spiritual blessings (*baraka*) of the Iranian Sufi master passed on to the Bahmani Sultan, but the latter was also initiated into the Nimatullahi order. In a reciprocating gesture Sultan Ahmad Shah accepted Shia Islam as the official form of Islam in the Deccani Sultanate. All this a year before Shah Nimatullah passed away in 1431.

In a second delegation to Kirman, Sultan Ahmad Shah requested Shah Nimatullah to send one of his progeny to the Bahmani court at Bidar.

Keeping in mind his old age, the Sufi saint refused to part with his son, sending instead his grandson Mirza Nurullah to Deccan. He was welcomed with great honour in the personal palanquin of the king, and was conferred with the title of *Malik ul Mashaikh* (King of Shaykhs/Sufis). Nimatullahi Sufis enjoyed a superior status in the royal court, compared to all other Sufi saints including the descendants of Gesudaraz. The Sultan gave his daughter in marriage to Mirza Nurullah thereby establishing a blood relation with the Nimatullahis of Persia who continued to enjoy state patronage till the survival of the Bahmani dynasty.

It was only after the death of Shah Nimatullah Wali that his son Shah Burhanuddin Khalilullah moved to Bidar. He too received a warm welcome at the court and his sons were married to the daughters of Sultan Ahmad Shah and Sultan Alauddin Ahmad Shah. When Khalilullah died in 1460 a beautiful tomb was erected on his grave carrying calligraphic inscriptions done by Mughis of Shiraz, who was brought to the Deccan, and especially entrusted with this task. The Iranian influence on the tomb architecture is evident from the slightly stilted arch of fine proportions and the margins of black stones carved in design patterns of rope, leaf and flower. The name of fourth Caliph Ali was engraved alongside the names of Allah and the Prophet Muhammad. One of the striking features of this architecture lies in the use of beautiful tiles of bright colours, particularly deep blue and deep green.

When Sultan Alauddin II succeeded to the Bahmani throne in 1436 Deccani society had split itself clearly between the Westerners and locals. The Sultan accentuated the situation by announcing that in the royal court Westerners will appear on his right while locals on his left. Such decisions lacked far-sightedness since not only were important administrative departments of the Sultanate, like army, revenue, run exclusively by the *afaqis*, such a decision created serious resentment among the local Deccani population leading towards an acute socio-ethnic crisis that would eventually ruin the Sultanate. In order to address the situation, the Sultan invited the grandsons of Gesudaraz to the royal court, hoping that it would pacify the local resentment. Sayyid Shah Yadullah Husayni I (d. 1448) refused to honour the request realizing perhaps the enormity of the social tension pervading Bidar. Instead he sent his brother Sayyid Abul Faiz Minullah Husayni (d. 1474). It appears, that the family of Gesudaraz, in course of their long stay in north India and then in the Deccan, had evidently ceased to carry their transregional character; rather they were now less Persian and sufficiently localized and could be used to diffuse the social tension among local Deccanis. In spite of such attempts on part of the Sultan, the situation failed to improve between Persian immigrants and local Deccanis.

SUFI PRACTICE OF *SAMA*

The presence of Sufi shrines in the Deccani landscape came to represent notions of spiritual sovereignty (*wilayat*). However when we speak of how these institutions operated vis-à-vis their own cultural world, one important aspect that emerges is that of shrine practices. Here we briefly look into one such practice of *sama* (listening to poetry and music for spiritual pursuits) which came to be recognized as the defining spiritual exercise of the Chishti Sufis, both in north India and Deccan.

Shaykh Burhanuddin was a strict follower of the Chishti mystical practices, *sama* being the primary among them. Sources attest that he invented a "distinctive style" of dancing (*raqs*) on reaching moments of ecstasy. His disciples termed this style as "Burhani" after the great Shaykh. Opinions differed as to what was precisely meant by the term "Burhani" — whether it signified the style of dancing or the epithet given to the disciples of Burhanuddin who participated in such a style of dancing. Such was the intensity of Burhanuddin's involvement in the practice of *sama*, together with his passionate style of dancing (*raqs*), that he often used to lose control over his conscious self. Some of Shaykh Nizamuddin's disciples, like Shaykh Nasiruddin Mahmud, who were also mystics of the same order, but possessed less passion for music and dance as spiritual aids, passed terse remarks on Burhanuddin's demeanour after his participation in *sama* and *raqs*. To this the Shaykh would retort back that such was the practice of his great masters of the Chishti lineage and that it was incumbent upon him to adhere to that hallowed tradition even if it did not find conformation in the widely read Sufi manual, the *Awarif-ul Maarif* by Shaykh Shihabuddin Abu Hafs Umar Suhrawardi.[14]

Sufis of the Chishti order repeatedly emphasized on the essentiality of *sama* as the ecstatic core of their spiritual order, and hence an indispensable practice in the path towards union with God. Their movement from Central Asia to north India and then to the Deccan never affected their strong preference for *sama*. Therefore it would be improbable that a mystic of the stature of Shaykh Burhanuddin could be deterred from participating in the *sine qua non* practice of the Chishti mystical tradition, over reservations from his fellow mystics.

Reservations toward *sama* drew its ideological origins from the works of Sufi theorists in the tenth and eleventh centuries, who in their elaborate manuals emphasized on the necessity of strict discipline, in the absence of which the mystic could end up in severe danger. Shaykh Usman al-Hujwiri (d. 1077) in his *Kashf ul Mahjub* (Unveiling of the Veiled), the earliest Sufi manual, elaborated

> Dancing has no foundation in the religious law or the spiritual path … but since ecstatic movements and the practices of those who endeavour to induce ecstasy resemble it, some frivolous imitators have indulged in it immoderately and have made it a religion. I have met with a number of common people who adopted Sufism in the belief that it is this dancing and nothing more … it is more desirable that beginners should not be allowed to attend musical concerts lest their natures become depraved.[15]

The rising fervour of orthodoxy pervading the religious ambience of the Delhi Sultanate did not escape the seasoned eyes of Shaykh Nizamuddin, who spent many summers under seven Sultans of Delhi. He taught Burhanuddin Gharib the value of accommodating Islamic theological doctrines, within the ideological framework of his spiritual practices and teachings, so that Chishti mysticism in the Deccan did not face an uncertain future. Thus, in spite of being an ecstatic believer in *sama*, Burhanuddin took great care to value Islamic learning and scholarship in his mystical circle, drawing references from classical Quranic commentaries, *hadith*, law, and treatises on Sufism. Sources enumerate quite vividly the popularity of *sama* in the mystical circle of Shaykh Burhanuddin in Khuldabad, continued by his disciple Shaykh Zainuddin Shirazi. In order to limit the growing degree of reservation against this practice together with upholding its sanctity in the eyes of fellow mystics, both within and beyond the order, and most importantly to ward off any sort of legal interferences from the ruling authorities, Shaykh Burhanuddin and his disciples took the onus of laying down a strict framework within which the ritual should be performed, quelling any doubt regarding its sacredness and permissibility.

Shaykh Burhanuddin divided sama into four types: *Sama* is lawful (*jaiz*) when the mystic turns his heart completely towards God, longing only for Him without leaving any room for worldly distraction. Second, *sama* is permitted (*halal*) when the mystic orients himself mostly towards God, longing mostly for Him, with little distraction towards His creation. *Sama* is disapproved (*makruh*) when the listener yearns mostly for worldly creations, rather than longing for the Almighty creator. *Sama* is strictly forbidden (*haram*) when the listener does not pay any attention towards contemplating for the Divine, and takes the exercise as an engagement in frivolity. However, the listener should know the difference between the four types prior to engaging in the ritual.[16]

Abu Hafs Suhrawardi (d. 1234), the author of the Sufi manual *Awarif ul- Maarif* elaborated on *sama*:

> Music does not give rise in the heart which is already not there. He whose inner self is attached to anything but god, gives in to sensual desires with music. One who is inwardly attached to god, is moved towards the love of god on hearing music. Common folk listen to music according to nature, novices listen to music with desire and awe. When Sufis listen to music it brings them Divine gifts and blessings. They are the spiritually perfect and god reveals to them through the medium of music which then becomes heavenly for them.[17]

Such theories continued to influence even later Sufi masters in the Deccan, the most important of them being Gesudaraz. Two very important aspects of *sama*, where Gesudaraz made a firm intervention, were those which concerned the issue of participation. First, was the problem of the common masses participating in *sama*. Like his illustrious predecessors in the north, Gesudaraz too did not impose a complete sanction on the participation of the lay in assemblies of *sama*. In fact, because people would throng in large numbers to his *khanqah*, became the pretext for Sultan Firuz Shah Bahmani to ask the saint to move away from the vicinity of the royal fort citing security concerns. Nevertheless, while elucidating on the qualities of listeners in such an assembly the Shaykh insisted that the listener (*mustami*) should be an individual of high intellect (*sahib-i firasat*) to be worthy of participating in such a spiritually charged assembly. The above preconditions make a clear distinction between lay individuals and those who possess sufficient spiritual training. Gesudaraz drew his conclusion that *sama* was not for everybody, and a Sufi who held a taste (*zawq*) for participation in *sama* should stay away from any such assembly where all sorts of people (*har jins*) gathered in to listen to words of poetry.[18]

Gesudaraz's reservation for the common masses participating in such a spiritual assembly is made amply clear when he stated that *sama* is "desireable" to the proficient (*muntahiyan*), "allowable" to the beginners (*mubtadiyan*) and intermediate (*mutawassitan*), but is completely "undesirable" for the common masses. Such clear categorization leads us to the second issue, that of the participation of novices in the assembly of *sama*. Gesudaraz made *sama* "allowable" for "beginners". But at the same time he left behind some amount of ambiguity by referring to Shaykh Junayd, founder of the Baghdad school of Sufism. Junayd was sceptical regarding *sama* and argued that if a novice participated in *sama* it signified that there was an element of idleness left in him. If Gesudaraz followed Shaykh Junayd, in this respect, then it was improper on his part to advocate the participation of novices in the ritual of *sama*.[19]

In the face of such debates Sufis of the Chishti order maintained that together with prayer, fasting and recitation of the Quran, *sama* too led an individual closer to the divine by allowing the Sufi mystic to interiorize the qualities of contemplation and thought — focusing on the attributes and essence of the divine. Though Gesudaraz was a strict follower of religious doctrines, he stood firm in his defense of *sama* against criticisms put forward by clerics. Rather, Gesudaraz emphasized that a combination of recitation of the Quran together with *sama*, brought more benefits to the mystic than ordinary prayers. Thus all his assemblies of *sama* begun and ended with a recitation of the Quran. However for Gesudaraz, remembrance, meditation and prayer — all of which emanate from a recitation of the Quran should be performed in conjunction with the exercise of *sama* for progress in the spiritual path. For those, like religious clerics, who are unaware of such secrets of the mystical path, observing silence is prudent.

Towards formalizing the tradition of *sama* in the Deccan, Gesudaraz drew inspiration from a number of early Persian mystics, the most important of them being Ayn-ul Quzat al-Hamadani (d. 1131) and his master Ahmad Ghazzali (d. 1126). Following the teachings of Ghazzali elaborated in his classical treatise *The Lightning Flashes of Indication Concerning the Refutation of those who Declare Audition Forbidden in General*, Hamadani in his work the *Tamhidat* argued that *sama* as a powerful spiritual exercise could emancipate the soul from the body preparing the wayfarer to receive illuminations from the divine realm.[20] In the process, Hamadani continued, the heart of the seeker would be transformed by the light of God that shone through it obliterating worldly desires. Both Hamadani and Ghazzali engaged in depth with the issue of *sama* given its controversial position among Muslim legal scholars. Both recognized the dangers involved in this exercise that could lead a novice towards deceit and temptation. As a result beginners and women were advised to keep away from this practice, since it could be read by them as popular acts of music. Drawing examples from the Quran, the life of the Prophet and his teachings (*hadith*), both these scholar-Sufis criticized the jurists and clerics who questioned the sanctity of *sama* and its worth as a spiritual exercise.

Recognizing *sama* as a spiritual practice not free from dangers, both Ghazzali and Hamadani did not advocate a complete ban on the exercise. Rather they argued that Sufis should engage in *sama* only under the proper supervision of their master, under specific physical and emotional conditions, in the company of individuals who are sufficiently trained in the pursuit of the ritual. The above regulations correspond to the preconditions of time (*zaman*), place (*makan*) and brethren (*ikhwan*), for organizing *sama*, emphasized repeatedly by Sufi masters of Persia in their advice manuals. The limb movements that accompany the ritual of *sama* express joy and elation as the heart experiences closeness to God. Different Sufis have their own style of gestures that involve the movement of hands, feet and head, and the whole body. The most identifiable style is that of the Mevlevis of Turkey whose typical bodily gestures label them as whirling dervishes. In this context it was perhaps not uncommon for Sufis like Shaykh Burhanuddin Gharib to have a particular dance style of his own, recognized as *Burhani*.

Regarding the use of language in assemblies of *sama*, Gesudaraz preferred Persian for "only in the sweet and tender melody of Persian poetry is it possible to do justice to the feelings and emotions surging in the heart of the singer".[21] In spite of characterizing *sama* as a practice unfit for the uninitiated, Khwaja Gesudaraz took measures to increase its popularity, together with making some of the verses intelligible to the common masses. Towards this end he encouraged the inclusion of Hindavi verses in assemblies of *sama* arguing that "Hindavi verses are usually soft, sweet and touching. The tunes are also soft and tender like the couplets, which induce humility and submission."[22] Gesudaraz realized the demands of the age and the social milieu he had situated himself in, and was one of the earliest Chishti mystics to use Hindavi and Dakhni Urdu as a means of active communication and expression of thoughts.

Notwithstanding the high standards of spiritual discipline and rules of conduct laid down by Gesudaraz, on the ritual of *sama*, attempts are made even to this day to organize *sama*, in compliance with all the regulations laid down by the Sufi saint. Such a *sama* that is held during the death anniversary (*urs*) celebration at Gulbarga, is termed as "Bund Sama" or closed assembly.[23] It is titled such so as to differentiate it from the more popular assemblies of *qawwali* that are regularly performed at the *dargah* complex participated by the common masses. *Bund Sama* is held strictly under the rules laid down by the Sufi saint himself. Being an assembly of great spiritual significance very few individuals, mostly Sufi adepts, are allowed to participate in it. The small size of the assembly make it easy to regulate, and moreover produces a conducive ambience for intense contemplation and meditation. The sacred *gaddi* (cushion), on which Khwaja Bandanawaz used to sit, is placed in front of the head of the shrine (*sajjada nashin*), who then initiates the assembly. The audition session is accompanied by only a pair of small tambourines (*duff*), with the strict exclusion of all sorts of musical instruments. The couplets are read out in the traditional form, both in Hindavi and Persian, as Gesudaraz preferred it.[24] Some of them being his own compositions and some by his devotees.

In the assembly of *Bund Sama*, these couplets written in Dakhni Urdu by the Sufi saint, and also his disciples are recited with the accompaniment of the tambourine, invoking the spiritual lineage of the Deccani saint.[25]

The fire of separation has kindled
Today in my body and soul
My Beloved is on the throne
Himself and His splendor on display
I am burning in the fire of love today

For Gesudaraz, and for many other Sufis of the Chishti tradition, *sama* remained an essential means to involve oneself in the thoughts of the Divine, through an intense feeling of love and devotion. Therefore Chishti Sufis in the Deccan never hesitated to uphold the integrity of the exercise in the face of strong opposition. Nothing illustrates this better than the breakdown of all cordial relations between Gesudaraz and Firoz Shah the Bahmani Sultan, when the latter could not come to terms with the elaborate musical assemblies in the *khanqah* of the Sufi saint. Though the Sultan dared not to ask Gesudaraz to discontinue such practices, he asked the saint to listen to the assembly in seclusion. Gesudaraz acceded and henceforth listened to *sama* from inside a room where a curtain separated him from the assembly. Later when the Sultan complained that the large number of people who visited these musical assemblies created chaos and a security threat near the royal fort, Gesudaraz showed no signs of compromise; he moved to the other end of the city. Similar would be the attitude of Shaykh Burhanuddin who chose to ignore the criticisms from some of his fellow Sufis on his ecstatic behavior leading to limb movements in an assembly of *sama*.

CONCLUSION

Throughout the fourteenth century, and also in the fifteenth, the larger cultural world of Persian was making measured advances in South Asia.

At a more micro level an important aspect of this Persian culture — its spiritual heritage — was formulated by Sufi saints coming from the north. Interesting to note that the creation of this spiritual heritage did not occur only through the numerous Sufi shrines that dot the Deccan landscape — creating an idea of a tangible heritage — that have been accessed by the elite and the masses alike. Rather the cultural heritage of Sufism in the Deccan came to rest on an inviolable set of practices and rituals. One would be the practice of spiritual succession that ensured a continuation of these Sufi orders through a strong bond of master–disciple relationship. It would be through this chain of succession that ideas of moral conduct and spiritual discipline be passed down over generations through the most adept Sufi master. In the absence of the latter the chain would end.

In a similar manner, specialized Sufi rituals would enable a deep sense of bonding within the community itself by bringing together a congregation of like-minded mystics in an eternal quest for the Divine. The organization of musical assemblies (*sama*) would be one such ritual, that defined the functioning of the Chishti order throughout South Asia, and also in the Deccan. Observed closely, it can be argued that both the above Sufi traditions played a crucial role in the process of adaptation of these north Indian Sufi masters within the region of the Deccan. It became an intrinsic component of their cultural environment, determining to a large extent how these masters would situate themselves in the unfamiliar terrain of the Deccan. In a region where Sufi orders rose parallel to political dynasties and on many occasions their paths would cross, it was due to the personality and spiritual charisma of these Sufi saints that no amount of political interference could compromise the integrity of the core practices that shaped these Sufi orders. Notwithstanding these tensions, seeking blessings from Sufi masters was a custom that the political elite increasingly engaged with from the period under discussion, bringing them closer to these saints and later their shrines.

Interestingly again, none of these practices were peculiar to the Deccan situation. Rather almost all of them had their roots in the cultural world of Persia and Central Asia. Both Sufis and the political elite of Deccan would draw their inspiration from a transregional cultural heritage. But their ways of appropriation would be starkly different. While the political elite would attach themselves to Persian traditions of kingship, authority, justice, art, architecture and cultural production; Sufis of the Deccan would trace their transregional origins to one or many among the numerous centers of spiritual activity spread across Persia, Central Asia and Afghanistan.

Sufi orders in the Deccan — Chishti, Junaydi and Nimatullahi — could not dissociate themselves from a cultural heritage that spanned regions beyond geographical boundaries. Regions from where these orders not only traced their lineage, but also the set of practices and rituals that they inherited from their predecessors.

Over the fourteen and fifteenth centuries therefore Deccan became an active site for inter-Asian interactions that connected it with some of the richest centers of cultural production across Iran, Afghanistan and Central Asia. All encapsulated within the world of Persian, not only as a transregional elite language, but a treasure house of art, architecture, literary production, aesthetics, and political discourse. Sufism came to constitute one component of this Persian cultural heritage in the Deccan: a significant one that rested on multiple networks and movement and mobility across Asia extending into the region of the Deccan which witnessed useful convergences between multi-ethnic and multi-linguistic traditions. Sufi saints, across orders, played a crucial role in sustaining this Persianized cultural heritage of the Deccan, so that in the coming days the region could strongly claim an identity of its own.

Notes

1. Leonard Lewisohn, ed., *The Heritage of Sufism*, vol. 2, *The Legacy of Medieval Persian Sufism (1150–1500)* (London: Oneworld Publications, 1999), Introduction.
2. Carl Ernst, *Eternal Garden: Mysticism, History and Politics at a South Asian Sufi Center* (New Delhi: Oxford University Press, 2004), p. 113.
3. Mahdi Husain, *Tughluq Dynasty* (Calcutta: Thacker Spink & Co., 1933), pp. 144, 173; H.K. Sherwani, *The Bahmanis of the Deccan* (New Delhi: Munshiram Manoharlal Publishers Pvt. Ltd., 1953), pp. 19–22.
4. Bilgrami, *Rawzat ul Awliya*, in Suleman Siddiqi, *The Bahmani Sufis* (Delhi: South Asia Books, 1990), p. 41.
5. Richard M. Eaton, *A Social History of the Deccan, 1300–1761: Eight Indian Lives* (New York: Cambridge University Press, 2005), pp. 33–58.
6. Richard M. Eaton, *Power, Memory, Architecture: Contested Sites in India's Deccan Plateau, 1300–1600* (New Delhi: Oxford University Press, 2014), p. 30.
7. Ibid.
8. Eaton, *A Social History*, pp. 60–61.
9. Eaton, *Power, Memory, Architecture*, p. 126.
10. Syed Shah Khusro Hussaini, *Sayyid Muhammad al-Husayni Gisu Daraz: On Sufism* (Delhi: Idarah-i Adabiyat-i Delli, 1985), p. 11.
11. Eaton, *A Social History*, pp. 63–64.

12. Terry Graham, "Shah Nimatullah Wali: Founder of the Nimatullahi Sufi Order", in *The Heritage of Sufism*, vol. 2, *The Legacy of Medieval Persian Sufism (1150–1500)*, edited by Leonard Lewisohn (London: Oneworld Publications, 1999), pp. 173–90.
13. Graham, "Shah Nimatullah Wali", p. 184.
14. Mir Khwurd, *Siyar ul Awliya* (Delhi: Matba i Muhibb i Hind, 1884–85), pp. 289–91.
15. Usman al Hujwiri, *Kashf ul Mahjub*, The Oldest Persian Treatise on Sufism by al-Hujwiri, trans. R. Nicholson (London: Gibb Memorial Series, 1959), pp. 410, 436.
16. Ruknuddin Kashani, "Shamail al-Ataqiya", in Ernst, *Eternal Garden*, p. 149.
17. Annemarie Schimmel, *Mystical Dimensions of Islam* (Chapel Hill: University of North Carolina Press, 1986), p. 182.
18. Ali Samani, *Siyar i Muhammadi* (Gulbarga: Gisu Daraz Academy, 1979), pp. 87–88.
19. Ernst, *Eternal Garden*, p. 129.
20. Firoozeh Papan-Matin, "Gisudaraz, an Early Chishti Leader of the Deccan and His Relationship with Twelfth-Century Mystics of Iran", *Deccan Studies* VII, no. 2 (2009), p. 118.
21. Ali Samani, *Siyar i Muhammadi* (Gulbarga: Gisu Daraz Academy, 1979), p. 71.
22. Ibid.
23. Syed Shah Khusro Hussaini, "Bund Sama", *Islamic Culture*, July 1970, p. 181.
24. Ibid.
25. Ibid.

11

ARCHAEOLOGICAL REMAINS AT NALANDA
A Spatial Comparison of Nineteenth Century Observations and the Protected World Heritage Site

M.B. Rajani and Sonia Das

The archaeological site of Nalanda has been inscribed in the UNESCO World Heritage List of 2016. One of the key requirements put forth by the World Heritage Convention (WHC) for such recognition is to geo-spatially identify core and buffer zones of the inscribed property. This essay analyses these inscribed zones in the spatial context of records and maps of archaeological remains at Nalanda created by Francis Buchanan-Hamilton, Alexander Cunningham and Alexander M. Broadley in the nineteenth century. Using recent satellite imagery and associated geo-spatial techniques together with ground observations, this essay firstly, identifies the geographical location of all features mapped and recorded by the three British explorers in and around Nalanda, secondly presents a visual comparison of the property inscribed as a World Heritage site and the expanse of archaeological features noticed in nineteenth century (some of which still exist, yet lie outside the core and buffer zones), and finally records the present land-use along those features (via visual interpretation of the latest satellite imagery and field visit) in order to identify locations where there is high potential for heritage conservation.

INTRODUCTION

Nalanda was a Buddhist monastery of considerable repute which attracted scholars from great distances. Accounts of visitors from China (dating from the seventh century AD) suggest that Nalanda was a large, thriving establishment whose physical dimensions were immense. This institution seems to have remained in existence from the fourth/fifth century to at least until the end of the twelfth century.[1] It is unknown exactly when this centre came into existence, and we do not have a continuous record for its activities. It must have gained a reputation for importance by the seventh century AD, attracting scholarly monks such as Xuanzang and Yijing from China. Tibetan monk Dharmasvamin records some lingering activity in the monastery with a handful of monks during his visit in 1234–36 AD. There is sparse historical documentation about Nalanda in the subsequent centuries, and the very existence of this mega monastery was forgotten in that region.

The site was visited by Francis Buchanan in 1812, a Scottish physician, who surveyed the region that would later be known as Nalanda as part of a survey of the territories forming the Presidency of Fort William. The first translations of the accounts of the Chinese travellers Faxian (337–422 AD) and Xuanzang (596–664 AD) into English[2] provided impetus to the growing interest in the discovery of Indian antiquity among British explorers. Aided by the translation of Faxian's accounts[3] Captain Markham Kittoe, an archaeologist, visited the site in 1847–48 and identified Baragaon as "Na Lo" of Faxian. Subsequently, Alexander Cunningham identified these remains as the ruins of the famous Nalanda that Xuanzang visited.[4] Thereafter, Alexander Meyrick Broadley visited Nalanda in 1871, exploring territory under his jurisdiction. Three of these explorers — Buchanan, Cunningham and Broadley — left detailed records of ruins, based on which the Archaeological Survey of India (ASI) has conducted phased excavations beginning in 1863 and most recently in 1983.[5]

These excavations have exposed a total of sixteen large structures: a row of four temples or *chaityas* on the west (numbered 3, 12, 13, 14), a row of eight west-facing monasteries or *viharas* (numbered 1, 4, 6, 7, 8, 9, 10, 11) parallel to the Temples and two smaller north-facing monasteries (numbered 1A and 1B), and to the east of Monastery-7 is Temple 2 and further east is the Sarai temple (Figure 11.1). The excavated site was inscribed as a World Heritage site by UNESCO in July 2016, with a 23 *ha.* core zone and a 57.88 *ha.* buffer zone.

This essay explores the graphical and textual records of archaeological ruins in Nalanda's vicinity made in the nineteenth century, identifies all features recorded therein, and precisely locates these archaeological remains in Nalanda's environs by correlating historical information with recognizable patterns in a variety of satellite images and reports the current condition of every location through on-ground observations. It also places this information in geospatial context with the core and buffer zones of the inscribed property as specified on the UNESCO website.[6]

FIGURE 11.1
Map of Archaeological Site of Nalanda Mahavihara and environs showing features within core and buffer zone inscribed as World Heritage by UNESCO

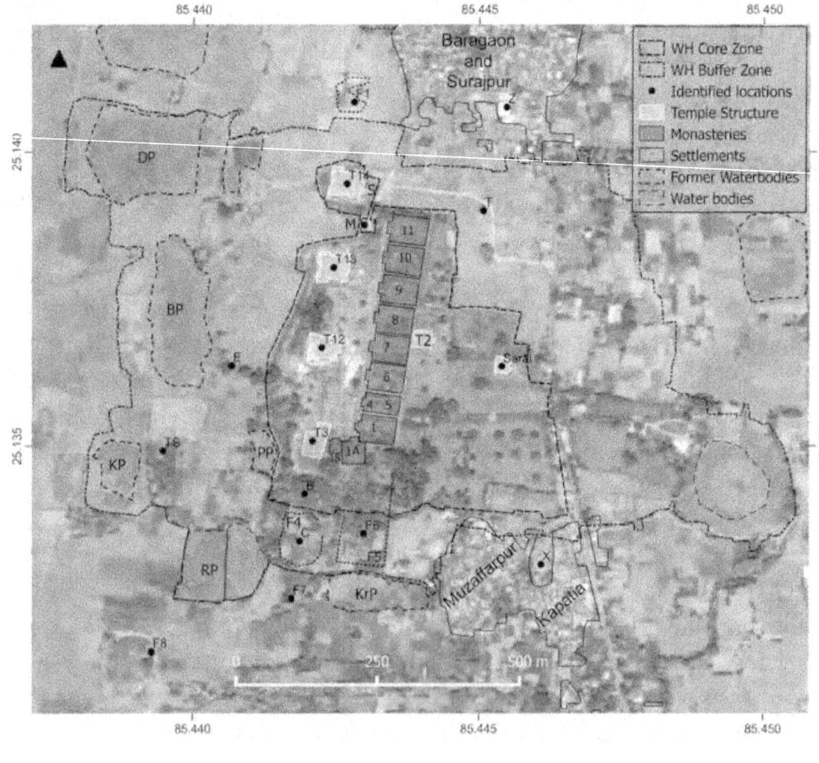

Source: Map prepared at NIAS, Bengaluru. *Image source*: Google Earth Digital Globe, 8 May 2010.

EXTRACTING GEOSPATIAL INFORMATION FROM HISTORICAL MAPS

Historical maps are an important source of spatial information, and are invaluable for understanding historical landscapes and identifying features of archaeological interest. In order to extract accurate spatial information, it is necessary to be aware of the methods used to create such maps and their limitations, as these can cause various inaccuracies that make feature identification difficult. Many eighteenth and nineteenth century maps use a mixture of survey methods. For example, distances between important landmarks were measured using triangulation, but dimensions between less important features were recorded as estimated walking distances. These methods have very different error margins, ranging from a few metres to several kilometres depending on the scale of the map.[7] For this reason, such maps are often distorted by software that attempts to geo-reference them using standard methods that take all spatial information into account. It is important to recognize the well-surveyed points and perform geo-referencing using only those, and explicitly ignore features that cartographers may have considered less significant such as roads, man-made tanks and settlements. Features of the latter type are often depicted on historical maps, and despite their possibly inaccurate representations, they can be very useful for modern archaeological exploration.

CONTEXT OF THE EARLY MAPS OF NALANDA

The earliest record of expanse of archaeological remains at the site of Nalanda and its environs are penned by Francis Buchanan. He visited the ruins of Kundilpur near the village of Baragaon on 8 January 1812 and evocatively records the expanse of ruins and details of antiquities he observed.[8] His daily journal includes a free-hand sketch of the ruins (with north aligned to the top of the page) marking tanks, heaps/mounds, temples, forts and settlements.This illustration measures 16 cm × 14 cm, a copy of which is available in the British Library.[9] It is likely that Buchanan made this drawing when he wrote the day's experience, since he has used the same pen and ink for the drawing and the text that surrounds it. The illustration is a remarkably good representation of the site, considering that map-making was not on his agenda, and that it was primarily drawn in a single attempt with very few edits. The drawing conveys the geographic spread of remains, and adds clarity to the textual account.

Cunningham first visited Nalanda in the winter of 1861–62, and conducted initial surveys until 1864–65. His famous diagram, "Sketch of the Ruins of Nālandā Mahāvihāra", was published in his report together with explanations for every feature he marked.[10] This map is also a good representation of the state of the site when he visited. The spatial distribution of mounds and proportions of distances between them are to-scale, suggesting that he used a trigonometrical survey with careful measurements. However, judging by their recorded sizes and shapes, it appears that the waterbodies, roads and settlement layouts received less attention because these were tangential to Cunningham's agenda to map ruins. In 1871, he was elevated from Director of Archaeology to the post of Director-General of the ASI. He focused operations in northern India, carrying out surveys and explorations and planned for additional explorations at Nalanda along with his assistants Beglar and Carlleyle.[11]

Before Cunningham or Beglar could revisit Nālandā, A.M. Broadley took charge of the subdivision of Bihar, Patna District as the Assistant Magistrate and Collector. In 1872, he had ready access to sites under his jurisdiction. With ample workforce and funds, he conducted independent explorations at Nalanda (and at other sites within the district), and had no hesitation in removing antiquities from their location. He regarded these efforts as assisting the official archaeological exploration rather than interfering with it, and he was an observant (if somewhat inconsistent) investigator.[12] He published a pamphlet with a diagram of the mounds, tanks and settlements at Nalanda entitled "Rough plan of ruins of Bargaon".[13] Despite not being to-scale, Broadley's diagram was clearly made with great care, and includes valuable annotations such as measured distances between mounds.

The illustrations made by Buchanan, Cunningham and Broadley are the only available early graphical record of archaeological ruins in the larger landscape of Nalanda. Subsequently, ASI has prepared an architectural drawing of the excavated structures "Nalanda: Excavated remains" published by Misra (1998).[14] More recently, a larger landscape visualization of these ruins were published by Rajani (2016) using satellite images to map the archaeological expanse.[15]

ARCHAEOLOGICAL FEATURES VISIBLE IN THE NINETEENTH CENTURY

Several features are common to the maps prepared by Buchanan, Cunningham and Broadley, but each map also includes unique features.

We tabulate a combined list of these features (see List 11.1): settlements in Table-1, waterbodies in Table-2, and all the archaeological features in Table-3. These features are also mapped with accurate geospatial locations in Figure 11.1 and Figure 11.2, and are shown on a Digital Elevation Model (DEM) or a height map in Figure 11.3. All figures also depict the core and buffer zones of the inscribed World Heritage property. Settlements are annotated with full names, large waterbodies have their name followed by the abbreviation P. (for Pokhar), smaller water bodies are annotated with abbreviations (e.g., BP for Balen Pokhar and DP for Dehar Pokhar). The structures within the ASI property are annotated with the nomenclature used by ASI, e.g., T2, T3, T12-14 for temples, and with the number prefixed with M for monasteries. The features outside the ASI property identified by Rajani (2016) are annotated as F1 to F9. The remaining features largely use annotations given by Cunningham, with the exceptions being the mounds TI and TS marked only by Broadley, and the mounds near Jagdishpur and Jeofardih annotated as Jg and Jf respectively. Within each table, annotations are arranged in alphabetical order. For place names, we preserve the spellings given by Buchanan, Cunningham and Broadley in their respective columns, and use commonly accepted spellings in our figures and Remarks.

ANALYSIS OF ARCHAEOLOGICAL FEATURES

Table-3 lists a total of 31 archaeologically interesting features ranging from single sculptures (e.g., the Vajra Varahi image at location T; Figure 11.4a) to individual structures (the temples) to clusters of similar and proximate structures (the monasteries) to large and complex features (e.g., the mound F9 which measures about 400 m × 400 m). Out of these, the features at S, W, V and RP no longer exist at the marked locations. The sculpture of Vishnu riding on Garuda at location V, recorded by Buchanan, Cunningham and Broadley, is now in the Indian Museum in Kolkata.[16] Among the remaining 27 features, 8 lie in the core zone (T2, T3, T12, T13, T14, Sarai, B and the monasteries) and 7 lie in the buffer zone (E, M, T, C, TS F5, and F6). The remaining 12 features are not within the inscribed property, even though several features show potential for archaeological exploration (F3 and F9).[17] Prior archaeological excavations at some of these locations (KKF, Jf and Jg) have yielded promising results.[18] This leads us to wonder whether the rationale for delineating the core and buffer zones is based on guidelines drawn by UNESCO. These guidelines are discussed next.

FIGURE 11.2
A view of Nalanda and its vicinity showing features discussed in Tables 1, 2 and 3

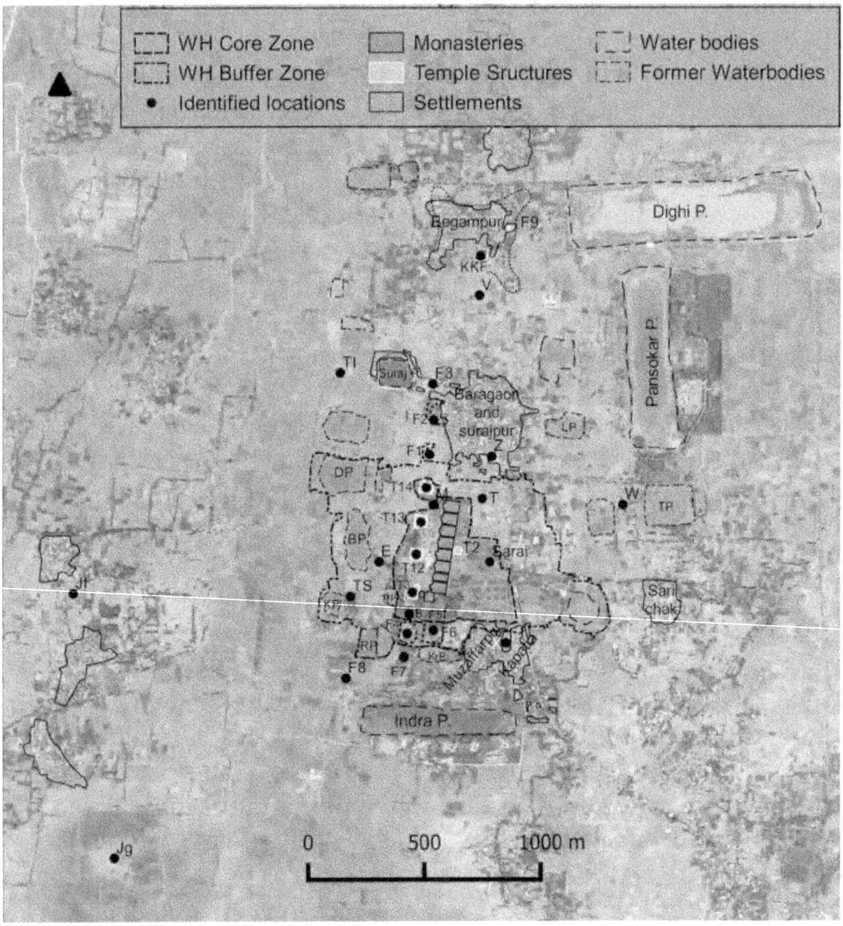

Source: Map prepared at NIAS, Bengaluru. *Image source*: Google Earth Digital Globe, 8 May 2010.

FIGURE 11.3
A view of topography of Nalanda using DEM showing shapes of mounds in the context of features discussed in Tables 1, 2 and 3

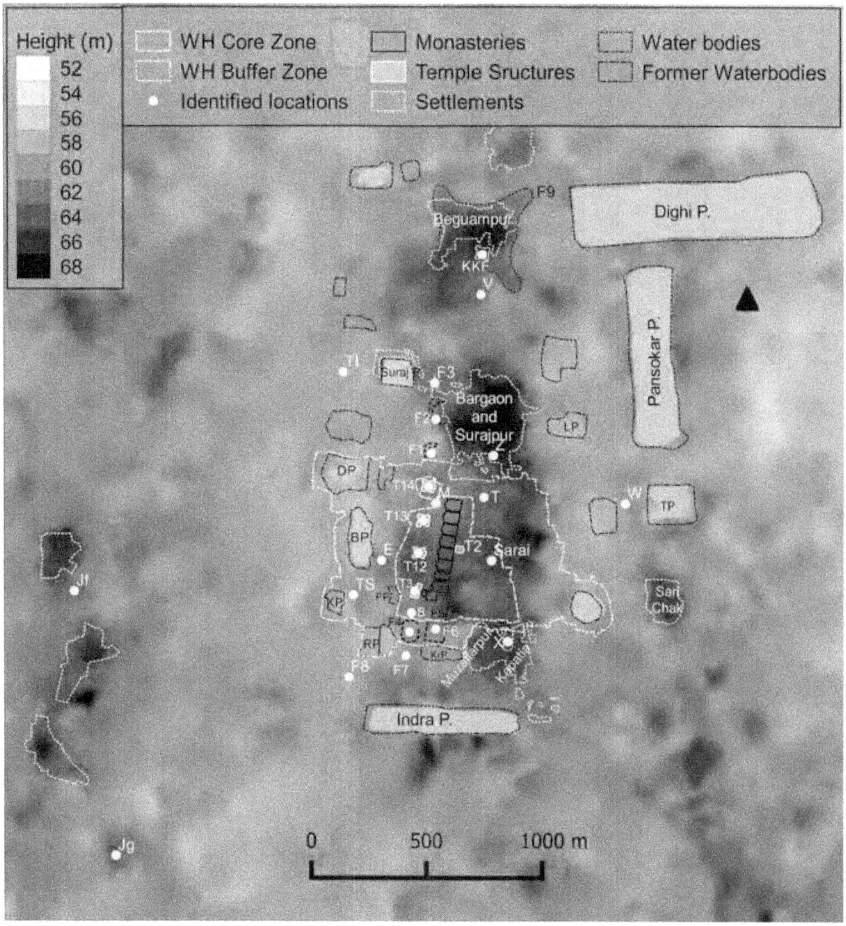

LIST 11.1

A comparison of spatial features mapped by Buchanan, Cunningham and Broadley at Nalanda and Environs

	Figure Annotations	Buchanan[a]	Cunningham[b]	Broadley[c]	Remarks
Table-1 Settlements					
1	Baragaon and Surajpur	*Baragang*	Baragaon	Burgaon	Baragaon: village on large mound
2	Begampur	*Begumpur*	Begampur	Begumpur	Begampur: village on large mound
3	Kapatiya		Kapatiya	Village of Kapterwari	Kapatiya: village on large mound
4	Muzaffarpur		Mozafurpur		Muzaffarpur: village with brick fragments
Table-2 Waterbodies (Pokhars)					
1	BP		Balen Pokhar	Ballen Tank	Active
2	Dighi P.	*Dighi*	Gidi Pokhar	Digee Poker	Active
3	DP		Dehar Pokhar	Deha	Active
4	Indra P.		Indra Pokhar	Inder Poker	Active
5	KP		Kunwa Pokhar	Suraha Tank	Seasonal
6	KrP	*Tank*	Kargidya P		Seasonal
7	LP		Loknath Pokhar		Seasonal
8	Pansokar P.		Pansokar Pokhar	Pansoker tank	Active
9	PP		Punwa Pokhar	Kundah Tank	Dried/cultivated
10	RP		Rahela Pokhar	Badhdeha Tank	Seasonal/partial
11	Suraj P.	*Surja Pukhor*	Suraj Pokhar	Suraj Poker	Active
12	TP		Tarsing Pokhar		Seasonal

continued on next page

LIST 11.1 — *cont'd*

	Figure Annotations	Buchanan[a]	Cunningham[b]	Broadley[c]	Remarks
Table-3 Archaeological features					
1	B*		B		Immediately south of Temple 3 within ASI wall; overgrown with trees
2	C**		C		Identified by Rajani (2016)[d] as F4; land used for cultivation
3	D		D	Tope no. VI	Mound identifiable on ground, annotated as F7 by Rajani (2016)
4	E**		E		Mound identifiable on DEM and ground; landuse: no activity according to RS images
5	F1				Identified by Rajani (2016); land used for cultivation
6	F2				Identified by Rajani (2016); land used for cultivation
7	F3	*"a conical peak of bricks"*	N	Tope no. I	Brick mound in Baragaon: Mahisa-suramardini temple on mound
8	F5**				Identified by Rajani (2016), over ground with trees, probably part of F6
9	F6**				Identified by Rajani (2016), over ground with trees, probably part of F5
10	F8			Tope (Near Satganti tank)	Mound identifiable on DEM and ground; overgrown with trees

11	F9	"… a very considerable space elevated with the fragments of brick"			Four cornered feature under Begumpur; identified by Rajani (2016)
12	Jf			Jowafir	Juafardih (Figure 11.5a)
13	Jg	*Juggispur "Yogeshpur"*	The sketch does not cover the location but indicates the path; details mentioned in this report.[b]	Jugdispur	Jagdishpur (Figure 11.6)
14	KKF	*"a small minous mud fort erected by Kamgar Khan"*	The sketch marks a four-pointed fort.	Fort	Kamgar Khan mound: mound
15	M**	*Botok Bhairub*	M	Boodhist Idols	Temple of Teliya Baba (Black Buddha) Figure 11.4b
16	Monasteries*	*Building with 5 courts*	Ruins of Monastery [south of Baragaon]	Ruins of the 8 courts	Monasteries 1A, 1B, 1, 4-11) excavated ASI property
17	RP			Ruined Pagoda (north of Suraj Pokhar)	Not available on ground
18	S		S, Ascetic Buddha		Not available on ground
19	Sarai*	circular heap	Y	Tope no. VII	Sarai: excavated/protected, ASI property
20	T**	*"three-headed Sakti"*	T, Vajra Varahi		Marichi Temple, stone sculpture with modern concrete walls; Figure 11.4a
21	T12*	*Heap opened,* circular heap, 3rd of 4	F	Tope no. IV	Temple 12: excavated ASI property

continued on next page

LIST 11.1 — *cont'd*

	Figure Annotations	Buchanan[a]	Cunningham[b]	Broadley[c]	Remarks
22	T13*	circular heap; 2nd of 4 Dorhars ref. in 4.4 above.	G	Tope no. III	Temple 13: excavated ASI property
23	T14*	*Dorhar*	H	Tope no. II	Temple 14: excavated ASI property
24	T2*				Temple T2; excavated ASI property
25	T3*	circular heap; 4th of 4 Dorhars ref. 4.4 above.	A	Tope no. V	Temple 3: excavated ASI property
26	TI			Tope, Inder Sing's field	Mound identifiable on DEM and ground; landuse: cultivation (Figure 11.5b)
27	TS**			Tope (Near Suraha tank)	Overgrown with weeds
28	V	*"Four smaller heaps"* One of them marked as *Bairubh*	V (two small mounds)	Small Topes (two of them)	Mounds south of Kamgar Khan fort: Low mound visible on DEM; land used for cultivation; location unidentifiable on ground
29	W		W *Three statues*		Not available on ground
30	X	small square *"Kapteswori"*	X	Top no. VIII	Settlement over brick mound
31	Z	*Parswanath*	Jain Temple	Jain Temple	Jain Temple: modern temple

Notes:
a. Sketch: MSS EUR/D87, p. 127, part of the Asia and Africa Collections, British Library.
b. Alexander Cunningham, *Archaeological Survey of India*, vol. I: *Four Reports Made During the Years 1862–63–64–65* (Simla: Printed at the Government Central Press, 1871), 28, pl. XVI, https://archive.org/details/report00cunngoog.
c. Alexander M. Broadley, *Ruins of the Nalanda Monasteries at Burgaon, Subdivision Bihar, Zilla Patna* (Calcutta: Bengal Secretariat Press, 1872).
d. M.B.Rajani, "The expanse of archaeological remains at Nalanda: A study using Remote Sensing and GIS", *Archives of Asian Art* 66, no. 1 (Spring 2016): 1–23
* Features in Core zone
** Features in Buffer zone

FIGURE 11.4
(a) Image of Vajra Varahi (Marichi temple) north of excavated site at location T;
(b) Image of Black Buddha (Teliya Baba) at location M

OPERATIONAL GUIDELINES FOR DEFINING CORE AND BUFFER ZONES FOR WORLD HERITAGE SITES

In 1972, the General Conference of UNESCO adopted a resolution for creating a "Convention concerning the protection of the World Cultural and Natural Heritage", hereafter referred to as the World Heritage Convention (WHC). The main objectives were to:

> define the World Heritage in both cultural and natural aspects; to enlist Sites and Monuments from the member countries which are of exceptional interest and universal value, the protection of which is the concern of all mankind; and to promote co-operation among all Nations and people to contribute for the protection of these universal treasures intact for future generations.[19]

FIGURE 11.5
(a) Mound of Juafardih;
(b) Mound TI

FIGURE 11.6
(a) Jagdishpur mound (Northwest view) 9 January 2014;
(b) Northwest view 16 December 2016;
(c) Southeast view of the mound 16 December 2016

The List now consists of 1,073 properties, of which 832 are cultural, 206 are natural and 35 are mixed categories. India is an active member state on the World Heritage since 1977, and 36 properties in India have been listed as World Heritage Sites (28 cultural, 7 natural and 1 mixed).[20]

The WHC notes that landscapes possessing objects of heritage were under increasing threat from new dangers: changing social and economic conditions. These factors potentially cause even more damage and destruction of cultural heritage than traditional causes of decay.[21] This has been particularly true in the Indian context, where heritage properties are increasingly being damaged and destroyed, or are vulnerable to mutilation due to the pressures of burgeoning urban sprawl and infrastructure development. The WHC recognizes that insufficient economic, scientific, and technological resources can be responsible for inadequate protection in some countries, but this is not true of India. The WHC also states that an effective system of protection has to be organized on a permanent basis and in accordance with modern scientific methods.[22] India is very well equipped to do this, provided resource allocation is focused.

The operational guidelines for the implementation of the WHC states: "delineation of boundaries is an essential requirement in the establishment of effective protection" of heritage properties and necessitates marking core and buffer zones.[23] The present guidelines for drawing cultural property boundaries have two main points:[24]

(1) boundaries should be drawn to include all those areas and attributes which are a direct tangible expression of the Outstanding Universal Value of the property;
(2) as well as those areas which in the light of future research possibilities offer potential to contribute to and enhance such understanding.

The analysis performed in this study has identified features in the immediate vicinity of Nalanda that clearly possess "outstanding universal value", such as Jf, Jg, KKF, F3-F9, E and TI, but are not included in the core or buffer zones.

DISCUSSION AND CONCLUSIONS

It is likely that important but unprotected features exist at each of the twenty-eight cultural Indian sites on the WHC List.[25] It is concerning to note that the UNESCO website lists no maps for three of these properties, and the core zone boundaries for each of the remaining twenty-two properties are identical to the area under current ASI protection. Several unprotected features around these sites have been researched in the past, and others have great potential for future research. As long as these features remain outside the core and buffer zones of inscribed sites, they face enhanced risk of destruction, especially since real estate close to world heritage sites is highly sought after for tourism and development activities.

The techniques using remote sensing images obtained from satellite/aerial platforms in this study can be applied to delineate appropriate boundaries for buffer zones in cost-effective and systematic ways. These techniques augment traditional techniques, especially when synoptic, multispectral views can discern tell-tale signs of archaeologically interesting features that are invisible to observers at ground level.

Notes

The first author thanks Nalanda University (NU) for a Fellowship in 2013–14, at which time she commenced research on Nalanda, Dr Anjana Sharma the then Dean at NU for encouragement; and the Homi Bhabha Fellowships Council for supporting her field trip in December 2016. The authors thank the financial support of SERB-DST Young Scientist grant which has supported fellowship and travel of second author. The authors are grateful to Dr Bijoy Choudhary, Director, Bihar Heritage Development Society (BHDS) for discussions; Kuili Suganya from NIAS for her input in UNESCO maps; Ms Shaashi Ahlawat and Azad Hind Gulshan Nanda from NU, Mr Ravi Anand from BHDS for accompanying us in field trip in December 2016; and Dr Viraj Kumar, PES University, Bengaluru, for his inputs.

1. The established chronology is problematic as the site may have had a longer antiquity going back to Maurya Period. B.R. Mani, "Excavations of Stupa Site no. 3 at Nalanda and Early Chronological Evidence", in *The Heritage of Nalandda*, edited by G. Mani (New Delhi: Aryan Books Intl., Ashoka Mission, 2008) pp. 13–22.
2. J.W. Laidley, 1848; Samuel Beal, 1884.
3. J.W. Laidley, 1836.
4. Diwakar Kumar Singh, "Sacred Sites and Sacred Identities: A study of Nalanda and its Vicinity (c. 600–1200 A.D.)", M.Phil dissertation, Department of History, University of Delhi 2010, pp. 43–44.
5. Excavated under the superintendence of Captain Marshall 1863: Alexander Cunningham, 1871, p. 33; A.M. Broadley 1871–72: Alexander M. Broadley, "The Buddhist Remains of Bihar", *Journal of Asiatic Society of Bengal* 41 (XLI) (1872): 299–312; David Brainard Spooner (1915–19), Hirananda Sastri (1919–21), J.A. Page (1921–29), M.H. Kuraishi (1928–30), G.C. Chandra (1932–36), N. Nazim (1936–37), A. Ghosh (1937–38), V.K. Misra, B. Nath,

B.S. Jha (1973–83): Diwakar Kumar Singh, "Sacred Sites and Sacred Identities", pp. 51–60.

6. <http://whc.unesco.org/en/list/1502/multiple=1&unique_number=2089> (accessed 20 January 2017).
7. Ralf Hesse, "Historical maps and ALS visualisations", presented at Cultural Heritage and New Technologies, Vienna, 16–18 November 2016 <https://www.academia.edu/29998719/Historical_maps_and_ALS_visualisations> (accessed 24 January 2017).
8. V.H. Jackson, ed., "Journal of Francis Buchanan (Patna and Gaya Districts)", *Journal of the Bihar and Orissa Research Society* VIII, part III & IV (1922): 266–73 <https://archive.org/details/journalofbiharre08bihauoft>.
9. MSS EURD87, p. 127.
10. Alexander Cunningham, *Archaeological Survey of India*, vol. I: *Four Reports Made During the Years 1862–63–64–65* (Simla: Printed at the Government Central Press, 1871), p. 28, pl. XVI <https://archive.org/details/report00cunngoog>.
11. Mary L. Stewart, *Nālandā Mahāvihāra A study of an Indian Pāla Period Buddhist site and British historical archaeology, 1861–1938*, BAR International Series 529 (Oxford, 1989).
12. Ibid.
13. Alexander M. Broadley, *Ruins of the Nalanda Monasteries at Burgaon, Subdivision Bihar, Zilla Patna* (Calcutta, 1872).
14. B.N. Misra, *Nalanda* (Delhi: B.R. Publishing, 1998).
15. M.B. Rajani, "The expanse of archaeological remains at Nalanda: A study using Remote Sensing and GIS", *Archives of Asian Art* 66, no. 1 (Spring 2016): 1–23.
16. Accession No. A25167/4012, Fredrick Asher, *Nalanda: Situating the Great Monastery*, Marg, March 2015, p. 39.
17. M.B. Rajani, "The expanse of archaeological remains at Nalanda".
18. Rakesh Tewari, ed., "Indian Archaeology: A Review", *Archaeological Survey of India*, Janpath, New Delhi, 2016; Juafardih 2006–07, p. 6; KKF in Begampur 2007-08, p. 23; Jagdishpur 2013–14, p. 20.
19. <http://asi.nic.in/asi_monu_whs.asp>.
20. <http://whc.unesco.org/en/statesparties/in (accessed 20 November 2017).
21. <http://whc.unesco.org/en/conventiontext/>.
22. <http://whc.unesco.org/en/conventiontext/>.
23. <http://whc.unesco.org/en/guidelines/> (2015), para. 99.
24. <http://whc.unesco.org/en/guidelines/> (2015), para. 100.
25. <http://whc.unesco.org/en/list> (accessed 20 November 2017).

12

A HERITAGE GEM SITS IN THE HEART OF A CITY, UNACKNOWLEDGED, INCOGNITO

The Case for Recognizing Kolkata Chinatown as a Historic Urban Landscape

Rinkoo Bhowmik

Blackburn Lane. It's a sleepy, time-forgotten alley in Kolkata's Tiretta Bazaar. Ennui hangs heavy, like Elliot's yellow fog, curling into every sleepy crevice. Suddenly, a thundering roll of drumbeats shatters the timeless languor — a gaggle of boys and girls in costume spill out of a weather-worn brick house in a raucous dragon dance. The street erupts into joyous celebration, the greys eclipsed by a riot of red. It is Chinese New Year in Kolkata's Chinatown.

Not many people are even aware of a Chinatown in Kolkata, much less that it is one of the oldest and the only surviving one of its kind in South Asia. The Chinese began settling in Calcutta (now Kolkata) over two and a half centuries ago, and for as long as the elders in the community can remember, Chinese New Year has always been heralded by dancing dragons in Blackburn Lane. The procession then winds its way to the newer Chinatown, the once swampy badlands of Tangra, now a warren of bumpy roads dotted with outdated Chinese restaurants and questionable tanneries. It finally ends up in Achipur in the city's suburbs where the community pays homage to the graves of ancestors in the place where the Chinese first settled. Where celebrations go, this is a pretty modest revelry, but it signifies something much deeper. A celebration of diasporic survival. Of continuity. Of a city's unique multi-ethnic heritage.

Today it's hard to tell that Tiretta Bazaar was once a bustling, vibrant market in a once grand, cosmopolitan city that was the "jewel in the crown" of the British Raj. Here you could buy the world: from crystal chandeliers to marble statues, from hookahs to cigars; it was where the Portuguese picked up the choicest fruits and the Armenians shopped for exotic birds; where the Baghdadi Jews selected Italian tiles for their mansions and where the Dutch bought shoes and the Greeks their olives. The large, colonnaded, cacophonous market was built by the flamboyant Venetian architect Edward Tiretta — friend of the infamous Casanova no less — who became Superintendent of Streets and Bazaars in Calcutta. The *Calcutta Gazette*[1] of 1788, described Tiretta Bazaar as occupying "nine bighas and eight cottahs of land, formed in two squares, with convenient shops, surrounded with a colonnade veranda, and the whole area of the square divided into commodious streets with pucka stalls". The market was valued at nearly 2 lakh rupees and yielded a monthly rent of 3,600 rupees. Today, nothing, not even a single pillar, remains of this vaunted market, except its name.

Tiretta Bazaar sat within colonial Calcutta's "Grey Town", the flourishing commercial centre that developed from the mid-eighteenth century. Scores of immigrant communities made the city their homes. Jews, Armenians, Greeks, Parsis, Chinese, Anglo-Indians and Muslims, all lived in this grey town in neighbourly camaraderie. To the south of this tract was the planned "white town" of wide avenues, grand buildings and mansions where the Europeans lived; to its north was the "black town", the less salubrious Indian quarter. Grey Town was the area that roughly spans Colootola, Tiretta Bazaar, Bowbazaar, Chitpur. Let's call it the "Heritage Strip". Today one can find traces of at least sixteen foreign communities scattered within a five square kilometre patch of that erstwhile grey town; of many other immigrant groups, not a whisper remains. It is a rich historical area that is crying out for preservation and revival.

The Heritage Strip is a fascinating glimpse into the city's very colourful and diverse past. Let's start with Tiretta Bazaar or Cheenapara, Kolkata's original Chinatown. Not just one, but multiple little-known marvels sit tucked inside its sleepy alleys — six Chinese temples (or churches as the

British referred to them) in a one square kilometre area — functioning both as religious sites and a social glue.

Just off Tiretta Bazaar, on Ezra Street, stands the first Parsee fire temple, built in 1839, once surrounded by gardens, now abandoned and overrun by shanties. The Parsis arrived in India some 1,300 years ago in Udvada, Gujarat, where the Holy "Iranshah Fire" was consecrated; subsequently many moved to Calcutta, then a gleaming entrepôt, capital of the British Empire. Some 600-odd Parsis still continue to live in Kolkata and their new fire temple has moved to the nearby Metcalfe Street.

One can easily miss the black marble plaque on Ezra Street commemorating the achievements of Russian Indologist, writer, musician, adventurer and translator, Gerasim Stephanovich Lebedev, the pioneer of Bengali Theatre. A Russian started Bengali theatre? Who knew that! An advertisement in November 1795 in the *Calcutta Gazette* announced the staging of an English comedy "The Disguise" translated in Bengali at "Mr Lebedeff's New Theatre in the Doomtullah, decorated in the Bengali style". It added that the characters were "to be supported by Performers of both sexes" and that it would commence with "vocal and instrumental music called the Indian Serenade". Tickets for boxes sold for 8 rupees: a king's ransom in those times.

On Brabourne Road stands the Portuguese Catholic Church and further down the Maghen David Synagogue with its chandeliers and ornate furniture. The city was home to some 10,000 Jews; today only 30 or so remain. The Magen Aboth Synagogue near Tiretta Bazaar area was demolished to make room for a characterless block of offices — an outrage that reflects the absolute dismissal of the city's rich, multi-religious and multi-ethnic past.

But, in this circle of neglect, just a stone's throw from the aforementioned Brabourne Road, on Old China Bazaar Street, is the well-appointed Armenian Church, the oldest church in the city, built in 1707, which is still an active place of worship. The courtyard is littered with tombstones, including one that is dated 1630 of an Armenian woman called Rezabeebeh, the oldest known grave in Kolkata. There is also a monument to the many Armenians who died in World War I. You get a glimpse of the past in the present and sense a continuity that is noteworthy in the general landscape of denial and the subsequent loss of heritage.

Just like the Armenian Church, in Chitpur there stands the house of another famous woman of Armenian descent — the resplendent Gauhar Jaan, born Angelina Yeoward. It was in a hotel room in Calcutta in 1902 that she sang a *khayal* in Raag Jogiya into a horn, making her the first Indian performer to be recorded on a 78rpm disc. It's an interesting historical fact that speaks of the immersion and integration of an Armenian community into the deep musical tradition that is wholly Indian. However, it is not just the musical first that makes this performer legendary, her flamboyance — she is known to have spent 20,000 rupees on a cat's wedding — situates her in the long line of artists and poets in India who show the same sense of panache and exuberant wealth! But Gauhar Jaan, steps beyond many of these luminaries as she also rode around town in a four-horse buggy reserved for Whites only, cocking a snook at the authorities by paying the exorbitant daily fine of 1,000 rupees for the deliberate transgression. Heritage, history, tradition, a sense of being Indian are all wrapped up in this daily encounter with colonial power and pelf and it's deliberate subversion. Unlike the actual record, a thing, it is this intangible heritage, located in the tradition of the tall tale that is found in all cultures, that becomes a signifier of the lost history of colonialism and its challenges, of heritage and its cultural ecology.

In the strip where the ghost of this prima donna still lingers, sits Bow Barracks, a row of red brick World War I tenements where a section of the now much-depleted Anglo-Indian community resides. A 2004 film *Bow Barracks Forever* tried to capture life in the enclave but earned the ire of the Anglo-Indian community for showing them as a bunch of idlers and drunks. Of course, this may be also since its tried to capture the historic decline of those who, at one time, would have been closer to systems of colonial rule: a decline which the present inheritors of an older heritage would have been keen to distance themselves from.

As we move onto Pollock Street, just off Ezra Street, there stands a grand Bohra mosque, where the Anjum, as the Bohra community is called, converges. There are about 4,000 Dawoodi Bohras living in Kolkata today. On Metcalfe Street is the Aga Khan Jamaat Khana, the place of congregation for the city's small Ismaili sect of Shias. Among the city's many settlers were also the Memons of Kutch, a community of Sunni Muslim traders who built Kolkata's principal mosque, the Nakhoda Masjid, an example of Indo-Saracenic architecture designed on the lines of Akbar's Tomb at Sikandra.

On Eden Hospital Lane there's a Myanmarese Buddhist temple, built in 1928, that finds mention in Amitav Ghosh's *The Glass Palace*. The building also provides lodging to visiting Burmese monks. The Mahabodhi Buddhist Temple in College Square was founded by a Sri Lankan monk Angarika Dharmapala who was also a delegate at the Chicago Parliament of World Religions with Swami Vivekananda in 1893. The temple upstairs, with wall frescoes and giant statues, has a Buddha tooth relic that is displayed on special occasions.[2]

On Nalanda Square near Bow Barracks is the Dharmankur Buddhist Temple, run and managed by the Bengal Buddhist Association set up in 1892 to revive Buddhism in Bengal. The large temple complex has a library and a guest house for students and for pilgrims on the Buddha Trail.

Preservation of this unique tract of land, a reminder of a once cosmopolitan Calcutta, is critical. Recognizing the area that was Kolkata's erstwhile "Grey Town" as a Historic Urban Landscape (HUL) that needs to be preserved in accordance to guidelines set by UNESCO is absolutely imperative.

The Cha Project (Cities • Heritage • Architecture) is bringing together scholars, historians, architects, designers, conservationists, urban planners, artists, private enterprises, government bodies, the community, NGOs et al., to bring about a community-driven, heritage-led conservation of this last surviving bastion of the city's multicultural past.

Beginning with Chinatown, the project hopes to set down a template for a holistic revival that goes beyond mere paint and plaster and addresses the entire problem space of urban revitalization, environmental improvement and economic empowerment which are too closely linked to be tackled in isolation. Although it starts with Chinatown, the revival includes all alternate cultural voices for it is the collective ensemble that is more engaging than a singular narrative of one migrant community. It is the absorption and integration of multiple ethnicities that makes the city what it is.

Letting this priceless piece of history crumble and die would be nothing less than a criminal offence.

*****

On a mercilessly hot mid-May afternoon, a group of students, some brown, some white, are seen measuring, photographing, sketching random old houses and Buddhist temples in Tiretta Bazaar. An old Chinese gentleman, watching from a distance can't take it anymore. He ushers them into the cool central room of the Sea Ip Church, chiding: "Why can't you do all this when it's cooler. Why in this heat? Why in summer?"

It's a Summer School workshop for architecture students from CEPT Ahmedabad and the Aarhus School of Architecture Denmark, led by The Cha Project's consultant architect Professor Kamalika Bose. This intensive on-site study had students documenting and analysing the spatial dimensions of the two-and-a-half centuries old Chinese settlement, and observing the various community interaction patterns embedded within. For The Cha Project, this context is extremely important; meticulous research is the bedrock of the revival blueprint.

Professor Bose feels that the on-site study, the first of its kind in the area, has been invaluable in evolving the revival project's methodologies to address key issues threatening the place and the community, and more importantly, it has provided a deeper understanding of this unique settlement, its institutions, living practices and community interactions. The primary objective of the study was to understand the culture, community, settlement and contemporary significance of the Chinese community in Kolkata whose strong identity is palpable even today.

Back at the Sea Ip Church, the old ceiling fans whir into action as the students and their instructors, Professor Bose and Professor Thomas Hilberth, take refuge from the scorching sun in the main room which has served as a social club and library for generations. The long black table has seen so much history, so many generations of Chinese families living and prospering in the area, the ups and downs in the fortunes of the diaspora, the post-'62 exodus on the heels of the Sino-Indian war, and the gradual decline. If only the walls of this modest, over 100-year-old building could speak of the long history: when Sea Ip was founded in 1882 by immigrants from four different districts in Canton and then moved to the current building in 1905.

Upstairs is a shrine dedicated to Kwan Yin, the Goddess of Mercy. Mr Ho Yuan That, trustee of the temple, remarks that visitors from China are always taken aback to see how people here still worship the old way. "We have been disconnected from China for such a long time, we haven't kept up with the changes", says Mr Ho. "We are continuing with the customs and traditions that our grandparents brought with them."

As heritage enthusiast Deepanjan Ghosh remarks, here sits a slice of China, unaffected by the Communist Movement, still preserving an ancient faith, replete with its age-old customs and rituals.

So, if it is a piece of China, the question that looms large is: Why does Kolkata Chinatown not look like a Chinatown? You could drive past Tiretta Bazaar without even realizing it is Chinatown. This is a one-of-a-kind Chinese enclave — unlike any other in the world. No ornate gate, no giant red lanterns, no screaming neon signs in Mandarin. Why, one asks?

Granted, much of Chinatown's character was lost during the mass exodus after the Indo-Chinese War in 1962, but even when Chinatown was a bustling enclave it never really had the trappings of Chinatowns in other parts of the world. Tourists are often disappointed. Professor Bose explains that it is only through an evolved understanding — of migration patterns, of imperialism, of alienation and displacement — that one can truly appreciate the uniqueness of this diasporic enclave. And once we get that, there's a fascinating living heritage waiting to be discovered.

Not only are there six tucked away Chinese temples but hidden in the urban fabric are also multiple native "huigans" or social clubs, some locked and forgotten, others with active members who meet regularly for a game of mahjong or a cup of tea. Each temple, and huigan, Professor Bose explains, belongs to one cohesive ethnic group, native to a specific region in China and thereby creating a subculture within the broader migrant community. And embedded in that chaotic urban landscape of alleys and by-lanes are also other ethnic groups who share space and livelihoods with the Chinese community, making it all the more fascinating.

As Professor Thomas Hilberth, says: "Kolkata's Chinatown is very distinct in that it does not visually declare itself; only when you start walking within it do you discover its hidden secrets."

*****

To help us understand why Kolkata Chinatown is so uncharacteristically understated, Professor Kamalika Bose offers a historical perspective. In nineteenth century colonial Calcutta, any expression of ethnic identity was frowned upon by the British rulers. As a migrant minority, the Chinese shied away from visual displays of culture. Quoting Mexican anthropologist Guillermo Bonfil, Professor Bose notes that in situations of colonial origin, such as old Chinatown, "any assertion of ethnic identity through architectural language was deemed to be undesirable by the dominant society." Minority groups therefore concealed their identity. There was a certain stigma attached to being a subordinate group, and shouting out one's selfhood was anathema to the established hierarchy.

Thus, it is interesting to see how the locals often used aspects of classical European architecture to please their overlords. The Toong-On Church, built much later in the 1920s, has a Neoclassical façade, the architectural choice of the ruling class and therefore *à la mode*. Both Toong On and Choonghee Dhong have Ionic and Corinthian orders, elaborate architraves, archways, pediments, and decorative stucco motifs. Nothing Chinese about them. But inside is a different story altogether.

It was in the interior spaces of the temples that the community got a chance to express its cultural identity through spatial elements, the use of colour and the decorations on shrines — from intricately carved roof hangings depicting war narratives of imperial dynasties and gods, to joss sticks and gilded weaponry. The temples were much more than mere places of worship; they were spaces where the community congregated, spaces that allowed for cultural expression and regional identity, spaces that were microcosms of the life they had left behind. For the various different clans and ethnic groups, the temples helped preserve the subregional identity of the diaspora in a foreign land.

The temples were hybrid typologies, not conforming at all to established frameworks of religious, social, or commercial building classifications. Today Gee Hing Church is also an office for Chen's Carpentry Works and a mah-jong club; the Choonghee Dhong Church has two noodle-making units and a warehouse inside; Sea Voi Church houses the Hupeh Association and a carpentry workshop; the Chon Nee Than Alms House was also a place for pre-funerary rituals. Most of the temples acted as temporary dorms for the newly arrived. Then there were the various commercial enterprises — Chinese provision stores, eateries, hairdressers — within the settlement that contributed to a self-sufficient community, albeit inward-looking. So functionality and usefulness was how this migrant working class community asserted its collective spirit, not through stylistic and visual expressions of cultural identity.

The question — does old Chinatown have to "look" Chinese? — then loses validity when understood from the above perspectives, emphasizes Professor Bose. It is not, and was never meant to be a recreated display of homeland where the urban theatre of a traditional ethnic community enacts itself, for viewers and tourists. The settlement is an accretive evolution of diverse Chinese subgroups — the Cantonese, Hakka, Hubei — who have come together, over centuries of hard work, trust and social enterprise to contribute to Calcutta society and its cosmopolitanism in a unique and irreplaceable way, she explains.

Kolkata Chinatown is a hybrid typology and its preservation needs to be anything but cosmetic. According to Professor Bose, the introduction of "commercial notions of touristy Chinatowns would be a terrible caricature and insult" to the place. The Cha Project has a difficult task of striking the right balance — between keeping the true essence of a two-and-a-half centuries old settlement intact and complying to the demands of a community wanting to finally assert its identity.

*****

It's been a very colourful history of migration for the Chinese in India. From those first long, arduous journeys that Chinese monks undertook to reach Nalanda, it's a story of indentured sailors, of opium, of war, of betrayal, of love, of tenacity. To understand the heritage of this unique diaspora, one must take a brief look at the history of the Chinese in Kolkata.

Of all the communities that dug roots in Kolkata, the Chinese have been the most significant outside influence. Theirs is a colourful history. They have been travelling to India since the time of the Silk Route. The first recorded Chinese visitor to India was Faxian in the fourth century, journeying by foot from China to India in search of Buddhist scriptures. In the fifth century, Chinese scholars thronged to Nalanda. In the seventh century, Xuanzang made his famous seventeen-year overland journey to India. The Chinese monk, scholar, traveller, translator left detailed accounts of his interaction between India and China in the early Tang dynasty. Modern movement between China and India began in the eighteenth century when Calcutta was an important port for the British East India Company, trading Chinese silk and tea in return for British silver. Trade through the city increased in 1778 when Calcutta became the capital of British India. It was the most modern city in the subcontinent at that time and the city everyone aspired to live in.

The first recorded Chinese settler in India was a tea trader named Yang Dazhao who went by the name Atchew. In 1778 he was given a plot of land by Governor Warren Hastings in return for a large gift of tea. There he set up a sugar mill with 110 Chinese men (mainly runaway sailors and indentured servants) who settled in the eponymous Calcutta suburb of Achipur. Atchew's men were representative of the first Chinese settlers in India — unskilled labourers who came on ships from Canton selling opium. The few skilled ones worked as carpenters on the ships. As Calcutta became a key part in the English opium trade, the influx of Chinese migrants increased.

The Opium Wars in the nineteenth century provoked a larger wave of migration as people moved to escape civil unrest back home. The population more than tripled in the next four decades. At the turn of the twentieth century, there were just under 2,000 Chinese living in India.

In 1910 the Indian government, pressured by the environmental concerns posed by the large number of tanneries, relocated the leather industries to the then-fringes of the city, to the area now known as Tangra. And a second Chinatown began to develop. A year later, the fall of dynastic rule in China caused many more to flee to India, and the population of the Chinese diaspora in Kolkata increased further.

The Japanese invasion and occupation of China caused many of the men who had settled in India to bring their families to India as well. The Sino-Japanese war (and World War II as a whole) also caused more people to move from China to India. By the end of World War II, there were more than 25,000 Indian Chinese happily living in India. Most lived in Calcutta, but there was a small presence in Bombay, as well as in the tea gardens of Darjeeling, Assam and Kalimpong.

In 1949, the People's Republic of China was established. This changed the situations of many Indian Chinese, who had papers from the previous Kuomintang government and may or may not have identified with the new Communist government. In order to remain Chinese citizens, they would have to renew their papers with the new government. The Indian Chinese population's approach to their immigration status was varied. Ten years later, in 1959, more than 8,000 Chinese in Calcutta were registered as foreign residents. Some had outdated passports from the previous government, while others identified as citizens of Communist China. There were also thousands of unregistered Chinese, who were born in India but did not possess birth certificates. They were, therefore, stateless.

And then came the Sino-Indian war of 1962. Much of the current state of the Indian Chinese community in Kolkata is due to this conflict, during which the Chinese in India came under scrutiny of the Indian government. Persons of Chinese ethnicity were regarded with suspicion, and often perceived as enemies. Their rights to free movement were restricted, and they were not even allowed to leave their residences for more than twenty-four hours.

Many Chinese were also dismissed from their jobs, both in the public and private sectors. Organizations funded and associated with the Chinese government were shut down, including the Chinese consulate, branches of the Bank of China, as well as schools that received funding from China. Hundreds of Chinese were charged with anti-Indian activities, and sent to internment camps in Deoli, Rajasthan, before being deported back to the China. Many Indian Chinese sent letters to the Indian government, pledging their allegiance to India and not the Communist government, but sadly the social repercussions of the conflict affected way too many lives. Covered by a blanket of suspicion and resentment, much of the spirit of the community was lost.

The events of 1962 still show their scars. Many of the Chinese in Kolkata left the subcontinent, and migrated to Europe, North America, and Australia and there are only about 3,000 Indian Chinese left in Kolkata today. In a city of 14 million, today's community is barely a whisper in the bustle of the metropolis. In 1995, the West Bengal government decided to move the tanneries from Tangra to Bantala, a suburb 20 kilometres away from the city. This move forced many tanneries to close and their Chinese owners to migrate to other parts of the world further asphyxiating the once-thriving Indian Chinese community. Chinatown, both old and new, became hollow shells of what they used to be.

It is exigent, absolutely imperative, that we preserve this unique cultural heritage before it is forgotten forever.

*****

Chiya. Chaha. Chaya. Theneer, Tī. Many different words for tea in different parts of India. Interestingly, in Bengali (spoken in Kolkata) it is Cha. As it is in Chinese. Although CHA primarily stands for Cities, Heritage and Architecture, it takes on an acronym that is really the essence of the project — a revival through teashops and cafes. Tea has had a rich legacy of being a catalyst for communication, culture, and creativity, bringing people, even nations, together, and it is through cafes and tea rooms that the project plans to revitalize the neighbourhood turning neglected by-lanes into vibrant food streets and night markets.

The Cha Project's approach to the revival is in tune with UNESCO's guidelines on Historic Urban Landscapes (HUL). It also incorporates the community's wish list, as well as the recommendations put forward by the CEPT Summer School Field Study. It is rooted in the premise that heritage conservation in isolation is pointless; a true revival is that which brings about economic revitalization and sustainability, empowers stakeholders, builds a sense of community, creates a better environment and better public spaces and preserves not only tangible heritage assets but the intangibles as well.

The Indian Chinese community's cultural traditions, food habits, festive celebrations, and architecture transcend geographical boundaries of the settlement to lend identity to the broader urban landscape of the city. The urban revitalization is being planned to empower the community, strengthen economic vitality and cultural identity, and leverage its historic value for the city.

In terms of tangible assets, a key element in the revival plan is adaptive reuse — unlocking the economic potential of unused and under-used buildings. Surveys by the Indian Chinese Association and the CEPT Summer School have identified several spaces that are currently vacant, underutilized or misused. There is huge untapped potential of these structures being repurposed for new uses. These uses will enhance the social, recreational, tourist potential of the settlement while introducing self-sustaining revenue models for them. With minimal new construction, existing assets can help re-instil pride and identity for residents, trigger enterprise and be an attractive point of entry for tourism.

Following the principles of HUL, the key to understanding and managing inner city settlements like old Chinatown is to recognize that the city is not a static monument or group of buildings, but subject to dynamic forces in the economic, social and cultural spheres that shaped it and keep shaping it. As stated by UNESCO:

> The historic urban landscape approach moves beyond the preservation of the physical environment, and focuses on the entire human environment with all of its tangible and intangible qualities. It seeks to increase the sustainability of planning and design interventions by taking into account the existing built environment, intangible heritage, cultural diversity, socio-economic and environmental factors along with local community values.

The HUL approach considers cultural diversity and creativity as key assets for human, social and economic development — which is also the mantra of the Chinatown revival plan. It is an alternative method to cutting the city up through "zoning" into separate conservation areas, which thereby become ghettos of historic preservation. The Cha Project's vision of food streets, walking trails, night market, better living conditions for the marginalized, traditional trades and crafts, cafes, performances will lead to a holistic regeneration of the neighbourhood which is bound to have a ripple effect on other areas in the city.

The revitalization cannot be envisaged without including the other communities and the marginalized population. The urban boundaries of old Chinatown integrate and absorb multiple ethnicities, which share space and livelihoods alongside the Chinese community. It is necessary to be inclusive of such alternate cultural voices as well to avoid insular narratives of a singular community.

As economic revitalization is the cornerstone of this revival, it plans to bring back the dying trades that the Chinese were once so skilled at. The Cantonese in Kolkata were excellent carpenters, Hubeinese were dentists, the Hakkas made bespoke handcrafted shoes. Those independent family-owned and run businesses have all but disappeared. Not only will the revival bring back these dying trades, it will help create a demand for those special skills.

*****

Speaking about skills, here's an interesting anecdote, a true incident that took place in an office building in Toronto:

Two total strangers enter a lift. One is an elderly man, possibly Caucasian, and the other a younger Chinese man. Suddenly, out of the blue, the Chinese man, asks:

"Are you from Calcutta?"

The older man, who it later turns out is Anglo-Indian, is completely taken aback. Remember, it's Toronto. And he doesn't look Indian at all.

"Yes, but how on earth did you know?" he asks in utter surprise.

The Chinese man smiles and answers:

"You're wearing Uncle Henry's shoes!"

This story, recounted by Dr Jayani Bonnerjee in her thesis paper on the Kolkata Chinese is a telling case in point of how distinctive their craftsmanship was — you could actually tell a Bentinck Street shoe by just looking at it.

There are hardly any of them left today. Most have migrated out of Kolkata and the few remaining have gone into factory production.

But things are changing. A new energy is creeping into the community. The Indian Chinese, a once inward-looking diaspora, haunted by the stigmas of the 1962 Indo-China War, are finally exorcising their ghosts and opening up to the hope of new opportunities.

And when all traces of resentment have been cleansed, and the Uncle Henrys begin returning back to roost in Tiretta Bazaar, that will be the true measure of success of the heritage-led revitalization of Kolkata's Old Chinatown.

Notes

1. The advertisement appeared in the 5 November 1795 issue of the *Calcutta Gazette*, a newspaper started by Francis Galdwin, an avowed Orientalist, to circulate government advertisements.
2. "Buddhist Temples of Kolkata", by Rangan Datta <rangandatta.wordpress.com>.

INDEX

A

Aarhus School of Architecture, 261
Abdul Kalam, APJ, 33
Abel-Rémusat, Jean-Pierre, 17, 142, 144, 149
Abrahamic scriptures, 102
Abu Hafs Suhrawardi, 232
Ādityavarman, 199–200, 203–04, 207–09, 214, 216
Aga Khan Jamaat Khana, 260
Agastyaparva, 211–12
"Age of Commerce", 209
Age of Faith and Doubt, 14
Ahilyabai, 95, 104
Ahmad Ghazzali, 233–34
Ahmad Shah, Sultan, 227–29
Ajatashatru, 34–35, 38–39
al-Palimbani, 'Abd as-Samad, 201
al-Siraj, Minhaj, 66
Alauddin Ahmad Shah, Sultan, 229
Alauddin Hasan Bahman Shah, Sultan, 225
Alexander, Sidney Arthur, 14
Almond, Philip, 14, 73, 83
"amateur antiquarianism", 77
Amoghapāśa Lokeśvara, 199, 214
Anaṅgavarman, 200, 204
Angkor Wat, 22, 54, 60, 62
Arabic loanwords, 215
Archaeological Survey of India (ASI), 38, 47, 73–76, 78, 80, 87, 100, 109, 240, 243, 255
"Archipelago Sanskrit", 215
Arjunavivāha, 210–12
Armenian Church, 259
Arnold, Edwin, 14
Aryans, 62, 155
Asian Civilizations Museum, 30
Asiatic Society, 76
Asoka, King, 20, 35, 58, 111, 161, 164, 167–70
Asokavadana, 167–68
Asrār al-Ārifin, 201
*Atharvavedapariśiṣṭa*s, 216
Awarif-ul Maarif, 230, 232
Ayn-ul Quzat al-Hamadani, 233–34

B

Baas, Michiel, 4
Baghdad school of Sufism, 233
Bahmani dynasty, 229
Bahmani Sultanate, 225–29
Bahman Nama-i Dakhni, 227
Balaputradeva, 66
"Bandung collection", 210
Bank of China, 266
banyan tree, 171
Barrett, T.H., 150–51

Batavian Society, 211–12
Beal, Samuel, 73
Becker, Catherine, 94
Beglar, J.D., 87, 91
Behar Herald, 82
Behar Times, 82
Bengal Buddhist Association, 261
Bengal Presidency, 71, 80
Bengali Theatre, 259
Bhabha, Homi, 24
Bhaṭāra Tumapel, 216
Bhimasorga, 212
bhujaṅga, 196, 198, 207, 214
Bhujaṅga Manik, 195, 197, 212
Bhuttacharjee, Babu Bemola Churn, 77–79
Bhuvanakośa, 205–06, 215–16
Bihar, 2–5, 7, 11, 22, 26–27, 33, 35, 39, 41, 46–47, 49, 61–62, 66, 70–84, 86, 97, 100–02, 137, 146, 151, 177, 243
  etymology of, 72
  framing of, 7, 70–71
Bihar and Orissa Research Society, 80, 82
Bihar Heritage Development Society, 26–27, 46–47
Bihar Museum, 7, 71–72, 76–79
Bihar State Religious Trust Board, 97
Bijayendravarman, 204
Bimbisara, 34, 38–39
"Biographies of Eminent Monks", 20, 109
"Biographies of Eminent Monks Searching for the Dharma of the Great Tang", 123
Biography of the Eminent Monk Faxian, 143
"Biography of the Tripiṭaka Dharma-master of the Great Cien Monastery of the Great Tang", 120
Birla Institute of Technology and Science, 67
Black Buddha, 249, 251
"black town", 258
Blackburn Lane, 257
Bloch, Theodor, 79
Bodh Gaya, 3–5, 7, 11–14, 34, 40, 72, 86, 88, 96, 161–69, 171–74, 176–78
  see also Gaya
Bodhi Tree, 11–13, 119, 161–78, 180
Bodhi Tree Worship in Theravada, 174
Bodhisattva Avalokiteśvara, 118–19
Bodhisattva Tārā, 119
Bohra mosque, 260
Bonfil, Guillermo, 263
Bonnerjee, Jayani, 269
Book of Bahman of the Deccan, 227
Book of Kings, 227
"borderland", 17, 149, 150–53, 156
"borderland complex", 17, 153–54, 156
Bortolotto, Chiara, 6
Bose, Kamalika, 261–64
Bow Barracks, 260–61
Bow Barracks Forever, film, 260
Brahma *kund*, 39
Brahmajāla-sūtra, 113
Brahmanism, 36, 74
Brahmi script, 8, 52–53, 57, 59
Bṛhatstotraratnākara, 216
British Discovery of Buddhism, The, 14
British East India Company, 265
British Empire, 170, 259
British imperial power, 7–8
British Library, 212, 242
British Museum, 9
British Raj, 258
Broadley, Alexander Meyrick, 2–3, 7, 19, 70–76, 239–40, 243–44

Broadley Collection, 71, 76–80
Buchanan-Hamilton, Francis, 2–3, 8–9, 19, 73, 87, 91–94, 96, 103, 106, 239, 240, 242–44
Buddha, 2–4, 11–15, 17–18, 22, 34–39, 53, 61, 88, 92, 103, 106–07, 110–13, 115–19, 122, 124–27, 130, 133–34, 142–43, 145–46, 148–50, 156, 160–61, 163–78, 180, 249, 251, 261
Buddha Trail, 261
Buddhaghosa, 107, 112–13
Buddhagupta, 53, 133
Buddhayaśas/Fotuoyeshe, 113
Buddhism, 13–15, 21–22, 23, 30, 44, 47–48, 53–54, 58–59, 61, 73–75, 83, 86, 136, 145, 150, 154–57, 161, 163–67, 169–70, 172–79, 184, 200, 208, 216, 261
Buddhist Art, 164, 175
Buddhist Canon, 157
Buddhist Councils, 27, 39, 41
Buddhist holy land, 163, 177
"Buddhist objects", 164–71
Buddhist temple, 98
Buddhist University, 6, 74
Bujang Valley, 57, 68
Bukka, 225
"Bund Sama", 234–35
"Burhani", style of dancing, 230, 234
Burhanuddin Gharib, 231, 234

C
Calcutta Gazette, 258–59, 269
Calcutta Museum, 8
Caliph Ali, 229
caṇḍāla, 147–48, 155
cargo, as instrument of cultural exchange, 163–64
Casanova, 258
"Central country", 146–47, 151–54
Central India, 142–43
Central Javanese collection, 211
Central Kingdom, 143, 150
CEPT Ahmedabad, 261
CEPT Summer School Field Study, 267
CHA (Cities, Heritage, Architecture) Project, 28–29, 261–62, 264, 267–68
Charleux, Isabelle, 166
Chaudhasaiya Gayāpal Samity, 97
Chicago Parliament of World Religions, 260
China–India dualism, 16
China, People's Republic of, established, 266
Chinatown, in Kolkata, 28, 257–69
Chinese diaspora, 29
Chinese population, in India, 266
Chinese sources, on Nalanda monastery, 108–11, 116–30
Chishtis, 223–24, 227, 235–37
  mystical practices, 230–31, 233–34
Chon Nee Than Alms House, 264
Chonvar temple, 98–99
Choonghee Dhong Church, 263–64
Christianity, 59, 156
Cities, Heritage, Architecture (CHA) Project, 28–29, 261–62, 264, 267–68
classical Malay, 215
classicism, 8
clypsedra, 107, 126
Cohn, Bernard, 87
"Collecting the Region: Configuring Bihar in the Space of Museums", essay, 7
Collège de France, 141–42
Collège Royal, 142
colonial archaeology, 74, 79
colonial narrative, 2, 70
colonial surveys, 86–87
colonialism, 4, 15, 28, 260

Communist Movement, 262
"Compendium of the Essence of Policy", 203
Compressed Stabilized Earth Blocks (CSEB), 42
Confucian centre of study, 65
Confucius, 61
"Continued Lives of Eminent Monks", 109, 122
Convention Concerning the Protection of the Natural and Cultural Heritage, 6
conversion ground, 179
Coomaraswamy, Ananda, 178
Council of Valabhī, 114
"country of *mlecchas*", 155
"cultural brokers", 2
"Cultural Heritage: Environment, Ecology and Inter-Asian Interactions", conference, 4
cultural imperialism, 59
cultural symbols, and elephants, 175–76
Cunningham, Alexander, 2–3, 8, 25, 73, 76–77, 87, 96, 106, 173, 176–77, 239–40, 243–44
Curtin, Philip, 52

D

Daṅ Hyaṅ Nirartha, 198
Daoxuan, 20, 109, 122, 129, 136
Daozheng, 150–52, 154
Darwin, Charles, 13–14
Das Kapital, 13
Datajieduojuduo, 116
Datang-Xiyu-ji, 116, 120, 123
Davids, T.W. Rhys, 145
Davis, Richard, 87, 94
Dawoodi Bohras, 260
"death of Sanskrit", 187
deforestation, 61–62
Delhi Durbar, 80
"demoticization", 193, 205
Dessicant Assisted Evaporative Cooling (DEVAP) Towers, 42
Devadutta, 39
Devalapa, 66
dharma, 106, 109, 111, 113, 116, 118–23, 125–26, 129–30, 151, 161, 194
  roots of the, 171–74
Dharma Pātañjala, 189–90, 212
Dharmankur Buddhist Temple, 261
Dharmapala, Anagarika, 3, 11–12, 173, 260
Dharmāśraya, 208, 214
Dharmasvamin, 240
Digha Nikaya, 49
Digital Elevation Model (DEM), 244
Dongguk University, 6
D'Oyly, Charles, 176
Drège, Jean-Pierre, 142, 144

E

"early modern", 184
East India Company, 265
elephants, as cultural symbols, 175–76
Elgin, Lord, 8
Elgin Marbles, 10
Elliot, T.S., 29
"epistemic break", 188, 210
Eurasia, 185
Eurocentric view, 6–8
Excavated Remains of Nalanda Mahavihara, 48
Ezra Street, 259

F

Fariduddin Adib, 224
Fasheluo, 116
Fawaid ul Fuad, 224
Faxian, Chinese monk, 3, 16, 17, 30, 36, 58, 73, 110, 142–44, 146–47, 149–54, 156, 240, 265

Felt, David Jonathan, 143, 156
Fergusson, James, 174
fig tree, 12, 161
Firoz Bahmani, Sultan, 226–27
Firuz Shah Bahmani, Sultan, 232, 235
Five Indias, 116, 125
Foguo ji, 142, 146
"folk etymology", 205
"Forest of Jewels from the Garden of the Dharma", 109
Forte, Antonino, 153, 156
Fotuojuduo, 116
Fotuoyeshe/Buddhayaśas, 113

G
Gait, Edward, 81
Galdwin, Francis, 269
Gautam Buddha, 14
Gaya, 86–87, 102
  see also Bodh Gaya
  history of, 88–94
  map of, 89
  temples, 94–98
Gayā-Māhātmya, 97, 104
Gayāsura legend, 97
Gayāwāla Brāhmaṇas, 97–98
gebang manuscripts, 194
Gee Hing Church, 264
General Conference of UNESCO, 251
  "Convention concerning the protection of the World Cultural and Natural Heritage", 251
George V, 80
Gesudaraz, *see* Shaykh Husayni Gesudaraz
Ghosh, Amitav, 260
Ghosh, Deepanjan, 262
Giriagrasamâja festival, 146
Glass Palace, The, 260
God of Illusion, 160
Golden Temple in Amritsar, 62
Government of Bengal, 70, 79
Government of Bihar, 26, 33, 46, 100–01
Government of India, 48
Government of Singapore, 30
"graphic breaking off", 210
"Great Chronicle", 161
Great Monastery of Nālandā, 106
Greater India, 59
"Grey Town", 258, 261
Guha-Thakurta, Tapati, 73, 167
Gunawan, Aditia, 189
"Gunung" script, 189
Gupta dynasty, 110
Gupta period, 36–37, 58, 115
Guru Nanak, 36
Guy, John, 176

H
Hadrami diaspora, 59
Hamzah Fansuri, 201
Han dynasty, 157
Harappan seals, 52
Hastings, Warren, 265
Hazrat Makhdum-ul-Haq, 39
Heluoshepanshe, 123
"heritage blindness", 8
"heritage" narrative, 2
Heritage of Sufism, The, 222
"Heritage Preservation in the Gaya Region", essay, 7
Heritage Strip, 258
"heritage tag", 101
"heritage value", 102
Higher Education Institutions, in India, 45
Hikayat Hang Tuah, 192, 213
Hilberth, Thomas, 262–63
Hindu religions, 53–54, 59
Hindu temple, 98
"Hinduised States of Southeast Asia", 202
Hinduism, 184, 192

Hinüber, Haiyan Hu-von, 144
Historic Urban Landscape (HUL), 261, 267–68
Historical Geography of Ancient India, 145
"History of the Dharma", 111
HMS *Beagle*, 14
Ho, Enseng, 59
Ho Yuan That, 262
Holy Land Reborn, The, 172
Hsüan-tsang, *see* Xuanzang
Huber, Toni, 167, 172–73
Huili, 108–10, 120
Hupeh Association, 264
Hurgronje, Snouk, 202

I

Imaduddin Kashani, 224
India–China dualism, 16
India Office Library, 211
Indian Asia, 59
Indian Chinese Association, 267
Indian Chinese population, 266
Indian Museum, 71, 76–80, 87, 244
Indian sources, in Nalanda monastery, 108–11
Indianization, 22
"Indianized" period, 186
Indic continuities, and transregional networks, 188–209
Indic Cosmopolitan culture, 187
Indic manuscript cultures, 186–88
Indo-Chinese War, 262, 266, 269
Indra temple, 96
Instituut Nalanda, in Belgium, 6
"Instruments of Cargo in the China Trade", 163
International Institute for Asian Studies (IIAS), 4
iqta system, 225
"Iranshah Fire", 259
Islam, 24, 59, 184, 188, 192–94, 196, 198–99, 208, 223, 228
  pre-Islamic Malay literary culture, 194, 203
  Prophet Muhammad, 224, 227, 229
  Shia Islam, 226, 228
Islamic
  culture, 21, 23–24
  mysticism, 227
  saints, 36
  shrines, 35
  structures, 73, 75
Islamization, 201

J

Jaffrelot, Christophe, 169–70
Jain, 9, 23, 34, 36–40, 46, 61, 73, 105–06, 110, 133, 135, 210, 250
  sources in Nalanda monastery, and, 111–15
Jalaluddin Rumi, 222
Jarasandha, 35, 37–38, 40
Javano-Balinese sphere, trans-regional networks in, 188–98
Java, topography of, 197
Jayanagara, 200
Jetavanavihāra, 125
Jiye, 130
Journal of the Bihar and Orissa Research Society, 81–82
Journey to the Western World, 48
Judaism, 59
Julien, Stanislas, 73
Junaydi, 228, 237

K

Kai Raga, 194
Kaka Sa'd Baksh, 224
Kalingabodhijataka, 170
Kamaluddin Samana, 224
Kashani, 224
Kashf ul Mahjub, 231
Kashi Prasad Jayaswal Research Institute, 88

Kemper, Steven, 173
Khalji, Bhaktiyar, 61, 66, 72
Kharavela, 36
Khmer Empire, 61, 204
Khwaja Bandanawaz, 235
Khwaja Burhanuddin, 224
Khwaja Hasan, 224
Khwaja Jamaluddin Kashani, 224
Khwaja Majiduddin Kashani, 224
Khwaja Umar, 224
King of Shaykhs/Sufis, 229
Kinnard, Jacob N., 9, 11, 39
Kittoe, Markham, 240
Kolkata's Chinatown, 28, 257–69
Koteśvaranāth Mahādeva temple, 99–100
Krishna, 35
Kṛṣṇadevarāya I, 213
Kṛtanagara, 214
Kublai Khan, 200
Kuja Ali, 204–05, 207–09
Kumārajīva, 154
Kumar, Nitish, 33
Kurkihar temple, 98–99
Kushana period, 36
Kyahi Tumeṅgung Puger, 211

L

Lahiri, Nayanjot, 93
"land of Han", 17, 149–53
"lands on the margins", 17
Law, Bimala Churn, 145–46
Law of the Buddha, 143, 149
Lebedev, Gerasim Stephanovich, 259
Lee, Risha, 54
Legend of King Asoka, The, 167
Legge, James, 143
Lewisohn, Leonard, 222
Li Daoyuan, 143
Li, Hwui, 62
LIDAR (Light Detection and Ranging), 18, 60–61
Lieberman, Victor, 185, 188
Light of Asia: Being the Life and Teachings of Gautama, The, poem, 14
Lightning Flashes of Indication Concerning the Refutation of Those who Declare Audition Forbidden in General, The, 233
Lion Capital, 170
"literary histories", 187
Lives of Indian Images, 10
"living heritage site", 177
lontar palm, 189, 210, 211, 212
"Lord of the Three Worlds", 200, 203–04, 209
Lotus Sutra (*Saddharma Pundarika Sutra*), 38
Lowenthal, David, 6–8, 29

M

Mackenzie, Colin, 211
Madhyadeśa, 17, 135, 143–49 151–52
Magadh-Bihar typology, 3
Magadh empire, 34
Magadha, 10, 18, 20, 22, 34–36, 46, 61–63, 109, 111–12, 130, 144, 166
Magen Aboth Synagogue, 259
Maghen David Synagogue, 259
Mahabharata, 35, 38, 216
Mahabodhi temple, 3, 11–12, 28, 173–74, 177, 260
  souvenirs for pilgrims, 176
Mahādeva temple, 96
Mahakasyapa, 39
Mahavamsa, 161, 164
Mahavira, 34, 61
Main temple, 98
Majapahit, 188, 192, 196, 198, 200, 213
Makhdum *Kund*, 39
Makhdum Shah Sharf'Ud-din, 36
Malay, Classical, 215

Malay inscriptions, Old, 199, 202–03
Malay literary culture, pre-Islamic,194, 203
Malay sphere of Sumatra, trans-regional networks in, 199–209
Malayapura, 200
Malik ul Mashaikh, 229
Mama-Bhanja image, 94
*maṇḍala*s, 192, 194, 198, 200
"mango grove of Pāvārika", 113
Maniar Math, 36–37
manuscript repositories, 189
Mara, God of Illusion, 160
Māra Piśuna, 151
Marcussen, Eleonor, 4
Maritime Museum, 60
maritime networks, 225
maritime trade, 57–60
Marx, Karl, 13–14
Maulana Ruknuddin, 224
Maurya empire, 61, 255
medieval temples, 98–101
Memons of Kutch, 260
Mentor Group, 33
Mevlevis of Turkey, 234
"Middle Kingdom", 142–43, 145
Ming dynasty, 166
Ministry of Defence, 40
Ministry of Tourism, 100–01
Mirza Nurullah, 229
"misappropriation", 70
mlecchas, 155
Monsoon Asia trade, 52, 54, 59
Morrison, Kathleen, 47
"Mosque of Fourteen Hundred Saints", 224
Mpu Dvijendra, 198
Mpu Tanakuṅ, 192, 206, 210, 213, 216
Mudgalayana, 39
Mughal Empire, 170, 222
Mughal, Rafiq, 52
Mughis of Shiraz, 229
Muhammad II, Sultan, 225
Muhammad bin Tughluq, 24, 223
Muhammad, Prophet, 224, 227, 229
Mukharji, Baboo P.C., 79
Mulagandhakuti Vihara, 171
Mulla Qutubuddin Kirmani, 228
Müller, Friedrich Maximilian, 16, 151
Muni, Kasyapa, 174
Muniśrī/Monishili, 130
"Muslim iconoclasm", 74
Muslim invaders, 66
Muslim tombstone, earliest, 59
"mystic synthesis", 193

N

Naga cult, 36
Nakhoda Masjid, 260
Nalanda Buddhist Society, 6
Nalanda Copper Plate, 36
Nalanda cultural festival, 6
Nalanda dossier, 5
Nalanda Geidge, 5
Nalanda monastery, 3, 6, 18, 20, 25, 27, 32, 37, 44, 47, 49, 61–65
  archaeological features, 244–50
  Chinese sources on, 116–30
  Chinese, Tibetan and Indian sources, in, 108–11
  layout of, 123–27, 241–43
  location and name, 106–08
  Pali and Jain sources, in, 111–15
"Nalanda Trail", 25, 30
Nalanda university, 3–6, 15–16, 25–26, 30, 32, 34, 37, 41–45, 47–49, 66–67, 131, 255
  list of schools in, 44
  Master Plan, 27, 43
  new location, 33, 41, 45
Narayan, Mahesh, 82
national identity, 81
National Library of Indonesia, 210–12

nationalism, 165
"native vandalism",70
"Nature of Buddhist Art, The", 178
Net Zero Energy Building (NZEB), 41–42
New York Times, 60
New York University, 67
Newdigate Prize, 14
Nicol, Janine, 143–44, 147, 149–50, 153, 155
Nigaṇṭha Nātaputta, 112
Nimatullah Wali, 222, 237
Nirenberg, David, 102
nirvāṇa, 61, 116
Nītisārasamuccaya, 203, 215
"Note on the Middle Country of Ancient India", 145
Notes on the Country of the Buddha, 142
Nṛsiṃha temple, 96
Nusantara, 185, 192

O

Ode to the Grecian Urn, 10
Okakura, Kakuzo, 4
Old Javanese
  inscriptions, 199
  language, 214
Old Malay inscriptions, 199, 202–03
Old Nalanda, *see* Nalanda monastery
"Ominous Great Residence of the Divine Nāga", 126
On the Origin of Species, 13
Opium Wars, 265
Ordnance Factory, 40
"Original Fragrance Hall", 126
"Outstanding Universal Value", 49, 254
overland trade, 52, 57, 60
Ozymandias, 1, 30

P

Padjadjaran, kingdom of, 194
Pala dynasty, 5, 107
Pali sources, in Nalanda monastery, 111–15
Pallava dynasty, 57
Pallava script, 56
palm-leaf manuscripts, 188, 195, 198, 210–11
"paradigm shift", 184, 210
Parameśvara, 208–09, 216
Partnership to Advance Clean Energy – Deployment (PACE-D) Program, 41
Pataliputra, 34–35, 47, 61, 75, 80, 86, 148, 152
Patna High Court, 97
Patna Museum, 71, 80
Pearson, Michael, 52–53
Pedanda Śiva, 198
Peking University, 47
Periplus of the Erythrean Sea, 52
Persianization, 223, 225
Peycam, Philippe, 4
Phillips, Carla, 51
Phillips, Richard, 14
Phillips, Wim, 51
pilgrim centre, 37
Pippala Cave, 38
Pir Mubarak Karwan, 224
Pires, Tome, 201
Poerbatjaraka, 212
Poluoadieduo, 116
Preface to the Sūtra of the Skandha-dhatū-āyatana, 153
Preface to the Sūtra of the Stages of the Path, 153
Preface to the Sūtra on the Twelve Gates, 153
pre-Islamic Malay literary culture, 194, 203
Prince of India and Founder of Buddhism, 14
Prophet Muhammad, 224, 227, 229
proto-university, 66

Provincial Museum, 81
"public temple", 97
pujaṅgas, 198
Puranic literature, 35
Pūrvaka Bhūmi, 198

Q
Qin dynasty, 149
"quadratic" script, 189–90, 199
Quanzhou temple, 54–56, 59
Quran, 231, 233

R
Ra Lotsawa, 173
Raden Saleh legacy, 210
Radha Krishna temple, 96
Raffles collection, 211
Rajgir, 3–5, 7, 15–16, 22, 25–27, 32–42, 45–48, 61–62, 72–73, 75, 86, 146, 151
  heritage walks, 47
  location, 33–35
  population, 45
Rajgir Archaeological Survey Project (RASP), 26, 46
Ramayana, 35, 216
raqs, style of dancing, 230
Ray, H.R., 167
"Record of the Inner Dharma Sent Back From the Southern Sea", 129
"Record of the Regions of the Śākya", 129
"Records of the Middle Region", 124
"Records of the Western Regions of the Great Tang", 108, 116
Reid, Anthony, 209
relic, tooth, 167, 261
relics of touch, 170
religious symbolism, 24
Religious Trust Board, 97
"Report Sent Back", 124
riverine trade routes, 57
royal patronage, 107
Ṛṣi Bhujaṅga, 198
Rumi, Jalaluddin, 222
rural temples, 98–101

S
Saadi, 222
Saddharma Pundarika Sutra (Lotus Sutra), 38
Safavids, 222
Said, Edward, 83
Śaiva literature, 190
Saivism, 53–54, 192
Saiyid Ali Hamadani, 222
Sakya-Muni: The Story of the Buddha, 14–15
Saluka Dipati, 204–07, 215
sama, Sufi practice of, 230–35
samadhi, 39
Samudragupta, 58
Sandalwood Buddha, 166
Sang Nila Utama, 208
Sanskrit Cosmopolis, 3, 185–86, 210
Sanskrit texts, 15, 20–21, 52–53, 56, 59, 113, 124, 126, 143–45, 149, 152, 155, 185–90, 199, 200–07, 210, 212, 214–16, 227
Sanskritization, 24, 205
Sanskritized Culture, 24
Saptaparni caves, 39
Sārasamuccaya, 204, 215
Sarai temple, 241
Śāriputra, 110–11
Sasanka, 173
Sayyid Abul Faiz Minullah Husayni, 229
Sayyid Muhammad al Husayni, 227
Sayyid Shah Yadullah Husayni I, 229
Schaffer, Simon, 163–64

sculptures
village shrines, in, 88–89
village temples, in, 90–94
Sea Ip Church, 261–62
sea trade, *see* maritime trade
Sea Voi Church, 264
Sejarah Melayu, 192, 200
Sen, Amartya, 4, 33
Sen, Gurupada, 82
Sen, Tansen, 4
Seth, Vikram, 156
Seven Luminaries, 155
Shah Burhanuddin Khalilullah, 229
Shah Nimatullah Wali, 228–29
Shahnama, 227
Shailendra Dynasty, 58, 66
Shaivite shrine, 37
shaman, 196
Sharma, Aviram, 4
Shaykh Azari, 227
Shaykh Burhanuddin, 223–24, 231
Shaykh Husayni Gesudaraz, 224, 227, 229, 232–35
Shaykh Junayd, 227, 233
Shaykh Nasiruddin Mahmud, 230
Shaykh Nizamuddin, 224, 228, 231
Shaykh Ruknuddin Kashani, 224
Shaykh Shihabuddin Abu Hafs Umar Suhrawardi, 230
Shaykh Usman al-Hujwiri, 231
Shaykh Zainuddin, 224, 231
Shelley, Percy, 1–2, 30
Shi Dao'an, 153–54
Shi Huiyuan, 154
Shi Sengrui, 154
Shia Islam, 226, 228
Shihabuddin Ahmad Shah Wali, 228
Shimizu, Yohei, 174
Shirazi, Hafez, 222, 226
Shuijing zhu, 143
Shuojialuoadieduo, 116
Sijzi, Amir Hasan, 224
Sikhism, 36
Śīlāditya, 122
Silk Route, 60, 265
Singh, Manmohan, 33
Sinha, Sachchidananda, 82
Sino-Indian war, 262, 266, 269
Sino-Japanese war, 265
Sinopoli, Carla, 47
Sisunaga, 35
Śivarātrikalpa, 192, 206
Sivasundaram, Sujit, 175–76
Smith, Horace, 30
Smith, Jonathan, 165–66
Son Bhandar cave, 36–37, 39
śrāddha rituals, 97–98
Sri Ajnyana, poem, 192
Sri Lanka, and Bodhi tree, 161, 164, 169, 176–77, 180
Śrī Śakrāditya, 123
Sri Tri Buana, 200, 208
Srimara-raja, 53
Srivijaya, 3, 199
Stein, Aurel, 60
Stewart, Mary, 17, 105
"Storehouse of Worlds, The", 205
Story of Gautam Buddha and His Creed: An Epic, The, 14–15
Strong, John, 167–69
Sufi, and practice of *sama*, 230–35
Sufi manual, 230–31
Sufi saints, 24–25
Sufi tradition, 24
Sufism, 222–24, 231, 236–37
Sultan of Delhi, 24, 223, 228, 231
Surya *kund*, 39
Sūtrakṛtāṅga, 114
Suvrata, 36
Śvetāmbaras', 114
"synchronisms", 186

T

talipot palm, 189
Tambo Kerinci, 215
Tamhidat, 233

Tang Dynasty, 58, 60, 265
Tang monasteries, 109
Tanjung Tanah codex, 185, 204, 206–07, 210, 215
Tantric Buddhist cults, 200
Taranatha, 66
Tata, Ratan, 80
Tathāgata, 118–19
Tattvajñāna, 190–93, 211, 213
temple architecture, 54
temples, rural, 98–101
Tengger community, 198
"Third Space", 24
Tian Xiaofei, 147
Tibetan diaspora, 172
Tibetan sources, in Nalanda monastery, 108–11
Timur, 226–28
Timurid Empire, 228
Tiretta Bazaar, 257–59, 261–62, 269
Tiretta, Edward, 258
Tirthankara, 34, 36
Tisyaraksita, 168
Toong-On Church, 263
tooth relic, 167, 261
trade by sea, 51–52
trade diasporas, 52–55, 59
Trailokyādhipati, 200, 204, 208
transnationalism, 22, 165, 208
trans-regional networks
  Javano-Balinese sphere, 188–98
  Malay sphere of Sumatra, 199–209
transregional Persian connection, 224–25
travelling cleric, 196
Treasure Trove Act of 1878, 78
Tree and Serpent Worship or Illustrations of Mythology and Art in India, 174
tree of enlightenment, 161
Tribhuvanarāja, 200, 215
Trinity College, 14
Tripitaka, 65–66
Tughluq Empire, 225–26
Tushita Heaven, 166

U

Ugratārā temple, 91, 93
Uncle Henry's shoes, 269
UNESCO World Heritage, 5–6, 17, 19, 29, 48–49, 86, 88, 105, 177, 239, 241, 244, 254
"uninformed native vandalism", 70
University of Cambridge, 16, 156
University of Minnesota, 51
Unveiling of the Veiled, 231

V

Vaishnavism, 53–54
Vakatakas period, 58
Vāyu Purāṇa, 97
Venerable One, 112–13
Vernacular Millennium, 185–86
Victorian England, 13–14
Vicziany, Marika, 22
Vijaynagar metropolitan survey, 47
Vijayanagara, 192, 225
village shrines and temples, sculptures in, 90–94
Vinaya texts, 142
Viṣṇu, footprints of, 97
Viṣṇu-Garuḍa image, 94
Viṣṇupada temple complex, 95–98
Vivekananda, Swami, 260
Voorhoeve, Petrus, 215
Vṛhaspatitattva, 190–92, 201
Vṛttasañcaya, 210, 213
Vulture Peak, 151

W

Wales, H.G. Quaritch, 55
water conservation, 42
Westerners, coming of the, 225–30
What can India teach us? lecture, 16, 156

whirling dervishes, 234
"white town", 258
Windu Sona, 211
Wisdom Lies in Places, 38
Wolters, Oliver, 186
World Heritage Convention (WHC), 239, 251, 254
World Heritage List, 49
World War I, 259–60
World War II, 265–66

X
Xiyu ji, 83
Xuanzang Centre for Asian Studies, 47
Xuanzang, Chinese monk, 3, 16, 18, 20, 30, 35–36, 48, 62–65, 73, 83, 106–10, 116, 122, 131, 133–34, 150, 154–56, 173, 240, 265

Y
Yale-NUS campus, 67
Yang Dazhao, 265
Yao Xing, 157
Yeats, William Butler, 27–28
Yeo, George, 4, 32
Yeoward, Angelina, 259
Yijing, Chinese monk, 3, 18, 20, 30, 62–63, 106–11, 113, 123, 134–35, 154, 240
"yoga" practices, 201–02

Z
Zafar Khan, 225
Zhi Qian, 113
Zhina guo, 155
Zhongguo, 17, 143–44, 148–49, 153, 155
Zhu Fonian, 113

Nalanda-Sriwijaya Series

1. *Nagapattinam to Suvarnadwipa: Reflections on the Chola Naval Expeditions to Southeast Asia*, edited by Hermann Kulke, K. Kesavapany and Vijay Sakhuja
2. *Preserving Cultural Identity through Education: The Schools of the Chinese Community in Calcutta, India*, by Zhang Xing
3. *Early Interactions between South and Southeast Asia: Reflections on Cross-Cultural Exchange*, edited by Pierre-Yves Manguin, A. Mani and Geoff Wade
4. *Hardships and Downfall of Buddhism in India*, by Giovanni Verardi
5. *Portuguese and Luso-Asian Legacies in Southeast Asia, 1511–2011, vol. 1: The Making of the Luso-Asian World: Intricacies of Engagement*, edited by Laura Jarnagin
6. *Anthony Reid and the Study of the Southeast Asian Past*, edited by Geoff Wade and Li Tana
7. *Portuguese and Luso-Asian Legacies in Southeast Asia, 1511–2011, vol. 2: Culture and Identity in the Luso-Asian World*, edited by Laura Jarnagin
8. *Sino–Malay Trade and Diplomacy from the Tenth through the Fourteenth Century*, by Derek Heng
9. *Tradition and Archaeology: Early Maritime Contacts in the Indian Ocean*, edited by Himanshu Prabha Ray and Jean-Francois Salles
10. *Civilizations in Embrace: The Spread of Ideas and the Transformation of Power; India and Southeast Asia in the Classical Age*, by Amitav Acharya
11. *India and China: Interactions through Buddhism and Diplomacy — A Collection of Essays by Professor Prabodh Chandra Bagchi*, compiled by Bangwei Wang and Tansen Sen
12. *Of Palm Wine, Women and War: The Mongolian Naval Expedition to Java in the 13th Century*, by David Bade
13. *Literary Migrations: Traditional Chinese Fiction in Asia (17th–20th Centuries)*, edited by Claudine Salmon
14. *Offshore Asia: Maritime Interactions in Eastern Asia before Steamships*, edited by Fujita Kayoko, Momoki Shiro and Anthony Reid

15. *Buddhism and Islam on the Silk Road*, by Johan Elverskog
16. *The Tongking Gulf through History*, edited by Nola Cooke, Li Tana and James A. Anderson
17. *The Royal Hunt in Eurasian History*, by Thomas T. Allsen
18. *Ethnic Identity in Tang China*, by Marc S. Abramson
19. *Eurasian Influences on Yuan China*, edited by Morris Rossabi
20. *The Sea, Identity and History: From the Bay of Bengal to the South China Sea*, edited by Satish Chandra and Himanshu Prabha Ray
21. *Early Southeast Asia Viewed from India: An Anthology of Articles from the Journal of the Greater India Society*, edited by Kwa Chong-Guan
22. *Asia Redux: Conceptualizing a Region for Our Times*, edited by Prasenjit Duara
23. *Buddhism across Asia: Networks of Material, Intellectual and Cultural Exchange, vol. 1*, edited by Tansen Sen
24. *Trails of Bronze Drums across Early Southeast Asia: Exchange Routes and Connected Cultural Spheres*, by Ambra Calo
25. *Buddhist Dynamics in Premodern and Early Modern Southeast Asia*, edited by Christian Lammerts
26. *Imperial China and Its Southern Neighbours*, edited by Victor H. Mair and Liam Kelley
27. *China and Beyond in the Mediaeval Period: Cultural Crossings and Inter-Regional Connections*, edited by Dorothy C. Wong and Gustav Heldt
28. *A 14th Century Malay Code of Laws: The Nitisarasamuccaya*, by Uli Kozok
29. *Esoteric Buddhism in Mediaeval Maritime Asia: Networks of Masters, Texts, Icons*, edited by Andrea Acri
30. *Indian and Chinese Immigrant Communities: Comparative Perspectives*, edited by Jayati Bhattacharya and Coonoor Kripalani
31. *Spirits and Ships: Cultural Transfers in Early Monsoon Asia*, edited by Andrea Acri, Roger Blench and Alexandra Landmann
32. *Bagan and the World: Early Myanmar and Its Global Connections*, edited by Goh Geok Yian, John N. Miksic and Michael Aung-Thwin
33. *Records, Recoveries, Remnants and Inter-Asian Interconnections: Decoding Cultural Heritage*, edited by Anjana Sharma